Wandering Between Two Worlds:

The Sacred Heart Seminary Class of 1965

Wandering Between Two Worlds:

The Sacred Heart Seminary Class of 1965

Edited by William E. Richardson

With a Foreword by Gregory Baum

And

A Concluding Afterword by Gerald Fogarty, S.J.

Van Antwerp and Beale Publishers

2222 Lloyd Avenue, Royal Oak, Michigan 48073-3849
(248) 541-1788 – E-Mail: gvanantwerp1@att.net
International Standard Book Number (13) 978-0-975941-65-2
International Standard Book Number (10) 0-9759416-5-8
Printed in the United States
Library of Congress Control Number: 2009922523

Each author separately retains all rights to his own story. Each story has been written by its author as a memoir. As such it represents the best recollections of the writer. The contents of each story are therefore the sole responsibility of the individual author. Neither fact-checking nor any form of censorship whatsoever was employed by the editor, the publisher, or any of the other authors. The contents and the facts of each story are the responsibility of each individual writer alone. Quotations from other sources used by the individual authors are attributed within the various stories.

The title of Kenneth Eason's story is taken from Bob Dylan's 1978 song "Señor."

Portions of Eugene Fisher's story earlier appeared in Carol Rittner and John K. Roth, editors, *From the Unthinkable to the Unavoidable: American Christian and Jewish Scholars Encounter the Holocaust* (Westport, CT: Greenwood Press, 1997) pp. 41-44, and in John C. Merkle, ed., *Faith Transformed: Christian Encounters with Jews and Judaism* (Collegeville, MN: Liturgical Press, Michael Glazer Book, 2003) pp. 130-138.

This book is dedicated to the memories of the fine men who graduated with us in 1965 but who did not live to see its publication:

To Jim Lavigne, who died during his theological studies, in 1967.
To Phil Calcaterra, who died in 1975.
To Jim O'Brien, who died in 2001.
To Fr. Bernie Schroll, who also died in 2001 and whose passing had a hand in bringing us together once again.
To Fr. Ron Cyprys, who died in 2007
To Ken Eason, who died in 2002 but lived long enough to write his story and encourage his "band of brothers" to endure and persevere in this project with joy and love.
.

Wandering between two worlds, one dead,
The other powerless to be born,
With nowhere yet to rest my head,
Like these, on earth I wait forlorn.
Their faith, my tears, the world deride;
I come to shed them by their side.

Matthew Arnold, "Stanzas from the Grand Chartreuse" (1855)

TABLE OF CONTENTS

PREFACE

There is an impressive building located at 2701 West Chicago Boulevard in Detroit. It has been there since the 1920s, when the Chicago and Boston Boulevard section of the city was a posh place for Detroiters to live. Its appearance gives away its purpose. This building is clearly a school.

The campus upon which the dark brick, Gothic-architectured building sits is bounded by three major Detroit thoroughfares: Chicago Boulevard, Linwood Avenue, and Joy Road. The fourth street completing its boundaries is the often forgotten Lawton Street.

When the building was constructed, the institution located within was called Sacred Heart Seminary. Its sole purpose was to train young Catholic men to become diocesan priests for the Detroit archdiocese as well as for several other dioceses in the state of Michigan. Its charter has since changed. It is now known as Sacred Heart Major Seminary and it trains more than just candidates for the priesthood. But in 1961, well before the change in charter, it was still simply Sacred Heart Seminary, known sometimes as SHS or the Heart by those who attended it.

Prior to 1961, and for a short time thereafter, the Heart consisted of two main divisions: the high school department and the college department. The program was, in reality, intended to be an eight-year continuum, leading up to the last four seminary years of theological studies elsewhere. For those that made it that far, most went on to St. John's Provincial Seminary in Plymouth, Michigan, an institution that eventually had to be closed because of the extreme drop off in vocations. But in 1961, things were pretty much what they had been for 40 years at SHS and for 400 years in the Catholic Church. The next year, Pope John XXIII would convene the Second Vatican Council and all would begin to change. The group of young men who began college at Sacred Heart Seminary in 1961 would be directly affected by the Council, as well as by many social changes in the United States and in the world in general.

Some of those entering college at SHS in 1961 were merely moving from the high school department to the college department. Others were joining the seminary from non-seminary high schools. Still others would join the class in the next several years, several of whom fell into the so-called "late" vocation category. Among these would be a lawyer and an urban planning expert.

In 1965, 43 men emerged from the other end of this four-year experience. Many did indeed go on to St. John's. A smaller number were sent to study theology in Rome and Louvain, Belgium. Still others decided against the priesthood as a vocation and left to pursue other paths. For those four years, however, the class of 1965 was a remarkably unified group of men, with a presumed common goal of eventually being ordained as Catholic priests. It is undoubtedly fair to say that the SHS class of 1965 was no more intelligent or gregarious a group than the classes that preceded it or came later. Nonetheless, it was a class that held a great deal of promise for the future, full of bright and friendly individuals who got along well with each other, men who were enthusiastic and ready to embrace the challenges of being Church leaders in the second half of the twentieth century.

But "things happened" on that road. The class with so much promise experienced what one member described as a "Diaspora." Although a majority of the 43 were eventually ordained, a minority still serve as priests. None has made it as far as monsignor, let alone bishop. Those that remain priests interact very little with each other. Those that left the priesthood after ordination, as well as those who were never ordained, had little contact with any of the others over the years.

"So what?" many might say. All college classes, indeed most groups of friends, eventually disintegrate as members go their own ways and form new relationships. This is true enough. But with SHS65 there were special forces at work -- social forces, religious forces, historical forces, factors that added to the difficulty of keeping everyone together.

Against all odds, in early 2001, the class of 1965 began to reassemble, not in the flesh at first, but electronically, via the internet. One by one classmates from literally all over the world began to reconnect -- exchanging email daily, exchanging thoughts and personal stories. One of the revelations of this reconnection was that class members found they still shared many of the same values, hopes, and dreams, even while differing greatly in many important life areas. Friendships, long dormant, were resurrected overnight. To many, it was as if the 36 years since that graduation day in the spring of 1965 had never intervened. It didn't take long for one member of the class to suggest a project wherein each class member would tell the story of what had happened in his life since 1965. This book is the product of that suggestion.

A perfect world, of course, does not exist. Although all were invited to participate, some class members chose not to join in the endeavor. These men undoubtedly have their reasons. Those that did participate represent a diverse group -- lawyers, educators, a federal prison official, an engineer, a lay theology professor, Vietnam war protesters and Vietnam vets, whites and the only black member of the class, priests and former priests, and more. All the authors agree that the process itself was worth the effort, even if the results had never been published.

The following pages, then, represent the story and stories of the 1965 college graduates of Sacred Heart Seminary, told in their own words, uncensored. Members of other classes and other seminaries might tell similar tales, but they have not done so as a group. As you read these stories, you should hear the echo of the 60's, overlaid by the changes of the following 40 years, reflecting in miniature what happened to the Catholic Church in the United States over that time.

William E. Richardson

FOREWORD
Gregory Baum

Sacred Heart Seminary in Detroit must have been an outstanding academic institution. This, at least, is how it is remembered by most of the seventeen men, whose autobiographical essays are collected in this volume. Having graduated in 1965, they now, some forty years later, recognize the profound influence that their years there have had on them. With one or two exceptions, these men praise the serious intellectual education they received, the competence of their professors, the spirit of openness that characterized their training, and the encouragement they received from their superiors.

Most of these men coming from modest backgrounds were the first of their families to receive a college education. They brought with them a conservative Catholic culture, obedient to ecclesiastical rules and conformist to what they regarded as the Church's official teaching. Yet since their years at the seminary coincided with Vatican Council II (1962-65), their priest professors, following the evolution of Catholic thought, made them into critical thinkers and encouraged an independence of mind. Sacred Heart Seminary, we are told in these essays, was regarded as one of the most progressive seminaries in the United States.

The seminary also created a community spirit among the students, including several members of the faculty. Some of the graduates recall their professors with affection and mention that they met many happy priests. Many members of the graduating class of 1965 remained friends. Even though they followed quite different paths, they felt that they had something in common. They had shared a formative experience in their youth. Because of this affinity, they were excited about this joint project asking each to reflect on his past and tell his story. Is this just a sentimental exercise, the reader may ask, or do these autobiographical essays have an historical value? I wish to argue that the essays document an important transition in American Catholicism, the entry into a new spirituality, the start of a new pastoral practice, the development of theological pluralism, the birth of tolerance, and the spread of some confusion. The changes that occurred, the essays tell us, created tensions among the seminarians, some welcoming the newness and others resisting it.

The Background

To appreciate the transition documented in these essays it is necessary to recall a number of facts. First, the nature of American Catholicism. In the second part of the 19th century the bishops had decided that the Church should become the Church of the immigrants. Accordingly they set up parish communities for them that would protect their identities and built schools for them to give them a Catholic education and enable them to succeed in American society. Catholics formed a subculture in the U.S., walled in partly by pervasive anti-Catholic prejudice and partly by the bishops' will to defend Catholics against the dominant Protestant and secular culture. This thriving Catholicism was a remarkable socio-religious achievement sustained by the generosity of the laity, the selfless dedication of nuns, and the direction of the clergy; yet it produced a conformist religious culture, an unchallenged clericalism, and an aversion to intellectual inquiry. This was the background of the graduating class of 1965. At the seminary they were introduced to a new vision of Catholicism.

In the U.S., Catholic education had been particularly faithful to the papal directives, especially after the Leo XIII's repudiation of Americanism in 1899 and Pius X's condemnation of Modernism in 1907. So while an important revival of Catholic thought took place in Europe beginning in the 1930s, Catholic thought in America did not move. The theological currents that preceded Vatican II did not reach the Catholic seminaries in the United States. Thus, in America the teaching of the Council appeared as a gift from above, a sudden re-orientation for which U.S. Catholics had not been prepared by antecedent theological debates.

This is the second reason why the graduating class of 1965 experienced a transition that was almost a leap into a new vision of Catholicism. The essays record their excitement at the time. As the Council went on, the professors followed the theological developments from afar and, recognizing that they could not rely on books, rewrote their lectures anew for every class.

The third reason for the transitional experience of these seminarians was the host of political events and the anti-authoritarian culture of the sixties. I will mention only a few of these: the civil rights struggle, the mobilization against the war in Vietnam, the assassinations of President Kennedy and Martin Luther King, and the youth movement for personal freedom in opposition to institutional constraints. The optimism and the new mobility of society were undoubtedly related to the great economic upswing of the sixties that touched even the lives of workers and the lower middle classes.

What influenced these seminarians the most seems to have been the civil rights struggle and the fight against racial prejudice. They became keenly aware of indifference to the race issue they had inherited and consequently decided to involve themselves in pastoral projects promoting solidarity with black people in America. They were saddened by the white racism that they found in many of the parishes.

Vatican Council II

Finally the leap into a new perception of Catholicism was provoked by the conciliar documents themselves. Let me mention two themes developed in these documents that had a great impact on the spirituality of the seminarians.

First is the divine call for solidarity with all human beings, beginning with the poor and afflicted. The very first sentence of *Gaudium et spes*, the conciliar document on *The Church in the Modern World*, says:

> The joys and the hopes, the griefs and anxieties of the people of this age, especially those who are poor or in any way afflicted, these too are the joys and hopes, the griefs and anxieties of the disciples of Jesus Christ.

This is new! No Council and embarrassingly few Christian writers of antiquity, the Middle Ages, or the centuries after the Reformation had ever expressed solidarity with humanity, including Jews, Muslims, and dissident Christians. Christian love was extended to Catholics, to "the insiders;" but we were not troubled by the suffering of "the outsiders." We drew a boundary line around the Catholic community and were cautious in our contacts with non-Catholics. We did not explore the meaning and power of Christian love in the pluralistic context of the world. We did not ask ourselves whether the outsiders were our brothers and sisters, whose hopes and anxieties demanded our response. Yet significant experiences of the Church in the 20th century - its relative silence during the Holocaust and the protest of Africans, Asians, and Amerindians against its identification with colonizing power - urged many Catholics to recognize the meaning and power of Christian love in their relationship to people outside the Church.

The divine call to universal solidarity announced in *Gaudium et spes* was made more specific in the conciliar documents on Ecumenism (*Unitatis reintegratio*) and the Church's attitude toward non-Christian religions, including Judaism in particular (*Nostra aetate*). While it is easy to draw a dividing line between the Catholic Church and outsiders in sociological terms, the dividing line is much less clear in theological terms. God's grace revealed in Jesus Christ addresses human beings wherever they are, often through the religious or sapiential tradition to which they belong. God is redemptively present in the whole of human history. Here is a sentence from *Gaudium et spes* (n. 22):

> Since Christ died for all human beings and since their ultimate vocation is one and divine, we must hold that the Holy Spirit in a manner known only to God offers every human the possibility of being associated with this paschal mystery.

Being inside and outside the Church is clear in institutional terms, but no longer transparent in terms of truth, salvation, and holiness. The Catholic Church, according to Vatican II, possesses the fullness of the gifts of Christ and is unique in this sense; but divine illumination and transforming grace are granted in the measure of God's mercy and maybe at times become more intense outside the Church. That is why the Church can learn from dialogue with other religious traditions and the wisdom of philosophers.

The call to universal solidarity and the discovery that the walls of the Church are porous had a profound influence upon the Sacred Heart graduates of 1965. They became ecumenical in the wide sense, both in their thinking and their actions.

The second conciliar theme that affected the class of 1965 was the ideal of participation. Before the Council, American Catholics did not reflect a great deal on the contrast between their democratic society that encouraged people's co-responsibility and the ecclesiastic order ruled by the top-down authority indifferent to people's values and aspirations. In the Catholic Church, the monarchical model of authority was predominant. Vatican Council I (1870) had defined not only papal infallibility but also the pope's universal jurisdiction. He was now empowered to rule the Church, if he so wanted, with monarchical authority. Since his jurisdiction was universal, he could legislate without consulting the bishops and establish rules and principles obligatory on all the faithful. And in their own dioceses the bishops themselves exercised monarchical authority under the pope without the participation of priests and people. Even in the parish, the priest exercised a one-man rule. This Roman ecclesiastical tradition was at odds with the synodal structure of the early Church and even more so with the ethic of governance that guided modern society.

Vatican Council II tried to move the Church government from a monocratic to a collegial model. Without contradicting Vatican Council I, *Lumen gentium*, the conciliar document on the Church, introduced the ancient concept of "collegiality" (nn 22,23). Under collegiality the pope was head and member of the body of bishops (the episcopal college) and hence ruled the Church together with the bishops, either as gathered in a general council or as consulted when they are in their dioceses. While the pope can act alone, the doctrine of collegiality asserts that the bishops are co-responsible, and hence the pope's action must reflect their pastoral concern.

According to a wider meaning of collegiality, Vatican Council II recommended the creation of i) diocesan councils of priests, ii) diocesan councils of the laity and iii) parish councils. Vatican II wanted to promote greater participation of Catholics on all levels of the ecclesiastical institution.

The emphasis on participation was expressed in another series of conciliar texts dealing with the vocation of the laity. Chapter 2 of *Lumen gentium*, entitled "The People of God," was added after a long debate at the Council, with the purpose of moving beyond the idea that the Church can be equated with the ecclesiastical hierarchy. The chapter presents the Catholic Church as the historical community of the faithful, God's people constituted by baptized Catholics. In this text, the Church appears as the body of Catholic men and women, the laity in other words, the Catholic people, who have been given priests, bishops, and popes to help them live their vocation to the full. Chapter 4 of *Lumen gentium*, on the vocation of the laity, specifies that, in virtue of their baptism, Catholic men and women participate in the threefold office of Christ as prophet, priest, and royal servant. While the priesthood of all believers taught by Vatican II is different from the priesthood of the ordained, the former empowers ordinary Catholics to participate in Church's mission in the world.

The new emphasis on the dignity and ecclesial vocation of the laity had a strong impact on the thinking of the graduating class of 1965. These seminarians believed that the summons of the Holy Spirit was addressed to the whole Church and hence that Catholic people were called to participation. They reacted negatively to authoritarian priests and bishops whose style and discourse suggested that they thought of themselves as solely responsible for the Church's life. The graduates of 1965 who eventually became priests considered themselves enablers and facilitators, helping lay people to assume responsibility in the running of parishes and to become actors in society promoting Gospel values. When other graduates decided not to move forward toward the ordained priesthood, they believed that their mission as lay people was to serve the Church and society as a whole.

Some of the essays in this collection reflect an unease with recent events, which have seen the movement toward collegiality and greater participation increasingly challenged by some Catholics, including some in the Vatican Curia. Indeed, the openness to change and the sense of participation in all levels of the life of the Church that permeates these narratives provides a refreshing, if indirect, counterpoint to the elements within the Catholic hierarchy who seem to wish a return to the pre-conciliar, monarchical mode of governance so at odds with the ethic of modern society and the vision of the Council itself.

Respect for Dissidence

Graduating from Sacred Heart Seminary offered the seminarians a Bachelor of Arts in the humanities and scholastic philosophy. Then it was up to the graduates and the seminary authorities to decide whether or not they should move forward to the study of theology and ordination to the priesthood. Some of these men were called to the ordained priesthood and exercised a productive ministry throughout their lives. Some received priestly ordination and decided in later years to leave and get married. Some decided to remain members of the laity and serve the Church in their own ways. And some moved to the margin of the Church and fulfilled their spiritual aspirations in other contexts.

What is remarkable in these essays is that leaving the seminary, or leaving the priesthood, or even leaving the Church is not presented as an act that deserves condemnation. This is new in the Church. A spoiled or defrocked priest was generally despised. What happened in the Church during the sixties, I wish to ask, that allowed the graduates of 1965 no longer to share the same feeling? Why has the generalized disapproval of laicized priests disappeared in the Catholic community? In many parts of the USA and Canada, priests who have left and are now married work in Catholic schools, are employed in Catholic diocesan offices, or offer religious education in parishes.

I wish to mention two developments that have led to this attitudinal change. First is the new respect for personal conscience. We used to teach that conscience should be our guide, emphasizing the duty to form our conscience in accordance with ecclesiastical teaching. The classical teaching added to this was that we were obliged to follow our conscience, even if it was erroneous. This principle, acknowledged in theological texts, never influenced the ecclesiastical attitude toward dissenters. It was Vatican Council II, probably influenced by the theology of Cardinal Newman, that expressed a new respect for personal conscience.

> Conscience is the most secret core and sanctuary of a person. There he is alone with God, whose voice echoes in his depth. In a wonderful manner conscience reveals the law which is fulfilled by love of God and neighbour. In fidelity to conscience Christians are joined with the rest of men in the search of the truth....Conscience frequently errs from invincible ignorance without losing its dignity. The same cannot be said of a man who cares but little for truth and goodness, or of a conscience which by degrees grows practically sightless as a result of habitual sin. (*Gaudium et spes*, n. 16)

Even though the graduates of 1965 have walked in different directions and arrived at different conclusions, they respect one another. Even the decision to leave the priesthood or withdraw from the Church is honoured if the persons in question "care for truth and goodness" and have not become "sightless" as a result of a will for power or wealth.

There is a second development that may explain the attitudinal change in the Church toward Catholics who disagree with ecclesiastical rulings and walk their own way. The generation of Vatican II is keenly aware that official ecclesiastical teaching changes. This was a particular shock for American Catholics, whose intellectual life had been steered toward unanimity. Now they witnessed that popes and bishops can change their mind. The Council of Florence (1442) announced that people outside the Catholic Church, even if of good will, were destined to eternal perdition, while Vatican Council II taught that, on the contrary, participation in the paschal mystery was offered to all humans, wherever they might be (*Gaudium et spes*, n. 22). In the 19th century the papacy condemned in the most trenchant way religious freedom and civil liberties in general, while Pope John XXIII's encyclical *Pacem in terris* and

Vatican Council II strongly supported human rights, including religious liberty. Pope Pius XI condemned the ecumenical movement, since it refused to acknowledge that Christ's historical body already existed indefectibly in the Catholic Church (*Mortalium animos*, 1928), while Vatican Council II recognized in the same ecumenical movement the presence of the Holy Spirit (*Unitatis reintegratio*, n. 1). These and other examples of self-correction convinced the generation of Vatican II that ecclesiastical teaching can change.

The Catholic Church never changes its teaching in the sense that it always announces the same Gospel of Jesus Christ and interprets it in the light of the classical creeds produced by the early ecumenical councils. To this saving truth the Church remains ever faithful. But the set of teachings and moral norms in which the Church applies this saving truth in different historical contexts is historically conditioned and hence capable of being changed under new circumstances. This happened at Vatican II.

John XXIII and the Council drew attention to "the signs of the times" as a new hermeneutical principle. We must interpret the tradition of faith in the light of the important historical experiences of the age. John XXIII mentioned three positive signs: the labour movement, the women's movement, and the struggle of the colonies for political self-determination (*Pacem in terris*, nn 39-43). In the light of these signs the Pope took a new look at the biblical teaching of creation and recognized that the high dignity of human beings created in God's image demanded respect and provided the theological basis for human rights. For the Vatican Council the Holocaust was a negative sign of the times. Rereading Scripture and Tradition in the light of this event allowed the Council to correct the anti-Jewish current in Christian teaching and recognize in Paul's letter to the Romans (ch. 11) the abiding character of God's covenant with the Jews.

Rereading Scripture and Tradition in the light of "the signs of the times" is a process that continues. The increasingly divided world and the fear of a clash of civilizations prompted Pope John Paul II to make bold gestures of solidarity toward the world religions, especially Islam, and offer new reflections, unheard of in the past, in praise of religious pluralism.

An inevitable consequence of this development is that Catholics recognize the conditional character of the ecclesiastical magisterium. This is true especially for the generation of Vatican II. Why? Because several theologians whose writings had been censured by the magisterium (Congar, Rahner, de Lubac, John Courtney Murray,...) worked at the Council and had their ideas endorsed by the Council. When the magisterium today reaffirms the old teaching on birth control or the ordination of women, Catholics take this with a grain of salt.

The existing pluralism within the Catholic Church has led to a changed attitude toward dissidents. What is honoured today is to be sincere, to listen to the inner voice, to search for the truth, and to respond to the divine summons for compassion and solidarity.

Since the sexual abuse scandals have become so prominent in the Church, I must make a brief comment on what the graduates of 1965 have to say about sexuality. They look back to their days in the seminary as a time of learning, friendship, prayer, and great fun. None of them remarked about observing any sexual indiscretions. At the same time, they acknowledge that the topic was avoided in their training. Seminary education bracketed the sexual dimension of the human condition. Most of the essays prefer not to dwell on matters of sex. None of them, even the priests, hold that celibacy is an essential dimension of the Catholic priesthood. They all know of married lay people and Protestant clergy where the wife supports her spouse in his ministry and helps him to make it more effective. Only one or two of the essayists are angry with the Church because of the sexual confusion in which many priests and many lay people find themselves. Priests leave the seminary without adequate self-knowledge. What they do later on, suffering from loneliness and frustrations, the harmless and the not-so-harmless, remains hidden. Men with pedophile inclinations don't recognize their need for psychiatric help. Dogmatism and the absence of open debate prevent the Church from rising above its own confusion. Again, the open-mindedness and sensitivity to their own pluralism exhibited throughout the essays of the class of '65 provides a model of living the life of Christian charity within the Church that is more and more needed today.

Allow me to repeat a sentence written at the beginning of this Forward. The present collection of essays documents an important transition in American Catholicism, the entry into a new spirituality, the start of a new pastoral practice, the development of theological pluralism, the birth of tolerance, and the spread of some confusion.

Despite their more or less polite disagreement with certain aspects of the Catholic Church, most of the graduates of 1965 write about their lives and their visions with serenity, the source of which is, I think, Christian hope. In spite of the terrible things happening in the world, they believe - as Christians have done throughout the ages - that God is good and won't let them down.

PART I:

LIFE AT SACRED HEART SEMINARY
IN THE 1960s

Wandering Between Two Worlds

LIFE AT SACRED HEART SEMINARY
IN THE 1960s

It is important that any reader who did not spend time in a pre-Vatican II seminary gain a sense for what went on in these institutions, what the routines and practices were. Even someone who actually *did* attend a diocesan seminary elsewhere during the same time frame might find the SHS experience a bit different. Sacred Heart had a deserved reputation of being among the most liberal seminaries of its day. Even so, many readers will find that life in such a setting was highly structured and quite restrictive. Frankly, that was exactly the idea.

The purpose of a Catholic seminary, then as now, was to prepare candidates for the priesthood, intellectually and spiritually. In the case of Sacred Heart Seminary's college department, there was a heavy emphasis on intellectual formation. Students there were indeed "in college." The seminary was an accredited institution of higher learning and, as such, had to maintain certain specific standards.

Still, there was more than adequate time for prayer and reflection built into the daily schedule. A seminarian's day began with an early morning Mass, at 6:30 AM. Each seminarian was expected to faithfully attend and participate, fully awake or not. Skipping the 6:30 Mass was not only frowned upon by the faculty, most of whom were priests; continuing disregard for this rule could get a seminarian expelled. For those in the first two years of college, skipping was hard to do anyway. Most of the freshmen and sophomores had roommates, thereby providing a check on each other in rising early. The juniors and seniors, however, had private rooms, making it easier to skip out. Few did.

The first two years of college were still considered part of what was called the "minor" seminary (the high school years comprised the rest). Proper attire for a minor seminarian consisted of a neat, open-collared shirt, slacks, and a light, zippered jacket, usually colored tan or blue. The jacket was to be worn at all times, except when the student was engaged in recreation or in his room. It wasn't exactly a uniform, but it was close.

The third and fourth years in college were part of the "major" seminary experience (the four years of theology comprised the rest). Juniors and seniors, therefore, wore cassocks with Roman collars wherever they went inside the seminary grounds (they did not wear this attire off campus). Known as "philosophers," since their main course of study was scholastic philosophy, centering on the works of Thomas Aquinas and related fields, these scholars were at the pinnacle of the SHS experience and were generally looked up to by the lower classmen.

After Mass, the student body went down to the seminary's lower floor to the Refectory for breakfast. Anywhere else, the name for where students took meals would be called a cafeteria. New students soon found out, however, that in a Catholic seminary, there were often special names for places and things, names seldom found in the outside world, names that recalled an earlier time and culture. Each class ate together, after which there would be a short period of free time before classes began.

During this free time, students could dash to designated areas where smoking was allowed. In those days, nearly everyone smoked. Smoking was so common, as a matter of fact, that designated recreation halls, where the students could engage in light activities such as ping pong, billiards, card playing, newspaper reading, or limited television viewing, were called "smokers." There were two smokers for the college department: the First and Second College Smoker and the Philosophy Smoker. This separation had the affect of further reinforcing the major/minor seminary division.

Classes were held every day except Sunday. On Wednesdays and Saturdays, classes ended at noon. Those afternoons were free. Each seminarian was given one or two "short permissions" and two "long permissions" each month. In this case, the *permission* was to leave the campus. The short permissions lasted only an hour. Many students didn't even use them, since the Boston/Chicago Boulevard area was no longer a posh district. Although the nice looking homes remained, the area around the seminary was almost entirely "inner city," meaning that it was indeed a rough neighborhood.

Long permissions, on the other hand, were *always* used. These allowed a student to leave the seminary grounds for the entire afternoon. Barring visiting parents, most used their long permissions for bus trips to downtown Detroit, still a thriving area in those days. Visits downtown meant everything from a ball game at Tiger Stadium to hamburger eating contests at an urban beanery to visits to Fuchs, the local Catholic supply store, where the famous seminarian discount (10% off!) was alive and well. Among the other popular hangouts was the J.L Hudson bookstore. It was there that one could buy any number of famous (and infamous) books, books the students couldn't find in the seminary library (or couldn't gain access to without special permission, since they were sealed in the "Forbidden Books" section). That bookstore was an education in and of itself.

The biggest thing about the long permission, however, was the fact that one was *outside*. It's not that the seminary was such a bad place. Furthermore, it was a self-contained operation. Inside the seminary grounds were a laundry, a bookstore (which also sold sundries), a barbershop (students did the haircutting), and an infirmary. The infirmary was operated by an old nun named Sister Sabina, who was empowered by school authorities to call in the seminary doctor for cases that ran beyond "Take two aspirins and see me in the morning." Still, after week upon week of those walls, most students longed to see *something else*. Long permissions were getaways, breaks from studies, a chance to see life on the outside. They were indeed welcome.

Outside of the short and long permissions, where one could actually leave the grounds, communication with the outside world wasn't very easy. There were no student telephones as such, except for two pay phones that received limited use. There certainly weren't any student telephones for *incoming* calls. If there was a family emergency back home, one had to rely on someone in the administration to relay the message. The seminary was equipped with an old fashioned switchboard, normally operated by an outside employee or one of a group of trained students. There were ways of getting messages privately through the student switchboard operators. Most routine communication with one's family, however, was accomplished by letter.

Academics at SHS were serious. The classes were serious. The professors (teachers or profs, as they were commonly called) were serious. And most of the students were serious. College seminarians studied everything from Latin to literature to liturgy, logic, speech, sociology, and, of course, philosophy. Most took another foreign language. There was one required science course. There were studies in the Bible. World and church history were also emphasized. In short, the world of academia at SHS was steeped in the humanities; and the teachers, the profs, were very good. Many of the profs were priests, graduates of Sacred Heart themselves; but there were any number of good lay professors as well. Some of these were former seminarians. When one left the college seminary by way of graduation, one held a degree that meant something, even if much of the outside world wondered just what the heck *scholastic* philosophy was.

At Sacred Heart Seminary, students were encouraged to ask lots of questions, both of their professors and of each other. Dialogues between students were frequent, animated, open, and often led to new insights on the parts of the participants. Outside lecturers were frequent. The Cardinal Mooney Lecture Series, for instance, introduced seminarians to the broader world of intellectual American Catholicism, people who wrote for *America*, *Commonweal*, and other important Catholic publications.

The philosophers were allowed, on occasion, to attend lectures off campus, at Wayne State University, for example. Once, an entire busload of seminarians made the trip from West Chicago Boulevard to the University of Michigan in Ann Arbor to attend a special lecture of important Protestant theologian, Paul Tillich. Constant intellectual stimulation was the rule, not the exception.

There were other outside activities that were not at all typical of the seminaries of that time. For instance, there was real involvement in the life of Detroit. Some seminarians went to high schools as Young Christian Students (YCS) moderators. There was a student-organized program whereby seminarians lived with African-American families for a weekend. In 1965, the entire student body marched from Sacred Heart to downtown Detroit, in support of the Selma civil rights march. Seminary administrators had the foresight and courage to make these important activities possible.

Each day, however, left plenty of time for reflection, informal discussion, and recreation. The back campus consisted of a large open grassy area surrounded by a stone walkway that tracked its perimeter. During free time, students could be seen walking slowly along the walkway, some by themselves saying the rosary, others in groups, conversing in quiet or animated ways. In the far corner of the campus, where Joy Road and Linwood Avenue intersect, there was a grotto devoted to the Virgin Mary. Students often paused there for a short prayer.

As far as physical exercise and sports went, inside that same walkway there could be a half dozen simultaneous intramural softball or football games going on. The seminary building contained a nice gymnasium where students could engage in basketball. The seminary was also equipped with a half dozen handball courts (racquetball hadn't been invented yet). Once a year, the seminary held a field day, organized by the college juniors, wherein students could display their track skills, among other things. The tennis courts disappeared when the new high school building was completed in 1960-61; and if one wanted to swim or bowl, a short walk to close-by Visitation parish and its recreation center was required.

Most of the recreation noted above occurred after classes ended in the late afternoon. During these times, however, the smokers were always open for those in the student body who preferred a lighter physical regimen. These free periods, of course, could also be used for study. Almost every seminarian, at some time or another, needed to put in a few extra hours to cram for an exam or finish a paper. Most of the studying, however, went on after the evening meal, which, like the other two meals, was served on a very specific schedule. If one didn't show up in time for a meal, one didn't eat.

Sunday was different, more set aside for spiritual matters. Instead of one Mass to be attended, the seminarians went to two on Sundays. The 6:30 AM Mass still was held, but it was augmented by a 10:00 AM High Mass, with full student choir (known in the seminary as the *Schola Cantorum*), incense, and all the trappings of such a celebration. In the late afternoon, the student body reassembled in chapel for Vespers, one of the hours of the Divine Office. This edifice, located in the very center of the seminary building, was pure gothic in its beauty. In the late Sunday afternoons, shafts of lights would pour in from the stained glass window over the altar.

Each day, not just Sundays, officially ended at about 9:00 PM with Compline (another part of the Office) or night prayers, again in the chapel. After that began the Grand Silence, wherein no speaking was officially allowed until breakfast the next morning. During Grand Silence, students were expected to return to their rooms for study or prayer, eschewing the smokers and other recreational areas of the building. This was, at least, what was supposed to happen. In the latter years of college for SHS 1965, the Grand Silence was almost universally ignored, unless one found himself in the presence of one of the faculty members, especially the priest assigned to act as the Dean of Discipline.

Like in the old English-model boarding schools, many of the priest faculty members were in residence full-time in the seminary building. Much of an entire floor of the gothic structure was given over to these priests for their quarters. Students needing to see a priest for academic or spiritual reasons were basically free to go knock on his door at any time. Priests' rooms were typically small, two-room suites, consisting of a sitting room and a bedroom/bathroom – fairly typical for diocesan priests, no matter where they lived. There was a lot of fun in visiting a priest in his quarters, mainly because of the incredible clutter found in most of them; and most of the clutter consisted of books, books, and more books. This stood to reinforce the importance of lifelong reading and studying in the eyes of the visiting student.

Student room policies, however, were quite strict. Visiting a fellow seminarian in his room was not allowed. Doors to student rooms were to be kept open at all times the assigned seminarians were not in them. A closed door meant that the seminarian was inside….alone, in the case of the third and fourth year men. Being caught in another seminarian's room, even for the most innocent of reasons, was grounds for immediate expulsion.

Despite the plethora of clergymen right there in the building, the seminarians were not necessarily encouraged to pick and choose among the faculty for spiritual advisors. The college department had an "official" spiritual advisor, a priest whose main duties consisted in counseling seminarians. Each seminarian was required to meet with this priest periodically for a review of his spiritual life.

Other spiritual activities that were routine in the seminary were the once-a-year retreat, normally conducted by an outsider, a priest not on the faculty, and days of recollection. The yearly retreat was a three-day affair, with constant silence as part of its aura. It was normally held early in the school year. Days of recollection, which sometimes reflected back to the theme of the retreat, occurred on selected Sundays throughout the school year. These were usually directed by a faculty member and included many religious exercises, such as a thematic series of sermonettes throughout the day, each followed by recollection time in chapel or walking the seminary grounds. Mandatory silence characterized these days as well.

The seminarians were also allowed a certain amount of entertainment, some self-generated, some from outside. Part of the self-generated entertainment were plays put on by the various classes. The first and second year classes were expected to put on a play each year. These mostly consisted in old Broadway plays from years before, plays like *Harvey, Brother Orchid*, and *Arsenic and Old Lace*. The major challenge encountered by the students was in picking a play where (a) either all the characters were male or (b) where any female characters could be transposed into male characters without totally straining credibility.

The juniors and seniors were responsible for the annual Passion Play, tickets for which were sold to the general public. Here, the sex of the various players was less of an issue, although more than one seminarian had to play Mary while wrapped, head to toe, in more fabric than a devout Muslim woman.

Relatively current films were shown in the auditorium on a regular basis. Selected by the faculty, not every movie being shown in local theaters made it to the seminary projection booth. The viewing of special television programming was also permitted, although run-of-the-mill sitcoms of the day were forbidden. If a student really wanted to see mass-media programming or dicey movies, he always had the long permission and his summer vacation (yes, the school year only lasted nine months!).

Even some of the entertainment had a true intellectual edge to it. On rare occasions, film festivals would be arranged, wherein a series of foreign movies, known then as art films, would be shown to the student body over a two or three day period. As expected, these films would generate numerous discussions among the faculty members and the student body. They were true learning experiences in their own right.

The seminarians of SHS also learned how to entertain themselves in an informal manner. There was a lot of clean horseplay and some outright practical joking. There were always individuals (or groups of them) who would try to dream up new ways of "topping" a prank pulled by someone else. The Feast of St. Patrick on March 17 normally was the top day of the year for pranks. On that day, the students formed into three camps: the Irish contingent, the non-Irish contingent (usually led by the seminary's large Polish population), and those just trying to stay out of the way of both groups. The humorous stories are too numerous to recount.

One of the truly "fun" things to do was to climb to the top of the Gothic Tower. The seminary is basically a four-story complex, but in the very front of that large building is a tall tower that adds an additional four or five stories. The top could only be reached by climbing a 60-foot ladder that went straight up the inside of one of the tower walls. Faculty permission had to be given for any student to attempt the climb; and no one was allowed to climb alone.

There was something daring about that 60-foot climb. More than one student got halfway up or down only to freeze in fear. Such students had to be coaxed or even gently led down by their fellow seminarians. Yet, the climb to the top was worth it. The tower was one of the tallest structures in that part of Detroit. From it, one could see a long way toward downtown, which was miles away. The view was magnificent, even stirring. One could see the world below, the people, the autos, the buildings; yet one was above it all, separated from the harsh realities of that world. The view only emphasized the oasis, both external and internal, that Sacred Heart was.

The journeys that were beginning or continuing in the building below were, in many ways, like journeys up and down that tower wall. Each had ups and downs, high points and low points. Each afforded the traveler an occasional view of "being above everything" and each required a return to reality.

The seminary was, in many ways, an unreal place. While it indeed afforded great exposure to the world of ideas, to the world of Catholic spirituality, there was also a lot going on outside that the students were insulated from. Further, much of what was going on outside was radical and revolutionary, especially the elements that bore directly on the Church. All had a direct bearing on the future of each student in the class of 1965.

William E. Richardson, with contributions from
Eugene J. Fisher,
John A. Dick, and
B. Thomas McCloskey

Wandering Between Two Worlds

PART II:

LIFE AFTER 1965

Wandering Between Two Worlds

CONFESSIONS OF A LAST
HOUR WORKER
Charles S. Fontana

In the argot of seminary speak I am a "lifer," having entered Sacred Heart Seminary High School in the fall of 1957 at the age of 14. This act alone made me a graduating high school senior in 1961 and a member of the SHS graduating college class of 1965, the focus of this book.

My vocation at times runs counter to many of the stereotypical ideas of the candidate for priesthood. I am a first generation American on my father's side and second generation on my mother's. I was born and grew up in Detroit, Michigan. I am the older of two children, my sister being four years younger than I. Both paternal and maternal lines come from the same small Italian village a few miles south of Rome. Its written records go back to the time of the Holy Roman Emperor Charlemagne, c. 800 AD.

My home environment was bilingual and bicultural and comfortably middle class. Dad worked for the Ford Motor Company Rouge Plant in Dearborn, and Mom was a homemaker. In my naive "Beaver Cleaver" days, I unconsciously categorized families as normal or dysfunctional. Sadly, dysfunction was a part of our family. Subsequently I have come to realize that there "ain't no such creature" as a "normal" family, merely varying degrees of dysfunction.

My parents were not regularly practicing Catholics in my early years, but they saw to it that my sister and I attended Mass each Sunday morning and religious education classes, catechism, each Monday afternoon. I have strong memories of my mother quizzing me on the answers to the questions in the *Baltimore Catechism*. I attended the local public elementary school from kindergarten through grade six, its highest grade. Then I transferred to our parish school, Nativity of Our Lord, on Detroit's east side. I quickly trained to become an altar server.

The conscious origin of my priestly vocation was rooted in my awe of the liturgical rites and in my admiration for our parish priests. Sadly in 2002 the press reported that one of those priests, now in his 80s, was sentenced to serve 30 days in jail after pleading no contest to a charge of sexual abuse of a minor committed decades prior.

In the late 40s and early 50s our parish was served by a pastor and three associate pastors, "assistants" in those days. My notions of priesthood were those of a child, both childlike and childish. They consisted of romantic ideas of mysterious men who went about doing good things as Jesus did.

When I was in the fifth grade, our family was on a trip to Flint, my mother's hometown, when, from the back seat of the auto, I announced, "I am going to be a priest."

Silence.

My only previous aspiration had been to become an archeologist, given my fascination with classical cultures. From the day of my announcement I never wavered in my desire for priesthood.

Not so for my parents who seemed bewildered by my decision. Only later would I come to appreciate some of their concern: no male heir to continue the Fontana name. Such a worry may underscore our Italian genes, but it is no less important for that. *Akeda,* the sacrifice of one's firstborn, in any form is not a joyful thought. It was not for Abraham and Sarah, nor for Luigi and Anita Fontana. I believe they consulted with one or another of our parish assistants who reassured them and got them to return to the practice of the Faith.

Wandering Between Two Worlds

From that point on I had my parents' support. At the same time, they told me that, should I change my mind, they would respect such a decision. I am grateful for their attitude, because in the seminary I saw more than one unhappy student who was there because mom or the "good nuns" felt he would make a good priest. I, on the other hand, experienced solid parental support along with the encouragement of our parish priests and sisters.

My pastor, a very stern man, took a keen personal interest in my spiritual and academic development. He did not hesitate to remind me of my responsibility to attend daily Mass during vacations. In this reminder he was supporting the motto of our seminary rector, Msgr. Albert Matyn, who would frequently proclaim in his booming voice, "There is no vacation from a vocation!" My pastor would also scrutinize my quarterly report cards.

I worked in the parish office on Sunday mornings during Masses, answering the doorbell and the telephone and preparing sacramental records for people requesting them. Gradually I came to know more and more of the inner workings of a busy rectory.

I attended Sacred Heart Seminary High School as a "day dog," the nickname given to those of us who lived at home and rode the bus to school six days a week. Boarding students were called "house rats." I loved the college prep courses and managed to be an honor student all four years. Ours was the first class to graduate from the new high school building, named in honor of the late Archbishop, Edward Cardinal Mooney. We moved into the new building after Easter recess in 1961 and graduated a few weeks later. In the fall of that same year I moved back across the campus into the College Department in the main building and became a "house rat," a requirement for all college seminarians.

The four years of college, like the four years of high school, provided an outstanding atmosphere for classical learning in the liberal arts. Ours was a unique institution, quite liberal for its day, yet maintaining an atmosphere of strict discipline and regimentation. For me it was, for the most part, a happy time with great friends, all sharing a common goal. We had professors who instilled in us a love of learning and who encouraged us to question and to explore. They provided us with a solid foundation and the framework from which to ask those questions and to launch that exploration. *"Nihil humanum mihi alienum."* "Nothing human is foreign to me."

Despite my love for my alma mater, Sacred Heart Seminary was by no means Eden or Disney World. As with all growing experiences, we had good times and painful times. Both of these situations centered on adolescence. There were the joys of developing new friendships, of sharing revelations previously thought to be unique, of realizing I was not alone. The pain came when over the years some of these same friends developed other ideals and aspirations and withdrew from the seminary.

I was and, to a great extent, still am an idealist. As such, I could be harsh, arrogant, demanding, and unforgiving and have been so for a good portion of my life. Only after I finally experienced weakness within myself, wallowing in the "muck and manure" of life, instead of imagining myself the impartial observer above the fray, did I learn forgiveness and compassion. Because I have on numerous occasions been the beneficiary of those gifts, I can now share them with others. Aeschylus's words mean so much to me: "He who learns must suffer. In our sleep pain that cannot forget falls drop by drop upon the heart and in our despair, against our will, comes wisdom through the awful grace of God."

I graduated from college in June of 1965, which qualifies me to pen these sentences. In September of that same year I entered St. John's Provincial Seminary in Plymouth to begin post graduate studies in theology and related disciplines preparing for my ordination on June 7, 1969, along with 41 classmates from all over the state of Michigan.

The transition to St. John's was psychologically difficult. The move from the inner city of Detroit to a far western suburb set the scene. At SHS we lived with the continuous cacophony of city life, the blare of sirens, the occasional gunshot, action all around. At St. John's all these sounds disappeared. For me the silence was deafening, broken only by the rumble of the train that passed next to our 180 acres.

Another adjustment concerned life within the house itself. The change from the relatively open atmosphere of SHS to the more rigid setting and rule of St. John's was taxing. "Great!" I lamented to myself, "I have moved from a place which gave me a great deal of freedom to a more severely restrictive environment. Here I am, 22 years old and treated like someone half that age." The rule specified that students could "walk the streets of town" only with a group leader, dressed in clerical garb, in odd numbers, and could not stop anywhere. The group leader was to report all infractions of the rule. For good measure, we were reminded that "spitting on the streets of town" was also proscribed. Odd numbers indeed! Thankfully, within a short period of time, the seminary rule would, as with so many other realities, undergo a radical transition.

The most jarring and challenging of all the transitions, however, was the one our class faced along with the entire Church, the Second Vatican Council, which closed during our first year of theology. Hesitation and hope coursed through the house, uniting some and dividing others. What a time of theological and liturgical ferment! The priesthood which had initially attracted me would not be the priesthood into which I would be ordained.

Almost overnight the traditional textbooks became obsolete, and nothing replaced them save the daily dittograph handouts prepared by our professors the night before class. Who can forget the sweet aroma of alcohol on the pages fresh with blue ink? They provided a cheap buzz lasting mere seconds. Of the professors who faced this daunting task daily I say with Genesis, "There were giants who walked the earth in those days. .... They were the heroes of old, the men of renown." For the most part they imparted to us an education that still holds up well after more than three decades.

I reached a critical juncture in my seminary career when, just prior to being "called" to orders, to being officially accepted as a candidate for priesthood, an underclassman slipped a letter under my door. The letter stated that, in his opinion, I was unfit to be such a candidate. He and I discussed the matter with no clarification or resolution. The fruitlessness left me in a state of rage and fear. The former was because I knew that the individual had himself been required to leave the seminary for a period of time. In fact he had been a classmate for eight years. The latter came from my own over-reaction. I after all had spent nearly my entire life preparing for one thing and was perhaps about to see it all for naught. "To dig ditches I am unable; to beg I am ashamed." What to do?

I met with my Spiritual Director/Confessor who assured me that he would himself investigate the entire matter. He spoke with my accuser and with other classmates. I know nothing of the nature of those conversations. The outcome speaks for itself -- ordination and nearly four decades of priesthood to this day. Even now, however, the entire event stirs me from time to time and has left scars.

My first assignment, from 1969 to 1976, was as one of two associate pastors at St. Suzanne Parish on Detroit's west side. There, at the urging of a dynamic laywoman, I developed a popular introductory course for adults on understanding the Bible. My love for Sacred Scripture is the legacy imparted to me by my late professor, Fr. John Castelot, during the St. John's years. I have always loved teaching and for awhile envisioned returning to SHS as an instructor. I did in fact return in 1978 for one semester and taught introductory Scripture to candidates for the Permanent Diaconate. I also place a high premium upon continuing personal education and enrichment. To this end I have taken courses such as intertestamental Judaism and have been privately tutored in Hebrew.

This first assignment also afforded me the chance to indulge in my love of global travel. I have visited in about 14 countries, including the former Soviet Union, the People's Republic of China and India; but it is Italy, land of my ancestors, that remains my favorite place. Far more than a root of Western Civilization, Italy has nurtured my own genetic roots. My first visit in 1966 was an emotional apex, something I had dreamt about for decades. I had the sense of returning home to a place I had never seen but which had always anchored my life. Each of the 13 visits I have since made there has always been a homecoming. My parents' generation has all but passed, but the blood that flows through the cousins that remain unites us. *"Alla famiglia!"* "To the family!" Wherever I have journeyed, I have made new friends and have grown intellectually. The idea of the global citizen defines my approach and outlook.

One of the most profound, life-changing experiences I had occurred at St. Suzanne and involved my relationship with the priest who became the second pastor. He arrived three years into my assignment. The founding pastor had decided to retire after 25 years at St. Suzanne. When the new pastor took over, the situation soon resembled the difficult adjustments that have to be made when a step-parent comes into a family. The transition was not an easy one. In hindsight, my reaction was puerile. Filled with resentment, I was unkind to him and did a great deal to thwart his acceptance by the parish. My behavior gave new meaning to the spiritual term "uncharitableness."

Meanwhile the new pastor ignored my childishness and simply returned kindness in the face of my nastiness. In time he broke down my resistance and won me over. We became good friends, and I seldom made major decisions without first seeking his counsel.

At the time of his silver jubilee Mass in 1984, he invited me to be the homilist. Ten years later he returned the favor. When I wrote to thank him for the opportunity to preach at his celebration, I recalled our initial relationship and all the difficulties I had caused and told him how it still embarrassed and pained me. In his response he wrote simply, "I remember only the good times." My own hope is that, when I appear before God on judgment day, God will respond to my failures with similar words.

In November, 2001, I underwent emergency quadruple bypass surgery. That same brother priest had me recuperate at his rectory during the first weeks of my recovery.

In the summer of 2002 this man was summarily dismissed from his pastorate, forbidden to represent himself as a priest or to function as one. This was the penalty given to him because of sexual indiscretions committed decades before. While many of us struggle with our vocations and battle low morale, this man, who was a priest to the very core of his being, who loved the priesthood above all else, sat idly on the sidelines dismissed from laboring in the vineyard. On a visit to his apartment, I glanced at his kitchen table and saw his chalice and a Sacramentary for the celebration of Mass, which he did by himself. My heart cracked at the sight. The loneliness of celibacy pales in comparison. His sudden death in 2006 has left a deep void. In February, 1976, I was transferred to St. Mary Parish, Wayne, and remained there 14 months. June, 1977, saw my arrival at St. Clement Parish, Dearborn, where I ministered to the large Italian congregation for one year. In late October, 1977, the regional bishop called me and asked me to be the temporary administrator of St. Andrew Parish, Rochester, where the pastor had abruptly resigned. My two-month stint at St. Andrew gave me the dubious distinction of being the pastor of pop icon Madonna. At the time I was unaware of this fact, and I am quite sure it meant absolutely nothing to her.

I returned to St. Clement in January, 1978, thinking I would remain there several more years, only to receive another episcopal call to consider a pastorate in rural Carleton, Monroe County, at St. Patrick Parish. After prayer and counsel, I accepted the call with trepidation. The assignment became the opportunity to bring some stability, healing, and peace to a community that had struggled with the temperament of the previous pastor. I remained in Carleton until 1985, when I felt it was time to seek a new pastorate. This time the parish was St. Pius X in Southgate, a suburb down river from Detroit.

This pastorate was not a pleasant one and left me with many harsh memories, which only recently have begun to ebb. I have over the years succeeded saints and SOBs and have concluded that replacing the latter is by far the easier task. My predecessor at St. Pius had been there nearly two decades. A workaholic, he felt that, if one Mass a day were good, three Masses would be three times better. He rendered extraordinary service to his people and established a very comfortable ambiance. In my efforts to trim and to create efficiencies, I suffered in comparison to him.

At St. Pius I came to understand the adage, "The only thing worse than being an associate is having one." My past sins against the pastor at St. Suzanne came back to haunt me in spades. I had three associates in as many years. The first one was somewhat brain-damaged from a head injury and kept a pet coyote. The second, a brilliant but troubled individual, taught me firsthand the meaning of addictive behaviors. The third was a recovering alcoholic who had been sober for many years but not before he had burned out several million brain cells. Even now I have no desire to live or to work with an associate.

In 1988 I assumed the pastorate of St. Timothy Parish, Trenton, another downriver suburb. I arrived an exhausted, wounded animal following the St. Pius experience and fell into the arms of a beautiful, supportive community. There is a balm in Gilead.

When I was in Carleton, I was also elected Vicar of the Monroe County Vicariate, which consists of 14 parishes in the southernmost area of our archdiocese. In that role I was the Archbishop's on-the-spot representative, troubleshooter, and delegate, the first line of contact with the central offices. For four years at the request of then-Archbishop Edmund Szoka, I was also a member of the College of Consultors, which met with him monthly to offer advice and consent principally on matters of finance. Finally I was also a member of the Incardination Board, which helped to consider and to process the applications of priests from other dioceses or from religious orders who sought to become members of the Detroit Presbyterate, a procedure which requires a number of steps over several years. In each of these positions I feel I learned far more than I contributed.

After eighteen years at St. Timothy I resigned the pastorate and accepted the position of Parochial Vicar or Pastoral Associate at St. Paul of Tarsus Parish, Clinton Township, where I have ministered for three years now. It is large parish with a substantial Italian population.

Wandering Between Two Worlds

The excellent education afforded me by Sacred Heart Seminary's high school and college has served to shape the path of my life. I am grateful for a visionary institution that was, in pre-Vatican II days, way ahead of the game, on the cutting edge. It was a small school but open to so many ideas, while providing a framework for critical analysis. It taught me independent thinking in a time of rapid change.

I am grateful to be a part of a Church which opened me, forced me, to contemplate the ultimate verities and to pare down to a very few what might be termed absolutes. The Second Vatican Council was a breath of fresh air wherefrom the unthinkable and the unchangeable became the possible and often the realized.

The 1960's taught me to be leery, wary, cautious, and critical. As a result I am a priest with a love-hate relationship with the "Mother" Church who nourished me. I find it an institution that can be insufferably controlling, even beyond the grave. Consider, for instance, the idea of indulgences or the rules for the disposition of cremated remains. Power does appear to be the ultimate aphrodisiac, at least for celibates.

Like Jacob I wrestle with God. As I move closer to the end of my earthly voyage, I cling to a few irreducibles: "I believe, Lord; help my unbelief." "There are no accidents, only grace." "The worst returns to laughter." "Never say never" "God is not fair, and thank God He's not." My favorite parable has become that of the last hour workers. I am one of them, and a poor one at that, in need of forgiveness, compassion, and mercy. Hypocrisy in all arenas -- ecclesial, political, and personal -- offends me greatly. Yet my quarrel with the Church is at base a lover's quarrel.

In the political sphere I count among the shaping events of my life the two Kennedy assassinations and that of Martin Luther King, Jr., Vietnam, and Watergate, all of which shattered any ideals and dreams I might have had in this area. As a result I am, for the most part, cynically apolitical, voting only in local elections and ignoring the self-serving individuals who style themselves our leaders. The late Scripture scholar, John McKenzie, said it best when he commented on Jesus' temptation in the desert: When Satan offered all the kingdoms of the world to Jesus, stating it was in his power to do so, it may have been the only time when the Father of Lies was speaking the truth!

As a priest for over three decades, I draw much comfort from the local church, the parochial scene. My prayer is that of the Rabbi in *Fiddler On The Roof*, "God bless and keep the Czar....far from my door!" At times I find myself in a state of mental schism from the hierarchical Church as I struggle with doctrinal and moral issues. If, by the farthest stretch, I were selected to become a bishop, I would indeed be flattered; but in no way could I in conscience accept the appointment.

My vision of priesthood is two-fold. The priest must be a seer, a witness to and an articulator of the reality that there is more to life than bread alone. The priest as leader must be the servant of all. I view the priest as the bard, the guardian of tribal myths and sagas, the inspirer of the people's communal hopes. I understand that such bards (Homer) often accompanied ancient armies in order to motivate soldiers before battle by their songs and stories. In a passage which I had printed on my ordination memorial card, Karl Rahner spoke in a similar vein: "My brothers, accept us as we are: the priest is not an angel sent from heaven. He is a man chosen from among men, a member of the Church, a Christian. Remaining man and Christian, he begins to speak to you the word of God. This word is not his own. No, he comes to you because God has told him to proclaim God's word. Perhaps he has not entirely understood it himself. Perhaps he adulterates it. But he believes; and despite his fears he knows he must communicate God's word to you. For must not some one of us say something about God, about eternal life, about the majesty of grace in our sanctified being? Must not some one of us speak of sin, the judgment, the mercy of God?" Fr. Paul Cioffi, another Jesuit, said it poetically: "The only priestly vestment Jesus ever wore was an apron at the Last Supper."

I am much like the curmudgeon who penned *Ecclesiastes* (McKenzie opined he may have been an atheist.) but with an essential moderating soupcon of St. Paul, "Eye has not seen, ear has not heard, nor has it so much as dawned on man what God has prepared for those who love him." And "How deep are the riches and the wisdom and the knowledge of God! How inscrutable his judgments, how unsearchable his ways! For 'who has known the mind of the Lord?'"

A funeral director-poet once spoke about grave markers. For most of us they will be quite simple: name, date of birth and date of death. Between the two dates will be a tiny dash. That dash represents our entire life, our autobiography. Martin Luther King, Jr., once said: "I am a sinner like all God's children. But I want to be a good man. And I want to hear a voice saying to me one day, 'I take you in and I bless you because you tried.'" Sufficient for me if my marker reads "I tried."

Personally I am more and more conscious of my sins and failures and of my emptiness before God. What this awareness has served to do is to make me more understanding and compassionate for the frailty of each of us who journey together. The hope-filled words of the 14th century English mystic, Juliana of Norwich, give me strength: "All shall be well. All shall be well. And all manner of thing shall be well."

FATHER OF THE MAN
Kenneth W. Russell

"The child is the father of the man."
William Wordsworth

Fall River, Massachusetts, where I spent my pre-teen years was, to me, an Irish town. My great-grandparents were all from the "old sod." Our neighbors all around were Irish. The Sisters of Mercy, who taught us at SS. Peter & Paul School, were Irish. Three priests staffed our parish. The pastor was Msgr. George Maxwell and the curates were Fr. John Hayes and Fr. Cornelius Kelleher. Can you get more Irish? The mayor, John Kane, a childhood friend of my father, was Irish, as were most of the city politicians.

The city was built on a series of hills. We lived at the uppermost portion of the hills on Tecumseh Street. Everything was downhill from home, which was great, until you had to pedal your bike back up. The street behind our house was so steep you dared not ride your bike down because you'd lose control. It was, however, a great sled hill. It was fairly safe since the cars, even with their chains, couldn't make it up the grade; so the police regularly closed it and we had it just for sliding. It was a factory town known for the manufacturing of cloth and thread. Beautiful churches with soaring domes and spires were scattered throughout the city.

We lived about forty minutes from the ocean. We spent many an evening at Horseneck Beach in the cool ocean breeze as well as many weekends at the shore with extended family. A visit to Cape Cod was always a special treat.

Although politically controlled by Irish politicians, the city's population was approximately fifty percent French Canadian in origin. The French built splendid churches, many schools, and a hospital. In our neighborhood some of the houses were owned or rented by Frenchmen; but pretty much we identified and hung with our Irish classmates. The French children typically went to their own schools, such as St. Anne or Notre Dame. Small groups of Polish, Italian, and Portuguese people lived in ghetto-like pockets of the city.

Protestant churches were few and far between; but I do remember St. Luke Episcopal since it was near a park where I spent many a summer hour. I did not know any Protestant children or adults, however.

At a far end of the city was a section unofficially named "The Highlands." Highland Avenue was the main street in the area. Large mansions, which were the homes of some of the factory owners, were located in this area. Many of my friends' mothers worked as domestics in this area of the city.

The newest immigrants to Fall River were the Portuguese from the Azores Islands. They were not well accepted; and, although they tended to live in certain neighborhoods, they also mixed into our neighborhood and a few of them attended SS. Peter & Paul School.

The Portuguese were extremely hardworking and willing to sacrifice good food and fancy clothes to achieve the American dream of home ownership. They built expansive churches and sponsored many festivals and processions for holy days. They sponsored many bands that slowly became a mainstay in Fall River parades. Dad's brother, Charlie Russell, played his trombone in the Portuguese band. It didn't matter that he was Irish as long as he could play well.

Most of us lived in tenement houses, which contained three flats per house. The rent was six dollars a week. The house we lived in was over one hundred years old when we left in 1956. The foundation was constructed of huge irregularly-shaped pieces of granite and the basement had a dirt floor. The houses had no insulation and no central heat. Heat came from large oil-fired space heaters in each tenement. Because of the cost of fuel oil and the danger that an unwatched heater could explode or burst into flames, the stoves were turned off at night. After hopping out of bed in the morning, I joined the rest of the family shivering around the oil stove.

Perhaps we were poor. I'm still not really sure. I know we were rich in friends and family to visit. As kids, we had the run of the city. We rode our bikes all over town and I, early on, found the library where I was allowed to go on my own. I always felt well nourished and always had decent clothing. Love of the ocean and the salt air are hard to erase from my memory. I remember this time of my life with great affection.

Catholic in a Catholic World

Catholic school was my destiny. We lived but a block away. Who ever heard of tuition? So off I went to SS. Peter & Paul School where, of course, my mother and father and numerous other members of the family had graduated. Learning to read in first grade was great fun for me and basically easy. First Communion was taken in first grade. How handsome I was in my white suit.

Because we lived across the street from the church I was often around the church playing and cutting through the property to get home. I made friends with the janitor and one of my first jobs was putting up the kneelers so that he could sweep on Monday morning.

I became an altar boy as soon as possible and rose in the ranks to become High Mass Team Captain. The curates of the parish trained us in our acolyte duties. At all times the priests of our parish were patient and kind and friendly. I didn't play Little League baseball or ride horses like my cousins. Serving Mass as often as possible became my passion. I substituted and volunteered to serve as often as possible.

On Saturdays we helped the sisters who served as sacristans to clean the altar area for Mass. The assigned sisters were of a younger age so as to be able to do the manual labor required. When they came to work they tucked their outer skirt up and over their leather belts, took off their big outer sleeves that buttoned at the shoulder, donned big aprons, and pushed their veils back and out of their way. They were happy-go-lucky and jovial and fun to be with. Sr. Lucia once asked me to make sure no one came into the kitchen because she was going to iron her skirt while she was still wearing it. She figured that anyone who caught her would think her a little daffy. Not too many people were allowed to see the human side of the sisters.

Rectory life was a mystery to most people. What does that big white clapboard three story house look like on the inside? Is the furniture antique or just old? Are the walls painted or wallpapered? What do the priests do in there all day? When I was in sixth grade Msgr. Maxwell, the pastor, died and was succeeded by Msgr. Kelly. Msgr. Kelly wanted to redecorate the rectory; and so he asked his nephew Ed Kelly, who was an art student, to apply his talents to the project. I got to know Ed and was at the rectory almost daily helping him. We had work to do in all the suites so I became acquainted with the priests' accommodations. Occasionally, I'd see the priests in their sport shirts. They never appeared in street clothes at any time or any place!

The priests lived quite well. They had a cook who prepared all their meals, someone to clean and to do their laundry. The rectory was centrally heated and each priest had his own bathroom with shower. At home across the street, we were still gathering around the space heater on cold winter mornings and taking tub baths from water heated on the stove.

I was invited to dinner at the rectory quite often. My dinner, of course, was taken in the kitchen with Ed and Helen the cook. But the food was the same that the priests ate and was really great. The dining room, with oriental rugs and a buzzer to summon the next course, was reserved for the priests. Not a bad way to live.

At school the sisters were very much reserved and serious. Some would call them strict. Occasionally, one of our Sisters of Mercy would beat the hell out of one of the students. They used a strap from first through fourth grade and the rattan rod for infractions of fifth through eighth graders. I escaped most of this punishment, getting just a few cracks across the hands with a pointer. The academic education we received was excellent. The Baltimore Catechism was taught but fairly even-handedly. Hell-fire and damnation were not pushed and things like telling children "not to bite the host or it will bleed" were not part of our training. Religion was not scary but embracing.

In seventh grade I was Safety Patrol Captain. During eighth grade I also was the office assistant for Sr. Mary Grace, our principal. We had no PA system, so all communications were handwritten and hand-delivered by me. One day I overheard a sister telling another that she had to finish sewing her summer wimple for summer school but she didn't want "Grace" to see her do that on school time as she would be upset. Just another peek into the human side of the sisters. I just naturally believed that they called each other "sister."

When Msgr. Maxwell was pastor he would come to the school on his birthday and we would all gather in the hallway and sing "Happy Birthday." After accepting the wishes of the students and a carton of cigarettes as a gift, he would treat us all to ice cream and give us the next school day as a holiday. I found that gesture to be very generous and was impressed that on his birthday he did something for us.

In this almost idyllic portion of my life I had decided that I wanted to be a priest. Growing up in a Catholic city, being touched by Irish culture, and knowing priests and sisters as human were big influences. I knew that priests had to go to school for many years; but in eighth grade education appealed to me. Also, I was big into responsibility and doing things for others, which I saw as a priestly characteristic. I must be truthful and admit that the "living" style of the priests had appeal when compared to the life style of my immediate and extended family.

A Midwesterner in the Making

Massachusetts had a depressed economy and my dad was always working part-time jobs in addition to his regular job as a refrigeration instructor at the New England Technical Institute. In 1955, he decided that he needed to live in an area of the country that had good paying jobs so that our family could live better economically.

Michigan was the place where he landed such a job. We moved to Michigan in 1956 at Thanksgiving time. I was in eighth grade and found it emotionally wrenching to leave my extended family of cousins, aunts and uncles, friends from my school years, and the church where I had been baptized, received First Communion, and so happily been an altar server hundreds of times.

Transition to Michigan was difficult since there were true regional differences at the time. My clothes were different from the norm in Michigan. I had what was called an "accent." Most of my classmates at St. Henry School had been together since first grade and were not willing to find a place for a newcomer. Nonetheless, I made it through the year and graduated but I did not establish a connection with the parish priests or become an altar server again. The Sisters of St. Joseph in the school were friendly and went out of their way to help me to feel accepted and welcome.

High School

If I had continued to live in Fall River I would have attended B.M.C. Durfee High School, a public school. My parents were both proud graduates of Durfee. There were no Catholic high schools for boys or any coed Catholic high schools available in the area. In Michigan there were several choices of small coed Catholic high schools. I chose to attend All Saints High School in Detroit. This choice was basically made because my closest friend at the time had made the same decision.

All Saints was a small school in a blue-collar neighborhood. Basically, it was a college prep school with a few typing and secretarial classes for the girls and a drafting class for the boys.

Socially, All Saints was a good place to be. With only sixty-five classmates there was an uncommon unity. The dances, held monthly, were attended by just about the entire class. Basketball games were well attended and there was always pizza or a Big Boy after the game with classmates. In high school I dated some and attended both the junior and senior proms.

Academically, All Saints was far from a challenge. Memorization and recall were the favored learning methods. Good grades were easy to obtain.

In high school, spiritually, we were prepared as most of the generations before us. We had a daily religion class, weekly attendance at Mass, and a yearly retreat. None of these seemed to have any great impact upon my life. I did belong to Sodality, however, and, in fact, was president in my senior year. The Sodality Moderator spent our time trying to form us into responsible self-motivated young people. To some degree I believe she was successful. While in high school I was a commentator at Mass in St. Henry Church, my home parish. Commentators appeared before the Vatican Council. We read the readings aloud in English for the congregation while the priest read quietly in Latin. Prior to this time the priest read the readings in Latin and then read them again in English from the pulpit.

My desire to become a priest persisted and became more of an entrenched part of my personality during high school. Throughout high school, I knew with an unwavering certainty that I would become a priest. No young lady that I dated, no beer party that I went to made me reconsider for even a moment my resolve to enter the priesthood. I made no secret of my intentions and received support from my teachers as well as the parish priests at All Saints and St. Henry.

Sacred Heart Seminary

My lifelong seminary dream almost did not come to reality, since my family did not have the tuition necessary for me to attend the seminary. St. Henry Credit Union came through with the necessary loan, however, after my dad explained its purpose. With all my laundry labels carefully sewn into my clothes and all my belongings folded in suitcases, I was dropped off at the back door of Sacred Heart Seminary. I had never been away from home for any extended period of time and was full of trepidation, but I knew my family would always be there for me if I needed them.

My assigned room was located in St. Edward Hall. This was a new residence hall converted from classrooms, since the number of seminary students was at an historically peak number. I was assigned to a four-man room. It was obvious that we were assigned according to alphabetical order. Two graduates of the seminary high school and two new men bunked together.

The living arrangements were a nightmare. None of us buddied up with each other or had anything in common. Our room had a large bay window area through which we could war with the rooms on either side. Water was thrown and squirted through the windows on a regular basis. Since we were at war with neighboring rooms, ours was often entered after lights out, and I spent a lot of time on the floor with my mattress on top of me. Sometimes I was a little wet under that mattress from a bucket of water. "Grand Silence," which started at 9 P.M., was a time when no one was allowed to talk. Those hours often became "Grand Bedlam." Our class president once knocked on our door to inform us that we were the worst room on the floor, that we were known to the Assistant Dean, and asked us to please quiet down! The Assistant Dean of Students was often seen patrolling the hallways. As my grades plummeted and the relationships in the room worsened, I asked the Dean of Students to find a new room for me. I was soon transferred to a single room in Immaculate Heart of Mary Hall. What a relief!

My first year was tough academically. I had Latin six times a week. Our professor-priest was soft spoken and never rose from his chair. Class consisted of correcting exercises from the textbook. European History was interesting but I was unable to reach the heights of understanding that the professor had hoped we would reach. My high school history class had consisted of a mere memorization of dates, names, and places; so I wasn't ready for the rigors of this class. I ended up failing the course and repeating it at the University of Detroit. At U of D the class was taught by the chairman of the History Department. This time I passed.

Our religion courses, Scripture and Apologetics, were taught by the Spiritual Director, who had not had any graduate training in the subjects beyond the normal studies in preparation for ordination. He also had a sleep disorder and could fall asleep at the drop of a hat. He divided up the book and we each taught a section. The texts were good but not a substitute for a learned professor.

In my second year I took more Latin from a professor who had had polio and was confined to a wheelchair. Though learned in languages, he was not a good teacher and students rarely paid attention to the constant correction of exercises. I never had the chance to take a foreign language, which the seminary high school grads were able to do, since they had taken Latin all through high school.

Second year was also the year we took a course on Liturgy. This course seemed vital and interesting to me and to most of my classmates. Because of the topics around Mass and the sacraments, we paid attention and often discussed the points from the class at meals and other free times.

The teaching methods used by the professors of the classes fell pretty much into a pattern. The majority of the professors, who were priests, would tell you they would rather be in parish life; but in holy obedience they were teaching at the seminary. The usual method of teaching was to regurgitate some notes from their graduate classes at Notre Dame, University of Michigan, Catholic University, etc. Professors who had studied in Rome or Louvain were forced to translate to the vernacular. We had many knowledgeable and well-educated professors who lacked the ability to teach. They knew no teaching methodology and lacked knowledge of the mechanisms through which people learn. They became sages on the stage rather than guides to learning.

Another of my favorite classes was Sociology. Again it was not that the professor was such a brilliant teacher but that I found great interest in the topic of sociology. There were not many private discussions about sociology, as the majority of my classmates hated the class. My graduate studies in psychology and counseling grew from my interest in the human condition that I first encountered in Sociology at Sacred Heart.

I will forever be grateful for the introductions to Gregorian Chant as well as classical music and opera that I was given at Sacred Heart. I was exposed to music both through class and during leisure time listening to records. The seminary provided a wealth of recorded music, ranging from classical and opera to musicals. This was a whole new world to me, one which I found fascinating. My interest continues to this day.

In our English classes we had a writing professor who did an outstanding job teaching us to write. His emphasis was on clear, concise, precise communication. The method of writing he taught served me well throughout my career in education. Nonetheless, I found him mean-spirited in his approach and heavy-handed in his grading and expectations. I truly did not appreciate him until a few years after I had left the seminary. I also received a broader knowledge and appreciation of European and American literature as a result of various English classes.

Third and fourth year of college were devoted to the pursuit of Scholastic Philosophy, which was our major. Our class was the last to have a forced major in Philosophy. The official texts for our classes were in Latin but most lectures were delivered in English. Most students had "ponies," which were textbooks written in English explaining the philosophical concepts we were studying. In Philosophy we had an upper and lower division based on ability levels. Not that anyone was lacking in ability but some could go further and deeper. Some students needed to be well schooled so that they could be sent abroad for study. In other words we needed bishop material. I was assigned to the lower division, which was good, since my interest in Philosophy was minimal. But like most other things we were asked to do, I jumped through the hoops because priesthood was my ultimate goal.

While at Sacred Heart I grew socially from an awkward teenager to manhood. At the end of first college I began to make a series of friends. I became more self-sufficient in many ways and enjoyed the camaraderie of my classmates. At the end of second college I began to stay at school to study or go places with classmates instead of going "home" at our permission times. I was secure with my path towards priesthood and secure with friends. Basically, where could you find a better group of guys? They were idealistic, hard working, fun loving people. On short permissions there was always someone to go with to the soda shop. When we turned twenty-one we went to downtown Detroit for pizza and a glass of wine. On long permissions we were granted a full afternoon and were often invited to the homes of fellow students for dinner. Who could forget the succulent homemade stuffed peppers, spicy lasagnas, and roast beef? What great times we had eating and laughing until our sides hurt.

On vacations I participated in a few trips with classmates. One Easter time we went to a classmate's cottage on Black Lake. One fellow brought his guitar and we sang hootenanny songs, which were popular in the early sixties. A classmate prepared a beef roast completely laced with garlic. You couldn't taste the beef for the garlic. On another Easter break we used a classmate's car to visit the Trappist monastery at Gethsemane, Kentucky. For most of us it was our first taste of monastic living, an experience to remember. We all chipped in for the gas but the joke was the car took a quart of oil at every fill up! Another time we traveled to St. Jerome Seminary in Kitchener, Ontario. Some of my friends had attended St. Jerome to perfect their Latin before entering Sacred Heart. For this trip we used one friend's station wagon. The trip occurred shortly after that classmate had fallen into a handball court and broken his back. By the time he drove to Kitchener, his back was so sore he couldn't drive any more; so he reluctantly asked me to drive back. Ordinarily this would not have been a problem, except that his father had said that no one else was to drive. We managed to keep it a secret from his father and get everyone home safely!

The regimen of the seminary was seen as necessary by the faculty but allowed for very little individuality. There were set times for classes, set times for recreation, set times for gym or physical education, and set time for meals. Most guys were anxious to see each other at mealtime, just to socialize. The seminary authorities never caught on to the fact that some good food might "soothe the savage beast." Some of our classmates who had spent time in the U.S. Army told us that the food served in the Army was unquestionably more palatable than that which was presented to us in the seminary.

One of the most abused seminary rituals was Grand Silence. Few found the concept useful, but I did know several fellows who followed the rule because they were fearful of dismissal. Many students were night persons, accustomed to studying late into the night. Some liked to prepare for exams through group study. The faculty accommodated none of these various or differing study techniques. Students risked punishment by talking during Grand Silence or staying up after lights out. We were told many times by those in authority that the seminary doors opened both ways. In other words shape up, follow the rules, or you can leave.

We had imposed upon us a system of self-reporting. If you broke a rule you went down to the dean's office and filled out a sheet with your name and your offense and put it into a box for the dean's reading pleasure. In second college the Assistant Dean called me in to his office. I had not been putting in any "sin" sheets. I was asked what I thought the faculty made of a person who never turned himself in. I mumbled some answers he wanted to hear. From that time on I made up some "sins" and turned in the required sheets. I never was talked to about this matter again, so I guess I found the magic number.

During my years at Sacred Heart, I developed many good friendships. I felt as though I was developing life-long friendships and that as friends we would sustain each other during our future priestly ministries. At one point the seminary authorities decided, however, that some of us had formed a clique. We were each called into the Rector's office and warned about the dangers of close, exclusive associations. We were told that we were like a flock of geese. "You see one and the rest were close behind." The interesting part of this episode was that when questioned by us as to whom they viewed as part of this group, they had missed one of our close friends. One of the irksome points about this incident is that the names were obviously turned in by a "stoolie" in our class. Because we all wanted priesthood, we were thereafter careful to be seen in the company of other students; but we never gave up our friendships.

Frankly, the seminary staff did not know us well enough to be fully aware of who we were, never mind with whom we "hung around." I was often referred to by another student's name by the staff. I hope he wasn't held responsible for my actions. Implied in the "clique" complaint was the veiled accusation that such close associations could result in sexual relationships, "particular friendships," as they were often called. All of this was implied, but the faculty never took the time to discover the true nature of our associations. In my opinion, our relationships were the "healthiest of the healthy." I believe that we all felt a kindred spirit that would last into priesthood, where the support of brother priests would be a lifelong need.

Often there would be young ladies inside the seminary building. They would frequently be there for Schola or theater performances. We ogled them unmercifully. On other occasions, a young girl would be seated on a bench in the front business section hallway awaiting an appointment with one of the priests or another staff member. She probably thought she was sitting in the only hallway that led anywhere. Most likely she grew tired of saying "Hi" or "Good evening." But once the word got out that she was there, the guys would begin to stroll by to take a look. Also, in our last two years, a new bookkeeper in the business office was certainly worth a look.

At the end of senior year, the faculty would meet and make the weighty decision as to whether or not a student would continue on to theological studies. I had received a number of clues through a series of meetings with the Dean of Students. These meetings foreshadowed a negative vote where my future as a theological student was concerned. The faculty was concerned about my scholastic progress, my limited friendships, and my quiet demeanor. Thus it came as no surprise to me when the Dean of Students called me into his office and informed me that indeed I would not be recommended by the Sacred Heart faculty for theology. He helped me to receive this news in the proper spirit and keep it in proper perspective in my life. No matter how well one knows that the possibility of disappointment looms on the horizon, until the negative event actually happens, its full effect is not felt. I was disappointed and wondered why I had worked so hard on studies when I could have been at the University of Detroit or at Wayne State University pursuing studies of my own choice and parceling out the rest of my time as I saw fit. As I worked through my feelings and disappointment, I realized that I had made the choice to stay and that in all my years at Sacred Heart I had stayed because priesthood had been a goal or a calling for as far back as elementary school in Massachusetts.

In subsequent conferences with the Dean, he offered me the option of switching to another Michigan diocese with the chance of joining my classmates at St. John Seminary in September. I informed him that I would take a year to weigh all my options, during which time I would also investigate the Glenmary Home Missionary Society, which was of longstanding interest to me.

Although I informed the Dean that I would take a year to ponder over my decision, I was simply being polite. I knew it was time to move on with my life. I was more than ready to begin a new life free from petty rules, lousy food, and courses I was not interested in and a faculty that I felt, with some notable exceptions, was lacking in teaching skills and uncaring. I had endured enough in pursuing my childhood dream of becoming a Catholic priest. By this time in my life, I had come to recognize that there are many ways to serve God and the people of God and that I definitely knew I would serve God's people in whatever vocation I chose.

A New Vocation and Focus

40

Faced with the need to support myself, I applied for a teaching position at Christ the Good Shepherd School in Lincoln Park, Michigan, where I taught seventh graders. Subsequently I taught at two other Catholic schools, St. Pius X Catholic School in Southgate, Michigan, and St. Henry Catholic School, my home parish in Lincoln Park. While working, I attended night school at Eastern Michigan University to obtain my teacher certification and a teaching major (English), since Philosophy was not considered a teaching major by the State of Michigan.

At Christ the Good Shepherd School, I met Catherine Anne Szynal, my wife, companion, and love for the past forty-one years. Together we have been through the best of times as well as the worst and will face the rest of life together no matter what it brings. We are faith-filled people sustained by the word of God, and we try to share our life with others.

Culminating five years of Catholic school service, I had the necessary teaching certificate to be able to secure a teaching position in the Trenton Public Schools as an English and History instructor at the junior high level.

One of the reasons that I transferred to the public school system was to become more financially secure, since we had applied for adoption through Catholic Social Services and Cathy and I decided that she would stay home with our baby for at least the first three years. On July 1, 1971, our son, Kenneth Andrew, arrived. Now thirty-eight years old, Ken is a graduate of Eastern Michigan University and works in the computer field for Computer Specialists, a local firm owned by one of his friends, a fellow graduate of Catholic Central High School. I'm proud to say that Ken is my son, my joy, and that our relationship has gone far beyond the typical father-son bond. We are, indeed, best friends. Ken is very spiritual and we have many sharing experiences. He attends yoga sessions as often as he can. He talked me into attending with him for about five or six sessions. Let's just say I don't attend currently.

Wandering Between Two Worlds

I was a classroom teacher in the Trenton Public School District for four years and, after obtaining a Masters Degree in Guidance and Counseling, I served as a guidance counselor for twenty-four years. I have always worked at the middle school/junior high level, a level I enjoyed tremendously.

When I first became a counselor, we were literally carrying students out of school due to the rampant usage of drugs. I became part of the team that was formed for drug education. The AIDS epidemic was another catalyst that increased my own expertise; and I became part of the AIDS education team within my school district. These were stressful times, since I truly cared about the future of my students.

I was a very active faculty member. I organized career nights for nine years; and, during my final five years, I was the team leader for School Improvement and North Central Association Accreditation. The school was accredited successfully for the first time.

I felt very much that I was doing the work of the Lord as I labored in the classroom and counseling office. Spending time with those students who had home, peer, or academic problems and helping them find solutions was rewarding and gave me the opportunity to act out my baptismal priesthood.

Retirement!

After thirty-three years in the educational field, I considered retirement. The pension ducks and the personal financial ducks were all in order and I felt I would have a full life without a formal job. Cathy made the same decision and we both retired in June, 1998. We took our first-ever cruise and bought a summer home on a lake in mid-Michigan. We are currently involved in a number of commissions at St. Mel Parish in Dearborn Heights, Michigan, including the worship commission, art and environment committee, and previously, the parish council, and choir. I coordinated the Rite of Christian Initiation for Adults (RCIA) program and taught five sessions as well. I continue to serve on the board of directors for The Guidance Clinic, which is located downriver from Detroit in a manufacturing rust belt area. My commitment to the clinic has spanned twenty-five years.

Our days are blessedly full and, like so many other retired folks, we wonder how we had time to work. It's a great life!

The person that I have become started, in my opinion, from my roots in Fall River. My formation continued both in my family and in subsequent experiences in high school and college. I was mentored by many fine educators and taught much by the children and families I counseled. I have met and discussed many issues with many caring and loving, hard working priests. I continue, even in retirement, to move to more fullness through discussions and sharing with a myriad of friends, with the candidates in the RCIA, and with my classmates from the Class of 1965 at Sacred Heart with whom I occasionally communicate through the internet and at alumni gatherings as well. We are all children in some facet of our being and we must continue to be open to growth as we move towards the full flowering of our manhood or womanhood.

In Peace

Perhaps, at times, my life story might appear to be negative. I am not, however, a negative person. None of the events of my life has caused me to become negative or sour. I firmly believe that the reason for this is my relationship with Christ, my friend, my Lord. It has been said that hope springs eternal in the breast of a Christian. I have always found hope for a new day even on the bleakest of days. I found in that hope the means to wade through the miasma of life. There were opportunities, like job promotions, that I wished for but that never materialized. Yes, I was disappointed; but, in the end, it always seemed that life worked out for the best. I attribute these events to the workings of the Spirit in my life.

I do have serious concerns about my beloved Church. It seems to be dying on the vine. Unable to deal with many issues for so long, it seems that the world and history is passing the Church by. The messages are more irrelevant to many more people. We have been told that the Spirit will always be here to guide the Church. I firmly believe this precept. I also feel, however, that the promptings of the Holy Spirit must be heeded. Are we committing sins against the Holy Spirit by our failure to listen? I observe that much of the non-listening seems to be among the authorities of the Church. We are again mired in rules and regulations that are quoted as answers for all situations. We need another John XXIII and subsequent popes who recognize the workings of the Spirit.

Recently, I reread portions of Church History and I was reminded that the Church has faced numerous obstacles and difficult periods—problems where Catholic leadership failed to listen to the Spirit. Nevertheless, the Church survived. May it continue to thrive!

May all the people of God find peace.

HISTORICAL CRITICAL THEOLOGIAN
John Alonzo Dick

How did an overly pious and shy Roman Catholic farm boy from Southwestern Michigan, who constantly dreamed in grade school about becoming a priest, end up married and a "lay theologian" in Belgium at one of Catholicism's most famous universities?

I grew up on a large farm in Southwestern Michigan. My parents, shaped by the Great Depression and by World War II, were strict, loving, and insistent that their kids (three of us) become independent and self-sufficient adults. My mother, Hellen Frances Fritz, was a rather average Roman Catholic and Waldo Emerson Dick, my dad, a rather critical Protestant. Ironically, in view of my later life, I come from a long line of strongly anti-Catholic Protestant ministers, starting in Chester, Pennsylvania, in 1684.

My home in Lawrence, Michigan, was a happy environment. I really did have a happy childhood. My parents were fruit growers; and they were also politically and socially active people, known by everyone in the local community. My dad was a county commissioner, a member of various boards, gave talks about soil conservation and fruit-growing on the local radio station. He and my mother were key figures in the Van Buren County, Michigan Republican Party. Although I was nurtured on a full Republican diet, I became a Democrat when I left college and have been one ever since, the only member of the family who is a Democrat.

For more than fifty years my mother was a volunteer campaign organizer, fundraiser, and instructor for the American Cancer Society. When my father died at age 88, a local newspaper described him and my mother as "activists." Dad would not have been pleased with that term. My mother was angry. "Activists" in my parents' eyes were liberal troublemakers and soft on communism. In fact, my one and only painful dispute with my parents was about being an "activist." In the summer of 1965 (just before I left the United States to study theology in Europe), I began to voice my opposition to their politics and to the war in Vietnam. They grew angry and disappointed as they listened to my youthful protest; and they began to fear their younger son was becoming a "liberal pinko activist."

As a child I often play-acted Sunday Mass, with a blanket over my shoulders, making abundant signs of the cross, mumbling Latin-sounding words, and blessing and sprinkling my sister with "holy" water. Religion always fascinated me. It has to be deeply imprinted in my genes, from some distant ancestor. My mother was not particularly devout. My dad was more of a Transcendentalist, like his namesake. Nevertheless, my family belonged to and regularly attended St. Mary's Catholic Church in Paw Paw, Michigan, although my dad did not become a Catholic until much later in his life. My dad did have a keen sense of the Sacred. On his death bed, he told me that he feared that liberal theologians, like his son, were stripping all sense of the Sacred from Roman Catholic liturgy. In some respects, of course, he was correct. (Before he died, he gripped my hand and whispered that he loved me.)

My paternal grandmother, to whom I was very close, had a small house on our farm. She was a wonderfully loving grandmother and a very devout Protestant. Her ancestors were French Huguenots, and she had an almost innate fear of Catholics. My maternal grandparents (for my grandmother's sake) attended Sunday Mass regularly; but my grandfather, John Sebastian Fritz, was outspokenly anti-clerical. He despised most priests, considering them crafty thieves. He saw what I would only see many years later: the inherently seductive danger of religion, when faith is exchanged for power and position. When I entered Catholic seminary after grade school, my paternal grandmother cried and my maternal grandfather threw a fit.

Wandering Between Two Worlds

My sister and I attended the local Catholic school in Paw Paw, Michigan, where Adrian Dominican sisters taught us. Those women were remarkable: intelligent, kind and gifted teachers. Many of them were regular visitors to our home and became my parents' close friends. On several occasions, those delightful sisters visited grandfather John, for whom they had great affection. He was a lady-charmer and they loved his "spunk." He thought it was terrible that such pretty and energetic young women never got married!

At some point when I was in sixth or seventh grade, I felt touched and called by God to become a priest. In fact, I still feel touched and called by God. I never became a priest.

I spent eleven happy years as a seminarian at two of the finest seminaries in the world: Sacred Heart Seminary in Detroit and The American College of Louvain in Belgium.[1] The events that directed the course of my life actually began to hit me shortly after I graduated from seminary high school in 1961.

In college, my eyes opened to the unfolding social and political dramas of the 1960s. The civil rights movement was gathering momentum in Detroit. I was there and part of it. My seminary professors marched in Selma. Civil rights, however, was just one part of a world that all around me was changing dramatically. My world-view was shaken in 1962 and 1963. On February 14, 1962, President Kennedy announced that U.S. military advisers in Vietnam would fire if fired upon. Then less than a week later, three times on February 20, 1962, John Glenn became the first American to orbit the earth. On October 1, 1962, James Meredith became the first black student at the University of Mississippi; and 3,000 troops were needed to put down riots. Then on October 28, 1962, President Kennedy informed the nation about the Soviet missile buildup in Cuba.

---

[1] The American College of Louvain, founded in Leuven Belgium in 1857, is one of two Roman Catholic seminaries in Europe operated under the auspices of the United States Conference of Catholic Bishops.

Events and people. Rachel Carson's *Silent Spring* launched the environmentalist movement. Civil rights leader Medgar Evers was assassinated on June 12, 1963. Martin Luther King gave his "I have a dream" speech during the March on Washington, August 28, 1963. Then South Vietnam President Ngo Dinh Diem was assassinated on November 2, 1963. And President John F. Kennedy was shot and fatally wounded, as he rode in motorcade through downtown Dallas, on November 22, 1963. Alone in my little seminary room in Detroit, I cried that night. His death was my 9/11.

Those people and those events shook my understanding of self, church, and world. They launched me on my own solitary walk through space, as I discarded old beliefs, rediscovered my faith tradition, and started, from scratch, to rebuild my understandings and my spirit. That process of rediscovery and rebuilding was slow and painful.

During my college seminary years, I also began to think about sex. Well, "Pious Dick," as my classmates called me, thought about sex a lot! (Something else I got from my maternal grandfather, no doubt.) But I have to say, in light of the current revelations and events surrounding the sexual abuse of children by priests, that I was never abused and never propositioned by a classmate or an instructor. (Only after leaving the seminary was I propositioned by a priest.) In my college years, I never questioned my own sexual orientation either. I liked girls and I knew that; but I was terribly shy and naïve around them. I was basically, in those pre-Vatican II days, a good seminarian, but continually talking about my strong sexual feelings with my spiritual director. I soon realized that, when it came to understanding sex, the poor fellow was more hopelessly in the dark than I! His continual advice never changed: "Pray and don't masturbate." Well I did pray a lot…

On the night before my college class graduated from Sacred Heart Seminary, I was officially informed that I would be sent to The American College of Louvain for theological studies. A few months earlier, I had understood that I would be sent to the North American College in Rome. Hearing about my Louvain destination on that warm June night in 1965, I was very disappointed. I had absolutely no idea what Louvain was all about. Today, of course, I know better and I am tremendously grateful that I was not sent to the old city below the Alps.

Louvain – Leuven, as it is called in Flemish -- is a wonderful place. It has now been my home for more than a quarter of a century. The Louvain "historical-critical method"[2] connected the past and the present for me in new ways and gave me a new vision on my own life. In my American College seminary days, Louvain was an energetic theological clearing house for the message and spirit of the Vatican II (The Second Vatican Council.) Working under the direction and inspiration of their own Cardinal Leon-Joseph Suenens, Louvain theologians left a lasting imprint on *Lumen Gentium* (*Dogmatic Constitution on the Church*) and *Gaudium et Spes* (*On the Church in the Modern World*) as well as on the shape and direction of the Council itself. In the days of Vatican II, Cardinal Suenens' theologians were known (and feared by some) in Rome as the *Squadra Belga.*

Vatican II thought permeated our official classes at the University of Louvain and enlivened informal discussions with our professors. Each day brought new insights and often colorful anecdotes about "the Council." Being a seminarian at The American College, in the final days of Vatican II, meant as well a continual flow of visiting U.S. bishops on their way to or from Rome. As one of my classmates from Michigan said one night, after listening to remarks from three visiting American bishops, "we are part of history …. in the making."

Years later, when I returned to Louvain to finish my doctorate in historical theology, Cardinal Suenens and I became good friends. For more than a decade, we had many wonderful visits, most of them at The American College. He died a few months after my own father. At

---

[2] The historical critical method, once called "the Louvain method," is an interpretative process that attempts to discover an author's original intent and meaning when he or she wrote the text. Historical grammar, syntax, literary forms and the historical-cultural situation in which the author wrote are all taken into consideration. One could call it historical contextual interpretation.

his funeral I felt that I had indeed lost a second father. I still think of him that way, as my adopted spiritual father.

Founded by papal decree in 1425, the Catholic University of Louvain gave its students a challenging and rich academic formation, along with abundant time to read and think. There were few papers, as is so common at a U.S. university, and all examinations were lumped into two weeks of anxiety-producing oral examinations at the end of the academic year! In my first year at Louvain, I had twenty such examinations. (At the end of the ordeal I was a zombie!) For the non-Belgians at Louvain, the geographic separation from country, family, and friends, as well as working in a foreign language (in my days it was French) led to moments of terrible homesickness. (On the morning of our first Christmas in Louvain -- and our first Christmas away from home -- I think all of my classmates and I wanted to cry but didn't. We were "new men" and had a sense of pride in showing our rugged masculine stuff.)

The Louvain experience also liberated us and gave us time and space to think, to feel, and to explore in new ways. It certainly liberated me through what was often an intellectual, emotional, and cultural baptism by fire. I was no longer a Michigan farm boy.

When I was at Louvain, the *National Catholic Reporter* was born back home in Kansas City. It became my progressive Catholic literary (some may scoff at that term) companion throughout the sixties and the seventies especially. (For a number of years in the seventies and eighties, I was a columnist for NCR.) During my third year at Louvain, issues of celibacy, marriage, and sexuality kicked in for me in full force. I began to suspect that ordained ministry, with mandatory celibacy, would not be my life goal after all. I discovered that the official church had tunnel vision when it came to human sexuality. (It still does.) When Pope Paul VI issued *Humanae Vitae* in 1968, that did it for me. In no way, I thought, could I be an ordained spokesperson for a teaching I could neither accept nor expect others to accept. (At Louvain we had been convinced that Pope Paul's response would be an open door.) I had also come to see a celibate lifestyle as meaningless and impossible for me. I did not want to live by myself nor spend the rest of my life living in a primarily male environment.

In the course of working out a new, non-ordained, direction for my life and determining the immediate steps I had to take, I corresponded with a few trusted priest advisors back in Michigan. They were men who had befriended and supported me throughout my eleven years of seminary formation. In the summer and autumn of 1968, I earnestly sought their understanding and their advice. All of them (with the exception of Father William Fitzgerald from Kalamazoo, Michigan) reacted in a surprisingly offensive and non-supportive fashion. These "friends" immediately accused me of sexual immorality, which, in their minds, had to be the only explanation for a seminarian's – one year before ordination!!! -- rejection of celibacy. I was told, as well, that I had no doubt lost my faith, had "surrendered to the flesh" and was no doubt living in mortal sin. One priest, one of my dad's friends, told me to grow up and face the facts. The facts were simple: as a priest I "could have a woman or a boy whenever I needed personal sexual relief." That remark, coming from my father's trusted friend, and a greatly respected priest in our diocese, was deeply disappointing and hurt terribly. I wonder still why I didn't become ragingly anti-clerical.

Little by little, more revelations were disclosed by my priestly advisors back in Michigan. They wrote with a frankness that was blunt and brutal; and they hoped their revelatory and judgmental letters (all of which I have destroyed) would re-convert me and bring me back to Holy Orders. I was assured that most marriages are unhappy, that sex gets to be boring "after a couple years of doing it," and that most married men end up estranged from wives and children. Bizarre. (At Louvain our moral theology professor Father Louis Janssens had had us on the edges of our seats, when, in his university classes he extolled the love relationship of husbands and wives. That kind of love, he had said with a twinkle in his eyes, best reflected the intimate love of the Holy Trinity.)

From my advisors in Michigan, I learned first hand that priests and bishops are afflicted with the same failings, sins, and temptations that afflict all sons (and daughters) of Adam. I wrote my parents that the church was sick, the priesthood a club of weird and crazy men, and that I wanted no part of that screwed-up mess. They really never understood what I meant, but they did love and support me. I thank God for my great parents. Their letters (which I did keep) are some of my life-journey treasures. I flew back to Michigan the summer of 1967 for a few weeks to meet with them (very felicitous) and with my bishop (not very felicitous). When I left for Belgium near the end of the summer, I was officially returning to the seminary; but I knew it was over.

I never told my parents that another of their close priest friends had tried to seduce me that summer. It was apparently his own way to keep me in the seminary and in the special boys' club. He had taken me for a drive in the country, so we could talk about priesthood and celibacy. He pretended he was lost, stopped the car, so he said, to get a map. In fact he reached for me and asked if I wanted to play sex games with him. I told him to take me home. That man, whom I have never seen since that summer, I later learned has corrupted and abused a number of young men in several dioceses across the United States. But we have heard more than enough about this type criminal in recent days.....

My final year in Louvain was anxious and full of turmoil. I knew that once I left the seminary I would have to face the war in Vietnam. I wanted to continue studying theology but had no money. My parents feared that I was on the verge of some kind of nervous breakdown. They were probably right. And I felt terribly alone. I tried to discuss my celibacy concerns with a couple of classmates. They agreed with me that it made no sense, but they were going to promise to be celibate anyway so they could be ordained. I told them I couldn't promise what I didn't believe. They found that rather strange. They promised. They got ordained. Today they are married. As long as this kind of behavior continues, the needed ecclesiastical change will never occur. If you don't believe it, don't promise it.

Most of my classmates, probably because they didn't know what to say, just stopped talking to me. So much for all those classes on pastoral ministry and the art of listening. Fortunately three mentor-type people did listen to me and could understand what was happening: Msgr. Paul Riedl, the rector of The American College; Fr. Harry Sikorski, the spiritual director; and Prof. Gustave Thils, the dean of the faculty of theology at the university. Over the years I have had wonderful visits and conversations with all of them. Riedl and Thils are now deceased. Harry later spent many years as a missionary in Latin America.

In the end, Uncle Sam never called me to Vietnam; and my parents made arrangements, through a friend in Kalamazoo, for a U.S. government student loan. Paul Riedl let me stay at The American College until I found a place to live. Gustave Thils allowed me to work on a master's degree at Louvain and helped me register, in the Netherlands, to do a one-year licentiate degree under Edward Schillebeeckx.

I moved to Nijmegen, took a crash course in the Dutch language, and spent a year working under my new theological mentors: Edward Schillebeeckx and Piet Schoonenberg. Great men. Great theologians. Their friendship over the years has been a tremendous personal support. A few years ago, in fact, when the then "New Catechism" came out, Schillebeeckx happened to be in Leuven and was invited to a little dinner party in my honor on my birthday. I asked him what he thought about the new catechism. "I try not to think about unpleasant things," he replied. Delightful. Schillebeeckx and Schoonenberg (now deceased) pushed my theological thinking to the limits with their continual questions: What does it mean to be a believer? How do people TODAY experience God? How should we THINK and SPEAK about God today?

When I went to the Catholic University of Nijmegen, I also became better acquainted with the girl of my dreams, who in 1970 became my wife. Joske was my Dutch language instructor. I fell off my horse the first day I saw her. I have been falling off my horse ever since - for nearly forty years.

After a year in Nijmegen, I had exhausted my funds. I packed my bags, grabbed my diploma, and moved back to Michigan. The same priest from Kalamazoo who had stood by me when I was in Louvain helped me find a job back home: head of the religious education department at St. Philip Catholic Central in Battle Creek, Michigan. A year later Joske and I got married. For the following thirteen years I taught high school, was a parish religious education coordinator, and traveled the back roads of Michigan as a diocesan teacher-education speaker. I was also a part-time instructor at Aquinas College in Grand Rapids, Nazareth College in Kalamazoo, and Kellogg Community College in Battle Creek. Truly an academic Jack-of-all-trades.

One day, as I was leaving my classroom at Aquinas College (where in fact I was a full time instructor but teaching only evenings and weekends), the president of Aquinas called me into his office. I walked in. He looked at me seriously and said: "Young man! Get your doctorate now!" A couple years after that meeting, in July, 1983, my wife Joske, our eight year-old son Brian, and I packed eight suitcases and headed to Louvain, Belgium.

The plan was that I would complete my doctorate in two years and return to Michigan. I did finish my doctorate, *magna cum laude*, and in two years; but I never left Louvain.

The day after my doctoral defense, I was offered a job as Director of Continuing Education and later Director of Academic Formation (academic dean) at The American College of Louvain. Back to my old seminary! (To my great joy, my old rector, Msgr. Riedl, was delighted when he heard the news. I would like to think that Alexander Zaleski, my diocesan bishop and an alumnus of Louvain, was delighted too as he looked from heaven.)

A few years after my doctoral defense, I became the third person to hold the Chair for the Study of Religion and Values in American Society, in the Faculty of Theology at the Dutch language University of Louvain: the K. U. Leuven (Katholieke Universiteit Leuven). (The first two holders of the chair were John Coleman, S.J., and Cardinal Avery Dulles, S.J.) That started my career at the university which I consider my true *alma mater*. For a number of years I was a member of the academic staff of the university's Center for Christian Ethics and was Managing Editor for the international journal *Ethical Perspectives*. For a number of years I was also editor for the international theological journal *Louvain Studies*.

Today, as a retired professor, I continue to research, write, lecture, and teach about religion and values in contemporary American society. I write a regular column for a Dutch language Catholic journal and teach one university course each year on "The American Way of Religion." And I am the executive secretary for the Jean Jadot Chair for the Study of Religion and Values in Society at both Louvain universities: the Katholieke Univesiteit Leuven and the Université Catholique de Louvain.

As of this writing, I am sixty-five years old. My wife Joske and I live in a lovely old house, built in 1672, on the edge of Louvain. An ideal home for an historian. Our basement contains the walls of a thirteenth century house, once part of a neighboring Norbertine Abbey. Erasmus had been here as well, but the house he knew burned down in the sixteenth century. Sometimes I still feel his ghost as I wander in my back yard. Our only child Brian is a young diplomat at the American Embassy in Brussels. His field is international relations. Like his dad he is a Louvain graduate as well.

Lest the reader think my life has been an easy and smooth move to where I now am, let me assure you that there have been a lot of unexpected bumps and detours along the way. I have learned through hardships as well. Each person, I believe, gets a special cross to carry. I have become humble by being humbled. There have been times of loneliness and paralyzing fear. I have stood in the unemployment and welfare lines, with low self-confidence and seemingly hopeless despair. I have had great friends and strong supporters. On the other hand, far too many people whom I trusted (bishops, superiors, and colleagues) have used and abused me and stabbed me in the back.

Life does have its ironies; and the Divine has a great sense of humor. I started out with a felt call to ordained ministry. In the end I have spent the greatest part of my life in ministry to the ordained!

I know that life is stronger than death, love stronger than hatred, and that goodness in the end conquers evil. I also know that the human journey at times comes with long and painful interruptions. That light at the end of the tunnel can sometimes be at the end of a very long tunnel. Nevertheless, and this is the best thing I have learned since my days as a farm boy in Michigan, for reasons I can only describe as a gift of grace, I have lived and walked in the shadow of the Transcendent. The Great Spirit, source of all we are and all we shall be, has never abandoned nor abused me. *Sit nomen Domini benedictum. Ex hoc nunc et usque in saeculum.* Yes indeed: Blessed be the name of the Lord. Now and Forever.

HOW I MET MY WIFE AND
ALMOST DIED WITH THE POPE
Anthony P. Locricchio

The old guy who shows up in my bathroom mirror each morning is as
foreign to me as the smiling face that has my name under it in the
1965 Sacred Heart Seminary graduation picture. I came to Sacred
Heart via an abnormal path. I was a lawyer in a large Detroit firm
when I shocked my family (and myself) by announcing that I would
be entering the seminary. Maybe the real question to ponder is how I
got from the courtroom to the Gothic halls of SHS and what it has
meant to my life since then.

My Pre-Seminary Years

I was raised on the east side of Detroit. As a small child my father
came with his family from Italy on the boat that helped rescue the
survivors of the *Titanic.* Dad became a wholesale produce seller who
sold to supermarkets and small stores in the outer reaches of the
Detroit metro area. I worked with him from my twelfth birthday. I
could lift a 100-lb. sack of Idaho potatoes with increasing ease as I
grew. I developed my love of education as a defense against a future
in potato lifting. I learned to drive a semi-truck before I drove a car.
After loading 100 watermelons daily into trucks during my summer
stints with the family business, I hate watermelon to this day.

My mother was from a well-to-do family. Her father, my grandfather
Joe Furnari, came from a small town in Sicily and amassed a
significant amount of money in the construction business after

arriving in the United States. He acted as a co-signer for some thirty immigrating families who were seeking loans to start their lives in America. He was recognized as a godfather (without the crime part) in the Italian community. When the depression hit, those loans could not be repaid. My mother's family went from very wealthy to very poor overnight, since Grandpa insisted on repaying every loan he had co-signed, even when he could have declared bankruptcy to prevent having to make the payments.

My grandfather's effect on me as I was growing up was pivotal in my "training" for life. I don't think I realized that fully until now. His philosophy was to take what comes and make the best out of life but above all to keep your dignity. Success was honor and not money. He had both, lost the money, but kept the honor.

My mother insisted that no matter how tough things were with our household finances, I should get the best education possible. I went to De La Salle high school, working two jobs to pay the tuition. I don't remember life being unpleasant or overly burdensome because of the work. I was a social success. I dated and danced. In fact, I was the best dancer at De La Salle. I did proms big time. All-guy schools attract invitations from all-girl schools for proms and dances. A date with Tony meant that your prom dress would definitely be noticed as you were lifted and spun around the gym floor.

My mom's vision shielded me from ever knowing that our life was tough. We dreamt Grosse Pointe while we budgeted lower east side.

I was the first one from either side of the large Locricchio family to go to college. There was never a question about it. Little money was not a consideration. I saved my money during high school, then ran out of funds after the first semester of my freshman year at the University of Detroit. I started night school, while working at the Grand Trunk Railway, various pizza restaurants, and as a clerk writing up truck repair jobs at International Truck Company. I made enough to help the family and pay my tuition.

I got a great job as a social worker type, working for the Polish Aid

Society in a racially changing neighborhood. This was my first
experience with the black (then called Negro) community. I never
noticed the strain of multiple jobs and school. I was a BMOC (Big
Man on Campus), Chairman of the Homecoming Dance, and
Chairman of the Spring Carnival. I dated homecoming queens. After
graduation I went to law school.

I ran out of money my first semester of law school. I began teaching
sixth grade at Our Lady Star of the Sea in Grosse Pointe Shores, the
richest community in the United States at that time. Sunday Mass
actually featured a doorman to open the Cadillac doors for the
parishioners so they could enter the church with some style and grace.

The average IQ of the students in my sixth grade class was over 130.
The challenge of keeping up with them while I went to law school at
night was difficult but great fun. Later, during this same period in my
life, I taught high school and grade school at St. Philomena's. When
word hit the press that there never had been a real St. Philomena, the
students were devastated and the parable of the non-existent saint was
born in my classroom. "I am sure there was a secret St. Philomena
that no one, except God, ever knew about; and that is why he has
allowed the story of St Philomena to go forth and multiply," I told the
students. The statue of the discredited saint disappeared quietly one
day to be replaced by a Virgin Mary of a neo-modernistic design.

I had always been the model Catholic. Daily Mass and Communion;
President of the Archdiocesan Counsel on Catholic Youth, etc. My
teaching of basic Church doctrine to high school and sixth graders
was conservative and deeply felt but without a strong intellectual
foundation.

I developed a lifelong friendship with the assistant pastor at Star of
the Sea He was searching in his priesthood and I was seeking a basis
for my beliefs. In many ways we were the blind leading the blind. Yet
we provided each other foundations for solutions we both needed.
George's doubts about priesthood opened the door for me to look at
that life in a way that was more realistic than most seminarians of that
day, those who saw ordination as the gateway to a trouble-free

lifestyle. George and I went on a camping trip up north together (my one and only time hunting), when my gun discharged and narrowly missed the priest. This lent a new depth to our discussions on life that night. George took his gun back and to this day I don't shoot.

It is important to admit that intellectually I had decided to enter the seminary before I was admitted to the bar. I was sure that this nagging idea would go away so I didn't pay any attention to it. I lived and loved the practice of law and being in the courtroom. The firm I was with threw me into the lake and had me swim on my own. I ran the American Society of Automotive Engineering Companies' legal division and acted as that organization's Executive Director as part of my duties in the firm. This status for a young attorney was heady stuff and I was sure that the nagging would go away.

One day I invited my parents to the law office so they could see what their boy had achieved. They met my secretary and saw my view of the Detroit River from 22 stories up. I took them out to lunch at the Top of the Flame restaurant and then nearly gave my poor father a heart attack when I told them I had decided to enter Sacred Heart Seminary that fall. My mother just sighed as though she might have been clairvoyant about what was ahead for me. It was a cruel thing to do and hadn't been thought out; but I had to stop the nagging. It would not go away. I saw the priesthood as the only way I wanted to live my life.

Sacred Heart Seminary and an Introduction to Church Politics

The radical change in my life started that summer, when I was required to go to John Carroll University in Cleveland to cram four years of Latin classes into one summer. Seminarians from all over the country and of all ages descended upon the lakeside campus to be Latinized. The teacher was the best instructor I ever knew. He became my role model for teaching at the college and graduate school level in later years. He used the classroom as an excitement zone that allowed him to make each student hang on his words and actions. One never realized that he was teaching one of the really dead languages.

The atmosphere at J.C.U. was electric. This was the time when the best and the brightest were entering Catholic seminaries across the United States. The intellectual level of the out-of-class discussions was boundless. I found that instead of missing what I had left behind, I was enthusiastically charging toward the priesthood, motivated by a caliber of men who collectively do not exist today. It did not matter if they went on to the priesthood or not. Their overwhelming desire to do the collective "good" was literally intoxicating.

Life at Sacred Heart was not like that at John Carroll University. It was the 12th century revisited, complete with appropriate Gothic sets and sounds and rules that made the lawyer in me laugh out loud (but never during Grand Silence). This life was so startlingly different to what I had been living. I did not think I would survive the first few weeks. Suddenly I had become a child. I needed rules and permissions to function, even in the smallest details of life. The authorities apparently felt that my fellow seminarians and I had to be protected from the evils of life outside the walls. It was assumed that we could not resist "TEMPTATION" unless it were completely physically and intellectually removed. Women and sex were forbidden topics; and discussions of sexuality were unheard of except when administration members pointed threatening fingers at normal relationships called "particular friendships." I re-read my letter from the law firm that kept open my job for me, while I again decided if this was the way I would spend my life.

In the wisdom of the Dean of Studies it was decided that I would start in second year college and retake many of the courses I had already taken at the University of Detroit (U of D). One of the teachers was the same person who taught me the same course at that Jesuit university. The result was that class-wise I could coast. That first year failed to challenge my intellectual capabilities in the classroom. As an alternative, I began to read and withdraw into a self-learning program with the aid of a spiritual adviser. I kept apart from my classmates. They were kids far younger than I and immature as only sheltered seminarians can be.

I don't remember when it happened, but it did. I found myself surrendering to seminary life and the required donning of a childlike cloak. I started to talk with the "younger ones." They were impossible to avoid. As I interacted with my classmates, I discovered that their basic goodness and fine personalities shown through their naivete and inexperience. For every immaturity they exhibited, I could count two profound insights or acts from them. For every "you got to be kidding me" was a polar opposite "you got to be kidding me" where their wisdom beyond years and experience would surface. I became childlike and played games and sports and interacted with men younger than I without noticing that was what I was doing. During intense discussions of matters that concerned the very purpose of life, my younger classmates exhibited a type of maturity that I had not experienced before. In becoming the child again, I was learning from basic texts the meaning of manhood in a way that had not been open to me before. Ironically, the absence of the opposite sex freed me from the traditional role-playing that was required in the outside world. Suddenly I was free to explore that nagging I had felt but could not describe, the nagging that led me to the doors of SHS. I remember a peace that I can still almost visualize, one that I miss in the hectic life I now lead, but a peace so clear that, when I need it, I can still find, even during the most difficult times of my life.

Nonetheless, I was appalled by certain faculty members and what appeared to me to be their abnormal views of marriage and life outside the walls. I recall a time in class when a professor chided those who were thinking that marriage was this great thing. "How would you like to wake up one night and find your wife had vomited all over you?" he asked. The sickening part of that statement was not that it was said at all, indicating a very unhealthy view of men and women, but that I was the only one that broke out laughing, because I thought he had to be joking. Yet, even given these types of incidents, I nonetheless began to fit in. I remember being very content and happy.

At some point I became active in the way that was to be my hallmark at the seminary. Because I was not being challenged in the classroom, I needed to occupy my mind by solving problems. It might have been my legal mind or merely a desire to start doing "good" now and not wait until ordination. Prior to my time in the seminary, I had put together a job-training project for one of our key law firm clients; so I was familiar with what had to be done to make such social programs work. Using that knowledge and those learned skills, I convinced former seminary rector Msgr. Albert Matyn's parish to fund a summer day camp program.

As it turns out, in 1965 the Detroit Catholic Church wanted a piece of the federal money being distributed under President Johnson's War on Poverty. Detroit had a head start on the rest of the country because Detroit had a poverty program before Congress passed laws creating the national program. The City of Detroit and the Detroit Board of Education had submitted proposals to the tune of tens of millions of dollars. Because of the day camp work I had done and other projects, pushing to get the Church involved in the black community, I was approached by Msgr. Thomas Gumbleton, a Chancery official at the time. Gumbleton asked me to write proposals on behalf of the Archdiocese to obtain some of the federal dollars. Whereas I had been scrounging for pennies to get that summer day camp project off the ground, suddenly Gumbleton showed up, asking me to write and submit multiple program proposals for federal dollars…and the Church would sponsor the programs. I was in seventh heaven. Gumbleton represented the weight of the entire Archdiocese. In so many words, he said to me: "Let your program ideas on how to work with the poor run wild. You can use this federal vehicle to get the Church involved." What would have taken me years to accomplish in small steps, I was now able to do in a few short weeks of writing program proposals.

Eventually I wrote five proposals, which the Chancery sent to Washington for consideration. During my senior year at SHS and my first year at St. John's Provincial Seminary, I was secretly sent to Washington to answer inquiries on the proposals. Gumbleton determined that these visits should occur without the faculty being informed of what I was doing or even that I was gone. Gumbleton, an advanced political player in the Church politics game (as I was to learn the hard way), told me that it would cause too much confusion if the faculty was made aware of what I was doing on behalf of the Chancery.

On the Thursday afternoon before my class graduated from Sacred Heart, I received word that one of the federal proposals had been funded. On that Friday I was informed that two more of my proposals had been funded. By the following Monday afternoon, I had learned *that every proposal I had written* had been funded by the Federal Poverty Program. The total amount was almost $2.5 M in federal funds. In those days that was a lot of money -- a million went somewhat further than it does today. These sudden approvals posed a serious problem, since I had been written in as the "in-kind" (free) project director for all five projects. This was important because in order to get the funds, the Church was required to come up with cash or "in-kind" (in place of cash) matching money or services as part of the overall federal funds award. I was a lawyer, so it was possible to value my work at what a lawyer would charge for his or her services.

I arranged an emergency meeting with Msgr. Gumbleton to convince him to select four other project directors to help run the projects. He refused to do so. He felt that I should run all five of the funded programs, since he did not want to have to ask the Archbishop to spend Church dollars assisting the poor in these programs. The Archdiocese would be happy to take the federal funds and run programs for the poor, but it did not want to spend any of its own money to do so. The Archdiocese would take credit for the programs but nothing else.

Suddenly I found myself being required to run five projects and hire almost 250 staff members, about half of whom were professionals, and find locations for the programs in Church inner city parishes (another part of the required match stated that the Church would provide the facilities for the programs). Gumbleton and I first argued over the ethics, or lack thereof, in double-dipping my hours, in effect charging for them five times over. Gumbleton thereby devised a plan that raised my legal hourly charge to cover the equivalent of three project director positions at a regular non-lawyer salary. Further, because of the burdensome workload associated with running five programs that had never existed before, I was working an average of 100 hours per week. This, plus the higher hourly fee, made the federal required match happen and made it legal.

I had to go out into the inner city parishes and nail down the locations for the programs. Gumbleton helped in some of the parishes where we had very receptive pastors, men who genuinely wanted to have these projects because their parishes were victims of "white flight." Such parishes previously had Italian, Polish, or Irish parishioners who had fled to the suburbs once the black population started to move into their areas. These "white flighters" would join and support suburban parishes but return for weddings and funerals to their previous ethnic inner city parishes. The pastors found they had few on-site parishioners; the new "residents" of the old parish were, in fact, black, often very poor, and by-and-large non-Catholic.

Some of the pastors were great; but others were bitter against blacks and frightened by them. One time I was negotiating for the use of one of the main Polish parishes, one that had incredible facilities: gym, swimming pool, bowling alley, athletic field, etc. During my initial meeting with the pastor, the wind blew open his office door leading to the walkway to the church. He jumped up and locked the door. "You can't be too careful," he said. "Those damned niggers are always coming here to ask for help! Now what was it you wanted to talk about?" I was left on my own in those cases and became pretty much hated by this type of clergyman. Here I was, a damned seminarian, putting pressure on pastors to open up their parishes to Negroes. Just who the hell did I think I was?

Nonetheless, we made incredible progress. We serviced thousands of kids and adults in the poverty area. Our neighborhood Youth Core job skills program became a national model, as did our early version of Head Start (someone else *did* get hired to run that program before it actually started up). We undertook a project with the Wayne County Juvenile Court whereby incorrigible repeat offenders were sent into our program to work in small teams with a staff person; they worked at assignments that trained them in work skills and job experiences. This project was an outstanding success; recidivism of those kids with a three-year follow-up dropped below 10%. We had projects at the Detroit House of Corrections that equipped prisoners with job training so that when they were released from the prison they were employable. No longer did they have to return to their criminal ways of making income, which had been their sole "job" training before these programs.

At the same time these young people were working for us in the project, the Negro population as a whole and the college kids in particular were moving through the initial stages of the Black Movement and major changes in their lives. I, as a white deeply involved in the inner city, was becoming a spokesperson for the Black Movement whenever the Movement leaders felt having a non-black saying the same things they were saying was of assistance. Controversy about the public statements I was making also added to my "baggage" in dealing with Chancery powers.

St. John's Seminary and Confrontation with the Archbishop

In my early years at St. John's Seminary, I was running these programs out of the back door while supposedly a full-time theology student. The St. John's faculty, which consisted of Sulpicians, not priests of the Archdiocese, was kept totally in the dark about what I was doing by order of the Chancery and my friend, Msgr. Gumbleton. My schedule often consisted of the following: I would sneak out of St. John's right after morning classes, miss Mass, go to my hidden car, drive to Metro Airport, fly to DC, and have a late afternoon meeting negotiating poverty program contracts or making presentations on the work we were doing. On behalf of the Archdiocese, Gumbleton would sign the contracts and I, as the Project Director, would also sign them. I would catch the last flight to Detroit around 6 PM and sneak back into my room at the seminary.

When Northwest removed that last flight from their schedule, I was forced to take the Eastern Shuttle to New York and wait there until just after midnight to take the red eye flight back to Detroit to get back for classes the next morning. (I must confess that, during that five or six hour wait, I would often go into Manhattan and see a Broadway play and have dinner at Mama Leone's restaurant.) These trips might occur as often as three times a week or as seldom as once every couple of weeks. I would sneak back into the seminary through the tunnel that linked the powerhouse to the main building and slip

66

back into my room. I made morning Matins so rarely that, when I did show up, my St. John's classmates applauded me on my presence. Because I was "secret keeping" with the Chancery, few in the seminary knew why I was such a "bad seminarian."

I knew that I was walking a narrow line between the seminary rule and the chance to do enormous good. It is important to note that seminary rules during this time period were changing. They had been changing for years. I had to balance those changing rules against the opportunity, as a mere seminarian, to obtain what was now over $3 M to work with the poor. In a way, it was I who was doing the "using." I was using the Church to pry loose some fantastic facilities from the fingers of some racist pastors. These facilities had been gathering dust and were decaying, and I could convert them for use by the poor. These inner city sites were so appreciated by the kids and parents of the poverty community that it was impossible for me to feel anything but elation over what was happening. Further, I was also working with some of the *best* priests in the archdiocese, ones who really wanted to do good and spread the Word through good acts. These fellows were not only role models for me but were my working partners at a time when I was a mere seminarian.

The secrecy *was* a problem because I was forced to lead a double life. In that sense I felt trapped. To this day some of my classmates have an extremely negative image of me because I was not able to explain what was going on. There were some guys who never got the whole story until years later and will read about it here possibly for the first time.

One night I arrived back from Washington via New York at 2:30 AM. A note was on my door from the rector (the late Fr. Eugene Van Antwerp). The note demanded that no matter what time I finally got in, I should come to his room immediately. I did not wish to wake him and went to see him the first thing the next morning. When I arrived he informed me that the faculty had met and voted to kick me out of the seminary. They were absolutely certain that I was living with a woman and spending most of the nights with her, since I had been observed sneaking back into the seminary in the wee small hours.

Finally caught, I explained what I had been doing and suggested that the rector call the Chancery and speak with Msgr. Gumbleton, who would verify my explanation. He called the good Monsignor and, true to real Church politics, Gumbleton's response was "Tony WHO??" Fortunately, I had kept our written correspondence and, most importantly, copies of the federal contracts containing Gumbleton's and my signatures. I gave those documents to the faculty. I also freed my confessor to inform the faculty that I had been reporting my activities to him all along, although not as part of my confession, of course. My discussions with him had helped me cope with my double life.

The reaction of the St. John's faculty members when they found out that they had been deceived by Gumbleton was one of the real rewards of my seminary experience. They moved immediately to protect me and to make certain I had the help and assistance I needed to learn theology and to do the work I was doing in the black areas. Instead of trying to squelch me, they supported me. I was permitted to teach both an undergraduate and graduate level seminar at the University of Detroit, speak at other universities and seminaries in other parts of the country, and to work on activities that grew out of the Detroit riot of 1967.

Nonetheless, at the time of the call to the subdiaconate, I was not on the list from the Chancery. The faculty sent a delegation to the Archbishop and told him that if I did not get the call, they would have to pull the Sulpician order out of St. John's because of the unfairness of the action of the Archbishop. I got the call the night before the subdiaconate ordinations. The Archbishop was furious, to say the least. From that point on, I believe he never intended to call me to the diaconate, let alone the priesthood. He merely went through the motions to get through the mess. The fury of the Archbishop was to gain in intensity, however, because of the following event.

I learned that money from the poverty program, intended to be used for the poor, was being diverted for illegal purposes. After

Gumbleton denied knowing me, I had been removed by the Chancery from most, if not all, of my activities in the poverty program. A monsignor with little skills in this area was appointed to replace me in the work I had been doing. The Chancery, however, was unable to stop my work in the black community that was not directly connected to the Archbishop's poverty program. As I stated earlier, in addition to my teaching, I had earned a reputation of being a savvy white guy who understood and could speak about the black movement in Detroit and across the country. I, a white man, had been elected to head the Model Cities Board of Directors, which was *very* unusual at that point in the black movement. Thus I had passed out of the direct control of the Chancery into the protection of the seminary faculty. I was too hot to keep quiet.

In my Model Cities position, I reviewed federal projects funded for Detroit, including the Archdiocesan projects. This was how I discovered the diversion of funds by the Archdiocesan Opportunity Program. Simply stated, salary checks were being written to people who were not working on the projects. Some of these people were receiving salaries from Church agencies such as the Catholic Youth Organization (CYO) and a second check for work they did *not* do from the Poverty Program. Some of these folks were, in fact, siblings of Chancery officials.

I documented the evidence, got around Gumbleton, and went directly to Archbishop Dearden to show him my findings. I fully expected that the misspent funds would be returned and the practice immediately stopped. I still very much respected the Archbishop and I trusted him to resolve the problem quickly. Instead, much to my shock and surprise, the Archbishop covered up the dealings and would approve no action to return the funds. It was made clear to me that, if I wanted to be ordained in the Archdiocese, I would be satisfied with the no-return-of-funds decision. To do otherwise would require the Archdiocese to make the repayments from its own coffers, thereby detracting from its ability to "carry out the word of God," or some such nonsense. I immediately filed a formal complaint against the archdiocese and named the Archbishop himself as having known what occurred and covering it up. This resulted in my banishment to

St. Clement's Parish in Romeo, Michigan, far from the inner city.

After the Detroit riots, I was asked to work on the Mayor's emergency team. My battle with the Archbishop made front-page news when we were both asked to state our opinions of the causes of the riots. I did not know the Archbishop's comments; but, as it turned out, for everything he said for publication, I held a directly opposite view, as printed by the press.

The final confrontation occurred at the seminary after a group of my classmates met with the auxiliary bishops to discuss my situation and demanded that the Archbishop come to St. John's to respond to questions. During the session with the Archbishop, I became frightened that certain fellows in the class were really sticking their unordained necks way out, since they were arguing directly with him. At this point I stood up and quit the seminary on the spot. The plan, I later learned, was for me to be quietly defrocked after the meeting, but I beat the Archbishop to it. Consequently, he stormed out of the room. I was right behind him.

In the end, after public hearings on the diverted funds, the Archbishop had to pay back the federal government a little over $80,000. He was very angry about having to do this. I too was angry. By exposing corruption in the Church, I was portrayed as a "bad" person. I later learned that the Archbishop had a press release issued while I was out of the country that stated I had been defrocked for reasons that were not available to the press. When my charges of corruption were proven, the Archdiocese had the political power to keep that matter from the press. I was so elated that the bad guys had to return the money to the poor that I did not bother to put out a press statement. Looking back now I realize I had been seeing so much good coming out of what I had been able to accomplish that I ignored the bad stuff and the bad folks. I had neither the time nor the desire to pay attention to them. I also knew that even if I did pay homage to the politics of the situation, Mother Church was not ready for my brand of "in your face" truth.

I was too involved with the real and exciting Church that I was living with every day to be concerned with the clerical political Church that rules the temporal. I am not sure whether I was smart or dumb or used or was a user. The only thing I know is that I could not have played the game any differently than I did. I also know that I had the time of my life during those days of riots, political upheaval, and Church politics.

My Near-Death Experience with Pope Paul VI

There was some humor that came out of the Dearden conflict. Well, maybe humor tinged with abject terror is a better description.

Right after the confrontation with the Archbishop, I got a call from a team from Harvard and MIT that I had worked with on the Archdiocese Poverty Program. The team had developed an innovative low cost housing system that we had used in one of our Poverty Program inner city parishes in Detroit to build the first models of a designed self- help housing project. Team members had been invited by a Colombian university group to come to Bogota and build similar housing in the barrios of the city. I had written them that I expected to be leaving the seminary shortly, voluntarily or involuntarily. They asked me to join them in Bogota as soon as possible. Since I was exceedingly ready to get out of town after the emotional St. John's session, I jumped at the chance and flew down there immediately. As fate would have it, and unknown to me, the Archbishop of Detroit was planning a trip there as well. The pope, Paul VI, was preparing to head that way too.

At that time Archbishop Dearden was the head of the U.S. Catholic Bishops Conference. As such, it was one of his duties to greet the pope at the Eucharistic Congress he was about to attend in Bogota. Hundreds of thousands of Colombians were expected to greet the Pope, since this was the first time a pope had come to that country or to any place in South America.

Against my better judgment, three of us on the housing team, including the director, Don Terner, who would later become the head of housing for the State of California, decided to make our way to the cathedral to observe the Pope's arrival. Since we would have no chance to get very close unless we were members of the clergy, we *dressed as* members of the clergy -- black suits, collars, the works. One of us was a legitimate priest from Boston. He supplied me and Don with part of our costumes. By tagging along behind a cardinal and his entourage, we were able to make it to the very front edge of the plaza of the cathedral, working our way through what was later reported as a mass of 800,000 people. We found ourselves in an open space between the masses, who were being held back by a thin line of soldiers from the Colombian army, and the front of the cathedral.

We were trying to decide what to do next when the roar of the crowd became deafening. The Holy Father and his entourage had entered the Square! The crowd was going wild. White handkerchiefs transmogrified into a wall of moving waves all over the plaza. I turned on a movie camera I had been carrying. I was spellbound by the crowd noise and its action. I began shooting the crowd's reaction because I was so overwhelmed by it. As my camera panned the crowd, Paul VI came into my viewfinder. I remember being surprised at how close he appeared to be. When I took the finder away from my eye, I realized that we were standing at the very spot that led into the cathedral. The Lincoln convertible was stopped, its door open. The Pope stood not more than ten feet from us.

When the rather short Pope stood up in the car, tens of thousands who could not previously see him suddenly got their first view. The already wild crowd went completely bonkers. Suddenly the three of us found ourselves pinned against the side of the Lincoln. The soldiers maintaining the barricade had abandoned the lines as they got caught up in the uncontrolled fervor. They rushed forward to get closer to the Pope. The sea of humanity, now no longer restrained, rushed right behind them. They were all headed for the Lincoln, Pope Paul, and our trio of clerically dressed fools.

I turned back to the Lincoln just in time to see a most frightening sight. A very tall papal guard had seen the soldiers breaking ranks and leave the lines. He screamed to the Pope to get back in the car, but Paul could not hear him. That guard, who had a cool that was beyond training, reached out and gave a tremendous shove, sending His Holiness, head of the Roman Catholic Church, the Vicar of Christ, sprawling across the back seat. When I saw the Pope's little cape up over his head and his rear end up in the air, I knew we were all going to die.

I cannot say for sure what happened next, or how. Here is what I think occurred. The group of Papal Guards, led by the head pusher, grabbed the Pope and lifted him from the car (I saw that part quite clearly), while somehow getting his little white cape back into position. They expertly formed a protective cordon around the Pope. I suddenly found that inside this circle was Pope Paul VI, myself, my fellow impostor Don, and one legitimate priest from Boston. I was pressed up against the Pope's back.

As we rapidly passed through the safety of the massive copper clad cathedral doors, the papal guard expertly peeled off the outer circle. The "huddled four" were suddenly unprotected. We all looked back to make sure we were not being followed inside. I remember having to move aside so that I didn't block Paul's vision to the rear. To comfort myself as well as His Holiness, I said to him, "It's all right. It's all right." My chance to speak one-on-one was limited to a final very clever bon mot: "No problem." I think I might have touched his shoulder to add to the effect of my reassurance. He looked as terrorized as I was.

A procession had already started up the central aisle of the Bogota cathedral. Huge lights were switched on as we came through the front doors, temporarily blinding all four of us. No one seemed to question just what our relationship with the Pontiff was, least of all the Pontiff himself. The Pope was clutching the arm of Don Terner, a 6-foot, 2-inch burly guy, who happened to be a devout Jew! We got about three or four rows up the aisle when we began to peel off into already-packed pews. Within a few minutes, after the procession had passed, the three of us left our pews and made our escape via a side aisle, up through a door in the communion rail, through the sanctuary, and finally out through the sacristy. As fate would have it, the first person we ran into once we got out of the Plaza area was Don's Bogota rabbi. Don had attended the synagogue since he had arrived in Bogota at the start of the project. In our excitement, we forgot to explain Terner's garb!

But the story doesn't end here. Not quite.

The next day, while our stalwart group was sitting together in a pre-Starbucks coffee bar at a local hotel, I was approached by a priest with a New York accent.

"Are you Locricchio?" He had pronounced my name correctly (a rare occurrence). "Is that you?" His eyes probed my face.

I responded with a slow "yes" that was more question than answer, letting my voice trail off, since I hadn't a clue who he was.

"Were you at the cathedral yesterday?" We admitted we were.

"Were you ... were you (long pause) with the Pope?" His eyes never left my face.

Again, one of our group said, "We were."

The priest leaned forward, partially blocking the others, intending to get the next answer from me alone. "Do you know Archbishop John Dearden from Detroit, Michigan?"

Of all the questions I have been asked in my lifetime, this was one of the most unexpected and, for obvious reasons, unwelcome. I mumbled that I knew the man.

He noticed my reaction and quickly explained. "I will never forget your name as long as I live. I was in the cathedral yesterday, up in the second row with my boss, Cardinal Cooke of New York. I am his Spanish translator." He gave us his name.

We exchanged head nods. I introduced him to the group. "The boss had me sit along side him during the ceremony yesterday so I could translate for him. I was between the Cardinal and Archbishop Dearden. We were looking at the television monitors near us when Dearden started saying, 'Locricchio, Locricchio, oh no, Locricchio!' He was pointing at the TV screen. He looked at me and asked me, 'Is that him? Do you think it's him?' I wasn't sure whom he meant, since the Pope had several priests around him. 'The Italian one. Black hair. It *is* him! Locricchio, Locricchio, Locricchio.'"

"Those sitting around us began to stare at the Archbishop," the priest confided. "I looked at the screen and this guy, you, were talking to the Pope and had your hand on the Pope's shoulder, you know, like you knew each other well." His tone had become reverential.

"When the Archbishop saw that, he became really upset. 'What is he telling the Pope? Can you translate it? Can you make it out?' There was no sound that I could hear coming from the monitors. I could not tell what you were saying to the Pope. What *were* you saying to the Pope?" He stopped when he realized that the conversation might have been personal, since we were old friends and all. I didn't even attempt an answer. I was nailed to the chair. I could not believe this.

He went on: "I told him I could not make out anything. I had to say 'no sound' twice before the Archbishop understood. His eyes were glued to the screen. Then he turned to look at me. 'You do see him, don't you?' I thought he was talking about the Pope, who was now walking in the procession.

"The Archbishop was now standing along with the rest of the congregation in the cathedral, but he was trying to look as far as he could up the aisle. For a second, I thought he was going to stand on the pew."

"He finally relaxed when he could see the Holy Father in person in the processional. 'He is not there. Locricchio is not there,' said the now-smiling Archbishop. He was embarrassed. He turned again and, in a low voice, said something about jet lag and how tired he was.

"Everything was fine again. The Pope passed by and was seated facing us. We took our seats and I heard the Archbishop give a short quiet chuckle directed at Cardinal Cooke, who had asked me to change seats with him. He had become concerned by the erratic conduct of his fellow bishop, one who was President of the American Bishops and was known for his calm demeanor. The Cardinal and I had exchanged worried looks that the Archbishop had seen.

"I watched as the Archbishop regained his composure. He told the Cardinal not to worry, that it was a long story and that he would fill him in later. We all sat. Suddenly, there you were again, not thirty feet away, standing at the communion railing on your way into the sanctuary. I didn't see you at first but I heard Dearden gasp. When I looked at him, he was staring at you and two other priests at that railing off to the side." Just then Pope Paul had turned as he saw you going through the gate and blessed you with a separate sign of the cross. When Dearden saw that he was beside himself.

By this time, the three of us had begun to laugh. The priest was confused until I told him my whole story. I told him about the confrontation at St. John's and the poverty program money having to be repaid. I explained that I did not know Dearden was even in Bogota until he, Cooke's translator, approached us in the coffee bar.

Once our new friend had the background, he could not help laughing himself. "Dearden was so certain that you had something going with the Pope that, when he saw you go into the sacristy, he thought you were going to be part of the Liturgy. For the remainder of the ceremony, he kept waiting for you to join the Pope at the altar! He was a mess.

"When Locricchio didn't show for the liturgy, he was sure that you were waiting at the reception in the residence, ready to point his finger at the him when he was presented to the Pontiff as the head of the American Bishops. We practically had to push Dearden forward to give the American Conference of Bishops' official welcome to the Pontiff. You and your name had become very well known among the American delegation staff. Dearden had us all on the lookout for you. He described you as Italian looking, on the chubby side."

"You certainly ruined his trip to Bogota" smiled the clergyman. "Do I get to tell him I met you and that he is worrying over nothing? Or not?"

After a long time, I said, "Father, I'm going to leave that up to you. I don't think he will believe you one way or another, but it's your call."

As it turned out, before that priest or anyone else could get to him, Dearden had suddenly returned to Detroit, due to pressing problems back home. The priest took that as a sign from God himself. "Don't tamper with divine providence or retribution," he told me later at another coffee shop encounter.

Re-Entering the Real World

Looking back at it all now, beginning at SHS, I made good things happen that would not have happened otherwise. I provided opportunities for a large number of seminarians to experience interaction with the poverty community, in particular with the community just outside our walls. I will always feel these were among the most important things I have done in my life. Yet they came at a high price. Even early in this drama, while I was still at SHS, the loss of solitude and non-responsibility and the peace that flows from that state were hard to replace. Small infusions of solitude and quiet were not enough.

Later in life, because of my seminary experience, I took on tasks that were not doable but I got done anyway, because I learned a calm at SHS that continues to amaze the people I work with. I don't suppress my Italian persona during those times, but I can control it, barely, and control the panic that should rightfully flow. I think that my lack of fear of failure allows me to accomplish more than I should be able to. That last year at SHS was impossible, yet it became possible because I had the luxury of the prior year to prepare my mind in the solitude and the peace I described.

I received a message one day at St. John's to call Sister Marie Bernadette at her convent at Nativity parish in the inner city.

Messages from nuns were not to be ignored; so I called the number and she answered promptly.

"Mr. Locricchio, I understand we are both speaking at the University of Detroit tomorrow on the same topic -- *Working with Youth in the Inner City*. So that we do not repeat each other, I thought it would be good if we met this evening to go over the areas we each will cover. If it would be convenient for you to come to supper here at the convent, we could review our talks afterwards."

She gave me the address and time and then suddenly yelled into the phone "Tony, honey, don't do that!!" I was more than shocked and said, "I beg your pardon, Sister?"

She started to laugh "Don't tell me your first name is Tony?"

"Yes, Sister, it is. I …I…"

She explained quickly, "I was typing up a paper for one of the boys in the neighborhood named Tony. He just sneaked in the back door and touched my shoulder and made me jump because I hadn't heard him come in."

Later I learned during dinner that the entire mini-convent of three women had heard the "Tony honey story" and they smiled a lot. The dinner had been cooked by Sister Marie Bernadette herself and was among the worst food I had ever tasted. What had not burned was of a strange flavor I thought it best not to inquire about. We had our meeting and staked out parameters for the talks the next morning. I offered to pick her up and take her to the University so she wouldn't have to drive.

The next morning I borrowed my father's black Lincoln Continental and arrived almost on time at the convent, an unusual pattern for me. I expected she would sit in the back seat, since I was garbed in my Roman collar and she was in veil and habit Instead, she jumped into the front seat with a warm "Good morning . You are only a little bit late." Off we went.

Wandering Between Two Worlds

During our talks it snowed quite hard. By the time I got to the parking lot, Sister had already cleared all the snow off the car and was ready to go. Somehow she managed to keep herself relatively snow free.

I went back to the convent a few months later to deliver some food packages for the Glenmary Order food distribution program. She met me at the door, a startling vision in her new habit. Her order had scandalized, yet intrigued, the Detroit nunnery communities by pioneering shorter skirts and short head veils that exposed the fact that nuns had hair. We conducted our food package exchange efficiently and made religious small talk and filled each other in on our latest programs. I asked more questions than were necessary but was very proper in my demeanor. I did notice, however, that she was really beautiful in a platonic sort of way.

I later ran into her on campus at U of D where she was about to graduate and I was teaching a theology class. She had been chosen to play the lead in a U of D Theater production of Goldoni's 18th century play "The Servant of Two Masters." She had been given permission by her order and by Archbishop Dearden to be in the play, since it was part of her graduation requirements for the theater degree she was taking for her order's work in the Appalachian missions.

Later, Rome's Head of Religious Congregations discovered that a Glenmary nun would be in a play at the University of Detroit (in a period costume, but with more cloth covering her than her order's new habit). The Roman cardinal demanded that the papal delegate to the United States fly to Detroit to order the Jesuits who ran the university to ban this nun from appearing in the play. The edict was delivered on the night of the second dress rehearsal to a cast whose lead actress had no understudy. Hundreds of stories from all over the world headlined "ROME BANS NUN FROM STAGE." Sister Marie Bernadette became a symbol in the 60's of Rome's overriding the decision of a local prelate.

The cast found an actress who fit into Sister's costumes with little adjustment. She was a quick study. Sister performed the role for the final time for her and during the run of the play was off stage coaching her replacement in the complex maneuvers required by the role. On opening night the new actress went on stage with a script in hand. I, being a wise cleric, sent a dozen roses. Six for Sister Marie Bernadette and six for the new leading lady. One dozen platonic roses.

Later, I found myself in the St. John's infirmary for trying to do too many things in too short a time. A flu bug had slowed me down. Sister sent me a get well card addressed to Mr. Tony Honey Locricchio. That envelope caused a stir at St. John's, but of course it was all platonic.

After my conflicts with Archbishop Dearden and my sudden return to the lay state, my life took on a new exciting direction. Foremost, I fell in love, head over heels, with Sister Marie Bernadette (Barbara Marie Kuess). The first time I spoke of that love was when I saw her at the University as the soon to be Reverend Mr. Locricchio. My sophisticated protective shell had been penetrated. Yet I temporarily fooled myself. I convinced myself that it was her work that I was so drawn to. Her potential. Her progressive order of missionary sisters. Her ability to retain her dignity and maturity during the stupidity of Rome's intervention in the play appearance. In reality I was quite simply in love with the most beautiful woman I had ever known, but too much in love with the idea of priesthood to admit how I felt even to myself. When I found that she had left the convent while I was stuck inside fighting tooth and nail with the Archbishop, I wrote her a very non-committal letter that could not survive the P.S. at the end. Out of the blue the postscript said: "Oh yes, by the way, don't do anything about your marital status; because if this archbishop keeps giving me a rough time, I will be down to propose. Yours, truly." That P.S. was *not* platonic.

I now realize that I may have subconsciously goaded the archbishop to move against my coveted priesthood because I wanted to "come down to propose." On our first official date I did propose and she said yes. We waited three months before getting married in a ceremony that is as sweet in my memory today as it was when it unfolded more than 35 years ago.

Wandering Between Two Worlds

When I think of the six years I spent in the seminary and the short parish work at St. Clement's in Romeo, I realize so very few of my years were spent inside the Church as a cleric. The story of my life is so much more than a recounting of that brief time. Even though Barbara and I married late, we have now reached the point where we have spent more time together than we lived before we met and married.

The transition from the clerical womb back into the world was a rather strange one for me. I had already been teaching theology at the University of Detroit and my separation from the seminary caused a stir in the press and among my students. Since U of D was a Jesuit institution, I expected a "cold shoulder" period after the blow-up with the Archbishop. Exactly the opposite happened. I became a "hero" in those rebellious 60's to my students and a large number of other young Catholics. My teaching expanded to two other universities. I lectured at non-Catholic churches and other schools. I was considered for a worker-priest movement project in Baltimore. Suddenly, I began to realize my transition was not a transition at all; only my address had changed. One morning I woke up and said to myself, "It is time to quit this new quasi-priesthood I am falling into and get on with life."

I jumped back into the practice of law full time, taking on the Chicago 15 case. Some of the defendants were former students of mine who, opposed to the Vietnam War, had broken into the country's largest draft board on the south side of Chicago and burned the 1-A draft records. The trial was the last of the "stand around events," where the defendants waited for police to arrive so that the trial could be used to speak out against the war. The atmosphere in the Federal courtroom in Chicago at the height of the Vietnam protests was frightening. Yet the courage of those students was something to behold. The honor to have been part of an excellent team of attorneys was one of the highlights of my legal career.

My love for legal work now demanded that I get into the field full time. I took a job as the Executive Director for Legal Aid in Flint, Saginaw, and Midland, Michigan. This became a way to stay involved in the poverty community and provide quality legal services through twelve lawyers to that community. Because we had offices and staff in each of the three cities, I spent a lot of time in my car driving between them and our home in Highland, Michigan. I put 50,000 miles on my car in one year. The time in the car allowed me a repeat of the contemplative quiet time I had learned to value in the seminary but had lost in the legal work and the heavy travel schedule I kept.

After about a year in the legal aid program in eastern Michigan, I was elected National President of Legal Aid Directors and Chairman of the Civil Division of the National Legal Aid and Defender Association. This position called for me to spend a great deal of time in Washington lobbying for federal funding for legal aid programs around the country. I also became a trainer of project directors for a new type of priority setting process, one that helped assign limited legal services funds to individual projects. I became the major attorney supporter of the National Clients Counsel. At national and regional training meetings, I would find myself socializing with the client representatives instead of other lawyers. I am very proud that, to this day, I am considered a lawyer who understands that real power must be in the hands of poverty clients to select the priorities for legal services to the poor. It has been a long time since I have held an official position with Legal Aid; yet I am still seen by my former clients from those days as their lawyer.

During this time the door to Hawaii opened. I became the Executive Director of the Hawaii Legal Aid Society, with offices and staff on all of the islands of the state. Despite our roots in Michigan, we packed up and flew to these isolated islands in a heartbeat, though it did take four or five minutes to adjust. Hawaii politics were a mess. Yet, in about two years, I was able to turn the Legal Services program, which had been essentially a divorce mill, into one of the most effective impact law programs in the country. After four years of initiating lawsuits, and with the State of Hawaii (which, ironically, was partially funding our project) as the principal defendant, we were able to form a very active client lobbying group to move on the state legislature. At this point my political position became very shaky. I was fired right after our program was selected as the best Legal Aid program in the country. Because I knew how political Hawaii was, I had a "no fire without cause" contract. In Federal Court I won more than $500,000 in a personal suit against the established powers. This victory allowed me to continue to select the type of law I wanted to practice and, for all intents and purposes, allowed me to continue to serve poor people without worrying about where the money would come from.

I subsequently became a specialist and something of an expert in the field of land reform law. The early Boston Protestant missionary families came to Hawaii to do good; and they did very well indeed. . . financially speaking, that is. One of the results of this was that much of the land, and especially land under people's homes, was owned by the large estates. A land reform bill to allow homeowners to buy back their land from the estates at a constitutionally fair price allowed me to go to court on behalf of groups of homeowners to seek a fair price for the land. The case I worked on, and the law that allowed land reform, went all the way to the United States Supreme Court, where the law was upheld. My son, Hoa David, whom we had adopted from Vietnam just before the fall of Saigon, went with me to Washington for the argument before the Supreme Court. Our side was headed by a top constitutional lawyer, a professor from Harvard Law School. After listening to the questions of the Justices, my son leaned over to me and said, "I think that means we won. Right, Dad?" He was twelve at the time and was still working on his English, but he had figured it out. We had won a landmark Supreme Court case in the field of states rights.

The national office of Common Cause says that Hawaii is one of the most politically corrupt places in the United States. Common Cause is right. Buying a politician here was inexpensive but had been elevated to a high art. Once the major economic invasion of the Japanese in the late 1980s and early 1990s hit, the influx of foreign campaign contributions were widespread but, of course, illegal. A group of us headed the efforts to stop the purchase of Hawaii by foreign political dollars. It took us five years to develop what is the largest case to this day in the history of the Federal Elections Commission (FEC). Fines against 120 Hawaiian politicians were issued. Several million dollars were forced to be returned to foreign contributors. The largest monetary penalties in the history of the FEC were levied. We were able to reveal major misdeeds by a leading candidate for governor. I feel we prevented his being elected. *Frontline*, a PBS television news program, and the *New Yorker* magazine did a rare joint expose on Hawaii politics called the Fixers and on our role in stopping part of the corruption. NBC also covered our challenge to the Japanese mafia during the economic invasion of Hawaii. *48 Hours* did an excellent piece on the plight of my clients -- several Hawaiians whose farms were destined to become golf courses through legislative corruption.

I received some death threats. I have a bullet hole in the stained glass front door of my house to remind me of that. One of the conspirators fortunately got scared and revealed to police a plan to have me bumped off while I was visiting family and doing work in Michigan. It was supposed to happen as a random freeway shooting by an unnamed black gang, far away from Hawaii. Newspaper coverage of the plan became an insurance policy for my safety. Life has not been dull out here under the palms.

The development of electric clean air vehicles has been my and Barbara's chief activity these past decades. The work has been tough, and the funding lately has been through a plan called "third mortgage on the house." Through the Department of Defense, the State of New York, and City of Los Angeles we have received over $11 M in funding for our work. We spent our own funds to keep the project going after the Republicans took control of the White House in 2000.

With the election of Barack Obama to the presidency, we have proposed a massive program called TIME IS OF THE ESSENCE, a secure bailout for the United States citizen. Our website is at evtransports.com. Visitors can let us know what they think by leaving a message at the site. The detail material covers our work of over 25 years in this field.

Our vehicles have four times won the world's largest electric vehicle race against vehicles entered by major auto manufacturers and universities. We had a team from the People's Republic of China drive one of our vehicles in the Tour de Sol. A second one was driven by a team from the Federated States of Micronesia. Both teams won their divisions and overall race first place awards. We have been invited by the United Nations Environmental Programme to demonstrate our vehicles at the United Nations Headquarters in New York and at Kyoto, Japan, and Johannesburg, South Africa, for the UN World Sustainability Conferences.

We never have had the luxury of a conventional life. Yet we have traveled all over the World and lived in the best places we can imagine -- a wonderful house on the bay in Tiburon near San Francisco, a great house we built in Highland, Michigan, in the middle of five square miles of state land. We owned horses and a one horse open sleigh with bells. We have lived in Manhattan alongside Central Park and for over 35 years in Kailua, Hawaii. We also have a great four-bedroom cabin we built in the state park on Kauai. We have been given the best of these lands and have lived on them well.

We have adopted three children, all of whom had serious problems prior to the adoptions. When we thought we could bear no more, new pain came. We lost two of them through early deaths. We have set high goals that threaten our security and place us at great on-going financial risk. But our son has brought to Hawaii a wonderful granddaughter for us. She makes us young and old at the same time.

While we have not forgotten the sadness, we know we can not let it direct our lives. Sadness, no matter how deep, is a luxury we just cannot afford. There is too much work yet to be done and too much joy in doing it.

Final Remarks

I, like a lot of "Catholics," attend few official Church functions these days. I remain a product of Christianity and of the Roman Church. I am a follower of Christ and keep bumping into him in my work and daily life. He is inconvenient to follow; and there are times I get very frustrated with the simple logic of his message, which is hard to rationally ignore. I am unhappy that I spent so much time being appalled at the things done in Christ's name by the Roman Church. Now I see this as unimportant. It is finally clear to me that the message of the life of Christ is very much alive in the Real Church that reflects the Mystical Body. The message of Jesus is so strong that it can easily withstand the worst abuses by the Roman Church and others who use the words of the message in rather sad ways. When I quit fretting over abuses, I realized that focusing on institutional Church conduct just wasted my time. I should have been focused on the vibrant real Church.

As for Sacred Heart Seminary, I have very different memories than most of my classmates. To me it will always be the Hightower Day Camp.

As part of my work in getting the Church facilities opened up to local residents through the poverty program, I undertook a campaign to make the great facility of Sacred Heart Seminary available to the kids in the neighborhood during the summer, when the seminary was virtually shut down. It frustrated me to no end to see this excellent recreational facility go unused in the midst of need. So with questionable ethics I suggested that the rector hold a one day open house of parts of the facility as a good will gesture. I shamelessly stocked the group attending the opening welcome session with black neighbors I was working with. The crowd was large. When the rector invited questions at the end of his talk and tour, the people already knew what to ask.

"Monsignor, this is such a great facility. Wouldn't it be wonderful if you made it available for the kids in the neighborhood to use when it is closed in the summer?" asked one specially selected sweet mother of four. The poor rector was momentarily caught off guard but quickly recovered: "That really would be a great idea," he smiled, "but unfortunately that would take a lot of money. I am sorry to say that our budget has no money for this type of thing." That was my cue to announce that we had just received word that the money for a large day camp project had been approved through one of the proposals I had written. The rector blanched.

My next plant then asked me, "Well, since you wrote the program and the rector thinks it would be a good idea except for the money, the problem is solved. Do you think this facility would work during the summer months when it is not being used?" I hesitated just long enough to make it appear I was thinking it over, taking care not to look at the rector who was glaring at me. Finally I said, "Why, yes, now that I think of it, the seminary grounds and recreational facilities would be excellent for that program. What do you think, Monsignor?"

He tried to make an effort to smile and stammered out, "Yes, it could work out if..." He never had a chance to say more as the prepared neighbors jumped to their feet with wild applause and rushed up to shake his hand and thank him for this generous offer. Poor Monsignor never had a chance. My ethics, as they say, sucked. I guess I might have felt bad about what I did but when I confessed it to my spiritual advisor, he laughed for a very long time. Later, just as our class of 1965 was about to graduate, the annual faculty-senior class softball game took place. I had avoided the rector as much as possible, sending in other seminarians from our staff team to coordinate arrangements for the Hightower Day Camp with him. Now here he was, barreling down on my second base position. By pure reflex I caught the throw from shortstop and tagged him out. He was "in my face" immediately and, using his arms to make a sweeping gesture that took in the whole campus. "Mr. Locricchio, look at this place! It is absolute beautiful, isn't it? After next week when you bring in those kids, it will be destroyed. They will ruin it. Remember, you didn't fool me. This is all your fault. You are responsible for what will become of this place!"

"Those kids" did not destroy SHS. They loved it. After that summer it became a part of the community. It was known in and around Chicago Boulevard simply as The Camp. The program continued with the support of the rector. Two summers later The Camp (SHS) was untouched, even though the Detroit riot started less than a mile away.

I have not been back to SHS for decades. The few times I did return, years after my poverty program days, the sounds I heard on the grounds and in the halls were not those of students returning to their educational institution but of kids chanting the Hightower cheers. I saw kids lined up to board excursion buses, all wearing their Camp Hightower t-shirts. I would gladly exchange the use of our cabin on Kauai for a staff Hightower t-shirt.

I think I may want to return to SHS soon. My memory banks could use a camp fix. Maybe the old guy could even climb the stairs to the Gothic tower, the "hightower," itself. I hope rational folks have closed down the access so I won't need to make a fool of myself trying.

You may wonder if I have matured and changed since those days. I am afraid I still "tag 'em out at second." I will know that I have finally reached reasonableness when I learn to occasionally drop the ball. Actually, when I calm down, when the grandiose plans for changing transportation and energy in America are in place, then I will be fine and ready to be an old guy. Upon retirement at 85, I plan to get some work done on the house and the cabin, lose that same weight I have been losing over and over again for decades, and write the definitive "no carbs" pasta cookbook. With only 14 years to go, it is time to start planning.

CHOICES AND DREAMS
William J. Clair

New lives begin from the dreams that arise from every choice we make.

<u>My First Dream – The Priesthood</u>

I entered Sacred Heart Seminary out of eighth grade with all the expectations of leading a most fulfilling life dedicated to Christ. I had an aunt and a cousin who were nuns, another cousin in the novitiate, and distant relatives who were priests. My parents were hard workers, achieving the American dream. They were also devoted practicing Catholics. There was nothing to stop me in achieving my dream - the priesthood.

In the 1950s and 1960s, the Detroit, Michigan, area had two parallel cultures. The majority were second generation, white Europeans. I belonged in this group, but I was actually a third generation European-American with German, French, and Irish roots. I lived a very secure life as an only child within a neighborhood where many of my cousins were daily playmates. My father was "color-matcher" for the second largest printing ink manufacturer in the world. He went to work every day in his new car, dressed in a suit, complete with white shirt and tie. After work, his life was his family and following sports. My mother was a bookkeeper for a large carpet cleaning business just down Linwood Avenue from the seminary. Her after work activities included housekeeping, being a concert pianist, and "buying and selling" homes.

Wandering Between Two Worlds

The other culture that was "moving on up" from the southern states to work in the automobile factories was that of the black people (we would have said "colored" in those days). These folks were moving into previously all-white neighborhoods. Some real estate agents were practicing "block-busting" methods (using scare tactics on white people by telling them that they had "better sell today, because tomorrow you won't be able to, since coloreds will be your neighbors.").

I enjoyed my high school years as a seminary "day dog" (one who commuted from home to school six days a week). I was part of the first class graduating from the new seminary high school – the Cardinal Mooney Latin School. I then moved on to the seminary college, where I was required to become a boarder.

The first two years of college were very pleasant. I was assigned one of the new rooms created from former classrooms on the second floor. Most of these were four-man units. My classes were very interesting, exposing me to new ideas of all sorts, in science, the humanities, and languages. I also participated in recreational activities such as handball, set off against more spiritual activities such as meditation and self-understanding. Even with all the in-depth studies, I decided that in the end "faith" in God was the ultimate answer to the questions "Where am I from?" "Is there a God?" and "Where am I going?"

The priest/professors were also intriguing: from the intense (Father Philosophy) to the comic (Father Gregorian Chant); from the apparently deeply spiritual (Father Advisor) to the apparently worldly (Father Financial); from the one in the wheelchair to the one on the motorcycle.

One situation that always puzzled me was why I wasn't openly accepted in my local parish life when I was off on vacation. I wasn't asked to serve at Masses even during Christmas and Easter (maybe they thought I had too much religion at the seminary and needed a break). During the summers, however, I would serve as lector every Sunday in the resort parish in Lexington, Michigan. There everyone knew that I was studying to be a priest and that for a summer job I parked cars at the local lakefront restaurant.

When the last two years of college were upon me, I knew it was time to make the decision of whether to continue or not. Celibacy was the issue. I enjoyed seminary life and all the classes, especially social science because the professor made it so human. I especially remember reading a book entitled "Man's Inhumanity to Man." By then I had a private room, which helped me to understand loneliness and to search for the answer to the celibacy issue. I had hope here because others had made the decision and become priests; and the Church was so alive with Pope John XXIII and Vatican II. This new era in Church history was exciting.

Seminarians had begun to become active in the social issue of equality. We marched down Woodward Avenue. We lived in black families' homes on weekends. We made Martin Luther King's dream our dream. I was also on the speech team that went out into the community. I took additional college classes at the University of Detroit. I had the total support of my family in every cause I took up.

Then in January, 1964, my father passed away from a heart attack. This event made me really consider the meaning of life, family, and my dream of the priesthood. After a grueling year and a half, I made the decision that I would not continue to St. John's Provincial Seminary, even though I had been given that opportunity. I could not lead the life of a hypocrite, since I thought that I could not guarantee myself that I could keep the promise of celibacy. I will never forget the day that I went into the rector's office, knowing that my dream of the priesthood was about to end. The rector listened and asked if he could be of any assistance in my reconsidering the decision, but I told him it was my final decision. I left his office wondering what my next dream would be.

My Second Dream – Careers in Education and Real Estate

Over the summer of '65, I decided to become a teacher. This decision was made even though I was earning $5,000 parking cars in 10 weeks during the summer; and I understood that a teacher's starting salary was $6,000 per school year.

Teaching was in my family. An aunt was a special education teacher; my grandmother was an elementary teacher in the Detroit schools; and an aunt and a cousin, both nuns, taught in the Detroit Archdiocesan schools. Furthermore, I had some fantastic teachers in Catholic elementary school and many exemplary teachers in the seminary.

I felt that I could "make a difference" in the lives of students at the high school level. I knew that I could help youngsters see that their dreams would come true with hard work. I also wanted to instill in them a strong sense of helping their fellow man survive in a just society. Thus, I began the journey toward achieving my new dream, this time in a secular environment.

In the fall I was off to Wayne State University in Detroit, where both my mother and her sister had been students. This was the time of the Vietnam peace rallies; and Wayne State's students were heavily involved. I enjoyed the excitement of the peace rallies and the new knowledge I was gaining by majoring in English, social science, and speech. After two years, I had my second bachelor's degree; and with 200 other graduating students, I enjoyed 40 days touring Europe (England, the Netherlands, Germany, Italy, France, Yugoslavia, Czechoslovakia, Switzerland), the Middle East (Turkey, Israel during the Six-Day War, Egypt, the Holy Land), and cruising the Mediterranean Sea to Corfu, Crete, and Greece. The Six-Day War presented a unique view of "war." I found myself touring Israel with the wife of a member of the Knesset and viewing an on-going war: the UN building being bombed; dead bodies on the sides of the roads; Chrysler trucks and tanks being used by both sides to fight each other; and finally, in the middle of the night, an Israeli helicopter taking people off the cruise ship I was a passenger on.

This trip also counted toward the first six hours of graduate school in sociology. A classmate and I wrote two major papers for credit. The first was on the contrasting sociology of the countries we toured and read about. Since the Wayne State professor was creative, the other paper was a time study of the red light districts in the cities we visited (17 minutes average time per encounter). Since this was my first trip out of the USA, my eyes and my horizons were really widened to a world that was not equal in values, religion, dreams, or economies.

When I returned to the United States, I immediately headed to the Fort Lauderdale, Florida, area where I was to have my first teaching job at Nova Schools. This system had a program from kindergarten through university, an 11-month school year, was in session from 8AM to 5PM daily, and drew from the entire public school student population across Broward County. I had applied earlier and received a Ford Foundation grant to teach there. At that time they were expanding their program, which was still in its infancy. Unfortunately, the buildings that were to have been ready were delayed, so I was given the opportunity to teach at a high school in Dade County.

I accepted the position of English/speech/forensics/debate teacher at Hialeah High School, which had 4300 students and ran on three shifts from 6AM to 10PM. There were many new teachers at the school and I made some lifelong friends. The year was extraordinary. I enjoyed the first shift, teaching English literature, forensics and debating. There was an AM principal and a PM principal but no assistant principals. The school had classes for every type of student interest, from college prep to vocational courses, from Shakespeare to aeronautics, from clubs such as Civitas to cooking, from sports to auto racing. The forensics/debate teams won the State of Florida championship and went on to finish fourth in the country. We spoke and debated all over the United States from Georgetown in Washington, D.C., to Macalister College in the Twin Cities. Fifteen thousand dollars in football team game money was used to sponsor the trips.

The school had a growing Cuban population. In my spare time between the first shift classes and late afternoon speech team practices, I started a class for students who were having difficulty with English as their second language. What more could I want from my new teaching dream?

I then read of a new teaching program sponsored by the federal government called the ES70s program. It was based on the theory that not all students learn at the same rate. Students could proceed through courses at their own rates if they were segmented into learning units. I agreed with the concept and applied and was accepted for a position with the Bloomfield Hills, Michigan, schools, one of the country's test sites.

I taught for two years at East Hills Middle School in a team teaching situation. After observing that a classroom would eventually have students on 15 to 20 different segments at one time and after experiencing a team partner who did not wish to team teach at all, I decided to look for an "All-American/mixed socioeconomic" school district. I found that school district in Farmington, Michigan.

I spent the next 30 years in Farmington working with all types of students. I served on an endless number of committees, co-chaired the committee involved in the restructuring of the high school, and served on the negotiating committee for just teacher contracts. During those years, I fought for the rights of all students, both the college bound and the technical bound, to receive appropriate courses for their interests and abilities. During that same time, I finally received an M.A. in curriculum and instruction from Michigan State University and completed the course work for a Ph.D. in the field of school administration.

My proudest accomplishment was leading a coup of teachers on the high school restructuring committee. After two years of study and debate, the administration wanted to exclusively focus the 68-page restructuring document on the college bound student. I held out for the technical (vocational) student's needs to be an equal part of the document. I had to threaten to write a dissenting minority report. In the final days, the administration gave in and the technical students' needs were included. My refusal to compromise what I knew to be right, however, cost me my aspirations of becoming an assistant principal or principal. After 19 tries, I was never chosen.

Nevertheless, I gained recognition when my team of six teachers and a para-professional won a $20,000 Chrysler Fund grant to create a technical program that connected English, social science, math, and science to a computer automated design (CAD) architectural program. The program, originally intended for developing one of the Little Caesars/Illitch properties, was cited by the Chrysler Fund and the State Board of Education as one of the top five in the state of Michigan (out of all 360 school districts).

After school, I sponsored the snow skiing club, which took trips to Aspen, Colorado. In the warmer months I taught water-skiing. One of my barefoot water-skiers developed the conceptual architectural views for a condominium project that I wished to build in West Bloomfield. The plans were submitted to the governing authorities and entered in the architectural high school state competition, where they were awarded first place.

My greatest accomplishments, however, were with the students. I was able to help my students believe in their dreams and achieve their potential. A number of my students eventually became very successful in life – both socially and personally. One became the president of a major local broadcasting enterprise. During his high school years I helped positively influence him while he was experimenting with drugs. Another student was involved with a much-publicized sex partying group. She told me about the situation before it broke in the newspapers and before she told her parents. She gave up the sex parties, testified against the organizer of them, and he went to jail.

Sadly, I was unable to help all my students solve their problems. One young man showed up on my doorstep on Sunday mornings periodically. He took his life with a gun within ten minutes of seeing me one fall day after school. Another student attempted suicide three times, but was unsuccessful, at least so far. But there are so many others who are leading good normal lives, as parents or singles. One of these is a girl who came from China with her father, a dishwasher in a restaurant. His daughter obtained a full scholarship to a university, where she graduated with a BS degree in engineering. She later obtained a MS degree and today is a noise and vibration engineer at the General Motors Proving Ground. (In 2000, I toured China for two weeks where I further experienced the diversity of values, history, people, and religion.) Another student of mine lost his father to cancer while in high school. His mother worked at a fast food restaurant to put her four children through college. He accepted the challenge to be the best and today is a vice-president of a Michigan bank.

Still another student totally bought into my "free enterprise, dog-eat-dog" economics course philosophy (Even though I really questioned some of that course's principles, the students never saw through my exterior until I told them at the end of the course. Even then, most would not believe me when I told them I didn't personally believe everything I had taught them.). Today my former pupil is a manager of a stock fund with a major bank. Finally, while English department chair, I taught creative writing, which I initially thought to be frivolous. One of my school's students, who was number one in math in the county, and later went to Harvard, is a co-creator of a cartoon which is a social commentary on America. You might have seen it on television. It's called *The Simpsons*.

During those 33 years of teaching, I believe I brought hope in the future, faith in oneself to take risks to better mankind, and equality of opportunity to over 5000 students. I always called **every** student "doctor," because I truly believed that each could be the best at whatever he or she wanted to be.

I had a parallel vocation - real estate. My parents mentored me in real estate as they bought and sold homes continuously. We moved to a new home at least once a year until I was in high school. We lived on every street in the Southfield / Outer Drive / McNichols (6 Mile Road) area. Even though both of my parents worked their "day" jobs, they also worked on the weekends looking for houses that they thought they could make a little extra money on when they sold them in a year. When I went to high school at the seminary, I asked my parents if we could stay in one house for awhile. They agreed and we lived in the same house for ten years!

Nevertheless, my parents then decided to build a cottage near Lexington, Michigan, where I had spent all my summers since I was in kindergarten. One aunt and uncle had a cottage just south of Lexington on Lake Huron. Their children, my cousins, were like siblings, since we lived in the same area of Detroit; and I spent every summer until college with them. Even in college I was nearby, working at both Camp Ozanam and at the CYO Camp, both just north of Lexington.

My real estate career took off as soon as I made my first commission selling a potential mobile home site in Novi, Michigan. I was hooked. I next bought some acreage in Southfield, which increased immensely in value in just six months. Eventually I bought and sold land in Ann Arbor for the expansion of the local landfill, land in West Bloomfield that I had rezoned for condominiums, and land in Wixom for single family homes. Along the way I continued in my parents' tradition of buying and selling numerous "fixer-uppers."

Even though I was diligently pursuing teaching and real estate at the same time, I felt that my experience in the real world of business brought an additional perspective to my teaching and for my students. I took my high school students to the G7 Trade Conference (when it was held in Detroit) and had breakfast with the governor and the participants at the Gem Theater. This was a field trip for a humanities class that had three focus questions: Who am I? Where did I come from? Where am I going? At another time, I talked my way into a symposium at GM's Warren, Michigan, Tech Center to hear Dr. W. Edwards Deming, the renowned quality expert, speak to 400 GM engineers live and 3400 GM managers down-linked world-wide. I used this experience to inspire my students to be the best in the world.

Along that same line, I used Alvin Toffler's *The Third Wave* in my humanities course. My field trips to see Toffler live when he was in the Detroit area were even written up in the *New York Times*, thanks to a *Detroit News* writer whose son I had in class. I surreptitiously tried to bridge the gap between textbook information and the real world -- the theoretical side and the human side, the right side and the wrong side, the good side and the bad side -- in my literature, social studies, and economics courses.

During the 33 teaching / real estate years, my faith was kept alive by seeing the faith of my mother in her everyday life. Her husband (my father) had died of a heart attack, but she remarried five years later to a very good man. He too died of a heart attack. Undeterred, she remarried again to another good man, and he survived her. Through all of her hardships, I never heard her once ask, "Why me, Lord?" She always prayed, attended Mass every Sunday, went to confession, and had the last sacraments many times in her life.

In my own life, however, I lost the fervor of the faith that I had from childhood through my college years. I still attended church, went to Communion, and would always say to myself "Lord, look what your kids are doing (on earth)!" I have even thought about writing children stories using that phrase as the title of a series. Some of the things that have really bothered me are the affluence in the Church, the celibacy requirement for most priests, the constant need to continue the modernizing spirit of Vatican II, the recently revealed sex scandals (which I never personally observed nor experienced), and the historical scandals of the Crusades, the Inquisition, and the buying and selling of the papacy. Today, I ask myself the more basic question of whose God is the true God, as I see the world at odds over the God of Mohammed, the God of Christianity, and the God of Judaism.

I have now returned to my college days when I decided that "faith" in God was the best man could do to "understand" the mystery. During my life, I feel that I have helped to "save the world" because I have helped mentor students in the right and good way during my teaching years and have always acted ethically in my real estate dealings. My most recent musing is about the division of the earth's resources between the first world, second world, and third world countries. I believe this is the triggering cause of today's current terrorist happenings.

My Third Dream – Retirement? (Not Yet!)

In 2002, the Farmington school district offered a buy-out for the teachers who had been with the district the longest and at the top salary. After much thought over four months, I decided to "retire," even though I didn't know what I would do in retirement. I needed a new dream.

I sold the home I had built on Upper Straits Lake in Orchard Lake, Michigan (oh, by the way, I also had a builder's license). Then I was off to Florida where I had built a house two years prior (Over the years I had also built homes for resale in Boca Raton and Jupiter, Florida.). In December, 2002, I moved permanently to Florida and began to work on defining my new dream.

I applied for an executive directorship of a new school for 200 high school students who were interested in a curriculum that was interdisciplinary and technological in focus. Unfortunately, I lost that opportunity to a professor from Florida Atlantic University who, after six months, resigned the position.

Then in May, 2003, I was inducted into the "Teacher Hall of Fame" in Michigan. Quite an honor! My remarks at the induction ceremony were:

"From Walt Disney's *Tapestry of Dreams*, played during the fireworks display, while the world globe crosses Lake Buena Vista at Epcot, Disneyworld….

"I feel it summarizes the teaching profession and my thirty years in the Farmington public schools. It will also serve as my thank you to all in Farmington public schools who have made my teaching dreams come true: seeing kids learn, grow, and dream.

"While listening, think of your Career / Life / Dreams.

**"With the stillness of the night,
There comes a time to understand,**

To reach out and touch tomorrow,
Take the future in our hands,
We can see a new horizon
Built on all that we have done,
And our dreams begin another
1000 circles around the sun.
We go on to enjoy
And through the tears,
We go on to discover new frontiers,
Moving on with the courage of the years,
We go on moving forward now as one,
Moving on with the spirit born to run,
Ever on with each rising sun,
To a new day-
We go on………………………..

We go on………………………..”

I, however, still needed to finalize my new dream. To most of my relatives and friends, I did not need a new dream - I had it: "retirement."

But this was not my dream at all, even though I did enjoy not getting up at 6AM and going to bed at 11:30PM. Then, in the summer and fall of 2003, my next dream came together. I decided to join the local school district on a task force to lower substance abuse (Martin County, Florida had the second highest occurrence of substance abuse in the state of Florida). I also continued buying and selling real estate, which came to an abrupt halt in 2007. I continued to work on my hobbies: photography, golfing, boating, and traveling.

But the establishment of a foundation to help inspire all types of kids to be inspired to take risks in all fields of study in order to better mankind has been on my mind for a few years. I hope I can start it now. As for the spiritual life at this time, I am now very open to the concept of a universal God without regard to any one "ritual." (This might seem like being a "cafeteria Catholic.") I still go to Sunday Mass, Communion, and work with Church organizations such St.

Vincent de Paul Society; but the "Prada and ermine trappings" of the Catholic Church seem too worldly when there is so much poverty in the world.

Even though most people lead lives of quiet desperation (especially during the current world economic crisis), to paraphrase Thoreau, I feel that I have been lucky to have led a life of dreams – most realized, some not. But if they had all been realized, they wouldn't be dreams, would they?

So I am still DREAMING,
        HOPING,
        QUESTIONING,
        STILL ALIVE.
May ALL THE WORLD have this choice to
        DREAM,
        HOPE,
        QUESTION,
        LIVE!

Wandering Between Two Worlds

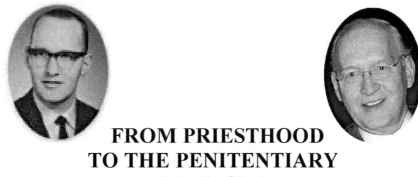

FROM PRIESTHOOD
TO THE PENITENTIARY
John L. Clark

In 1969, I was thrilled to finally be out of the seminary as a newly minted young priest in Flint, Michigan, working hard serving my bustling working class parishioners, but also keenly interested in social justice and anti-Vietnam activities. Twenty years later, I was the warden of the U.S. Penitentiary at Marion, Illinois, the first federal supermax facility, responsible for the daily operation of the most constrictive federal prison in the country. I was in the middle of a 30-year career in prison administration, having made seven cross-country moves with a growing family of four kids.

It is surprising to some that I see this transition not as jolting departure, but as part of a consistent flow in a journey shaped by several forces, but especially by indelible values and lessons I took from my four years at Sacred Heart Seminary. That abiding influence has not dwindled another twenty years on, as I scale back my work as a government consultant, while also finding myself entrenched in Catholic parish leadership and an assortment of other service-based volunteer work.

Over the intervening decades, my winding journey has been compelled by a religiously-rooted sense of vocation, of being called to do something good, even important -- to fix what is broken, working to solve institutional problems in both the criminal justice system and the local Church. And yes, just as surely, by a desire to take the lead, to be in charge.

My professional experience and religious values have converged over the years into certain core, motivating beliefs. A short-hand summary would be something like this:

> Public functions and organizations, particularly in the criminal justice arena where I have worked, affect the lives of people, for better or for worse. So often it is the underdog, the person on the margins of society, who is most impacted by the system's rules and outcomes. Even when it requires intense bureaucratic maneuvering, genuine public service improves "the system" by helping vulnerable people in tangible ways. Thus it is holy work bringing about God's Kingdom.

My First Vocation

I was lucky to be raised in the supportive atmosphere of a large extended family, most members living close at hand around my native Jackson, Michigan. I was sheltered in the setting of Catholic parishes and schools, with the focus of that community often split between religion and athletics. During my formative years, I felt the seeds of a vocation, of a responsibility to achieve, lead, and do good things. The influence of nuns, coaches, and family left the strong impression that much was expected of me. The ultimate role models held out in that environment were the parish priests: admirable young parish assistants, as well as several strong, old-school Irish pastors.

So when the time came to declare for college, after several years of very private struggle, off I went to the seminary, convinced I was following this call to give my life over to doing God's work. In retrospect, my vision of Catholic priesthood was just as surely clouded by the place of honor and esteem I saw accorded to priests.

That fall of 1961, I moved from small town Jackson to Sacred Heart Seminary in Detroit's inner city. Though in a seemingly confined setting, I felt my world thrown wide open in so many ways beyond the content of the liberal arts curriculum. I was excited by the broader vision of the faculty regarding life, society, and the Church. I quickly felt comfortable and ultimately loved my whole time there.

Wandering Between Two Worlds

Academically, I worked fairly hard and did well. Not being a particularly conceptual thinker, I was not a good fit majoring in philosophy, but that was the unquestioned program of the day.

Of particular influence on me were the frequent guest lectures on a wide variety of subjects. I was especially attracted to topics of social and racial justice, building on the continuing themes of a number of our professors. Likewise, having grown up in a sheltered white environment, I was influenced by Sacred Heart's setting right there in the heart of a thriving big city black community. Walking those neighborhood streets or riding the bus downtown had an emotional impact on me, making the issue of racial injustice much more real. I became increasingly fascinated by the civil rights revolution that dominated the news of the day; and I wanted to be a part of it.

In 1964, the summer before senior year, my classmate Gene Fisher and I engaged in a singular experience, one which profoundly influenced my subsequent life and career. To a great extent this cemented a friendship with Gene which endures 45 years later. Looking to raise our awareness of racial problems, we signed on for a one week program for seminary students sponsored by Friendship House in the crowded South Side of Chicago, coincidentally in an area near where Barack Obama became a community organizer two decades later. I lived with and learned so much from a working class black family, the Turners. From Friendship House, Gene and I were exposed to a daily variety of committed people and savvy Chicago organizations. At the conclusion we were challenged to return to our seminary and work in new ways for racial justice.

That summer trip led to my most memorable experience at Sacred Heart, and it is telling that it was neither academic nor directly religious. As soon as classes resumed, Gene and I organized the Student Human Relations Education and Action Committee, or SHREAC, a group of about 15 or 20 students pulled together especially to raise the awareness of the student population on racial issues. SHREAC remained very active as a student organization for some years. We sponsored various educational programs and organized a local march by the entire student body and faculty in support of the 1965 Selma to Montgomery march. We focused on setting up weekend home visits by the student population to the homes of black families, mimicking our Chicago experience. These families invited in friends to share their views and experiences with our students. Almost the entire seminary population participated in these weekends. It was generally agreed that the impact of those personal experiences in the black community of Detroit was deep and lasting on the student body and on the seminary as an institution.

I recall my personal elation in successfully organizing the logistics for the weekend family visits. Over 200 families all over Detroit had to be found and briefed on plans. Transportation was needed. The seminary administration had to be kept constantly in the loop. For many weeks, my studies were secondary, while I kept various balls in the air, coordinating innumerable details with a variety of folks from the Archbishop's Committee on Human Rights. In retrospect, this, my first real taste of organizing a significant endeavor from start to finish, put me in a comfort zone. I liked organizing and managing a project that made Sacred Heart and the Detroit Church better institutions.

At the same time, the sweeping new insights of the Vatican Council, combined with the wonderful direction provided by our faculty, profoundly changed my personal understanding of the Church and of the priesthood. I saw a new vision of my personal vocation.

After graduating from Sacred Heart, I breezed through four years of theological studies, frankly putting more energy into a number of outside activities in the area of civil rights and community organizing than into my studies. I do not recall having any particularly difficult crises of doubt about my faith or my vocation to the priesthood. I had occasional periods of loneliness, but I was too busy for them to last. At the same time, the prospect of life-long celibacy was always an emotional struggle, causing me considerable resentment. But I balanced this against my strong sense of vocation, of being personally called to do God's work and to lead and serve his people as a priest. With open eyes and a grudging heart, I eventually accepted the package deal: celibacy was a part of the sacrifice tied up with my call to be a Catholic priest.

A Young Priest – For Awhile

Having finally been ordained in 1969 in Lansing by Bishop Alexander Zaleski, I learned quickly that I loved being a priest, particularly in the circumstances of my first assignment. For three years, I was a junior member of a new experiment in ministry, a seven-priest pastoral team assigned to three very different parishes in Flint, Michigan, a General Motors factory town then at its zenith in so many ways. I lived with two of the priests and did most of my work at St. Luke's, a very busy parish in a working class neighborhood, challenged by rapid changes in its racial composition. The other two parishes we served, each with older pastors in failing health, were in the inner city. I especially loved helping in the education and formation programs designed to implement the reforms and vision of Vatican II at the grass-roots parish level.

It was a time of great hope and palpable vibrancy, making me proud of the Catholic Church in our diocese. My peers and I sensed we were on the cutting edge of inevitable changes -- changes which would shape the Church and the lives of so many of our people for decades to come. We could never have imagined what so many of us now in retrospect view as the great disappointment with the subsequent path of the institutional Church, as its leadership has moved away from the vision of John XXIII and his Council. What an enduring heartbreak!

But I still consider that period as a high point in my life. I loved being a priest and am convinced I was a good one. I took little time off, working hard on many "priestly duties." I received lots of favorable reinforcement from the people and from my fellow priests. I was convinced our work on racial and social issues was part of a pattern of broad-based changes that would leave our society a much better place, especially for the poor and minorities. On a personal level, I found that there was a close sense of fraternity among many of the priests of the diocese.

After about two years of getting my feet on the ground as a young priest, a new opportunity further opened my eyes to another aspect of my personal aspirations, or to be more frank, my personal sense of ambition. Father Don Eder, St. Luke's pastor and my mentor, was granted some months away on sabbatical. The bishop's office showed unusual confidence in overlooking my relative inexperience and appointed me at the age of 28 to be interim administrator of this large, complex parish.

I found that I was not intimidated at all by the administrative and leadership roles, and things went well. As in the past, I loved having leadership responsibility thrust upon me. In a real way, those months foreshadowed my later experience as a prison warden. In each case, I was responsible for leadership of the many facets of small but complex communities.

Torn by Personal Conflict

On the broader scale, the winds of post-Vatican II sweeping the Church fostered independent thought and the questioning of accepted structures. One of the most obvious areas of challenge was the mandate for a celibate priesthood. The pace of change in so many other aspects of the Church increased the naïve hopes of so many of us that there might be some change in this discipline. This unsettled atmosphere in the tenor of the times surely contributed to the relative brevity of my tenure in the ranks of the ordained. Very soon I found myself facing an intense personal dilemma that changed my life – the result of a priest-nun love story not uncommon for the times.

During my second year in Flint, Sue -- that is Sister Sue Collins, O.P. -- was sent to teach fifth grade at St. Luke's parish school, where she quickly developed a reputation as a talented and popular teacher. Sue and I worked together in the normal course of events on school-related activities and gradually developed a closer friendship while working on liturgy planning and on peace movement activities with a local interfaith group. I was struck by her upbeat and self-reliant spirit, generous and not stuck on herself. I thoroughly enjoyed being around her in those group activities.

Late in that school year, she stopped by the office and mentioned to me that she had been struggling for some time and had decided to leave the Dominican order that summer. She had found a job teaching mentally disabled kids at a school in South Bend. I found myself upset and conflicted about the prospect of her leaving the area and my life. Slowly we started spending more time together in the weeks before she moved.

Several times that following year I quietly took the three hour trip to see Sue in South Bend. It soon became clear that we were in love with each other, head-over-heals, struck-by-lightning. At the same time, I loved my life and work as a priest and felt a strong sense of loyalty to the Lansing Diocese. In no way was I looking to fall in love, cheat on my vows, or leave the priesthood. Yet, I was beset by this overwhelming personal conflict and did not know how I might proceed.

<u>Struggle to Transition</u>

In the normal course of things, I was transferred after my third year in Flint. In the bishop's wisdom, I was sent to be chaplain at the Ypsilanti State Psychiatric Hospital, a huge old 2000-bed facility near Ann Arbor. After Sue and I talked about her moving nearby as we tried to sort things out, she took a job teaching at a parish school in Ann Arbor. We saw each other with increasing frequency and kept growing closer.

At the state hospital, I became immersed in the forgotten world of the acutely ill and the chronically insane, initially finding myself overwhelmed. During some of my early days there, I was close to being repulsed and shocked, particularly by the seemingly hopeless situation of many hundreds locked in the back wards. To put this assignment in perspective, at the age of 29 I found myself for the first time in my life in a "secular" environment, outside a closed Catholic setting. I soon adjusted, however, and began to thrive on the hectic pace and the rough give and take of this complex institution. Little did I know that this would only be the precursor to a long career serving in, and eventually managing large, secure human institutions.

Wandering Between Two Worlds

For two years, Sue and I struggled mightily with what course to take with our developing relationship -- our flat out love for each other. This situation, which I had freely pursued, became my great joy and a confusing burden. I had two great loves that could not long coexist. Part of the burden was that I felt two-faced, projecting the public persona of a committed priest, while maintaining a private though blossoming friendship with Sue. At one juncture I was moved to tell Sue I was going to stop seeing her so that I could give my best "single-minded effort" – my exact term to her -- to renew my commitment to the straight and narrow priestly life to which I still felt so deeply called.

That "single-minded" endeavor did not last long. Hard though I tried, I was a mess. Over a period of several weeks, I was totally distracted and missed Sue terribly. I finally decided to sever my most central commitment after only five years – to abandon something I loved and to which I had devoted my adult life. Still, I felt a certain sense of liberation at having resolved this two year dilemma. I was overjoyed at the prospect of openly sharing my life and my love with Sue and of relieving her of the patient waiting, of her agony with our crazy situation.

A few friends and family members gradually came to know of our relationship. There was understandably great consternation among some of the elders on the Catholic side of our families, while others were immediately understanding and supportive. My mother had recently remarried after more than twenty years as a widow. She and my new stepfather, Pete, were wonderful throughout this time. I think the situation was not initially easy for my mom. She had put so much of herself into supporting me through the long seminary years and was so proud to have a son serving the diocese as a priest. But she and Pete quickly accepted and loved Sue, being especially kind during the difficult private time of our sorting things out.

First I had to resolve my situation with the Church and with the Diocese of Lansing. In June of 1974, I met with Bishop Zaleski to tell him of my resignation and pending marriage. This proved to be a very emotional conversation for me, one of the toughest of my life.

110

Wandering Between Two Worlds

This was a man for whom I felt much affection, since he had been very good to me. During this unsettled era for the Church, I knew he had held many similar conversations with other priests; and I did not relish adding to his burdens. As we talked, he was kind but seemed weary and sad.

In short order, then, so very much happened. I dealt with numerous family issues in the wake of my departure from the ministry. I filed my papers requesting laicization, having decided I wanted for reasons of conscience and family to stay as close to harmony with the institutional Church as possible. Sue quit work, moved a few miles to a small flat in Ypsilanti, where she entered graduate school in special education at Eastern Michigan University. We had no money, I was out in the cold without many of my prior supports, and I was struggling with personal identity issues. I started a low-wage job in a tough new situation and began commuting nights to graduate school at Wayne State University, 35 miles away in Detroit.

Still, Sue and I both remember this initial period as a good time. For me, it was a very simple time after several hectic years of being pulled by competing polarities, a time to just concentrate on my new work and to be with Sue. Sue and I found our situation was made easier when my papers from Rome arrived in less than six months, allowing us to be married in the Church. We were married a few weeks later at St John's in Ypsilanti, with several priest friends concelebrating the Mass for a rather small party of our family and friends.

One year later to the day, our first child, Peter, was born. By the time our sweet fourth child Mary was born five years later in New York's Hudson Valley, we had spent fifteen months in Florida and two years in Atlanta, Georgia, moves brought on by my job transfers. And this brings me back to the portion of the journey involving my decision to catch on with the Federal Bureau of Prisons.

Now Called Behind the Walls

Like others in my situation, I was intimidated by the prospect of finding a new career. My long training in philosophy and theology would provide limited credentials. I considered many options, including work within the Church, maybe as a Catholic school administrator, a director of religious education, or some other staff role. An Episcopal priest friend lobbied strongly for me to join him as a priest in his tradition. But I decided that if I was leaving the Catholic priesthood, I wanted to go with no sense that I was hanging onto some part of that vocation. For my own sense of identity, I realized I had to make a clean break to another career. By intuition and conviction, I also felt drawn to move beyond the narrower Catholic world where I had spent almost my entire life and into the broader secular world, though I still felt a strong sense of a religiously-rooted vocation. I also harbored a gut feeling that for some time I had been preaching to others how they should be. Now it was my turn to find a way to live those words.

During those two years at the state hospital, I had occasionally served a few hours a week as substitute chaplain at the nearby federal prison in Milan. Having grown up in Jackson near a huge 6,000 bed state penitentiary, I had for years been fascinated by prisons. I now found myself drawn to the prospect of prison work, not just for a paycheck but as a way to live out the words of my own preaching. Here was a concrete way to work to improve our system of social justice for the underdogs of society, to find a place in a public institution that exercised great influence on the lives of the down-trodden and minorities -- in this case on the lives of prisoners and their families.

In sorting out a new direction for my life, I reflected on lessons I first learned from the priests at Sacred Heart Seminary. As they educated us in the Vatican II document on the Church in the Modern World, we learned that all of God's creation was holy. Engaging, rebuilding, and humanizing that world and its institutions was holy work. "Thy kingdom come...on earth as it is in heaven." I wanted to embrace and impact "the system" from within.

And so it was that I took a job as an entry level uniformed officer at the Milan federal prison, doing shift work in housing units, the yard, and the towers. What a jolting, difficult transition from the sheltered

112

life of a Catholic priest! Harboring natural fears and doubts as a
rookie uniformed officer, I received a stiff reception from some staff
and frequent testing from many inmates. These were many of the
same staff and inmates who had treated me with deference just a few
weeks earlier during my weekend stints as a substitute chaplain. It
was a blunt blow to my ego, reminding me that much of the esteem I
had enjoyed in the priesthood was in deference to my collar, not so
much to my personal qualities.

In great part, I was willing to take an $8,900 job in 1974 as a low
level uniformed officer in the federal prison system because Sue and I
were ready for a change of scenery beyond Michigan. We saw this
as a first step in a career with a large nation-wide organization that
was known for transferring staff to prisons in various parts of the
country. Little did we know what awaited us – eight interstate moves
with our growing family in one 14-year period. As they say, be
careful what you ask for!

After the initial shock and adjustments, I benefited from the friendly
mentoring of some of the senior officers and managers. I gained a
comfort level and within months was convinced I wanted a long
career in the Federal Bureau of Prisons, or the BOP. Truthfully,
another reason I found the prison system attractive was I knew that I
wanted to eventually be the boss – the warden – to run something.
And from the beginning, I sensed that once I got some experience and
training, my talents would be well suited for this environment. After
more than 30 years in corrections, after so many unexpected
challenges and twists on the journey, I know I made the right
decision.

Occasionally over the subsequent years, the question understandably
arose as to how I could square my previous background and values
with a profession whose basic work is holding other men captive. I
often went back to some of the core convictions built on early
insights from my years at Sacred Heart. I came to see that, although
work in law enforcement and prisons is difficult and too often fraught
with stress and ambiguity, it is also the ground for noble, even holy
labor. During my years in prison work, especially in the most

113

contentious settings, I have found it important to maintain the vision that both staff and prisoners are all God's children, though surely our roles are distinct. Even in the highest security penitentiaries, most prisoners simply want to do their time in peace – in an atmosphere of safety and civility, often seeking practical opportunities to better themselves.

Tough odds can work to undermine prisoners' normal desires, however. In this setting, it is the unique calling of prison workers to foster conditions of civility and safety, to establish an atmosphere where hope and personal restoration can blossom. To achieve such ends, we must control predators and mitigate gang conflict. Effective educational and addiction programs must be refined. Humane, mature attitudes must be modeled among often unsteady younger staff. I am sure that I and many others have been more effective prison workers by drawing on the strength and model of Christ, who continually reached out to the outcasts and the sinners and who never hesitated to wade into life's toughest, most confrontational circumstances with His gentle but determined spirit.

Eventually I became profoundly troubled and embarrassed by the wrong-headed expansion of incarceration during the era of the so-called "war on crime." I hated the unprecedented growth in the number of men confined due to the use of very long sentences in this country, especially among poor minority and immigrant populations. During a twenty year period, our agency found itself forced to grow by five-fold, from a modest sized system with about 25,000 prisoners in the late 1970's– about the same size as in 1950 – to over 130,000 when I retired from the agency in 1997.

Like many of us in corrections, though certainly in the minority, I am not a proponent of capital punishment, which became a troubling prospect to some of my BOP friends as it returned to the federal system in the 1990's as a practical responsibility. In 2008, I took the opportunity to testify in favor of abolition of the death penalty before a blue ribbon panel appointed in Maryland to make a recommendation to the governor and the state legislature. I have also worked with the Maryland Catholic Conference lobbying the legislature for abolition.

Crisscrossing the Country with the Bureau

If Sue and I wanted to see the country with the prison system, we got more than we bargained for. After spending three years at Milan doing lower level work and completing a master's degree in public administration, I set out along with Sue and two babies on the first of a series of eight rapid fire transfers across the country. After a brief tour at a minimum security facility in Eglin, Florida, I was assigned to a much more challenging job at the big old penitentiary in Atlanta for two years. This was a rough place with a hardened staff. It was the scene of a number of inmate homicides during those times, my first exposure to such violence. I was shocked at the senseless stabbing death of a young female dietitian the day she was to travel home for Thanksgiving in 1978.

In the spring of 1980, we found our facility impacted by the Mariel boatlift, which brought 125,000 Cubans to the Florida shores. Many of the prisoners Fidel Castro had forced on to the boats had been disrupting various resettlement camps and committing other crimes around the country; so a large segment of the Atlanta penitentiary was converted to house hundreds of problem Mariel cases. They gave us a run for our money every day.

Next it was on to three years in New York's Hudson Valley, at the newly-opened medium security facility at Otisville. At this facility, I was tasked with a unique challenge -- setting up and managing the Bureau's first large prison unit for federally-protected prisoner witnesses, a self-contained high security prison-within-a prison. Secrecy was the order of the day. Most of my staff were not permitted to even know the prisoners' names. As things got up and running pretty smoothly, I enjoyed the chance to be innovative in establishing a unique new operation.

The Supermax: Marion Penitentiary

At the beginning of 1984, along with our growing family of four young children, Sue and I made our fourth move, transferring to southern Illinois. A profound challenge awaited me as I was assigned to the management team at the highest security federal prison in the country, the maximum security penitentiary in Marion. The mission of this unique prison -- relatively small at less than 400 inmates -- was to confine the key gang leaders and the most dangerous, predatory prisoners in the system. These were men who could no longer safely function in any of the other high security penitentiaries. With certain cold, calculating souls there, I sometimes felt I was as close to experiencing the dark side of humanity as I would ever want to get.

Marion was in a state of crisis following a series of major disruptions over the previous several years. Just weeks before my transfer took effect the disruptions culminated in the calculated, ruthless murders of two respected officers by leaders of the white-racist prison gang, the Aryan Brotherhood. After the staff killings, Marion was in a virtual state of siege, resembling a daily battle-zone. Though locked down in their cells, prisoners flatly challenged staff at every opportunity. The level of sustained stress took a toll on even this very hardened staff.

The long-time Director of the BOP, Norm Carlson, realized that this was a critical moment, not only for one institution but for the entire federal prison system. Whereas Marion had previously operated with a certain degree of free prisoner movement, Director Carlson and the agency leaders concluded the only option was to permanently operate the facility in a very tightly controlled fashion, with most prisoners locked in their cells much of the day. Inmates who did not need this level of control were transferred out. The rest moved from place to place only in cuffs and chains, accompanied by officers carrying batons. The pace for every function and activity was very slow. Unquestionably security and personal safety were paramount.

Our plan was well conceived and implemented by Warden Jerry Williford, who quickly became a strong mentor and friend to me. Eventually, the plan succeeded. Over the course of about a year, we found that our message that resistance and disruption were counter-productive and would not be tolerated finally got through to this unusual population. A key ingredient of our equation was providing a carrot, an avenue of hope, wherein compliance would lead to transfer to an open prison. Almost all the original prisoners eventually slowed down and complied, being transferred out within three years. The cycle continued, however, as others in the rapidly growing federal system worked their way up to Marion by their disruptive or violent behavior at other prisons.

Unfortunately our experience at Marion was part of a trend in the 1980's, when there were growing confrontations at state prisons across the country by violent prison gangs. The precedent set by our legal and operational success in the "Marion Model" led to the establishment of a string of what are now called "supermax" prisons in other systems. By chance, I had been on the ground floor helping develop a very controversial but effective operation in American corrections.

<u>Plucked from the Trenches into the Washington Swirl</u>

Twice over the next few years Divine Providence coincided with the wisdom of the federal prison system to send me to work in the agency headquarters in Washington. From Marion, the family packed up the boxes and off we went for what I figured would be a rather brief, obligatory exposure to the central office prior to a permanent return to the field operations. Little did I know that this move brought me to the arena that would dominate most of my subsequent life: the Washington bureaucracy. It was my good fortune there to work under and be mentored by Dr. Gil Ingram, the agency's revered assistant director. A clinical psychologist not much older than I, he was the acknowledged master of the ways of Washington, but especially of how to achieve positive changes in an expanding system of 70 or 80 prisons scattered across the country.

This was a whole new world to me after eleven years in the day-to-day operations at five different prisons. Our office was a busy focal point, since we were responsible for most of the operational areas of the prison agency, including such functions as security, emergency response and inmate classification. When problems occurred anywhere inside the federal system, the bad news came through our hub, as did the plan for a response. The pace was usually hectic, as we simultaneously balanced work on an assortment of long term systemic changes with the immediate demands of the sprawling agency's daily incidents or emergencies. My role involved regularly coordinating operations with a number of outside agencies, such as the FBI, the U.S. Marshals Service, and the Department of Justice.

Lives on the Line -- Dealing with Riots and Hostages

In November 1987, after two years in Washington, I was snapped out of my bureaucratic routine by the largest hostage situation in American history -- a searing event in my life, an experience to which I can hardly do justice here. Two simultaneous and interconnected riots broke out among the 3,000 Mariel Cuban detainees held at our prisons in Atlanta, Georgia, and Oakdale, Louisiana, resulting in over 125 of our staff being taken hostage for the better part of two weeks.

I spent most of the next twelve days, including Thanksgiving Day, living at our downtown office, helping coordinate the crisis management response of the Bureau of Prisons and the Department of Justice. Our management of this delicate crisis was complicated because the prisoners complaints did not involve prison conditions within our control but rather their grievances over the threatened return of many of them to Cuba. Under a newly minted, historic breakthrough, an agreement between the U.S. and the Castro government, Cuba would begin accepting back Cubans convicted of crimes in the U. S. in return for other concessions on the part of the American government. As part of the boatlift exodus of 125,000 from Cuba to Florida in 1980, Castro had forcefully unloaded the worst criminals in his prisons and in Cuban society. Now these men in our custody were desperate not to return to Castro's control.

The Atlanta and Oakdale prisons went up in a fury of fire and homemade knives, as prisoners systematically destroyed and burned much of the two facilities. Ringleaders made wild demands and threats to the hostages. Thousands of military troops and law enforcement officers surrounded the prisons. Hundreds of news media and their trucks camped out, as the ongoing riots dominated the national and international media. Logistics and interagency coordination were a nightmare. And for myself and so many in our agency, this situation was as much personal as it was professional, since most of us had colleagues and even close friends held captive with knives to their throats.

After many days and complicated negotiations, first Oakdale and then Atlanta were peacefully settled. Along with so many who had worked for resolution of this horrible crisis, I was unimaginably relieved and drained by the final outcome. No hostages were lost, though most were badly scarred, some for life. Interestingly, the goals of the rioters were to a great extent met. There were no prosecutions for rioting and the process of returning Mariel detainees to Cuba was interrupted, resulting in a large proportion never being repatriated.

Unfortunately, this resolution was not to be the last time the Bureau or my life was to be disrupted by an almost identical Mariel Cuban hostage situation. In 1991, just after I moved back to Washington after two other field assignments, things flared up again in Talladega, Alabama. I was dispatched to be deputy site commander at the relatively new prison at Talladega where a group of Mariel prisoners had taken over the high security unit along with 13 staff hostages, including several women. This incident occurred the day before 40 of these men were to be flown to Havana. Some of these men had been ringleaders at Atlanta less than four years before. They were now dealing with some of the same FBI hostage negotiators from the Atlanta crisis.

Despite our best faith efforts, we were not able to peacefully resolve this crisis; we needed an assault by the FBI Hostage Rescue Team and special BOP teams. They were successful in rescuing all the hostages, with only a few minor injuries to the prisoners. The storming of the fortress-like cell block at the quiet hour of 3:40 AM, complete with powerful explosives to force entry, was the single most dramatic event I hope I will ever be a part of. A few minutes later I was present for the families' reunion with the now-former hostages. I was also glad to be present at the Birmingham airport the next morning as the INS plane with those 40 men departed for Cuba.

The Priest Becomes a Warden: A Different Sort of Conflict Resolution

Only a few months after the 1987 Cuban hostage situation was settled, I began the next challenge of my prison life, that of serving as warden of two complex facilities, first in Miami, Florida, than back to the penitentiary in Marion. Especially in my years as a warden, I found that many of the fundamental values and life lessons in which I had been formed at Sacred Heart stood me in good stead. A particular satisfaction was the opportunity to work daily at conflict resolution. Prisons are fertile grounds for such work – whether the conflict is between inmate groups, staff and inmates, labor and management, or prison authorities and prisoner advocates. Such conflicts can be mitigated or resolved in a hundred ways every day, but most especially by the tone of moderation and respect set by the leadership of the prison. I found that contrary to stereotypes, success in prison management comes less from hard-edged personal toughness than skill at human relations work. Again my core seminary training was great preparation.

Parenthetically, in the closed community of staff and inmates, I often was struck by the similarities between the strong leadership role of the successful warden and that of the pastor in a parish community. The same qualities that helped or hurt you in one setting would have a similar effect in the other. Also, as a rookie warden, reminiscent of my experience as a rookie priest, I was pleased to find that I was immediately supported and welcomed to the ranks by the more senior wardens at other prisons, a number of whom were helpful in providing concrete tips on everyday problems. There was a real bond among the agency's 80 or so wardens, whose ranks by this time included a number of very talented women – a resource that unfortunately goes untapped in the ranks of Catholic pastors.

In my two years at Miami, I especially enjoyed the non-stop pace of the crowded facility that served as the federal jail for the exploding caseload of the local federal court, then besieged by the 1980's

Miami drug phenomenon. As I grew into the role of warden, we survived two serious but unsuccessful escape attempts from my prison. Once, a Colombian drug trafficker climbed into a large trash compactor in hopes of getting a quick ride out of jail to the landfill. We didn't find him until the next morning when we had the trash company remove the container to the landfill. The man, half dead in the stink from having been compacted, came tumbling out -- grateful for a breath of fresh air and for some medical attention.

The other incident landed us on CNN. A small helicopter had swooped down in dramatic fashion to try to remove a high profile prisoner. Ben Kramer, a millionaire world champion off-shore power-boat racer, was serving a life sentence for his world class drug running operation. The plot would have transported him to a nearby small plane and then safely out of the country. One of my brave young officers ran in pursuit as the pilot and prisoner hurriedly lifted the helicopter off a small recreation area. In their rush to get away, the tail rotor caught a security wire at the top of the fence, unceremoniously dumping them down, nose first. They were so close to success. That morning, thankful I would still have my job, I pondered the old adage that "it is better to be lucky than good."

Our family had no desire to leave the color and sun of Miami. Still I was pleased to be asked to return to Marion Penitentiary as warden in late 1989. Things had calmed down considerably, but the mission was still to deal with the highest security cases in the system. We kept things quiet and safe during my time as warden there. No one was killed or seriously injured, though the inmate population would never let things become dull. The staff was professional and dedicated but could be stubborn and tough to deal with on labor issues and various policy changes. By this time I could be pretty tough myself, though I like to think I had also gained a bit of polish. To be honest, I fully enjoyed the rough and tumble of working at Marion.

In those times, life at Marion was a bit colorful. The prison was a lightning rod attracting media attention, due partly to our controversial mission and partly to certain high profile prisoners.

Baseball player Pete Rose served his five months at our work camp, bringing us continuing attention. Due to the notoriety of some of the spies, mafia chiefs, and international drug lords housed there, a parade of network news celebrities, including Mike Wallace, Diane Sawyer, and Maria Schriver, traveled to rural southern Illinois for interviews during my time, In that vein, my background as a "priest-turned-supermax-warden" caught some media attention, bringing me my fifteen minutes in the sun with features by the *Chicago Tribune* and the *Today Show*.

Man of God and Supermax Warden: A Paradox?

Over the years, I have had to address the apparent paradox that I considered myself a human rights advocate, yet I also helped to shape and later to administer the prototype of the controversial "supermax" prisons. I find no inherent conflict. I am convinced that placing necessary though strict controls on a few men at Marion allowed many other prisons to function more safely and openly. Thousands of other inmates could live with less fear, able to work at their daily jobs or to participate in self-help programs without arming themselves or joining prison gangs in self-defense.

I have maintained great respect for, and a sort of kinship with, most prisoner advocates. They keep us as correctional administrators honest and on our toes, often pointing out legitimate problems. At the same time, I have refused to yield the moral high ground in the correctional world to these advocates, including those who are religious leaders. Prophets and preachers do holy work, but so do those who carry their moral vision into the public square to work for excellence and change – often struggling with inherent ambiguity or with the necessity of compromise to achieve realistic goals. I worked with many men and women -- some rooted in explicit religious motivations and some not -- who brought their values into the arena of corrections, determined to make the system safer and more humane.

Though surely an aberration, on several occasions at Marion I had the distasteful experience of being accused in the press in false but

122

colorful terms of perpetrating human rights violations on my
prisoners. My background in the ministry was publicly thrown in my
face with calls of hypocrisy. Once during my time as warden there,
my then twelve year-old son Charlie came to me looking upset and
asking, "Dad, do you have enemies here?" He was quite distressed
to overhear an abrasive local attorney utter a series of biting remarks
about me at a social gathering at the home of mutual friends. By this
time, of course, I understood and accepted that all of these things
came with the path I had chosen years before.

The Final Move: Back to Washington and Maryland to Stay

In 1991 I was transferred from Marion back to Washington to become
an assistant director of the agency, charged with establishing a new
division primarily focused on community corrections, the far end of
the spectrum from the high security penitentiary. This challenge of
helping prisoners at a crucial time in their lives was actually much
more in line with the original motivation that drew me years earlier to
a career in prison work. I found it great fun to assemble a staff and to
take on this mission for the final six years of my federal career. I felt
we made steady progress over those six years in bringing innovation
and energy to the expansion of a system of community halfway
houses and drug abuse programs for inmates leaving prison around
the country.

When the time came after 23 years to retire and leave the Bureau, I
was left with indelible lessons and many good friends. Just as surely,
I was confident that on my watch I had been a good steward of the
public trust, leaving the agency and its prisoner population better than
I had found it. I have often reflected on how the lessons of my
experience at Sacred Heart Seminary formed the foundational values
for my public management career. The following might summarize
those reflections:

> In grappling with the daily demands of prison operations, in spite
> of the gray shades of ambiguity and the need for periodic
> compromise, there is no essential conflict between Christian
> principles and effective management. If you honestly sort things
> out, the ethically right way to act will not be at odds with the most

effective way to achieve the goals of the civil agency.

A Chance to Jump into the D.C. Fray

In 1997, I was able to retire with a pension from the federal prison system while still in my mid-50's; though with four kids of high school and college age, it was necessary for me to look for new employment. There were good opportunities to catch on with one of the private for-profit prison companies, as many of my close friends had done. But in sorting it all out, I found my heart would not have been fully in it. I recognized that at my core I was a government guy, still possessed of a sense of public service and a vocation to influence and improve public institutions.

Providence smiled again. I had the occasion to take a newly created position in the government of the District of Columbia as Corrections Trustee. Sue and I love Washington, D.C., and I was proud to have an opportunity to help in rebuilding the city and its local government. Congress had passed legislation ordering closure of the District's troubled system of seven prisons in suburban Lorton, Virginia, the District's rough equivalent of a state prison system. Under appointment by Attorney General Janet Reno, I was charged with supervising the orderly transfer of the 8,000 sentenced felons into the federal prisons of my old agency over a five year transition period. We also provided financial oversight for about $150 million in yearly Congressional funding to the District during the transition and coordinated a lot of technical assistance and resources in upgrading the operations of the District's remaining municipal jail system. I enjoyed setting up our small agency from scratch and making our way in the rocky landscape of local D.C. politics. In the end, we successfully engineered the transition, getting good grades both from the District government leaders, as well as from our Congressional overseers.

As part of my job in shutting down Lorton, I was asked by the Attorney General to lead a review of a controversial private facility that housed 1500 D.C. felons on contract. This new private prison in Youngstown, Ohio, had experienced a significant series of problems,

124

including two inmate killings and the escape of a group of six murderers one bright Sunday afternoon. There was a cry from the governor of Ohio and a number of Congressmen for an investigation. We assembled a team and in fairly short order produced a well-received 300 page report which attracted wide attention in the corrections community and led me to testify before the District's City Council and at Congressional hearings. The report did not make me the darling of the private prison industry. A few days after we released the report, Ed Bradley brought a *60 Minutes* TV crew to my office for an interview as part of an expose he was finishing on problems in private prisons. I survived the interview, only afterward noticing that I had sat for an hour before the cameras with my fly open. Thank goodness for close up face shots! (In the spirit of full disclosure, I have to note that I had set up my own video camera to tape the entire interview. I knew from experience how, after all the editing, brief comments taken out of context can get you into trouble, in this case potentially with Justice or Congressional folks. So when I got up from my seat and turned to a corner to zip up, I forgot I was facing right into my own camera. My staff had a hoot over that and stashed a copy for future blackmail purposes.)

For the subsequent seven years I have put my contacts and experience to work as a private consultant, again limiting my work to federal and D.C. government agencies. I have also become involved with several pro bono volunteer boards and activities in the area that help inmates and their families or contribute to the improvement of the local justice system in Washington.

The Family of Six Surviving Eight Cross Country Transfers

Our family is close, having endured quite nicely the many moves and changes brought by my selling my soul to government service. When we made our final government move, we landed back in Gaithersburg, Maryland, where we bought our eighth house since leaving Michigan. We have treasured settling into one community for going on two decades.

Each move generated its own story, along with its challenges and opportunities. Sue and I enjoyed every town and neighborhood we lived in, though by the last one or two moves we found the rapid changes were wearing us down. By then, our older kids were at the stage where we wanted to settle in for high school. For the most part, everyone did very well as we moved. The kids prospered and were broadened. From their earliest years, moving regularly was the only life any of them knew until we landed back in Maryland. Now the four Clark kids are grown and prospering in a variety of careers.

Through all the moves, Sue was the loving glue that held our family so close. While the family learned to make adjustments to the transfers, Sue always faced the most demanding ones. I could just trot off to work in another prison on Monday, and the kids soon got immersed in school and new friends. She settled each house, got things set simultaneously at two or three schools, checked on available orthodontists, and on and on. Sue found that doing tutoring gave her a flexible way to keep her hand in teaching and to supplement my government income. But then, too soon, the call would come, and we would be on the road again. What a demanding routine!

Sticking with the Church We Love

In our vagabond existence moving around the country, we always jumped into the life of the local Catholic parish, finding this a quick way to get anchored in the community and to make new friends with similar backgrounds and values, not an easy task in a new town. Sue often became very involved in a variety of ministries, mostly in serving the poor and helping with religious formation. In what might be a soft touch of irony, after we landed permanently in Maryland, Sue moved into the role as a pastoral associate at St. Rose of Lima parish near our home in suburban Gaithersburg, doing much of the type of work I started out to do decades ago. She had also done similar work at St. Rose when we lived here in the 80's.

St. Rose is a wonderful welcoming community of genuine diversity and Gospel values -- a great place to celebrate life and liturgy. For almost fifteen years until her recent retirement, Sue was a natural whiz there, covering so many bases at the parish and being loved and respected by everyone. After all the moves and adjustments she had to make over the years to accommodate my career, I took immense satisfaction in seeing her success. And in being known around St. Rose as "Sue Clark's husband."

Although Church involvement and striving to be guided by Gospel values have played a central role in my life, I long ago became disheartened and lost interest in the politics and personalities of the larger institutional Church. I choose not to waste much energy carrying around anger at the disintegration and abdication of leadership by the Church hierarchy, now seemingly paralyzed by a conservative choke hold. The bishops' handling of the sex abuse scandal in so many places horrified me.

More broadly my heart is broken by the impact of our leaders' continuing obsession with maintaining a celibate male clergy. This fixation has succeeded in losing much of the vigorous Eucharistic leadership for local communities. I am despondent over the loss of vitality of the Church I love. I grant that the long, continuous demise of the ordained clergy has led to the development of many wonderful lay ministers, like my wife Sue. But without the quality of ordained leaders that I admired as a youth, I am concerned about our ability to pass along to my granddaughter's generation the richness we received.

I have chosen to focus my personal relationship with the Church on this blessed local community of St. Rose of Lima. From there I draw my spiritual inspiration and challenge. Over the years I balanced my urge for action by regularly participating in a small faith community where I could learn, meditate, and grow. My major commitment over 15 years has been coordinating the annual fall festival, known as the Fiesta. I love this old-fashioned Catholic parish event that reminds me of my Jackson roots. Appreciating the difficulty of being new in a parish, I also enjoy helping with the monthly welcoming program for newcomers to the parish.

More recently, I felt called to involvement in parish leadership. I just completed two very intense years as the chair of the pastoral council during the course of a rocky pastoral transition. Our long-time pastor moved on and was replaced by a pastor who brought a very different management style and philosophy. During this time, I found myself again making extensive use of my conflict resolution skills. Thankfully, things seem to be sorting themselves out, and I am able to step back, letting the next generation pick up the reigns.

It is now clear to me that from the earliest days of junior high athletics through my time in the priesthood then on to my work in criminal justice administration, I have especially enjoyed the challenge of being in the action. I love motivating, implementing, getting conflicts resolved and seeing organizations change for the better. Rather than working in the realm of theory or ideas, I am so glad I have been able to follow my heart and my vocation to the rugged give and take of the game - the planning, plotting, and mid-stream adjustments of the public square and the local parish. *Thy Kingdom Come, Thy Will Be Done.*

CAN YOU TELL ME WHAT
WE'RE WAITING FOR, SEÑOR?
Kenneth M. Eason

The day I graduated from Sacred Heart Seminary was one of the high points of my life. I can still remember the anticipation I felt on that morning before the graduation High Mass. Everybody was finishing up, packing suitcases, busying around, tying up loose ends, saying goodbyes, and getting ready to hit the bricks. I felt great. I put an "H" in front of "Alleluia" as we sang the Mass recessional hymn, making it "Hallelujah", as you would hear in a Baptist church. I thought that inserted "H" would make the whole recessional feel more jubilant. Fr. Thaddeus J. Ozog, the choirmaster, would not have approved of this departure from the rules; but at that moment I didn't care. It felt too good including it; besides, nobody could hear me anyway, as loud as we were singing.

Like so many other guys in the class of 1965, I was the first in my family to graduate from college. It felt great doing that, but I knew that I was only halfway to where I personally wanted to be. I had completed the first leg of the journey to my chosen destiny, or the destiny I thought at the time was mine. Four more years at St. John's lay ahead, and I had hoped they would be the formative years they were intended to be. I had hoped they would become the forge and the press that would mold me for ordination.

I felt a little edgy all summer long about going to St. John's. Just days before graduation, I suffered through the exit interview with Fr. William Sherzer, Dean of Men. As I thought he might, he let me know that the faculty had given me approval to go forward to St. John's. There was no joy in his face as he said this, however; and only his doubts concerning my dedication to purpose and the probability of my success came through his voice. I left the room somewhat saddened that, in the four years I had been at Sacred Heart, I could only muster this kind of response from the Dean of Men. Yet I also knew that unless the faculty was reasonably sure about my chances for ordination, I certainly wouldn't have been going anywhere past graduation from Sacred Heart.

As I look back at it now, I feel that everybody in the class should have had the opportunity to go forward, as long as they were convinced that they wanted to. There would be plenty of time in the next four years to test conviction, fitness, and dedication to purpose. Not everybody matures at the same pace. When all is said and done, only God really knows for sure. As it were, there were plenty of empty rooms at St. John's that first year, rooms that could have been filled by promising candidates. There may have been some very good candidates for the priesthood who were left by the side of the road after graduation for very flawed personal or political reasons.

I grew up in the Baptist faith and became a convert to Catholicism at age seventeen. My immediate family was, and still is, Baptist. And, while they spoke of being proud of me and my accomplishments at Sacred Heart, they never really supported the idea of my becoming a priest. It was a foreign concept to them. Their lack of support was a big disappointment for me. Without the real support, understanding, and encouragement of family members, it was difficult for me to maintain the conviction that the course I had chosen was the right one.

During my early years as a Catholic, I had become quite enthralled with the beauty and solemnity associated with the celebration of the Eucharist. Later, at Sacred Heart, Holy Hour, Vespers, Compline, and everything else we did in chapel would only add to the enjoyment I felt for things liturgical. I thoroughly enjoyed singing Gregorian Chant. I had been allowed to join the seminary choir, better known as the Schola Cantorum. Church music became something I identified with because I could do it and because I loved its sound. I had no special singing talents beyond the ability to stay on key while singing a cappella. I enjoyed singing many of the a cappella four-part harmony compositions chosen by Fr. Ozog. Besides that, the Schola was physically positioned in the nave of the chapel, occupying three rows of elevated pews that flanked the left side of the sanctuary. Consequently I had a close-up view of everything going on in the chapel.

It came as a surprise to me that the faculty did not object to the hootenanny-type singing group that five of us had formed. The group, composed of myself, classmate Jim O'Brien, and three fellows, John Larsen, Jim Szymaszek, and Paul Kuebler, from the classes immediately behind ours, provided musical entertainment for the entire seminary during periodic informal social gatherings called "smokers," named after the locations in which they were held. As I look back at it, this was about the time that the liberal concepts of Vatican II had begun to work their way into seminary life. To my knowledge, this was the first and only effort of this type ever allowed at Sacred Heart and probably any other seminary in the country. The administration didn't come out and formally approve of our forming the singing group; they just never said we couldn't do it. It really had nothing to do with why we were in the seminary at all. I think that since the Singing Nun had gained both approval and notoriety with her Top Forty hit, the faculty probably decided that it couldn't do any harm to also let us sing and let a little air in. Besides I don't think they wanted to be completely outdone by a nun!

It was a lot of fun putting on the songs, and I think most seminarians enjoyed the live music. Songs of that time by Peter, Paul and Mary, Bob Dylan, and others, those not necessarily romantic in nature, were "safe" enough for us to perform without drawing criticism from the faculty. We dubbed ourselves the Rumrunners probably for two reasons. No known band had used the name before and it spoke of Detroit's shady role in the old days of Prohibition. For the Christmas concerts put on for the whole school as well as parents, the Rumrunners prepared and performed a couple of songs. The group played music together at various events until Jim and I graduated in

1965, and then the group dissolved.

At that time I was still convinced that I wanted to serve the Church as a priest; but I didn't realize that I had an extremely idealistic view of the Church and of what life would be like for me as a priest. Life for me as a priest in Detroit was not going to be about music or just about the celebration of the Liturgy. My life as a priest was going to be very hard. It was going to be a much harder road to travel than the roads my white classmates would experience. Maybe Fr. Sherzer and the rest of the faculty could see that I was somewhat blind to the cold realism of the world that waited for me outside the walls of Sacred Heart; and consequently they were hesitant to send me on, given that I believed the world would warmly welcome me.

My first year at St. John's proved to be very revealing of what life as a priest was going to be like for me as a black man. We had the opportunity that first year to assist in the parish census at one of the parishes in Detroit. This involved going to the homes of parish members dressed in black suits, roman collars, and attempting to update that family's parish records. For the most part, my presence was unwelcome. People were even reluctant to talk to me at the door. I can remember being invited into only one home to warm myself as we talked on a winter day. I was cut deeply by what I learned that first year. Perhaps this experience was a rare and isolated event. But it allowed me to see that acceptance as a priest by the people I was going to serve was not going to be easy. It would take a year or so after my leave of absence at the end of that first year, however, before I knew for certain that there was no call to the priesthood for me.

My first and only year at St. John's passed so quickly. I thought my classes were going well for the most part. I enjoyed all of them and felt that I was learning the things I would need to know as a priest. I won't say much here about the Canon Law professor. I look back now at what I experienced in that class, similar experiences in Church History class at Sacred Heart, and isolated experiences with two other faculty members at Sacred Heart as turning points in my conviction to continue in the seminary. Simply stated, I felt that some of those priests had real problems with racial prejudice, hatred, and discrimination. The term "non-Christian" comes to mind. I didn't think they wanted me to become a member of the clergy at all. I was sadly disillusioned.

Don't get me wrong. The actions of those few men should not, and have not, reflected on the other faculty members who treated me very fairly. There were some that I considered to be truly holy men. They were the kind of men that I wanted to emulate in my life. Since the road to the priesthood was rocky and difficult, I had expected all those who had successfully made the journey to be above such an evil thing as racial bias. I had blinders on then, however, and maybe I still do to a certain degree.

I was invited back for the second year, but my spiritual adviser at St. John's told me that I should think about taking a leave of absence first. The faculty was concerned about my conviction and dedication. Fr. Sherzer had brought up the same matter just a year earlier at SHS. It occurred to me that maybe the faculty was right. Maybe I didn't belong. They obviously saw something I didn't see. How many times would it take for their message to sink in? I was getting tired of everything not being completely right. Everything seemed conditional. Maybe I needed to step back and reconsider my choices before going on to the second year. And so I did. I took a year's leave of absence to reassess things. I didn't know it then, but I would never return to the seminary.

I worked from July, 1966, to January, 1967, at Ford Motor Company's Transmission and Chassis Division General Office, located in Livonia, not too far from St. John's. It was an office job at an assembly plant. From the quiet of the office located up front, I had to make daily trips into the deafening din of the plant, which was a mix of stamping, pressing, broaching, drilling, grinding, and assembling machinery in a facility that was a quarter mile wide by a half mile long. This was a good experience for me as a transition to the outside world. I was in a workforce with people who worked hard for a living at repetitive and dangerous tasks. There was nothing attractive about the job or the kind of life I would live by remaining there. That kind of work was definitely not for me, and I was looking for my next transition in life.

It took almost no time at all to begin my life in the secular world.
There were young women, and Detroit's nightclubs and outstanding
live music, to experience. All of this was new and pleasant for me,
and I was having a ball. Music in Detroit in 1966 has told its own
story, and I thoroughly enjoyed every minute of it, up close, several
nights a week. In those days, I needed a break from the
disappointment that came with ending my seminary days; but the job
at Ford and the party life after work were not taking me anywhere I
thought I wanted to go. I wanted more at the time. I didn't know what
would be next.

Sometime in January, 1967, I received my draft notice to report for
induction into the United States Army. NOT. This was a twist I
hadn't prepared for. I was not going to join the Army as a private. In
fact, I didn't want to join the Army at all. At the time, my brother
was on his third tour in the United States Marine Corps. He had
joined in 1955, right after high school. If I had not gone to the
seminary in 1961, I would have joined the Marine Corps also. Now
that opportunity would come to me again. I knew that with a college
degree, I could probably qualify for Officer Candidate School with
any of the services, but I chose the Marine Corps. I signed up and
took the oath before I had to comply with the Army induction notice.
As a consequence, I would experience more combat in the next year
as an infantry officer than most men do in twenty.

Receiving my initial set of orders in February, 1967, to report to
Quantico, Virginia, for Officer Candidate School was a very proud
moment for me. I had wanted to be a Marine as far back as
adolescence, when one first starts to consider what to do in life.
During high school, the idea was there, but toward my senior year,
the Church and the loftier goal of priesthood overshadowed
everything. Now I was actually joining the Marines.

I trained very hard at home, with many repetitions of pull-ups, push-
ups and endurance running, to prepare myself for the upcoming
challenge of OCS screening. Waiting to get to Quantico first would

have been a huge mistake. You had to be in good physical shape in order to have any hope of successfully completing the ten-week course. In 1967, when the recruitment offices of the other services were full of hopeful officer candidates, the doorway in front of the Marine Corps Officer Selection Office had been vacant for so long that it almost had cobwebs. The Marine Corps recruiting staff would tell you at the front door, before you signed anything, that, yes, you would be going to Vietnam, and soon. During the ten weeks of training before commissioning, my OCS class of 800 candidates would be reduced to 400, either by Marine Corps dismissal from the program or by the dreaded Dropout On Request (DOR). This was the scenario, even at a time when Marine Corps recruiting numbers were at an all time low. They did not let it become easy to get through the program at all. I knew that the Marine Corps had always had these high standards, and I wanted to be a part of it. Again, the stage was being set for me to be blinded by yet another idealistic pursuit.

My training at OCS, and the subsequent six months of training at the Basic School in Quantico, prepared me for duties as an infantry officer. I had a great time at Quantico. I trained hard, but I also played hard. Washington D.C. was only 30 minutes driving time from Quantico, and it was a good liberty town. If one knew how to find it, there was some outstanding live music in a couple of places, in addition to the more traditional tourist attractions.

The riots that had taken place in Detroit in 1967 had not spilled over to Washington. Yet those were hot and uncertain times. Vietnam was dividing the nation. Talk of the war was everywhere. Most black people I encountered in those days were against black men voluntarily joining the service. Lessons had been learned from all the preceding wars, including Korea. The majority of black men had gone, fought, and returned, only to be disillusioned and frustrated by the unrelenting racism and discrimination this country provided in abundance. In my OCS graduating class of 400, there were only five black candidates, four of whom were commissioned. I had made my choice, however, to be active as a fighter in the war. I didn't address the issue of stopping communism. I was never concerned with this propaganda. I saw my duty at the platoon and company level as providing for the individual Marine, especially in combat. I felt that I had certain abilities that would allow me to be a good platoon commander. That job had nothing to do with propaganda at all. During the summer of 1967 at Quantico, we all watched the incoming battle reports on Con Thien, the Rockpile, Hill 881, and other battles.

By the end of November, I had graduated from the Basic School, received my orders for WestPac Ground Forces, Vietnam, and had said goodbye to everybody I could. There were three days of orientation in Okinawa, at Camp Hansen. Hansen was a transition base for Marine Corps troops going to and arriving from Vietnam. It was here that I saw for the first time men just arriving from a combat unit. They were standing there in platoon formation, wearing brown, used-to-be-green, dusty, muddy, ragged and torn jungle uniforms you could only obtain by surviving in combat or a combat environment. I found out later that you could get that same look after only a few days in combat. The wear and tear and the mildew would literally rot clothes right off you in a very short time. This was how I was going to look should I be fortunate enough to come back. I was in awe of these men. They were younger than I, yet they were so much older than I. They looked at and through us new guys, wearing our new stateside starched green sateen cotton uniforms, not so much wishing us well, as speaking of celebrating their return to the world. They were happy. I can remember them shouting the battle cry to us, "Get some," as we parted ways. And for Marines, this was as close to "Best Wishes" as it gets.

For these guys, unless they came back for a second tour, it was all over. Life would be sweet again. Somewhere along the line, I had read an inscription on a cigarette lighter: "For those who fight for it, life has a flavor the protected never know." I tried to garner what I could from this inscription in the hope that it would help me keep it all together for the next 13 months. At that time, it was hard for me to conceptualize lasting the 13-month tour in a combat environment. I was assigned to the 1st Marine Division in I Corps, South Vietnam. I arrived in country 17 December, 1967. Only with the help of God and a few fellow Marines did I depart on 30 December, 1968. In between those dates, events would occur that would change my life forever. I tried to meet the challenges that came before me with the courage and conviction every Marine Corps officer should have, and there was no time to show fear. But inside me there were storms of fear, especially after firefights. I confided in the Company First Sergeant once, early in the tour, during a brief lull in the preliminary actions preceding the Tet Offensive. I told him that I was scared. He looked at me and said, "So what, Lieutenant? Everybody's scared. Don't you know that? Get over it." That was all I needed to hear to realize my fear was nothing special. I learned to put it in its place and go about doing my job to the best of my ability.

I spent my entire tour assigned to an infantry company in the field, both as platoon commander and later as company executive officer. On two occasions, I assumed command of the company in combat when the company commander was wounded and medivaced out. I was never assigned to the rear or to a desk job. My unit participated in seventeen named combat operations from December, 1967, to December, 1968. Some of them were worse than others. All of them were bloody.

For Operation Hue City during the Tet Offensive, I was detached from my company and assigned, along with two squads of my platoon, to ride as armed "shotgun" support for a truck convoy. We were to travel from Hue City to Phu Bai, ten kilometers to the south, and back again with a resupply of badly needed ammo. The officer in charge of the convoy was 1st Lt. Jerry Nadolski, my seminary classmate! We had a chance to talk for a day during the trip, and then we parted ways, when I returned with my two squads to the rest of the company fighting along the eastern wall in Hue. Strangely, although we both survived the war, we have not seen each other since.

Along with a few other Catholics, I tried to attend Mass in the field whenever the chaplain would come out there. I think all of us wanted to have all the Grace we could get going for us, knowing what could happen at any time. Death was everywhere, and we all knew that. The only thing we could do was pray and ask to see another day.

137

I thought about the chaplain's position a lot after the first few months. I took my R&R very late in my tour. It was November 20 when I went to Hong Kong for five days. I had only one month left in country upon returning to Vietnam to finish my tour. First of all, I made sure I had a great time in Hong Kong treating myself well. I then went to a tailor shop and bought two suits, one of them black in color. Why? I had been influenced by the actions of a chaplain, Fr. Vincent Capodanno, who had served in Vietnam before I arrived. Fr. Capodanno, a Maryknoller, was with 3rd Battalion 5th Marines and had been involved in a combat operation which included elements of 1st Battalion 5th Marines, the unit I was to become a part of. The action took place on September 4th and 5th, 1967, two days before the start of Operation Swift. I never thought a priest could be so courageous and so devoted to duty in the face of such prolonged peril. I don't recall that the Church brought mention of his actions to the attention of the faithful; but the Marine Corps certainly thought highly enough of him to see to it that he was awarded the Congressional Medal of Honor. When I got to Vietnam, three months after Operation Swift was over, the men were still talking about the severity and intensity of the action that preceded it. They also continued to speak of the bravery of the three men who earned the Medal of Honor in the course of the battle. I have never heard of another chaplain of any faith that showed the kind of passion and devotion to men in need that he obviously showed that day. He didn't have to do what he did. He could have stayed back in the safety of the battalion command group with the other "important" people, but it appears that he wasn't that kind of priest. His actions that day truly were above and beyond the call of duty and were in keeping with the highest traditions of the Marine Corps and the United States Naval Service.

Companies K and M, 3/5, along with the battalion command group, were making their way through the Queson Valley to provide support and relief to Companies B and D, 1/5, located four kilometers away. This contingent had been hammered for two days by a large enemy force. First Platoon of Company M 3/5, covering the flank of the advancing unit, became pinned down in a wide, open rice paddy by heavy small arms and automatic weapons fire from a large North

Vietnamese Army (NVA) force deployed in an L-shaped ambush. As the 2nd Platoon crossed over a small knoll to come to their aid, a full company of well-entrenched NVA attacked them. First Platoon managed to pull back and take up positions with the rest of Company M at the top of the knoll. The NVA quickly surrounded the 2nd Platoon, pinning them down with heavy mortar, small arms and automatic weapon fire, and inflicting heavy losses on the trapped men. When the fighting started, Fr. Capodanno rushed across the bullet-swept knoll to the 2nd Platoon. As casualties were mounting in the battle area, Fr. Capodanno repeatedly braved the enemy fire to give aid to the wounded Marines. Several times he left the 2nd Platoon's perimeter to carry seriously wounded men uphill to Company M's main position. Even after being wounded himself, Fr. Capodanno refused to give up. Ignoring his wounds, he continued to treat casualties, pray with the dying, and pull men to cover, until he was finally cut down by a burst of enemy machine-gun fire. The fight raged on, continuing the next day until evening. There were 130 NVA soldiers dead, 54 Marines KIA and 104 wounded at the end of the two-day battle. Operation Swift started the next day and continued until September 15, 1967, when the enemy finally withdrew from the area.

I never met Fr. Capodanno, of course; but I've never been able to forget him either. It was him that I was thinking about when I bought the black suit in Hong Kong. Even if the Church never mentions him, I'm sure the men who saw his acts of courage, and those whose lives he saved that day, consider him a saint. The recount of his bravery rekindled a desire in me once again to consider the priesthood. It would take me several months after my return to the United States to realize that even if I did go back to the seminary, and even if I were to be ordained, no bishop in his right mind would allow me to leave and become a Navy chaplain. At the time, I felt that the military might have been an ideal place for a black priest with combat experience. Again, my idealism was out of touch with reality. With some regret, I never wore that black suit.

When I returned to the States, I found a different America than the one I had left a year earlier. I was assigned as a Marine Officer

Selection Officer (recruitment) and had the opportunity to make visits to college campuses all over the eight western states. This was during the time of the Kent State massacre. Marine Corps recruiters on campus were being demonized by young college age America as representatives of the "baby-killers." This was no way to come home. There was, of course, no welcome. There was only resentment, mistrust, and disdain. I had a rough time dealing with the way all of us still in uniform were being treated. I felt that young people my age were neither cognizant nor appreciative of the efforts so many guys had made, including those guys that had given everything there was to give. I didn't realize it then, but it would take years to sort through some of the issues that arose out of my Vietnam experience. Some of them I still deal with and will always deal with.

I left active duty in 1970 to attend law school at the University of San Francisco. I needed an advanced degree in order to stay in the Marine Corps past the rank of major. I had intended to stay with the Corps, but the Commanding Officer and I disagreed on exactly when I would be given an opportunity to get that advanced degree. I decided to leave active duty, get the law degree on my own, and return to active duty with two service codes: Infantry Officer and JAG Officer. I graduated in 1974, but during my senior year I had become disillusioned with the way I saw justice meted out to people of color in this country.

I had a chance to clerk for a small law office during that last year. I saw justice played out not in the courtroom, but like a crooked card game back in the judge's chambers. This was fine, I suppose, for those that could live with the system. I knew that I could not. I didn't want to have anything to do with jailing people, the people that were being jailed unfairly anyway. If you had money and could afford expensive legal counsel, there was better than a good chance that you could get justice. But if you were indigent and had to rely on the court-provided system, like most of the young black and Latino offenders and alleged offenders, then you were toast, victims of the system of plea-bargaining. There are those that would argue with me on this point; but there are more than enough facts to support my contention that without money, you have a poor shot at getting the

140

kind of justice reserved for only those with money. Even under the rules of the Uniform Code of Military Justice, you were basically guilty once charges were brought against you, unless and until you were subsequently proven innocent in a court-martial. I realized I was not going to be able to save many combat veterans still in uniform from any of their minor misdeeds. Nor was I going to make an impact as a criminal lawyer in the civilian criminal court system, which I mistakenly considered at that time to be my only alternative. I was disillusioned once again, this time with the idea of changing things, especially when change was clearly not an option.

Unfortunately, I had given up. I was throwing in the towel. For a number of years, I resigned myself to bartending, in jazz clubs, hotel bars, and local bars, for only one reason. Help-me-to-forget-drinks were free for the bartender. At the time I was convinced that I had a lot to forget…and to forgive. I had gotten married during law school. There was nothing wrong with that, but she was just the wrong woman; and I kept trying for seven years to see if she would ever become the right woman. Wrong. I was disillusioned really badly that time. It took me some years and many bottles to recover from my losses, to forgive and forget. Later I realized that I was probably just feeling sorry for myself, and that I needed to heed the words of my old 1st Sergeant and "get over it." I finally did that.

There were several bright spots in those years behind the bar. There were times, and I remember many, when I was able to have a positive impact on some of my customers during their darkest hours, as they sat alone at the bar talking to me about their troubles. In a way, I was fortunate to have the full extent of my background, without their knowing it and rejecting me as an out-of-place do-gooder. A lot of it involved just listening. But a lot of it also involved having the right things to say to help that particular person find the answer to the problems that he or she was looking for. I'm sure I helped some people try once again to look at that half empty glass and see it as half full; and I'm sure some of them climbed out of the hole like I did and regained their lives. I still have some of the "thank you, bartender" letters that I've saved over the years. They have come to me from all over the country. Indeed, there were some very rewarding moments in those days.

Sooner or later, you have to leave the bar business just like you have to get away from the battlefield. Your time is up. Something goes sour about the whole thing and you lose your perspective. Fortunately for me, I was able to return to a fairly low-pressure kind of life in government service as a contract specialist for the USDA for ten years and now the Coast Guard. While I'm working 40 hours a week, I still consider myself retired from anything that might disillusion me in the future. Real money jobs have always evaded me, so I don't even think about them anymore.

I've found a Michigan woman close to my age that likes me and enjoys spending time with me. Our two dogs also seem to get along well. I busy myself now with downhill skiing at Tahoe in late winter, fishing all year long, walking my dog along the San Francisco beaches, and trying to live as quiet and easy a life as possible. I have returned to hunting pheasants (from my youthful days in Michigan), and hunting ducks with my female black Lab, Noche I find true solace in the duck marsh at first light, when the changes in the colors in the sky and on the water defy description. There are veterans who would find this scene too much of a reminder of the kind of terrain we had to deal with in Vietnam, but I see something different there. The marsh, the beach, the empty woods and streams have all become a cathedral for me. I suppose I go there to worship in my way, to pray, and be truly thankful that God has allowed me to live so long and to see these wonders for just one more day.

My thoughts and prayers go out to all my brothers, and I hope they continue to have happy and peaceful lives.

Editor's note: Shortly after he penned these words, Ken was informed that he had terminal liver cancer, possibly caused by an exposure to Agent Orange during his service in Vietnam. With his family at his side, he died on December 27, 2002, at the Veterans Administration Hospital in San Francisco. One of the eulogists at his funeral Mass was his good friend from his Sacred Heart Seminary days through his final illness, Bob Thomas.

SOJOURNER
Robert R. Thomas

"The weight of this sad time we must obey.
Speak what we feel,
Not what we ought to say."
  --The Duke of Albany in *King Lear*

In my dotage I have taken up with aphorisms rather than doctrines to describe what a pundit called my "lack of belief system." Scattered throughout notebooks and journals are snippets like:

This is certainly not
Like we thought it was!
  --Rumi

Some lost their faith,
While others lost their nerve.
  --Mark Tiger Edmonds, from a poem

The list goes on like little Post-it® notes sprinkled all over my life.

Much as I like aphorisms, I recognize their sound bite limitations when describing the complexity of beliefs, or lack of same. But it's also the element I like best, that cryptic haiku thing that articulates the Zen ideal that finds the spiritual in the ordinary.

People coming, people going
Over the spring moor–

For what, I wonder?
   -- Shiki

How I got to Post-it® notes from a degree in philosophy from Sacred
Heart Seminary College in 1965 and to aphorisms from theology, is a
long, strange trip, not unlike the stories of each of my brothers from
the SHS Class of '65. I believe one's life is one's art. Therein resides
redemptive challenge. Our stories exemplify redemptive art,
individually and collectively.

In describing my sojourn for this collection, I'll focus on events
pivotal to the evolution of my current reality construct, my "lack of
belief" system.

It is important to note early psychological footprints in my clay.

Prior to my seminary time I was raised from birth to be a good
Catholic boy by a long-suffering, passive/aggressive mother and an
abusively domineering father. Her agenda was obedience to the
church and his was control—both motivated by fear. I was their
firstborn of eleven.

Guilt and fear were big staples of my childhood. I was afraid of
pissing off my father and disappointing my mother. I was afraid of
dying *and* going to hell, just like everyone around me. Eschatology
was a real concern; the future was as scary as the present. I was
repressed and depressed. And the God of Salvation my religion
offered as a panacea wasn't in much better shape, what with
earthlings crucifying his son and all.

My mother's Nebraska Catholicism verged on Jansenism. My father
wore his Catholicism on his sleeve, but it was more show than
substance. The dogmatic catechesis of pre-Vatican II Catholicism
added to my claustrophobic gloom despite its offer of heaven. Life
reeked of fear. Preoccupation with death and hell will do that. "What
the hell is this all about?" was an abiding childhood concern.
Negativity ruled my world. "Don't do that!" was the dictum of the
day. I worked at memorizing the rules and obeying them, expecting

this inherited path would lead to some answers.

In fact, a deeper immersion into Catholicism did shed light.

A Catholic belief system was all I knew. In need of an operating manual, I clung to my Catholicism religiously. The seminary offered opportunity to steep myself in those beliefs. I was, after all, a born believer. The seminary seemed the logical extension of becoming a good Catholic boy. By learning more I'd become a better believer and maybe even a priest, a noble vocation. Plus, maybe I could save my immortal soul?

But more than anything, the seminary got me out of my childhood milieu and on a path away from the God of my childhood—a monumental first step in developing my own point of view. It was escape from the provinces down a holy road at thirteen years old.

Sacred Heart Seminary, home for the next eight years of high school and college, was my first experience of leaving one life behind and beginning another based on a decision I made. Another thirteen years passed before I effected the next transformation, but I never forgot the power of that first molting. Existentially it set the stage for all my subsequent evolution.

My new home was an institution. I thought *The Dead Poets Society* film accurately captured several essential boarding school lessons about authority, competition, friendship, loyalty, power, and the individual versus the institution. Camaraderie was a major factor in my surviving the institution, faculty warnings about "particular friendships" notwithstanding. My fondest memories of the Heart revolve around the friendships I experienced. To this day some of those friends remain my saving grace.

Sacred Heart taught me the value of endurance over the long haul and the importance of stick-to-itiveness and self-discipline in the process of personal accomplishment.

Educationally, Sacred Heart offered the goods. I learned to think --

critically. In terms of belief, this education proved a two-edged sword: it did allow a thorough examination of Roman Catholicism, but it also offered glimpses into other belief systems and religion's role in some of human history's horrors. My curiosity was piqued.

"In human society," Mr. Ringold taught us, "thinking's the greatest transgression of all."
"Cri-ti-cal thinking," Mr. Ringold said, using his knuckles to rap out each of the syllables on his desktop, "-- there is the ultimate subversion."
    --Philip Roth, *I Married A Communist*

My love of learning and intellectual curiosity grew symbiotically throughout my Sacred Heart curriculum, eventually leading me to an intertwining of various intellectual disciplines. Instead of achieving a unified field theory, however, my search for intelligent signs of life in the universe broadened when I discovered an important tool for further investigation—the literary light. Fr. Gerry Martin's American Literature course and the appearance of existentialism in a History of Philosophy course were critical turns along my intellectual path. Mark Twain's *Letters from the Earth* and Sartre's *Being and Nothingness* blew my mind. In pronouncing the failure of reason and the death of Western philosophy, the existentialists challenged both God and Reason. I began to perceive and think in refreshingly new ways outside the box of my religion. Although my faith in Roman Catholicism was not yet an issue, a seed was planted. There were other ways to think. Intellectually I became more catholic and less Catholic. Existentialism caught my attention with its emphasis on free choice and responsibility in a hostile or indifferent world that cannot be explained. Twain's bitterly acerbic attack on some of the more garish manifestations of anthropomorphic divinity impressed me with the power of satire and delighted my iconoclastic predilections.

A mind once expanded by a new idea never again returns to its original dimensions.
    --Anonymous

Concurrent with my growing intellectual curiosities were the times,

146

the turbulent Sixties. The turbulence was not confined to America. The world was getting smaller. And so was the Roman Catholic Church. Vatican II refreshed my Catholic faith as much as Sartre stimulated my intellect. Despite these apparent contradictions, my idealism flourished. My belief system was changing from negative to positive, from dogmatic to dynamic. All the signs and portents seemed electric with the hope of fresh possibilities.

Knowledge humanizes character and does not let it be cruel.
-- Translation of the Latin motto of a South Carolina university

In such a state I matriculated to St. John's where my intellectual pursuits focused on Christian theological constructs.

Jack Castelot's scripture classes illuminated some radical Christian messages, like the fullness of life and the NOW, by introducing me to scriptural critical thinking, just as Gerry Martin's classes had introduced me to literary critical thinking. Learning to read the literature critically was a basic theological and literary lesson that continues to inform me.

Theology identified and refined my questions about life and religion's role. I began to differentiate between Christian and Roman Catholic. My theological argument wasn't with God as much as with those who spoke for Him—organizations, humans like you and me. Studying the prophetic aspect of priesthood attracted and enlightened me. So did the Book of Revelation. I examined Old Testament warnings of false gods and New Testament rages against the moneychangers, while remembering Twain's attacks on idols.

Church history confronted me with the secularism of ecclesiastical power. Sacramental theology opened me to the magic of ritual in ontological pursuits. Moral theology illuminated the gray at the expense of black and white by introducing me to situational ethics— more akin to existentialism than the dogmatic catechesis of my youth. Fresh perspective was the lesson here, derived from a growing awareness.

St. John's was a testing ground for emotional and cultural collisions as well as intellectual and spiritual ones.

Involvement in the civil rights movement continued from my Sacred Heart experiences. Privy to a glimpse of American poverty, racism, ghettos and hatred, I did a double take on this brave new world outside. I looked hard at politics and agendas, many of which had little in common with truth, justice and the American Way. Chicago's south side, Jim Groppi's Milwaukee and my classmate John Clark's Peter Claver Center in Jackson, Michigan, assured me this was no longer Kansas, Dorothy. I was not surprised by the urban ghetto explosions. I was surprised by the polemics of many Christian churches. "Love One Another" took on some perverted misrepresentations; I got my first real taste of Christian fundamentalism. Nonetheless, I had the hope of the true Christian message and the idealism of youth. I believed that would be enough to transform the political process.

While grappling with political consciousness, I got involved with the University of Detroit Retreat Program. Using teams composed of seminarians and university students, the program offered weekend retreats for U of D students at a facility near Brighton, Michigan. I enjoyed being away from the institution with the opportunity to practice some ministerial skills and mingle with college students in the real world. Because U of D is a coeducational institution, I was introduced to coeds. Being around young women in a social situation proved how stunted my social development was, while providing lessons the seminary was not equipped to adequately teach. My abiding fascination with interesting women blossomed in Brighton. After living in a male environment for too many years, discovering women was breathtakingly foreign and mysterious. I was still too much the geek to be sexually active, but I found unexpected pleasure in the company of women. I felt more human. Socially, things were looking up.

My socialization and politicization occurred in the glow of faith and hope. I happily anticipated the impending challenges of a pastoral ministry.

Wandering Between Two Worlds

May 18,1968. My brother Gary was killed in Vietnam while awaiting extraction from his final mission as a recon Marine. Life would never be the same for me because death, my great fear, had come home to roost. Burying my brother shattered illusory explanations for the unknown and confronted me with the inevitability of mortality. Nothingness loomed as I walked through the gloom while clinging to my Catholic coat of faith, a coat now beginning to fray at the edges.

Getting the news about Gary's death was the shock you imagine, but the demolition of my previous life wasn't over. When I reached my parents' home, I found lost souls. I remember the look, the thousand-yard stare that cried out, "What do we do now?" I did what I was trained to do: I ministered to them.

Three weeks or so elapsed between notification of death and the arrival of Gary's body and the funeral. Pardon the indiscretion, but that's a lot of dead time with a family looking for some solace. I was guided by the Christian scriptures. I can't remember chapters and verses, but they revolved around resurrection and the fullness of life and how that relates to the living rather than the dead. I was dealing with survivors, not the deceased. I was certain of my area of responsibility here. I was equally certain my brother's death taught me how much I wanted to live. I tried to convey my newly-found passion for LIFE while offering a shoulder to cry on and an encouraging word. Again, nothing miraculous or particularly noble here; this is what ministers are trained to do. What I didn't have for them and for myself were any answers.

The funeral sermon was more than a duty I had just been ordained to the diaconate to perform. Many remember the sermon. They (myself included) don't remember the words, but they remember the sermon performance. From my perspective as preacher the entire experience was one of being in a zone of instrumentality. It didn't feel particularly religious or enlightened; more like I was tuned in and flowing with the Force. I was along for the ride just like the audience. It was a graced moment that I knew had direct linkage to acceptance, not explanations. Spirituality for me was becoming more existential, less theoretical. Riding the ride was as instructive as analyzing it.

Wandering Between Two Worlds

1968 was a very bad year -- from Tet, through the deaths of Gary, Dr. King, and Bobby Kennedy. I was lying on my parents' couch, still awaiting the shipment of Gary's body, when

Kennedy died in Los Angeles. With Nixon and his thugs waiting in the wings, my political idealism eroded rapidly.

On the ecclesiastical political level, the business with Tony Locricchio sickened me, emotionally and politically. I felt disconnected from everything familiar, including the camaraderie of my classmates. The class fractured into political and theological factions. We no longer all believed the same things, but then we probably never had. Polarization was a nasty experience. We were now the Class of the Diaspora. Like it or not, we were growing up.

My beliefs and the world had collided in a most unholy manner, assaulting my privileged ivory tower reality construct with malevolence. Consciousness became a lot less myopic and much more alert. In the aftermath much of my youthful idealism was dead. I wasn't cynical, but I was a lot more realistic. I examined creation with less certainty.

Theocratic tyranny seemed so intertwined with ecclesiastical tyranny as to be indistinguishable. I questioned not so much what, but whom I represented. I lost confidence in ecclesiastical management's ability to properly execute its philosophy. I no longer felt good about being a company representative, but I wasn't quite ready to shed my institutional skin. Basic cowardice and confusion, I suppose. What else was there to do? Other career options, like the military or the factory, paled significantly in contrast. Getting ordained, what the dozen years of preparation was all about, was right around the corner.

Ironically, ordination could not have occurred at a more auspicious time. The challenges of being a parish priest gave me purpose, and several parishioners loved me enough to renew my grounding in the human community. Healing had begun. Day by day I gained confidence in my humanity. All the while, the ecclesiastical authorities barely bothered me. Priesthood was the best job I've ever had. I particularly enjoyed the one-to-one of confession and the grander scope of the bully pulpit.

Preaching caused me to contemplate, to ponder. I pondered the implications of practicing what I preached. And what was it I preached? What did I believe?

I preached against bondage and tyranny. I believed that no one should be terrorized by man or god. I believed the secular and religious structures of authority, hierarchy, and domination should be challenged regularly to increase the scope of human freedom. I believed in personal responsibility and freedom. An aberrant aspect of the priestly role, one I loathed, was the abject dependency of the faithful on the clerical caste. I encouraged the priesthood of the faithful. I was suspicious of organizational power and thought the solution to abusive power was to take it away from managers who often saw the medium as more important than the message. But such a revolution, I knew, began with individual metanoia. It didn't take long for this line of thinking to curl around and face me in the mirror one morning.

During this period I somehow ended up spending time with a few classmates who were, as someone put it, "having trouble with their vocations." An abiding observation I took from these visits was that while celibacy, ecclesiastical power, lousy assignments, etc. were debated, everyone I talked with wanted something more for his life— a woman, a family, "a fuller life," as one man stated. So did I, but I was not so interested in a wife or family as slaking my growing thirst for more personal freedom. I saw my institutional role as a serious hindrance to my burgeoning individualism. I was feeling less like belonging and more like becoming. I faced taking responsibility for my life.

The morning I confronted myself in the mirror about practicing what I was preaching, I knew what I had to do. There was no time like the present to put up or shut up. Another emphasis of my preaching was the importance of, and appreciation for, the NOW. It was my time to cut bait and stop fishing, and I knew it.

I have often been asked about how difficult it must have been to leave the priesthood. It was no more difficult than picking up the phone to arrange a meeting to tell the bishop my decision. While the meeting was a courtesy call (I had already decided I would leave), my exchange with the bishop was a fascinating experience in power, albeit a brief one. As soon as the bishop understood my decision was final, he dismissed me. His only concern was that I not do anything priestly to embarrass the Church. I remember watching myself calmly settle affairs with my bishop and my church. It was another experience of being in the zone, centered in the moment. Walking away from the Chancery, I remember smiling and muttering to myself, "So this is how it goes: They have no power as soon as I choose to not give it to them." I knew I had made the right choice as surely as I knew I had stepped outside the box of Catholicism in both thought and deed.

Remember, there's a big difference between kneeling down and bending over.
--Frank Zappa, from a song

Shaking off a former life including religion was exhilarating and scary. Seeing life with fewer religious filters was refreshing For the first time in my life I was in charge of the paths I would take, freed from the expectations of others. The challenge seemed daunting, but I was happily committed. I stepped into the outside world excited about my new life. It felt like resurrection. "Free at last!" had existential significance.

So did being broke without a home or a job. But I was young and restless, and I had the unconditional support of several parishioners, hardcore believers in the priesthood of the faithful, to whom I remain bonded. They took me in until I got a job as a social worker in Flint. Then they continued to love and support me.

The year spent as a caseworker with the Genesee County Department of Social Services was exciting and enlightening. I had a savvy boss—middle-aged, female, black—who taught me a lot in a hurry about the street and the bureaucrats. She also partnered me up with a man who introduced me to writing for pleasure, among other bohemian delights. He remains one of my dearest friends and guides. To understand my evolution is in great part to understand the guides along the way and my penchant for bohemian delights.

What they tell me
I should want
Isn't what I need.
    --Linda Perry, from a song

Moving to San Francisco provided me with a cornucopia of guides and bohemian delights. My early years in San Francisco were exciting. Everything was new. Baghdad-by-the-Bay was the perfect base for reinventing myself; it offered stimulation, anonymity, and tolerance. I could be Anyman. I morphed through several manifestations.

While in my wannabe bohemian state, I hung out in Ferlinghetti's *City Lights* bookstore and *The Vesuvio Café*, the famous Beat watering hole across the alley. Delving into Beat literature in the dank basement of *City Lights* offered further credence to my individualism and added Allen Ginsburg's *Howl* to my pantheon of apocalyptic scriptures. Engaging conversations with the habitués of *Vesuvio* introduced me to anarchism. It wasn't at all what I thought. To get a better handle on what I was learning in *Vesuvio,* I returned often to *City Lights* for a review of anarchist literature. I identified viscerally with the anarchist belief that the burden of proof must be placed on authority. If that burden cannot be met, offending authority must be dismantled.

QUESTION AUTHORITY was more than a hippie bumper sticker. A later discovery of Noam Chomsky, the MIT linguist, critic, and proponent of anarchist traditions, refined my American belief that tyranny in any form is unacceptable. I once heard anarchism described as "taking democracy to extremes." *Manufacturing Consent*, a documentary film about the art of controlling opinion, highlights the potential of anarchism and the anarchist idea. The anarchist tradition inspired me with its faith in the power of the individual and common decency.

The Beats' credo encouraged individuality and freedom of expression; it did not encourage fulfilling anyone's expectations or mouthing company lines. Blake's *Songs of Innocence* and Rimbaud's road of excess in search of enlightenment were set against the Puritanical ethos and dogmatism of the dominant culture. I felt simpático with the Beats' rage against the machine. Turn on. Tune In. Drop out. Altered states and expanded consciousness became soul food. Increasing consciousness begat freedom. Awareness became my daily prayer.

The mystical always enticed me in a spooky way, like a really good Halloween tale. I wasn't so much curious about the supernatural as I was about the extent of the natural. The dimensions of this life intrigued me far more than the hereafter. Aldous Huxley's *Doors of Perception* and Dr. Andrew Weil's *The Natural Mind* informed my experiments with mind-altering drugs and their role in various cultures, particularly the sacramental role. An old pal used to pop a couple magic mushrooms, head out onto my deck to sit staring at the Bay and, as he put it, "converse with God for a few hours." Those who have ridden with Brothers Psilocybin or Mescaline understand my friend's description. Psychotropic drugs bring existential meaning to mystical. They not only opened doors of perception for me, but left the doors permanently ajar. What I saw was vast impermanence. No answers. An even bigger mystery than I imagined or hoped for. I was excited. I introduced myself to modern physics and dug more deeply into Eastern thought.

Alan Watts was my first encounter with an attempted synthesis of Eastern and Western beliefs. A colorful sybarite and former Episcopalian priest, Watts had a regular 30-minute program on local radio. From Watts I learned of "the wisdom of insecurity"—how to live with doubt and embrace it. I learned that a koan (in Chinese, *kung an*) is a riddle meant to short-circuit all logical connections. With the koan we learn to have questions without needing answers because it is not about knowing anything; it is beyond logic and language; it is about being, not knowing. The Knowing of the West is all about the Being of the East. Zen holy fools consider one thing to be holy: their moment-to-moment Zen. Being requires constant homage to the eternal now.

Buddhism spoke to me about the path, the *dharma*, in meditative tones, surprisingly realistic and calming despite beginning with the somber realities of suffering. The Eight-Fold Path is as noble an operational manual as any. Known as The Middle Way, Buddha's path rekindled my appreciation for the realism of the Thomistic *via media*.

Modern physics was another can of worms. I'm not your math guy, first of all. I didn't know the language and was certain I wasn't going to learn it in this lifetime. Thanks to my collegiate introduction to cosmology, I got a tenuous handhold on the subject and searched out physicists who were writers and writers who were physicists. What I learned was that the cosmic doors of perception opened via psychotropic drugs bore an uncanny resemblance to the revelations of contemporary physics.

While investigating modern reality constructs and the implications for belief systems, I was experiencing secular diversity in a multicultural milieu outside the box of Christianity.

My first California love was a Jewish American Princess, the daughter of an Oakland doctor, who graduated from Berkeley, then covered the anti-war student uprising there for public radio. Susan introduced me to Judaism and taught me how to use chopsticks. She deftly escorted me through new worlds filled with artists, psychiatrists, eccentric bohemians, flea markets, gourmet cooking, rich people and poor people. She offered entree to worlds I never knew existed. Susan's soirees were festive, stimulating happenings punctuated by gourmet grub and fascinating conversations with a raft of characters. Sharing her life and her lovely studio in Pacific Heights expanded my horizons every bit as much as psychotropic drugs.

I never quite knew what Susan saw in me, but initially she was intrigued by my apparent lack of guilt, especially considering my priestly background. Catholics and Jews have similar considerations of guilt's oppression. Susan delighted in introducing me to her more neurotic Jewish psychiatrist friends as "My friend, Robert. He doesn't do guilt." Attempting to offer perspective on Susan's take on me and guilt, I explained that the further I got from the sources of guilt, like my parents and my religion, the less guilt I experienced. I likened my experiences with inbred guilt to aversion therapy: I had so overdosed on guilt in my childhood that it no longer overpowered me. The shrinks liked the aversion therapy analogy. I enjoyed the therapeutic effect and the realization that every instance of casting off a former life resulted in an exponential diminution of misguided guilt. I did not feel amoral; personal freedom demands its own moral responsibility. Susan and I parted company because she wanted a future and we both knew it wasn't me. I had no idea what I wanted to be when I grew up. Susan met a good man and married happily. I went on a trip around the world.

Traveling around the world was realizing a youthful fantasy incited by *National Geographic* magazine and my fondness for maps. At thirty-three, opportunity knocked and I opened the door.

Overlanding the planet along the old international hippie trail with very little money, especially in the unknown and mysterious East, truly opened me to the world and permanently transformed me. It was like being on LSD for six months. My nose was rubbed in patience and acceptance and the NOW. Some of Buddha's lessons became very experiential. I saw there were too many people, and too many of them were impoverished and suffering. I saw the land was worse for the wear. My political and economic perspective turned more international and less regional. Reading about the United States in the foreign press was enlightening. Regular contact with Islam and Hinduism and Shamanism extended my theological curiosities.

The stimulations of the trip reverberate thirty years later as I continue to learn about all that I saw during those six months in 1976. The trip was a perfect compliment to my formal education, bringing my existential curiosities up to speed with my intellectual pursuits. I became an abiding student of the world. Nationalism got discarded into the pile of its loser pals— fascism, capitalism, and communism. International experiences and observations permanently inform my personal belief system about everything from politics to religion.

Religiously, I felt less beholding to a specific deity and more grounded in the pulse of this life, more incarnated and less cerebral, more connected with the mysterious process of life. Insights interested me more than answers. I looked toward common linkage and away from divisive dogmatism. I believed we were all trying to talk about the same thing -- the mystery -- despite our various constructs. Defining a supreme being seemed a false summit. The anthropomorphic dilemma appeared insurmountable dogmatically. Art seemed a more effective expression of mystery than anthropomorphic religion, and recognizing divinity in humanity seemed a more expeditious path.

I returned from Asia gaunt, weakened by months of dysentery and parasites and the most grueling road trip I've ever taken. Several friends commented on my being a shell of my former shell. Despite my weakened state, exacerbated by a serious dose of culture shock, I couldn't malinger. I was broke, in debt, and without a home or a job again.

Very shortly after landing back in San Francisco, I received a letter from the city personnel department informing me that my name had come up on the eligibility list for transit operators, a list I had forgotten I'd applied for two years earlier. A month after returning from Asia, where I'd ridden all manner of buses, I was driving a bus for the City and County of San Francisco.

Living and working in San Francisco steeped me further in the multicultural world. The City not only sports a multicultural residency but is an international caravansary as well. My apartment and my job put me squarely in the heart of the action. The multiculturalism is so normal to me that whenever I travel to less diversified sections of the country, I often feel foreign.

Aside from my inherent boosterism of San Francisco, this locus of the middle years of my life has been as important to my evolving beliefs as any. The daily rubbing of shoulders with a plethora of beliefs offers refreshing perspective and facilitates understanding and change. Living in a melting pot for thirty years has been a daily reminder of basic universal connections. Breaking bread together is commonplace, but never tedious.

For thirty years San Francisco offered me such happenings in an intelligent nondenominational community. Hope was grounded in daily communal experience and faith in the path of tolerance. San Francisco was home because it is an encouraging environment and a noble urban experiment.

Working as a transit operator literally put me on the streets, down in the trenches with the salt of the earth in a multicultural setting. Fodder for several novels resides in those years featuring characters from beyond Central Casting. Camaraderie forged under common fire from the public, the bosses, and a corrupt union blessed me with new friends. Wage slavery in a bloated bureaucracy that spawned moronic behavior was a trial that did nothing to weaken my affection for the anarchists. John Lennon's "Working Class Hero" became my blue-collar anthem, and plenty of my fellow transit operators and lots of our passengers sang right along with me. The money the job offered allowed me to play in San Francisco and travel extensively. It paid for lots of adventures from here to Bangkok. I always felt I got my money's worth.

When I retired I expected to reflect on all that went before in splendid isolation from mundane demands. But reflections leading to what? Conclusions and credos? Hmmm? Not likely, what with the wraith of anthropomorphic dogma constantly lurking over my shoulder like a cross. But I will hazard to say that any divinity worth consideration must be bigger than a construct, no matter how essential to the human psyche such a construct might seem. In my theological process, explanations and descriptions gave way to attempts at awareness. In very real ways I am no more enlightened down the paths I have followed than that kid in Davison, Michigan, who wondered "What the hell is this all about?" Now, however, I'm not as worried about answers. "Seek and ye shall find" gave approbation to my process. One finds in the seeking, not in the finding. The journey is the journey, not the end of the journey.

Never was this more evident than in 2002, a horrible year for me. It was even worse for my old pal and classmate, Ken Eason; he died, and he did not go peacefully. I was with him from the day he learned he had terminal cancer. The death march lasted eight months, ending shortly after Christmas. Still fresh in my psyche, I see no purpose in reliving the nightmares of those days, but there were notable saving graces relevant to my personal development and the Class of '65. For as long as Ken was ambulatory, he and I would wander out to Land's End behind the V.A.'s Death Hotel, sit on a log under a giant Monterrey Pine overlooking the entrance to the Golden Gate, and share a joint, our mutual sacramental for many years. Sometimes we'd talk; other times we'd be mostly meditative, but comfortable in each other's silent presence. I can't recall who first dubbed our visits to the cliff "holy," but we both agreed that's what they were. Life and death permeated our awareness, our friendship, our brotherhood.

During one of our holy conversations, Ken recommended I rent the HBO series *A Band of Brothers*. This recommendation came on the heels of a conversation we'd had about our seminary comrades and Ken's Vet buddies. The conversation was stimulated by the support both Ken and I were receiving from both bands of brothers, priests and warriors united in common cause. No matter how down Ken might get, visits from his brothers always lifted his spirits. I particularly remember refreshing visits from classmates John Clark and Bill Sumner when Ken was spiraling down physically and psychologically. There were many other examples of support from the brothers in the form of phone calls, e-mails, cards and letters. Ken was a contributing member of the class reunion and book project. He was one of the first to visit classmates in Ohio and D.C. He submitted an autobiography for the book project. He told me that he hoped that after he died I would continue to work toward bringing the project to publication. The more support he received from the Class of '65, the more strongly he felt about the class book.

Our conversations about our class led to conjectures about the mandala, which means "disk" in Sanskrit and connotes reincarnation, the ultimate in recycling. Ken and I agreed that we were getting to live our seminary brotherhood again in its reincarnated class reunion form. Our holy conversations bore remarkable resemblance to the seminary conversations I once dubbed "intellectual" conversations. They were, of course, much more than simply intellectual; they were the means by which many of us bonded; they were holy cement, just as were the holy conversations between Ken and me on the Land's End log.

After Ken died the doom and gloom that had dogged me for the previous two years lay like a flatiron on my depleted spirit. I was numb. To alleviate the psychic stink by getting outside myself, I turned to an old reliable in my bag of survival tricks, a trip. As soon as I decided, I felt a new lease on life, a burst of spirit much like I'd experienced after my brother died. The death march odyssey had again led me to a new life. Some say, "Allah be with you." I prefer, "Let the path continue to blossom."

The path was the Amtrak tracks from San Francisco to Florida, then up the eastern seaboard. The plan was to let the trip blossom, to have no preconceptions other than visiting old friends along the way. Unlike all previous spins on the sojourner mandala, this one had no destination or time schedule. I was retired and unencumbered of responsibilities. I did not have to return to another life at some point. The sojourn was now my new life and where I was on the sojourn was my home.

Little did I know.

The trip lasted nine months and far exceeded my lack of expectations. Allowing the trip to evolve was a wonderful elixir in itself. Sharing quality time in the lives of friends was a great solace and inspiration. Being warmly invited into the lives of several seminary brothers offered a reappreciation of our bond and the redemptive art of each of our sojourns.

As winter approached Boston nine months down the road, I scurried back to San Francisco by plane. Riding the trip's good energy, I spent the next nine months enjoying the peace and quiet of an uncomplicated life on my rooftop. This was what retirement was meant to be.

In early summer my father's death returned me to my Michigan roots for the gathering of the clan and the funeral. I expected to be there a week. The trouble with expectations is they bear little resemblance to reality.

The reality was that for reasons worthy of its own story, I lived in Flint, Michigan, with my mother, as her primary caregiver for the next two and a half years. The possibility that such would happen to my retirement bliss was no more on my radar than finding a pot of gold at the end of a rainbow or the great love of my life in my golden years.

Being a sufi is to put away what is in your head–
Imagined truth, preconceptions, conditioning–
And to face what may happen to you.
-- Abu Said

The first summer in Flint was hellish, none of it caused by my mother or Flint. The best demons come from within and mine are no exception. Accompanying seething self-pity at my plight was a panic that I'd lost control of my retirement plans and my life, which, of course, I had. I resented my sudden lack of freedom, even though I had freely chosen my path. As usual, I had attributed to myself much more freedom than I actually had.

Sometimes I go about pitying myself and all the time I am being
carried on great winds across the sky.
--Ojibway Saying

By summer's end I had tired of living with my woeful self. Sitting quietly for hours outside on Mother's backyard deck watching the birds and bees and squirrels cavort in the yard and long walks in a nearby nature preserve had as much to do with my rebirth as my disgust with the daily pity party plaguing my spirit. Reconnecting with the natural world got me outside myself, reminding me that in nature we learn the vital lessons of just being.

As for locus, lessons learned in twelve years of boarding school and a trek around the planet returned to pay dividends in the patience being stuck in a place demands. Home, I reminded myself, is where I am in the here and now. Having been true in Afghanistan, then why not in Flint? Having no rebuttal, I reacquainted myself with Flint, Michigan—its history, its people, and it's present state—with the same curiosity and fervor I'd immersed myself in Herat, Afghanistan.

While reconnecting with nature and my hometown, I began teaching myself to cook, immersing myself in the importance of the meal. Having cooked for a large family for years, Mother was adamantly finished with cooking. Left to her culinary devices, she'd gladly exist on mac and cheese and popcorn, especially if it meant she didn't have to cook. And I didn't cook because I'd never had to learn more than the rudiments. As with my choice to stay in Flint caring for my mother, there was no choice. If we were to survive, I had to learn to cook. So I did, a Zen exercise which did us well both nutritionally and spiritually.

Not only was I losing my woeful self in these immersions, I was learning acceptance again.

To the Zen master, truth and salvation are a matter of acceptance. One day while doing my mother's laundry, remembering how much laundry she'd done on my behalf, I burst out laughing. Paybacks are a bitch even in a labor of love, where acceptance is the only approach that makes sense. It was back to basics: one day at a time in the here and now as artfully lived as imaginable.

...but I might learn something of mindlessness, something of the purity of living in the physical senses and the dignity of living without bias or motive.
     -- Annie Dillard

As with Ken's dying, friends were anchors of love and emotional support. Several were brothers from the class of '65. They had been there with me at my brother's funeral and during Ken's death march. Again, at my father's death and my mother's dying, there are those same brothers. Their solidarity on such occasions is palpable. There is nothing like proven old friends.

It was the old friend who had introduced me to bohemian delights in the aftermath of my religious life who thirty years later introduced me to the love of my life.

You never find happiness until you stop looking for it.
   -- Chuang Tzu

Long ago I had learned that neither Ms. Wonderful nor a pot of gold was going to make me happy. By sixty-three I had traded those illusions for peace of mind. Not only was I not looking for Ms. Wonderful or gold, I was not interested in either. But the uncertainty principle and guides again exerted their simple twists of fate.

Initially introduced by our mutual friend as the definitive Flint guide, Ingrid is indeed that. She tutored me in Flint history and politics as I peppered her with questions about my hometown. She single-handedly turned around my attitude toward Flint, reminding me there is life after GM, the UAW, the Rust Belt, and Michael Moore. A mutual appreciation for being out in nature blossomed into a mutual appreciation for each other during lengthy walking conversations during which we gradually revealed ourselves. Like me, Ingrid had created a peaceful life on her own without need of a significant other. While neither of us could imagine someone in their daily life 24/7, neither objected to new friendships. We became friends. There was no danger of 24/7 because I was committed to daily life with my mother, while Ingrid had daily responsibilities for her eighty-six-year-old mother and ailing sister. Plus, my home was San Francisco, hers was Flint.

Nevertheless our contacts gradually increased to daily, usually with Ingrid joining Mother and me and sister Kathleen, when available, for dinner. The dinners quickly became very beneficial to all of us. The meaning of the meal increased exponentially with daily practice. There was no glumness in these gatherings despite knowing Mother was definitely dying of multiple myeloma. Eventually we all recognized we were in the presence of unconditional love. It's what we gave each other. In this milieu it is no stretch to understand how Ingrid and I fell in love, despite our proclivities for the single life. It was Ingrid who first recognized her love for me as "the first time I have ever loved anyone without holding something back." Her recognition resonated with me, and I readily admitted she was the first person I had ever loved unconditionally. I hadn't recognized it as such until Ingrid spoke the word. The end result is a breath of fresh air and an odd freedom for each of us. The night Mother passed I left her home on Twilight Drive for good and moved in with Ingrid. That was one year ago. I've never been happier with the here and now. Delighting in Ingrid's company 24/7 turns out to be a delight.

So now, at sixty-five, several full reincarnations around the Great Mandala and a few addenda later, followed by a stunning surprise of the highest magnitude, finding the grand love of my life in my sixties, how does this old philosopher out of Sacred Heart, Class of '65, take stock of this long strange trip to this point?

I've learned to never say never because you never know.

We are here and it is now.
Further than that all human
Knowledge is moonshine.
    -- H. L. Mencken

I have reached no conclusions other than being there is the way it was no matter what I say.

After all, the personal story is just another aspect of the fleeting scene.

I leave.
You stay.

Two autumns.
	-- Buson

"What's it all about, Alfie?"

"Just this," replies the Zen master.

Wandering Between Two Worlds

WARRIOR AND CAREGIVER
B. Thomas McCloskey

Deciding for the Seminary

I come from a religious family in the small town of Howell, Michigan. It is part of the Lansing diocese, 58 miles north and west of Detroit. I have an older sister who was married in 1955. My two older brothers were both good athletes and I looked forward to playing on the high school sports teams as they were doing. My nine-year-old brother Pat would later enter the Franciscan Order and serve as a priest with them. My father was a dentist and took a special interest in our education. In our dinner table discussions, when we would come up with a question no one could answer, his response was always the same: "Look it up in the World Book Encyclopedia!" After dinner we would always make good use of that investment in the family library. My mother was a librarian and had a great curiosity about many things.

From about the third grade on, I had occasionally entertained the thought of becoming a priest. By the eighth grade, however, I was more interested in sports and girls. It was during this time that a missionary priest came to our class and talked about "vocations." As I listened to him talk about "having a purpose in life and doing good," I decided that I should pursue this calling. One of my good friends had entered the seminary two years earlier and he seemed to like it. When my mother asked me whether I wanted to be an order or diocesan priest, I was a bit confused and so I responded: "I want to go where Jim is." That keen bit of ecclesiastical insight brought me to Sacred

Wandering Between Two Worlds

Heart Seminary High School in the fall of 1957.

The assistant pastor at our parish was certainly a big influence on this decision. He had a great sense of humor, loved sports and was very personable. Both of my parents were quite active in the church and they were proud of my decision to enter the seminary. It was always clear to me, however, that they would be supportive of me whether I chose to remain or not. Later on I often described my seminary years as a kind of Cinderella story. I was attracted to the priesthood and my seminary days became a time of "trying on" the shoe to see if it fit me. It is safe to say that, at the age of 14, I was somewhat naïve, but I never thought of it that way at the time.

The Formation Years

In our high school and college years, we students were blessed with some remarkable men who taught us, shared their stories of their lives as priests, and served as examples and mentors for us. Two of them deserve specific mention, since they had a big influence on my formation.

Fr. Ed Scheuerman was the assistant dean in high school and taught us basic and advanced algebra. While mathematics was my least favorite subject, Ed always had a sunny disposition, was a great storyteller, enjoyed music, and took a personal interest in me. Although my contact with him was limited in college and non-existent during my four years of theology, I asked him to preach at my First Mass in June of 1969. He was most gracious, well prepared, and very personable with my friends and family for that occasion. His basic text was the section of Paul's letter to Corinthians where he describes the proper celebration of the Eucharist. Ed did his own reflection on that passage, which included some dreams and challenges for the modern parish community. His presence and remarks brought to full circle the journey that had started for me twelve years earlier when I attended my first math class as a 14 year-old high school freshman.

Fr. Jerry Fraser became the high school librarian once I started college. Nonetheless we struck up a friendship. In the 50's he had been chaplain for Young Christian Workers, Young Christian Students (YCS) and Christian Family Movement groups in Detroit. Fr. Fraser spoke Spanish and was quite bright and articulate. He was very committed to connecting faith and social justice and had a big influence on my thinking and how we needed to form small communities of believers in our parishes. Using similar techniques, a number of us in college formed a cell group out of the Mission Society. We would go out and give talks at various high schools in the Detroit area. If possible we would try to establish YCS groups in those schools, and then maintain contact as chaplains or advisors. One of our graduates was a young woman who would go on to do pastoral migrant work with some of us in western Michigan. Later she became the director for the Social Justice office of the Archdiocese of Detroit. Another student would go on to work full time at the YCS headquarters in Chicago, ultimately getting involved in anti-war civil disobedience actions there. She was sent to a Federal Women's prison in Alderson, West Virginia, where two classmates and I visited her in the spring of 1970.

During these years of formation, we were challenged to the dream of being "warriors for Christ," while we were given the tools to do our part in the battle. Part of being a warrior was to have a vision of what was possible and then the courage to stay with the task until you had achieved your goal. We looked to our leaders for some direction and our comrades in arms to help give us strength. The macho man image came in for a lot of criticism. "Real men" were warriors tempered by compassion.

Cardinal Newman's definition of a gentleman - a man who gives no offense – was often on our minds. Our professors believed in that principle and lived it to the best of their ability. Often they would speak of a sound mind in a sound body. They encouraged us to take part in sports as a break from the serious pursuit of our studies. In many ways the seminary culture put a great deal of emphasis on sports and physical activity. In retrospect this emphasis provided an outlet for a lot of energy in a healthy way. It appeared that many of us were attracted to women, but we were a "band of brothers" committed to Jesus and in service to the Church. Some of the newly ordained would return on their days off to play handball, and then go off to spend the day together enjoying a movie, dinner, and good conversation. We were taught that this type of friendship would be our salvation someday as happy and productive priests. In my later seminary years I would play hockey with some priests who were among the most dedicated and gifted men in Detroit's inner city parishes. They were joyful, confident, bright, and personable, with a strong sense of social mission.

While we were warned about homosexuality and "particular friendships," we did not really talk about this area of life. Since we were living in an all-male environment from an early age, there really was not a good opportunity to grow in our sexual identities. It would appear that American culture in general and Church culture in particular had a conspiracy of silence with regard to homosexuality. The central problems of priests seemed to revolve around either women or alcohol. The proper remedy was prayer, confession, and spiritual direction, discipline of the senses, hard work, and making sure to take a day off.

In my twelve years of seminary training, there was not a single discussion of homosexuality, let alone pedophilia, among priests. Sex was for those who were married, and we were taught that we could live without it, if we had a proper balance of prayer, study, and caring for our people in a proper way. I have encountered other priests in ministry who made use of therapy to work out sexual dysfunction. This lack of an open discussion on sexuality was probably the single biggest failure of that seminary system. Nothing that we were taught about sexuality was incorrect – it is just that we were taught very little. In place of discussion there was a huge silence. We observed Grand Silence following our evening study hall until breakfast. In retrospect, perhaps that Grand Silence extended to the area of sexuality as well.

Immediately after my ordination in June of 1969, I received a call from a good priest friend to join him for dinner. He was leaving the priesthood to receive some therapy in another state and was not very specific about his difficulties. Later I found out that he was guilty of pedophilia and that our diocese had made an arrangement with the local prosecutor to keep him out of that county and put him into a treatment program. Most likely some damages were paid to the family involved. He later married, had a child, and has enjoyed a very successful career in business. I am aware of just one other case of priestly pedophilia in my diocese from 1969 to 2002. That other priest served time in a state prison located in a town where I served.

Mexico and Migrants

In our college years, Professor Gordon Farrell came over from the University of Detroit to teach Spanish. He was a very lively man with a good sense of humor and a great love for the Spanish language and culture. He inspired us and challenged us to learn Spanish well. During our second year we found out that we could join a group of high school students who traveled to Mexico for the summer, lived with local families, studied Spanish, and enjoyed the people and the culture. I went on this journey with my classmates Larry McCulloch and George Wesolek and had a profound experience in the summer of 1963. Pope John XXIII had just written *Pacem in Terris* and John F. Kennedy was our smart, witty, and urbane president. The "two John's" began the Peace Corps and Papal Volunteers for Latin America. We had a chance to see some of the worst poverty in Mexico and to view ourselves as others see us from abroad. We college seminarians were on a separate track. Most of us stayed with families and had a month of intensive Spanish in Mexico City. In our second month we went to parishes in the boonies for a first-hand experience of the lives of people in poverty. We became inspired by some of the priests we worked with. Our vocations were more grounded from that point on.

I had tried on priesthood in my imagination after being around many good priests in high school and college. Now by doing a little bit of pastoral work myself in that summer experience, I discovered, as did the others, that I was good at it and liked it. In the image of the Cinderella story, "the shoe seemed to be a good fit." I had now decided as a young adult that I *really* wanted to be a priest and if the

Church didn't want me it would let me know. Life was much simpler after that.

I spent the following three summers with a team of Mexican priests and Cuban seminarians working with migrants who had come from south Texas to pick western Michigan strawberries, cherries, and cucumbers. It was a continuing schooling in life, Hispanic culture, and some of the challenges of social justice. We had a few confrontations with growers whose housing was way below the standards that our state had recently legislated.

Since others in the class had undertaken different summer assignments, when we returned to school there were shared stories about voter registration in the south and work in the inner city. John Clark had started the Peter Claver Center as an outreach to the black community in Jackson, Michigan. Some worked in anti-poverty programs in Detroit, while others had once again gone to Mexico. It was a very lively interchange among young men of high ideals. The harsh realities of institutional poverty we had experienced became part of a political climate where the dreams of the Great Society now clashed with the death and destruction of Vietnam.

By the day of college graduation in 1965, most of us in the class were seeking our own niches in life and communities where we could love and be loved. While many of us continued our seminary studies, several men left to pursue other careers and the possibilities of marriage. There were about fifteen of us from that original high school class of 150 who went on to study theology. A few studied in Rome and Belgium, but most of us went on to St. John's Provincial Seminary, in the Detroit suburb of Plymouth, where we did our graduate studies in theology. There we were taught by members of the Society of St. Sulpice, Sulpicians, another group of gifted priests whose special calling was seminary education and formation.

That summer before my studies in theology began, I made a weekend retreat called a Cursillo. I observed carefully how the priest served as chaplain during a Cursillo, even though it was up to the Lay Director to organize and carry out the weekends. That method was to become my model of how a priest should usually operate most effectively. The trick was to be not so much an organizer as an enabler and support person. Such an approach later seemed to be the thrust of Vatican II pastoral theology. When we began our study of *Lumen Gentium, The Dogmatic Constitution on the Church*, in the fall of 1965 in our theology classes at St. John's, it all fell into place for me. My personal vocation in having a purpose in life and doing good was now spelled out very clearly by the Church, in both theory and practice. My role as priest was to be a catalyst for change in helping to bring about an educated and inspired laity. Lay persons were to assume their proper roles in working for peace and justice in our society.

This document on the Church was the foundation, but the other Vatican II documents would specifically address issues surrounding priests, laity, religious, ecumenism, scripture, liturgy, and religious freedom. *Gaudium et Spes, On the Church in the Modern World*, was a fantastic analysis of the interplay between the Church and the world and the need to fight for social justice. My personal sense of vocation and calling was already taking a specific shape through my involvement in the migrant ministry; and I was receiving a blueprint for how to carry it out in my life as a priest. I enjoyed being on the cutting edge and was looking forward to the challenge ahead.

Ordination and Those First Years

After ordination I spent my first seven years in and around Flint, Michigan. Two of my classmates were nearby. George Wesolek was assigned to a parish on the western side of Flint, a better part of town. John Clark was part of a novel pastoral team approach that covered a middle class white parish, an aging Slovak parish, and a black parish. We all had the opportunity to try to put some of our dreams into practice as we got our feet wet.

It was both a frustrating and exciting time for the Church as a whole. As an individual I shared in that strange mixture of hope and despair. Many of us had high expectations coming from our vision of a post-Vatican II Church; but we had low success rates in moving that vision into a real world that was slow to change. The Church had a heavy institutional investment in Catholic grade and high schools, many conservative pastors were firmly in place, and there was a lot of anger in the black and Hispanic community. The divisive war in Vietnam was tearing apart our country, and lay people were trying to make sense of a new style of Church. Any one of those forces was a huge challenge in itself but the combination was formidable if not impossible. It is no wonder that the time of the greatest exodus from the priesthood was in the late 60's and early 70's.

There were three operating principles that I had "absorbed" through my training and they became a core focus for my own vision and energies.
1) Lay collaboration meant a serious effort at parish councils, sharing a vision and shaping the future.
2) Adult education meant Cursillos, Marriage Encounters, weekend training, and the formation of a core group of lay leaders in Bible studies and a spirituality that flowed from it.
3) Reading the signs of the times and identifying with the "joys, hopes and sorrows of the poor" were actions that flowed from the Gospels, Vatican II, and the Church's long tradition of social justice activism, sometimes referred to as one of our Church's best kept secrets.

In the downtown Flint parish, we had an active parish council. The other priests worked with the Administration, Education, and Liturgy Committees while I was given the challenge of Parish Life (social events and communications) and the Christian Service Commission. I claim no great accomplishments in those areas. Nonetheless, we made an effort to revive an annual summer Bible school where we brought in the black children of the area and then visited their parents at home to try to open our doors to them. We set up a summer recreation program as an outreach to the teenagers in the area as well.

One of my pastor's constant refrains was that you needed to maintain your facilities with pride, give good service, and let people know what you were doing. While there, I began a parish newsletter that I continued in other parishes for the next twenty-three years. I enjoyed teaching Scripture classes for adults and this too became a constant throughout my ministry and to this day. I discovered a hunger for the Bible among the laity, although it seemed confined to a chosen few.

After three years in the city, I continued to focus on some of these same priorities in the gorgeous setting of a country-suburban parish in Fenton. That parish had twice as many families as my previous parish, most of them with young children. The pastor had assembled a fine staff, and there was a whole different dynamic compared to the urban parish. I found it a lot of fun. After the fall of Saigon in 1975, our parish adopted a Vietnamese family that found a new home in America. This was a special joy because many of our neighboring parishes had selected members of the same family (parents, in-laws, cousins, etc.). They all made us welcome at their joyful family gatherings. It was somewhat reminiscent of my college days with migrant workers, and I was very much at home.

On a personal level, during those years I enjoyed playing a piano that I had purchased. I attended some plays and got together with family members and friends. I took great delight in joining a hockey league, skiing, and learning to sail. I developed some strong and lasting friendships with certain couples in the parish that remain to this day. It was a good life but there was pain as well. Some of the pain came from losing four of my Lansing Diocese priest-classmates within five years of our ordination. Was the attraction to a wife and family a fleeting or a permanent feeling in my own heart?

Cristo Rey (1976 – 1986)

In December of 1975 Bishop Kenneth Povish came to head the Diocese of Lansing. The following month I went to a Priests' Senate meeting to try to get a sense of his priorities. I almost fell off my chair when he announced that parish council development, the formation of a Diocesan Pastoral Council, and a special outreach to the poor would be his top priorities. Upon discovering my interest in those areas, he asked me to be in charge of revising and updating temporary parish council guidelines for the diocese and to help him form the Diocesan Pastoral Council. In June of 1976 he asked me to

leave my comfortable suburban parish and take over Cristo Rey
Church in Lansing. Seeing my reluctance, he said: "Tom, you are
young. You need a challenge!" Only later did I appreciate the truth of
that observation. Over the next ten years I saw him somewhat
regularly at our Monday priest luncheons and at some occasions at his
residence, where two of my best buddies were in residence. He had
wonderful vision, a great sense of humor, and an amazing ability to
connect with people from all walks of life. In addition he was
personally affirming of me. Since I had made somewhat of a sacrifice
to take an unwanted post, I felt that in the future I could call on him
for full support when the time was right.

In the early 60's I had been around Cristo Rey as a seminarian
working with migrants. I spent some time in the parish itself. Harvey
Cox had just written *The Secular City*. Many of us in the seminary
had read it and concluded that the social mission of the church was its
primary mission. At the time, the pastor of Cristo Rey had decided
that Hispanics badly needed education, jobs, health service, credit
unions, and counseling more than a Spanish church. So, when the
parish plant was razed to make room for highway construction, the
big questions became: (1) Are we needed? (2) What form should we
take? (3) Where do we go? The decision was made to take the
operation to north Lansing, where the primary focus would be on
serving social needs as "Cristo Rey Community Center." The Center
would also contain a chapel to be a kind of way station to get
Hispanics into their area parishes. It was a great idea but the pastoral
part never took off. After ten years there was just a remnant of about
fifty families that held together as the parish. When I arrived as
pastor, we had to either sink or swim, because we couldn't go on in
the same way.

One of my first actions upon arrival was to kneel down in the chapel
with a feeling of helplessness and pray: "Lord, you put me here, so I
am relying fully on your power to help me make good things happen
or we are in deep trouble." I have to admit that in the back of my
mind was the thought that nobody would be too critical if we failed,
since priests weren't lining up to take this spot. For the next year and
a half I did a lot of listening and tried to identify some potential

parish leaders. In February of 1979 we moved into our own church. Here the parish was truly reborn. It became a center for spiritual renewal, community awareness, and a broad network of personal friendships and what became to be known as Small Christian Communities.

There were two key events in my "Spanish Church education." One was taking part in the Segundo Encuentro in Washington in the summer of 1977 with a gathering of Hispanic leaders from around the country. Listening to their stories and experiences inspired me to try some things back in Lansing. Then, in 1978 I took a three-week intensive formation course in pastoral ministry at the Mexican American Cultural Center (MACC) in San Antonio. During the next eight years, we started *Quinceaneras*, Sweet 15 celebrations for girls coming of age. We revived a tradition of Christmas *Posadas*, where we would go from house to house on the nine days prior to Christmas for prayer and sharing as we celebrated the journey of Mary and Joseph to Bethlehem. We developed an annual Good Friday procession on the riverfront that was open to the whole community.

We started an annual Fiesta that was a fundraiser and community wide event. During the Fiesta we would always tell people: "If you like our party, you will love our church." This became another means for our growth. We sponsored an annual Passover potluck meal with a Jewish/Spanish overlay. Every year we formed a nice class of adults who were not baptized or missed out on their confirmation. Our Easter Vigil was a joyous celebration when we baptized them by full immersion using a baptismal tank we had inherited from the Baptists. We had an active senior group, and many young people who got involved as well. We were family in the best sense. Many of our leaders began taking summer courses at the Mexican American Cultural Center in San Antonio. Borrowing an idea from San Antonio, we established a state-wide Hispanic Choir Festival where ten other Spanish church choirs from around the state would gather on a Saturday in May for a kind of jam session in which we each shared some of our best songs, enjoyed a meal together and had a teaching on the role of the choir in the liturgy. We had such an enthusiastic response from the other parishes that the custom continued by rotating this day and having a different church host us each year.

During a sabbatical in Madrid in 1981, I had an experience of personalizing and reflecting on the Nicene Creed. Out of this experience I was inspired when I returned to try to get my leaders to write their own Credos. After my return, I collaborated with a parishioner who was a cartoonist; and we developed twenty-five booklets a year in Spanish over the next three years. These booklets consisted of a single sheet of 8x11 paper folded into four pages. They contained drawings and a brief summary of the points we were covering in our presentations, with some questions for discussion. The culmination was a process where the participants wrote their own personalized CREDO, which they then shared with the group. The illiterate were able to speak their beliefs to a friend, who in turn put them down on paper. Later we had these typed and framed for display in church and gave each author a copy for his or her home. When members of other denominations knocked on their door they could now take their CREDO down from the wall and explain their own beliefs to their guests. This obviously came from the heart, and it gave me more pleasure than anything I had ever done. Their story was in place. I just provided the vehicle for them to share it.

During my last three years at Cristo Rey, I was a participant in a Doctor of Ministry program through St. Mary's Seminary in Baltimore. This got me reading again in a way I had not found time to do since my seminary days. My major project was an expansion of some of my materials from CREDO in a new format suited for small group discussions. My publisher sold over 6,000 of these booklets in the United States and in El Salvador, where I later did some work. There are motivational writers and speakers today who encourage people to tap the potential of the "giant within." Through the power of the Holy Spirit and the inspiration of some powerful mentors along the way, these projects came about. One of the things I learned over the years is that everyone has a story of their dreams and the price they paid to make them come true.

The longer I was involved in Hispanic ministry the more I promoted the theme "*Yo soy hispano y catolico – orgulloso de mi raza y mi religion.*" ("I am Hispanic and Catholic – proud of my race and religion.") Over the years my own Irish roots have come to the fore, and one of my prized possessions today is a license plate from Cristo Rey which has the Mexican flag with a shamrock superimposed. I am proud of those Irish roots, but I have grown immensely through my immersion in Spanish culture. I would like to think I am more Catholic because of that experience. There is a lot of "warrior" in me. The hammer (not a nail) was often at work in my life, and my belief is that there is something in me as a man that cries out to be a creator. Two of those creations are the CREDO series and the community from which they came. Thirteen years after my departure, Cristo Rey had outgrown its old facility and purchased a complex twice as large to accommodate the growing community.

In 1986, Msgr. Tom Kleissler invited me to join the gifted staff of the International Office of RENEW in Plainfield, New Jersey. Tom had begun RENEW in Newark, and it achieved such great success that people came knocking on his door to learn how to replicate the experience throughout the world. I now had the opportunity to work in the development of Small Christian Communities in English and Spanish across the country and in two dioceses in El Salvador. My training under Fr. Jerry Fraser at Sacred Heart Seminary in the early 60's had grown into sharing in an exciting vision of Church as part of a movement that had global dimensions. My move to New Jersey and a totally new kind of work was both stimulating and traumatic. While I looked forward to a new challenge, I did not realize how much I would miss family, friends, and especially parish life. I was now part of a team of fifteen men and women from across the country that worked out of a center to provide inspiration, organization, and support for local diocesan efforts to develop communities of prayer, Bible sharing, and social action in each parish in their area. We would have a three year contract with a diocese in which we would come in at specified times to offer training for their diocesan staff and then go out into parishes with them to help them do evaluations and prepare for the next season of RENEW with their people.

During the years from 1986-1989 I worked in dioceses in English and

Spanish in Massachusetts, North Carolina, Tennessee, Texas, and California. Back in New Jersey, I was part of a writing process where we reworked our original materials from the late 70's to make sure that we were theologically accurate and to incorporate suggestions from the participants. RENEW had taken on world-wide dimensions; and during the summer we did intensive training on site for diocesan staff who came to us from Africa, England, Australia, New Zealand, Guam, Samoa, and El Salvador. Their stories were incredible and it was a gift and joy to be part of the dynamics of the interaction of such gifted and educated people. I now had the opportunity to see the Church up close and personal on a global scale but using a method that I had helped fashion on a local level. I was most impressed with the vitality of the Church in places like Raleigh and Nashville, where Catholics had previously been very small in number but were now experiencing rapid growth due to population shifts and the hard work of local parishes. A high point of this period was making two trips to work with people in El Salvador while a civil war was in progress.

Closing a Chapter

In July of 1989 I returned to pastor a parish in the inner city of Jackson, Michigan, according to my agreement with my bishop. In the first month of my return, Bishop Povish gathered the priests of our area for a "listening session" on our suggestions for diocesan and parish renewal. I was amazed at the vocal and unanimous consensus of about fifteen of us that there had to be a change in the rule of priestly celibacy if we were to attract younger men to lead in the Church. In many ways that Church was very vibrant at the grass roots level but was becoming aging and sickly in terms of priestly leadership. This was not an especially radical group of priests. I had come to the point where it did not make much sense to me to even bother discussing the issue since nothing was going to happen. The bishop, however, was very honest in asking his priests their primary concerns, listening attentively to them, and promising that he would relay that message to the Vatican. I tried to be very careful to not become too involved in the discussion because it was such a deep and personal issue with me. While we expressed our concerns in private, in public we felt bound to maintain a positive aura of hope and confidence. I was, however, a strong believer in the adage that you made the best of a bad situation and did the best you could on a local level. Accordingly, I rolled up my sleeves and went to work.

I was replacing a good man who never accepted the vision of Vatican II and who had not been well for ten years. We had a staff of thirty, many of whom were quite good, six aging buildings, a mid-sized K-6 school. There was a lot of catching up to do on deferred maintenance of the buildings, a regular message to write for the Sunday bulletin, and meetings with core staff (school principal, CCD director, priest associate, outreach worker, deacon, and liturgist).

Our challenge was to maintain services to long time parishioners and to work to attract new members outside of our geographical area through what we had to offer. We had a beautiful old church, and so we concentrated on our music and community spirit to attract more people. We began a stewardship program to raise our income, while continuing various existing fundraisers and adding an annual parish festival. We began a quarterly newsletter, Cursillos, Bible studies, and faith sharing groups in homes. My priest associate and I worked with the parish council and its committees of education, liturgy, finance, and social concerns. We developed an active group for the Rite of Christian Initiation of Adults (R.C.I.A.) and brought a new spirit to the parish.

My description is a personal one, and I am not trying to suggest that my own efforts were all that special. Many priests in the diocese handled a load that was heavier than mine and I salute them. Part of the strategy that many of them used to deal with these realities, however, was to develop a strong "filtering process" in which they simply set aside ninety percent of these concerns and focused on what they could do reasonably well with a limited amount of time and energy. As a result we saw a significant drop in the development of parish councils, in involving parishioners in helping to set some direction for the parish, and in any serious efforts at evangelization.

In spite of the education and development of many excellent lay staff people, in my judgment we are still prisoners of a system in which too much depends upon the pastor. We are losing our vision of implementing the Second Vatican Council on a parish level because of a lack of vision on the part of our bishops, the diminishing numbers of priests, their lack of skills in leading a parish, and their lack of energy to do much beyond keeping the ship afloat and retaining their health and sanity. In my own life as a priest, I experienced a sense of failure in an impossible situation that was surely compounded by my own limitations and identifying my personal worth with a priestly identity that was all consuming. My own longing for a personal relationship, for friendship and love in a marriage were part of the problem ("let's pretend") and not the solution in a Church setting. Rather than continue in such a situation, I concluded that it was better for me to leave and get on with my life.

Thus, in Holy Week of 1992, I found myself closing a major chapter in my life. I had spent twelve years of preparation for the priesthood, which led to 23 years of priestly service, 35 years in all. It was a very painful decision to leave that life and calling. Probably the biggest pain I bore in leaving was from the personal guilt. I had made a sacred promise that I could no longer keep. I failed where I had never failed before in my vocation. In addition, I had let down family, friends, and parishioners who had given me their love, trust, and encouragement. Why? As I approached my birthday that year, I was torn by two numbers. I was two years away from my silver anniversary of ordination, which was very important to me. I was also getting older, fifty was fast approaching, and I was becoming more depressed. I looked at a life ahead of me without a marriage partner but with impossible job expectations. I felt a cloud from the public surrounding me, a public that wondered whether I was celibate or gay or perhaps even a pedophile.

Celibacy was a relic of another age, far from life-giving to me and a good number of my priest friends. It was turning many of us into peculiar old bachelors who, as a group, were not very healthy, physically or mentally. When we were preparing for ordination and accepting celibacy, we discussed why the Church asked this of its priests. When the subject of *total availability to service* came up, one of our professors raised the question: "Is this a more demanding job than that of being president of the United States? Presidents seem to combine a demanding job, marriage and family. Was priesthood that much more difficult?" For me the answer was no. I can honestly say that I have always had love in my life, but somehow I needed the particular love that only marriage and family can bring.

Just before Holy Week, I met with my bishop and informed him of my decision. I was a basket case of guilt and tears, since I felt I had let down a man who had been extra supportive of me and my ministry in the sixteen years we had worked together. My biggest fear was that he would put some roadblocks in my path, asking that I take some time or do some things that would prolong the agony. Imagine my surprise when he responded simply, "Tom, you have given 23 years of your life in good priestly service and it sounds like it is time to move on. Here are the benefits you will get in your transition. Your retirement pension will be 23/40th of your normal retirement at age 70 based on your years of service." I couldn't believe what I was hearing, since I had not given much thought to retirement benefits. I loved the priesthood but I also wanted to grow as a man and marry. The two were not compatible. My bishop had just taken a five hundred-pound weight off my shoulders and I was a free man. I walked out of his office on a cloud, having made one of the most significant passages in my life.

At the end of June my two older brothers drove over to take part in the last Mass that I offered. We then left for a round of golf and lunch. I did not expect this gesture of support on their part, but it was very moving to me. I was much happier that day than they were. My big brothers stood by me, even though they had some serious doubts about the course I was choosing for my life. During that time, my life was on fast forward. I said my goodbyes, packed my bags, made a temporary move to my brother's house, found an apartment in New Jersey, moved my belongings (including my baby grand piano), found a job, and made new friends.

Once I arrived in New Jersey, I felt a physical and mental peace that I had not felt in years. I was amazed at how cluttered my mind had been with the details of running a parish and how all-consuming that task was. There actually had been a slight physical quivering in my body that soon gave way to a new tranquility. I had not anticipated this but gladly embraced it. I did not realize how much mental baggage I had been carrying around in trying to run a parish and function as a priest. The gradual unloading of that baggage was even more liberating than I had imagined.

That summer I returned to New Jersey to establish myself and pursue a relationship. Valerie is a vivacious, fun-loving Italian-American with lots of energy and a deep spirituality. We married in October of the following year and moved to North Jersey with two of her three children (two sons, 14 and 22). Her daughter chose to get an apartment of her own at this time although we were very much together as a family. Marriage into a ready-made family comes with its own blessings and challenges; but we have enjoyed both together.

For priests who consider marriage an easier path, I now have a bit of a laugh. There are major challenges for a man and woman forming a new life together. The addition of children can raise the stress level considerably. The results, however, have been most gratifying for me. As I now observe our three grandchildren, I can see that children have minds of their own from day one and are capable of adding monumental stress to a marriage. Thank God for the love, joys, pleasures, and blessings which flow from that union to help keep the family strong.

As I made my transition from the priesthood to married life, I often reflected on Joseph Campbell's advice: "Follow your bliss." There is also an Irish proverb that says: "Where your heart is, your feet will follow." I came to the conclusion that I would still try to live my life in accord with the vision of Jesus and as a man of faith willing to fight for those on the margins of our society. It is even more exciting and fulfilling with a good woman at your side. My quest continues and my journey is the same in many ways, but along a rather different path.

Life as a Married Man and Reflections on the Priesthood Today

In the summer of 2008 I had the opportunity to reconnect with about fifteen of my old priest friends back in Michigan. Seven of us gathered for dinner one night and it was a great joy for me to be with them and feel a strong bond of friendship and support that was still present sixteen years after my leaving priesthood and the area. Most of them are retired now and it was fun to share old stories, new experiences, and their current adventures. Many of them shared the joys of priesthood but their frustrations with a new generation of young priests who did not appreciate the vision of Vatican II but followed a new path that seemed to emphasize personal devotions and the importance of the clerical state.

In the past ten years I have worked for a pharmaceutical company, sold real estate, done project work for a diocese and church organization, developed my own church consulting business, served as a parish business manager, taught theology and scripture in adult education in parishes and through our local library, taught Spanish, philosophy and the American Experience in four universities as an adjunct professor, and worked as a therapist in Spanish for a "Strengthening Families Program" in an urban setting. This has been quite a contrast to a career of 23 years in Church work with a single steady employer, food, housing, benefits and a regular paycheck. While I have been comfortable in secular occupations, my heart has remained in Church work.

We have discovered a local parish with a very supportive, wise, and enabling pastor. Valerie has served as a lector and participant in parish life, while I have plunged in by developing a parish web site, establishing a parish newsletter, organizing publication of a parish pictorial directory, teaching adult education sessions, working with a ministry of Small Christian Communities, and establishing an overnight retreat for the men of the parish. We are fortunate and proud to be part of a loving and caring community of believers. Another ministry which is really more my therapy has been serving in our parish choir under the direction of a musically talented and prayerful director of music.

Occasionally I return for a visit with Valerie to Cristo Rey. I am no longer "Father Tom." There is a saying in Spanish: "Cuando tenia dinero me llamaban Don Tomas. Ahora que no tengo nada, soy

Tomas no mas." ("When I had money they used to call me Mr. or Fr. Tom. Now, they just call me Tom.") That sums it up well for me and I rejoice in being a brother to my good friends.

While leaving priesthood is still somewhat painful to me, my new life has been a gift and a joy. Valerie and I have worked together in preparing couples for marriage. I have been fortunate in finding good priests who welcome and use my gifts according to the needs that they are seeing. In recent years I have worked through the Center for Lifelong Learning in our local library in coordinating and team teaching courses in religion, philosophy, and medical ethics, drawing from the gifts of rabbis, ministers, and imams from the surrounding areas. We have received a broad response and this brought me great joy. In many ways it is easier to bring people to these topics through the library than through the parish.

As a man, I am much more settled in my identity as a person who can express that love in a sexual way in loving my wife. The Church has much wisdom in the area of marriage and family life which Valerie and I enjoy sharing now as grandparents. In the year 2007 I turned 65 and started a "semi-retirement." I have several classmates who are now enjoying a retirement that is not far off for me and Valerie. I find it scandalous and unbelievable that the median age of our priests is now 63, priests who continue to take on more jobs with less help and a growing Catholic population. There is no other group of people that I know who comprise such an endangered species. My heart aches for good men doing impossible jobs with a limited support system. There are more priests in the United States who are over 90 than are under 30! That is pretty pathetic for a Church which is vigorous in so many other ways.

We grew up in a system where we received a marvelous education but limited opportunities for psycho-sexual development. The vast majority of men coming through that system have performed well and are responsible for tremendous accomplishments in the Church in the United States. Some individuals have turned to pedophilia and have caused a huge amount of damage to our Church. It is our own 9/11 Twin Towers tragedy. In its past response to pedophilia abuses, the Church had worked for the rehabilitation of these men, but this is now seen as a cover-up. To me that effort was consistent with our belief that there is no such thing as an unforgivable sin. Many dioceses have failed to protect our children, however, by continuing to give such men new assignments after unsuccessful efforts at rehabilitation. This pseudo-solution will not continue, as we move into a policy of zero tolerance in not allowing abusers to remain in ministry. While such incidents are not caused by celibacy, they are a symptom of a serious problem with our current system. We need good, healthy, married *and* celibate priests. That's why I have been an active participant in CORPUS, which advocates a married priesthood and provides a gathering space for those of us who have left clerical ministry. Today, of those who leave the priesthood in their 30's or 40's, most seem to prefer to make a clean break and not bother with a group such as ours and the battles we wage. Perhaps I have unconsciously become part of another endangered species!

Over the years I have maintained close personal friendships with three of my classmates, and their support and understanding has been very helpful to me. Valerie and I can better appreciate how our own children keep us young as we try to support them in the challenges of education, careers, relationships, finding a partner, and establishing a family. While they are often in another world with their music and movies, there is a particular joy we find in family, in our meals and special celebrations that we share with them and their friends.

In June of 2000, the McCloskey family gathered in Cincinnati for the twenty-fifth anniversary of my brother Pat's ordination to the priesthood. This gathering gave us the opportunity to do some story telling that always includes the gift of our parents, their strong faith and encouragement in our education, and the impact it has had on all our lives. Pat is a member of the Franciscan Order and has spent his priesthood teaching in a high school, serving in Rome at the Order's headquarters and currently as editor of the *St. Anthony Messenger*. This publication has the largest circulation of any Catholic magazine in the United States. We have stayed close over the years, and he is a good example of a religious order priest who has a strong supportive community in living out his own celibacy.

As I reflect at this point in my life I am struck with the image of the sculpture of Don Quixote and his faithful companion, Sancho Panza, that resides in the heart of the Spanish Plaza in Madrid. Don Quixote is a national icon in Spanish lore and his story was popularized in the Broadway musical *Man of La Mancha*. The two of them went forth to fight evil and live by the vision of a better world. Don Quixote was the warrior and man of impossible visions. Sancho was his faithful companion, more concerned about picking up the pieces following the last debacle, binding up his master's wounds, looking for the next meal, and finding a bed for the night.

Idealistic warriors do well to have practical caregivers at their side. Head and heart are two sides of the same coin. Sacred Heart Seminary provided me with the vision and the tools to try to combine warrior and caregiver in my own life, one that has had its own share of adventure. For some of us the limitations of the institutional Church have put up considerable restraints, even opposition to a dream we had been given. In many ways the class of 1965 was called to "dream the impossible dream" of reconciliation, social justice, progress for underdeveloped countries, and a renewed and vibrant Church where all could offer their gifts and share in a strong community of faith.

In Holy Week of 2002, on Good Friday, I decided to bake some "Easter bread" under my wife's careful supervision. We were sharing stories of past Easters. In one of my first parishes, I was introduced to the Polish custom of blessing Easter baskets in church. This recollection naturally led to others of my ten years in pastoring a Spanish church, where we had the custom of a public way of the cross along a beautiful river and finishing in the city streets of a predominantly poor and mixed population. Then it struck me – "It is a beautiful day and in an hour that same celebration begins in Passaic!"

Valerie agreed to finish the bread as I raced down to the location and joined the people at the third station. What a glorious celebration! Young and old, mothers pushing baby carriages, teenagers and grandparents, all carrying crosses from home and joining in the prayers and songs of Good Friday and our Lord's journey to the hill of Calvary. We were 1500 strong, marching down closed off streets in front of merchants and residents along the way who were looking out from their shops and apartments and bowing their heads in respect as we passed by. We alternated the prayers and songs from English to Spanish and followed the young people of the parish who wore robes and carried 14 large crosses at the head of the parade. I had done a little work with the pastor in the past, and he gave me a warm greeting as I congratulated him on a beautiful, prayerful, and moving ceremony. "Tom, what are you doing here?" he said. He was genuinely concerned about how I was doing, given my strange appearance. I was unshaven and a bit grubby after my mad dash to Passaic, and I am sure I looked more like a street person in need of some help. On my drive home I decided that the Holy Spirit must have brought me there.

Perhaps our leadership could listen to the voices of the people in the streets of Passaic and other Spanish communities across this country from New York to Los Angeles, Detroit to Miami and San Antonio. Part of personal and institutional growth is to admit past mistakes and take corrective action to develop some good strategies for keeping that faith alive with a strong and vibrant priesthood. I have a crazy dream that someday our bishops will listen to the voice of the people, sing this song, and chart a new direction so that this faith might grow and flourish.

"Peque, peque Dios mio, piedad Senor, piedad, si grandes son mis culpas mayor es tu bondad."

("I have sinned my God, send your mercy, although my sins are big ones, your mercy is even greater.")

Wandering Between Two Worlds

TALE OF A POLISH PRINCE
Edward L. Nowakowski

I began my training for the priesthood at Sacred Heart as a sophomore in high school in 1958. Previously I had attended St. Ladislaus, located in Hamtramck, Michigan, for grade school and one year of high school. As the name of the school and the city suggest, I come from a thoroughly Polish background. When I told my pastor I was going to attend Sacred Heart, he was disappointed and didn't have much to say to me for awhile. I was *supposed* to attend St. Mary's Seminary in Orchard Lake, which was the Polish national seminary, you see.

The reason I started as a sophomore was because I was a little late in deciding to go to the seminary. I "kind of" made my decision after graduating from the eighth grade. My uncle was a priest in the Lansing diocese. I observed the respect that he received from my family as well as the people of his parishes. In the Polish culture a priest was put on a pedestal. My father was thoroughly Polish and religious. What a way to be the "apple of his eye"! The priesthood afforded esteem and privilege.

Perhaps an example can best describe my feelings. I was an altar boy; and, as a result, I experienced more personally the prestige of the priesthood. Because of my father's influence and sense of pride, I was "a good altar boy" -- always punctual and knowing the Latin prayers well. As a result of being one of the best altar boys, I was often chosen to serve for funerals. Starting time for funeral Masses was typically between 9 AM and 11 AM. This meant that I would have to get out of school to serve those Masses or perhaps even arrive late for school. At times we would have to accompany the priest to the cemetery, which extended the "out-of-school" time. The frosting on the cake, so to speak, was that often the family would give each altar boy $5 for serving the funeral (more if it was a wedding). Such a deal! I got to be a person of privilege (and, as such, was always treated well), got out of school, and was paid. Not bad for a 12-year-old Polish boy.

Another great influence in my deciding to go the seminary was a priest by the name of Fr. Bob Werenski. When he came to our parish he was newly ordained, young and enthusiastic. He was thoroughly loved by the parishioners. I got to know him better because I was an altar boy. He was very kind and approachable, and when I got into a couple of jams (which is beyond the scope of this literary endeavor), he became my hero. He was the parish hero and a personal hero. There was no doubt priesthood was for me. He stayed at St. Ladislaus for about two years and then went off to get his doctorate in Sacred Scripture. Many years later, interestingly enough, Fr. Bob became my Scripture professor at St. John's Provincial Seminary for two semesters. He since has died.

At any rate, by the time my thinking about the priesthood turned to soup, I was late in applying for the seminary. My father and I talked to Fr. Ed Scheuerman, the Dean of Students. He suggested I attend St. Ladislaus High School for one year, then, if I still wanted to come to the seminary, I could enter as a sophomore. We all agreed. Needless to say, my decision brought me a great deal of respect from the pastor, the nuns at school, and of course my family, including my uncle, the priest. I felt like the Polish Prince, at times to the detriment of my relationship with my sister, who wanted attention too.

My one-year at St. Ladislaus High was quite normal. I still maintained my relationships with classmates whom, for the most part, I had known since kindergarten. I didn't tell them that I would be going to the seminary, because that wasn't looked upon as a popular career choice among my high school friends; and I worried that I wouldn't be included in normal high school activities such as sports and dances. But I was a hero with the nuns, although they sometimes questioned my intentions because I didn't really act like someone who was planning on becoming a priest.

The seminary admission process appeared easy, basically consisting of an entrance exam along with letters of recommendations. The exam actually showed me I was smarter than I thought.

There were two types of students at Sacred Heart Seminary High School: day students and boarding students. I was a day student, taking the bus to school each day. Still it was an adjustment, because in the past I just walked a few blocks, and I was at school. The drop-off point at the other end of the bus line provided me with the opportunity for another adjustment. It was in a black neighborhood, and I had to walk about ten blocks to Sacred Heart. The area is where the 1967 riots took place in Detroit. But I had only one incident in three years. Needless to say, I didn't like the long walk in the wintertime, carrying what felt like a ton of books.

Being a day student felt like I was attending a Catholic Central or a DeLaSalle High School, which are all boys' central high schools. I arrived at school, and after school I went home to Hamtramck. I didn't get involved in school activities much. The boarding students had their own friendships and culture. The day students came from the entire metropolitan Detroit area; but since I didn't have a car, I had little contact after-hours with other day students. One of the fellows with whom I *did* develop a friendship, Jerry Nadolski, years later became my brother-in-law. And all along I thought he was coming to the house to see me!

I was too provincial. I went to Sacred Heart but maintained my closed cultural life style. I continued to maintain my friendship with my old classmates at St. Ladislaus, attending sporting events and dances and other normal teen-age activities, like cruising Woodward Avenue. As I progressed at Sacred Heart, however, I found I had less in common with those friends, and some of the relationships deteriorated.

There was no doubt that going to Sacred Heart was academically more difficult. There were some very bright students in my class. I really had to study hard in order to maintain about a 2.8 average in high school. Most of the teachers were priests from the Archdiocese, and they were demanding. In fact one of the priests came to our house in Hamtramck to make sure that I had my own study area.

Looking back, my attendance at Sacred Heart Seminary High School was my first exposure to the outside world. My closed world of "Hamtramck" said I wanted to be a priest. When I pursued that calling, it meant that I had to leave that closed world that was Polish and narrow. But I sure didn't know what it meant to leave a closed world. Not yet, anyway.

In the fall of 1961, I began college at Sacred Heart Seminary. Things had been going well and I thought that I would just go on. The boarding experience seemed to be acceptable and got better as the years went on. I had to get used to starting school in September, with my next visit home, for all practical purposes, being the Thanksgiving Day vacation. The rest of the time was spent on campus and that time was pretty well scheduled. We had no cars. I was a healthy 18-year-old and confined. Needless to say, the social activities with my friends from St. Ladislaus soon began to disappear; and by the end of my college career, they were gone.

The classes were difficult, yet I was able to raise my GPA to 3.00. In order to keep occupied during my free time, I got involved in sports, such as intramural basketball. I learned how to play handball. Sacred Heart Seminary had some of the best indoor handball courts in the city. I also got involved in drama. Each class had to put on a play for the rest of the school. I tried out for a part, got it, and then it was practice, practice. The best thing about this was that the plays got me out in front of people and definitely helped me form some friendships. One of these friendships was with Phil Calcaterra, who was in charge of constructing the stage. This friendship would prove most important in my life and had consequences unforeseen at that time by either Phil or myself.

The big dramatic event at Sacred Heart was the Passion Play, staged for our families and for the general public on the two weekends

194

before Easter. I had parts in the Passion Plays for four years. During one of the performances, which was done in a theatre in the round environment, I was Caiphas. I was apparently so convincing that a lady from the audience started to hit me with her cane for taking part in the killing of Jesus. My family came to those plays, and they were proud of the "Polish Prince."

The first two years at Sacred Heart Seminary were pretty confining in that most of our activities were in house. During our junior and senior years, however, things began to open up due to the Vatican Council. We were encouraged to get involved in outside activities. There were various opportunities to do so, such as hospital visiting. I became involved in the Young Christian Students program (YCS). Today we would call them youth groups, with a spiritual component. I was able to sign out a car, go to various Catholic high schools and organize the students. As I recall, I was able to organize YCS groups in about fifteen high schools. The seminary was opening up, and I began to exercise my priestly calling.

Moving into the final two years at Sacred Heart Seminary was a major turning point, because it seemed that we were finally and formally moving toward our objective, the priesthood. We wore cassocks, collars, and birettas. The classes were not just "general" but more specifically geared to the priesthood -- ethics, metaphysics, and other courses in philosophy. The philosophy classes were to prepare us for the theology classes at St. John's Provincial Seminary. The basis for both was Thomism, which is based upon the writings of St. Thomas Aquinas and his commentators. Some of the classes were taught in Latin, with Latin textbooks. The Schola Cantorum, or choir, sung beautiful Gregorian chant and the liturgies were filled with ceremony. All of this led to a perpetuation of that special aura surrounding the priesthood. Further, all of it continued to fuel my fantasy. Lurking in the background, however, was the *aggiornamento* (updating) that was going on in the Church. At first I didn't see the need for the changes that were introduced by Vatican II. Although the Mass was in Latin, Polish songs were sung during the Mass in the parish I attended. I guess you'd have to say that the vernacular was already present, so I didn't see a reason to change things.

The "ante" certainly went up when I got home with the cassock and collar and biretta. My father was definitely proud, and I was given more respect and a greater role in the parish. I was no longer just an altar boy. I assumed the role of Master of Ceremonies at the great liturgies of Christmas and Easter at St. Ladislaus. I was able to hang around the rectory more with the priests. I was definitely getting there and with that came greater respect and notoriety. It was ego inflating. It felt like I was a doctor or lawyer, in a respected profession.

Graduation in 1965 meant that I was *really* on the way to fulfilling my dream. College was behind me, and I had "only" four more years to go before ordination and those boyhood visions would be made real.

When I entered St. John's Provincial Seminary in the fall of 1965, it was like regressing. Sacred Heart Seminary had really opened up because of the Vatican Council. But when I went to St. John's, it was as if I were a freshman in college at Sacred Heart all over again. Perhaps an example would best describe what I'm trying to say.

The first day of school, we got our room assignments, class schedules, and a glimpse of what life was going to be like at St. John's. There was a knock at my door, to which I responded, "Come on in." That's the way it was at Sacred Heart. But no one came in. After a period of silence, there was another knock, and I again said, "Come on in." No response. A third knock irritated me; and I got up to answer the door, thinking that it might be a classmate who just wanted to bother me. So I opened the door with an attitude and said, "What do you want?" Standing there was the rector of St. John's.

He said, " I smell smoke." That was an accurate observation, because I was holding a lit cigarette. He said, "You'll have to put that out, because we don't allow smoking in the rooms. You can only smoke in limited designated areas. Also there are only specific times during the day that you're allowed to smoke. I'll let you go this time because you're new, but don't let it happen again." He then left. I felt like an adolescent trying to sneak a smoke, but being caught by his parents. I had smoked at home since I was about 17 or 18 years old. Here I was,

196

22 years old, being told when and where I could smoke. The funny thing was that the rector was a smoker. For awhile St. John's took that same approach with other areas of our lives.

Again, I was back to coming to school in September, not getting home till Thanksgiving vacation, and having my day regulated in a closed society. There were no plays to keep me sane. But I learned how to play golf (the seminary had a nine-hole golf course surrounding it) and I ice skated in the winter on the pond that was on the eighth hole. The seminary had a professional woodworking shop. Phil Calcaterra was a master craftsman, and our relationship continued to develop. He taught me how to use the tools, and I made a chalet-type Christmas crib for my parents as a Christmas gift. In order to make some extra money, I set bowling pins (the seminary had a ten-lane bowling alley). And the food was much better.

The classes were difficult, all theologically oriented. We had "to read and translate" canon law, which was written in Latin. As I recall, I studied two years of Greek in order to understand the New Testament better. Some of my classmates were chosen to take Hebrew; but, unlucky me, I wasn't smart enough. Yet I was now in the Major Seminary, and that was the price I had to pay to become a priest. The classes were at least geared to my chosen profession.

My visions were furthered as I saw the fourth year students become deacons and shortly thereafter ordained as priests. There were various steps, or orders, that led up to the priesthood -- tonsure, acolyte, and several other minor orders, followed by subdeacon, deacon, and then priesthood. The progression meant I was moving along. By this time, I had lost all contact with my friends at St. Ladislaus High School; and I was so into the program that the subdiaconate (when one makes the promise of celibacy) didn't really seem to be a problem. My attention was diverted. As the time for each new order approached, some of the students left the seminary. Those that remained were of the same mind and focus. The culture of St. John's and the Roman Catholic Church of the time furthered my personal program, and I moved along. That was on one level.

On another level I was being de-toxed. That first year at St. John's, in order to keep them alive, I maintained some contact with the YCS groups that I had worked with at Sacred Heart. During that time my classmate Tony Locricchio approached me to work in the Church's anti-poverty program. This was part of President Johnson's Total Action against Poverty. The Church was granted several million dollars to run programs for the inner city, such as day camps and programs for juvenile delinquents. The Church's contribution was the donated use of their facilities, which for the most part were being underutilized because of the white members' flight to the suburbs.

Tony asked me to be a director of one of the day camps. I couldn't believe it. I certainly didn't feel I had the talent and ability to do something of that caliber. But he pointed out what I had accomplished with the YCS programs, which indicated to him that I did have that talent and ability. After several conversations with him, I decided to take the job, even though I had some real hesitation. All of a sudden I was responsible for approximately 600 black kids all day long, all of this in light of the Pennsylvania/Kercheval incident.

That incident occurred in 1966 and was a "rehearsal" for the 1967 Detroit riots, which were symptomatic of what was happening across the country. The Pennsylvania/Kercheval incident was a small "riot" that occurred on the east side of Detroit. Directors of the various programs met with city officials and the police department to develop contingency plans, that is, what to do with the kids if a riot broke out. In one sense it was ego inflating meeting the Chief of Police of the City of Detroit. I was an altar boy from Hamtramck, but my vision was quickly and forcibly expanded. Here was this Polish boy with his provincial Polish Catholic thinking at the cutting edge of a national social development. Perhaps this can be better explained by a very personal example.

The job for the poverty program took a lot of time. My father objected because it meant that I could no longer help him around the house painting, cutting the grass, and that he would have to do things himself. At twenty-two years old, I had my first rite of emancipation. "A man has to do what a man has to do." I had to stretch what I thought at the time was beyond my limits. It was one of the greatest experiences that I have ever had. I certainly came to understand the extent of racism in our country.

The Church loved the publicity that came with being responsive to the plight of the inner city. But it also meant that the Church had to stretch. It's like letting a cat loose in the house. The situation then has a life of its own. The Church was criticized for its social policy by the membership. There was also some administrative mismanagement of funds, which proved embarrassing. This ruffled some feathers in the local hierarchy, and did not make Tony very popular when he pointed out the Church's incompetence. His pursuit of the truth made Tony a threat to the local institutional Church.

Tony's whistle blowing continued into our final years of classes at St. John's. It was also at the time that the Student/Faculty Council was formed, and I ended up becoming its president. The intention was to give the students a voice in what was happening in the seminary. The first and main issue was Tony. There were various small meetings at the Chancery offices as well as a big meeting when Cardinal Dearden came to the seminary to confront what amounted to a student rebellion. Needless to say, Tony was going to be asked to leave the seminary; but I think he saw the writing on the wall, and he decided to leave on his own. I found this situation personally difficult, especially since the Cardinal became quite irritated with me when I tried to stand up for what I felt was right. What I found out then was what the people of America discovered in 2002/2003 with the priest pedophile scandal. The institution had to cover up its mistakes to protect an image, and it would go to quite an extent to do so. This was an awakening for me, and my fantasy was tarnished. (As an aside, I felt that I must have gone to a different school, when all of the homosexuality and pedophilia in the priesthood surfaced. Some of those accused, even convicted, were priests I had gone to school with; yet I had no idea what they were doing at that time. Talk about being unconscious!)

Part of the training at St. John's was to take a work assignment in a parish to gain experience and understanding of what the priesthood would be like. My first assignment was to help a priest start a new parish. Needless to say, I immersed myself in the work, and my fantasy was brought back to life. Before I knew it, it was time to go back to school.

My second assignment was as a deacon. I was sent to a large parish with a high school. The pastor of the parish was a former chancellor of the Archdiocese, a sickly but wise man. A priest who was assigned to the parish was just a few years ahead of me, so I had a friend and mentor. I was now really "hyped" because as a deacon I could do more, such as preach and baptize. Preparations were being made in my home parish for my First Mass and reception. My father was on cloud nine.

The ordination was like a Polish wedding. I was treated literally as the Polish Prince. I certainly basked in the glow.

My first assignment was in Hazel Park with an old Irish pastor. The parish was dead because of its leadership. What the Cardinal had told me when he sent me there was to bring it back to life, and he would back me up. I wasn't too sure about the backing up part, when I remembered what happened to Tony. To give you an idea of my start there, another example is appropriate.

We were supposed to report to our assignments on a Wednesday, but I was also supposed to go to a Founder's Day event at St. Mary's of Orchard Lake with a classmate of mine. We were going to play golf, have dinner, and play some cards; and I knew I might be late coming in. So I came to the assignment on Tuesday to introduce myself, get a key to the rectory because I was going to be late, and of course to see what Mass I was going to have the next day. The pastor asked me when I would come in on Tuesday night. I told him probably after midnight. He told me that was not acceptable, that the boys (other assistant priests that were there before) had to be in by 9 PM. I told him I was not going to be in by 9 PM, and he said that he had no key for me. I then told him that I would not be in till some time on Wednesday, when I was to report. He finally gave me his key, and I came in after midnight. I hadn't been in by 9 PM since I was 12 or 13 years old.

The pastor gave me the job of handling the religious education program. I met with the lady who had previously done this, and she gave me two cardboard boxes that contained some paper, crayons, and few books. There was no money with which to run the program, except what was obtained through a 50/50 drawing by the usher's club. This was not going to work. So I consulted with my old friend Phil Calcaterra, who had left the seminary prior to subdiaconate and was a religious education director at a suburban parish.

At that time I found out that Phil was being let go by his pastor because Phil had developed cancer. I told Phil that as far as I was concerned he had another job, being religious education director at my parish. I then told my pastor that I needed a minimum of $15,000 to run the program and that I wanted to hire Phil as the Religious Education Director. The pastor told me that was not going to happen, so I told him I wouldn't handle the program. He told me that I was arrogant, wet behind the ears, and he was calling the Cardinal about my insubordination. I felt "confident" because of my earlier conversation with the Cardinal, so I told the pastor to call him. Apparently he did. I got the money and Phil was hired as Religious Education Director. The pastor retired the following June, after having a heart attack. Despite our confrontation, that old Irish pastor and I had developed a friendship. I went with him in the ambulance to the hospital when he had his heart attack. After he was stabilized, I went to see him. He said, "Ed, that was a close one. By the way, you got a cigarette?"

The new pastor was a little stiff but open, and he allowed me to exercise my priesthood and talent. The parish then just rocked and rolled. A team was formed that included Phil, the school principal, and one of the teachers at the school. The team, along with the youth group and others in the parish, put on the play *Jesus Christ Superstar* for the parish and community. A local juvenile delinquent (supposedly) played Jesus Christ.

I also got involved in the community of Hazel Park, with the Lions

Club and Youth Protection Committee. With some members of the community, I founded Threshold, which was an alcohol and drug abuse center. I wrote the program and obtained a grant from the city and county. An old building that was owned by the parish served as the site. Fr. Ed became the "Polish Prince" of Hazel Park. I was given the Citizen of the Year Award and received several other commendations. My father was extremely proud.

On March 1, 1975, my friend Phil died of cancer. We had been through a lot together as far as the parish went, but also as far as the cancer went. I got to know his wife, Penny, and their son Jeff. At times I would take Phil to the doctor, visit him at home or at the hospital, and tried to be supportive of Penny, who was also part of my social group at the parish. I vividly remember his funeral. Much more could be said here, but I feel that it would go beyond the scope and in a different direction than this article is intended. I truly lost a great friend. John Mulheisen, another classmate of mine from Sacred Heart, was then hired as religious education director to replace Phil.

Assignments by the Archdiocese were meant to last for about five years, and my term was supposed to be up. I also felt that it was time for me to move and do something different. I was transferred to William Beaumont Hospital as the chaplain. Beaumont Hospital is a large major metropolitan hospital (approximately 1,000 beds) in the Detroit area. I followed another classmate of mine, Bob Ruedisueli, who was there just a couple of years. The priest prior to him was an alcoholic. No longer was I the "Polish Prince" in Hamtramck, nor the local hero of Hazel Park. Instead I felt like Fr. Mulcahy in the TV series *M*A*S*H*.

It took me several years to build up my credibility for the chaplaincy program. It meant showing up for countless emergency calls and working with patients who were sick for the first time to people who had chronic conditions and were in the process of dying. The emergency room was very active. There was no doubt that the price of the priesthood went up, and often times I was sleep deprived. I set up a program of volunteers from various parishes in the area to help in giving Communion to the patients, because there was no way I could do it all. I got involved in the Recreation Committee at the hospital in order to get to know more employees and gain credibility. As part of closing my "credibility gap," I set up group trips to Tiger Stadium for those employees and played basketball with a group of residents.

Eventually, I gained their confidence and was invited to in-house Mortality and Morbidity conferences and ethics conferences. I felt I was being included in practicing team medicine. The problem that arose for me was that my education was limited. The Thomistic framework that I had been given in the seminary didn't connect with my current work. While I was in Hazel Park, I finished a Master's degree in Religious Studies; but I still thought I needed to go back to school, especially in light of the fact that I was dealing with a highly educated parish. I started to go to the University of Detroit for their M.A. program in Psychology, later transferring to Wayne State University in the Master's of Social Work program. I was then a full-time chaplain and a full-time student. I was able to convince the administration that another Catholic chaplain was needed, and another chaplain was hired, a Franciscan priest. That made things a little bit more humane.

I had maintained many of my social contacts with a group from the parish in Hazel Park. One of its members was Penny, Phil's wife. My contact with the group was irregular because of my job and school. In 1980, things changed. I was involved in a racquetball tournament at the hospital, and it was to be co-ed. I could have asked several interested nurses, but I needed to maintain propriety. So I asked Penny to do me a favor and be my partner. I felt "safe" in our relationship. I thought that we would lose, and that would be it. But that was not the case. We won several rounds, and my feelings toward her (and much to her surprise) changed. "Ed, I feel like you've just been a brother and not someone to date." Still, our relationship changed, and we started to date. I also had a positive relationship with Jeff, her son. I had known him since his birth.

Going to school, working at the hospital, and dating Penny, I spent less time at home. My father became suspicious. As I was about to tell him what was really going on, he had a massive heart attack and died in February, 1981. Maybe he had guessed what was going on. I preached at his funeral, which was very difficult.

In May, 1981, I graduated from school, resigned my position from the hospital, and got a job at the Wayne County Circuit Court, in the Family Division ("Divorce Court"). The job entailed making custody and parenting time evaluations for the judges. Part of the irony is that one of the judges is the Honorable Michael J. Callahan, who was a classmate at Sacred Heart and is also a former priest. During that time, I had a 45-minute meeting with Cardinal Szoka. He said that he would be willing to give me some time off with pay and that someone would be contacting me from the Office of the Clergy. But no one called or followed up.

In August 1982, Penny and I were married, and I moved to her house in Hazel Park, where we lived until 1983. We then moved to Southfield, a northern suburb of Detroit. The reason for that move was that Jeff, who is a very good athlete, wanted to go to Brother Rice High School, which was noted for its great sports programs. He played football and baseball for the school. He subsequently got a scholarship to play baseball at Indiana University and after his senior year was drafted by the Yankees. He played rookie ball with Derek Jeter. Jeff was a catcher; but because he could throw the ball well to second base, the Yankees wanted him to be a pitcher. He was unfortunately injured; and during his third year, he was released. He then returned to Indiana University, finished his degree, and became an assistant baseball coach at Indiana University. He is now married, has two children, and is the head baseball coach at the University of Hartford in Connecticut. As you can tell by my talking about Jeff, I really got into my marriage and family life. As a husband and father, I never looked back.

In the fall 1984, I was asked by a priest friend to provide some counseling services at his parish. He said he had been getting a number of requests but had no time. Further, some people couldn't afford a fee. I could use the parish offices rent-free and charge what I wanted. I agreed. Before I knew it, word got around; and I was providing counseling services to several parishes in the area and had to get a partner. I subsequently limited my private practice, providing individual, marriage, and family counseling services to three parishes. I'm a licensed Marriage and Family Counselor.

I began at Sacred Heart Seminary to become a priest, but I sure didn't think I'd be exercising my "priesthood" this way. What is really an irony is that I gave the "sermon" at all of the Masses on the December 7th weekend in the parish that I attended in Detroit. I was asked to do so by the Liturgy Committee. Much to my surprise, some people who attended were from the parish I worked at in Hazel Park; and they were glad to see me, telling me that I hadn't "lost my touch." My priesthood was still being exercised but surely not in the way that the Polish boy thought it would be – not with a cassock and collar and biretta, but with a shirt and tie, by a married man with a son.

I've since retired from the Court (October, 2002), and my private practice (August, 2006). In 2006, Penny and I built a home in the woods in West Michigan, one mile from Lake Michigan. Penny is an interior designer, with an active practice. I went back to school to develop a new interest, that of graphic design and digital photography. Thus far I have had one exhibition of my work, with others in the planning stages. Since "retirement," I can't believe how quickly the time goes.

Sacred Heart Seminary provided me with an excellent basic education. I was able to go on and get a Master's degree in Religious Studies from the University of Detroit and also a Master's in Social Work from Wayne State University. Not only was I provided an education but also the discipline necessary to further that education and then practice my profession with integrity.

Sacred Heart Seminary provided me with a brother-in-law, Jerry Nadolski, as well as my wife. Jerry has been my brother-in-law for close to 40 years and definitely has been a important part of my family. Because of my friendship with Phil Calcaterra at Sacred Heart Seminary, and the later crossing of our profound paths, I married

Penny, his widow. My marriage to Penny and raising Jeff, "my son," has truly and profoundly enriched my life. Sacred Heart provided me with extremely close personal relationships.

My life is certainly different than I originally thought it would be, but it is also very full. Maybe the same thing is happening to the Church today. I, too, had to let go of the thoughts and ideas of Polish Prince/Priest thinking. I bare no ill will toward the Church and have no ax to grind; but sometimes I feel sorry for the Church, because it uses the past to prevent the present revelation of God from dawning. It is trying to use time against God. The choice is not whether to see the past or the present; the choice is merely whether or not to see God's continued revelation. What the Church has chosen to see has cost her vision. Yet we say that the saints of old had visions. Maybe that's how they got to be saints.

Sacred Heart Seminary prepared me for a different kind of priesthood than I thought. But judging from the events of my life, it turned out (unknown to my seminary professors and to me) that it prepared me for a contemporary priesthood that is based on more indestructible and unchangeable values. Sacred Heart Seminary provided me with the foundation to go from illusionary thinking to maturity. I have not practiced my formal "ordained" priesthood since I resigned, and I have no interest in doing so. Yet, I feel that my practice of the "priesthood" is more expansive, an archetype for the future, truly more. It was not always easy making the transition, nor is it for the Church, obviously. But when I "let go, and let God," it worked out better than I thought. It has helped me to bring to completion the God inside of me and I'm still at it. That would be my advice for the Church. That cassock of old, though, could have been a casket for me. Much more could be said, but that's for the next book.

A LIFE IN DIALOGUE
Eugene J. Fisher

Late on Friday of the third week of Lent, 2003, through an article in Catholic News Service (CNS), I learned what had happened in Rome a short time before. During the weekly Lenten homily given by the pope's personal preacher to the Holy Father and the Roman Curia, my name had come up, and not positively. The Papal Preacher, Fr. Cantalamessa, had gone out of his way to caution against what he felt were the deviant theological views of some Catholics who questioned the wisdom in our time of organized attempts by the Church to convert the Jews to Christianity. An article written in 2001 by one Eugene Fisher in *The Tablet* of London was singled out by the Preacher as a most egregious example of this dangerous trend.

I must say that there is nothing quite like learning one has been publicly denounced for heresy to the pope in front of the Curia, which is to say, the whole world. With visions of Giordano Bruno (burned at the stake for supporting Copernicus, since he was not quite as well connected as Galileo) dancing in my head, I hastened to try to contact CNS to get the particulars. I was unable to do so until Monday, however, which rendered my anticipated peaceful weekend just a tad nerve-wracking.

It has all been worked out now. The good Fr. Cantalamessa had not, in fact, read my article in *The Tablet*. He had only read about it in an article published in a conservative Catholic magazine. Written by an overly zealous Jewish convert to Catholicism, the article rather badly twisted what I had actually said,   with the apparent purpose of

207

polemicizing against me. I have been the brunt of a lot of attacks from such sources over the years, so while I knew about the article, I had not (and still have not) bothered to respond to it. I did, however, respond directly to Fr. Cantalamessa on the advice of a good friend of mine, himself a Cardinal of the Curia, who had started in Rome in Catholic-Jewish relations at the same time, now a quarter of a decade ago, that I took up a similar position with the United States Conference of Catholic Bishops (USCCB). Fr. Cantalamessa responded warmly, and we are now in friendly dialogue, albeit not in total agreement.

Such incidents cause me to reflect on how a guy from suburban Detroit ended up becoming the "lightning rod," as one of my colleagues put it, for international attacks from those Catholics still unreconciled with the teachings of the Second Vatican Council. I am now more able to put perspective on how I got where I was in the spring of 2003.

How I Got There – Let's Start from the Beginning

One Christmas some years ago, my mother (nee Caroline Damm, as in "Here comes the whole Damm family!") gave me a beautiful present. Looking at my wife, Cathie, and my 12 year-old daughter, Sarah, Mom said, "You know, Gene, I don't think you lost your vocation when you left the seminary. I think you followed the path to your true calling from God." My leaving St. John's Seminary in 1967 was quite hard on her, since she hoped very much that I would become a priest. This statement, then, some 35 years in the making, meant a lot to me. And I believe it is true. I thank God for my six years in the seminary, and I thank God for guiding my path ever since. Any mistakes, as authors say in prefaces, are of my own making.

I had a wonderfully happy childhood in Grosse Pointe, Michigan, despite accidentally starting a fire with Christmas lights when I was five that caused serious damage to our house and coming down with acute rheumatic fever when I was 13, the kind that would have killed me had I been born just a bit earlier in the century before World War

Wandering Between Two Worlds

ll gave us penicillin. I was a dead average American kid for our upper middle class neighborhood, the politics of which were framed by such classic ditties as "Whistle while you work, Stevenson's a jerk." I played "Bombs Over Tokyo" by throwing pebbles into puddles and worried every Saturday morning at 11 AM, when the air raid sirens were tested, that that was the best time for the Russians to launch their missiles at us, when we would be least likely to head for the underground shelters.

I was the second child in our family, three years younger than my sister, Carolyn, my prime sibling rival, and five and eight years older than my two brothers. Interestingly, while our parents' families had both lived in the Detroit area for some generations, all four of us wound up making our lives elsewhere: one brother, Bob, in San Francisco; my youngest brother, Dick, in Atlanta; and my sister and myself in Washington. My sister held one of the highest positions ever attained by a woman in the political analysis branch of the CIA.

Both of us were voracious readers as kids. I introduced my sister to the Oz books and she introduced me to Tolkien, years before he became popular in this country. I discovered science fiction. The sense of limitless horizons for human potential in good science fiction and fantasy opened my mind at a young age to the idea that any system, seen from a wider perspective, can and should be changed for the better. This ideal is at its core profoundly biblical. The Bible is essentially "counter-cultural" in any given period of history. It always measures the present by the yardstick of human and, indeed, cosmic perfection of the End Time of universal justice, harmony, and peace. Such a concept is guaranteed to make the people of any generation restive and uncomfortable with the human institutions, whether political or religious, in which they find themselves. I don't think I'm alone in this.

And then came the sixth grade. I stopped growing in height and kept growing in girth. I got my first set of glasses. I fell in "puppy love" with Sr. Laurentia at St. Clare's Grade School and started getting all A's so she would say nice things to me and give me sentimental holy cards. In short, I became a pious geek. In the eighth grade I got a part time job at the rectory, was deeply impressed with the life-style and spiritual commitment I saw there, and have been quite literally working for the Church ever since.

My father, I was told at his funeral, was the first Catholic to have joined a major law firm in the city's history. As a rising young attorney, my father had shortly after the War applied for membership in the Detroit Athletic Club, a downtown facility where big business was done and deals were made over lunch and in the locker room. He was black-balled, however, when it was discovered that despite his English name, he was really mostly Irish and very Catholic. It would not do to have "them" polluting the club with papism, now, would it? There are other stories, but I think the point is made. I played happily with all the kids in our neighborhood. "Protestant" and "Catholic" didn't matter much to us kids. But in the larger environment the process of breaking down the social barriers among ethnic and religious groups was only beginning. To grow up Catholic in the 1940's and 1950's was to know you were "different" and to have to prove things to yourself and to the world at large that others did not have to prove.

It was World War II which began the process by which society's invisible but well-understood social barriers were, gradually, one by one, broken. The reasons are doubtlessly complex. The underlying one, I believe, was simply that America desperately needed us immigrant types to win the war. Hence, the culture became far more accepting of those asked to die to save it. One can see this reflected in the war movies of the period: A WASP lieutenant heads a small platoon composed of an Irish guy, an Italian (or Jew or Hispanic), and a black, one of whom will die saving the WASP's life. I saw a lot of these movies on TV as a kid. In any event, the soldiers came home to the GI bill, the Marshall plan for ethnic America; and many of them became the first in their family's history to go to college. Education as revolution.

I went to an all-boys high school, Austin Catholic Prep, run, as was St. Clare's, by the Augustinians. There my sense of having a vocation became strong. Rheumatic fever kept me first in the

210

hospital and then at home for most of my freshman year. A good friend faithfully brought me my homework assignments and then handed them in for me. Ironically, since I was on penicillin throughout high school, I never missed a class after that and ended up with a "perfect attendance" medal among the five I was awarded at graduation.

I was on the slow end of the adolescent male cycle, not hazarding to ask a girl for a date until the junior prom pretty much forced me to. My entry into social life was a bit less than suave. The dance was at the local war memorial. I had to park my Studebaker in the auxiliary lot, which was separated from the entrance by a glossy hill of icy snow. Gallantly, I offered to carry my date, who was a bit unsure of her high heels, over the hill. About half-way down the other side I slipped. She landed in a bush and ripped her dress, unhurt but unhappy. We went in and she hurried off to the ladies room to mend her dress. When she emerged we went in to the ballroom. As we went in, the music stopped between songs. A friend said hello. I turned and waved, and in the process knocked down a large, standing ashtray, this being in the antediluvian period when people were still allowed to smoke indoors in the winter. The crash in the silence made every head turn. Ashes and sand were spread in a large area of the dance floor. A few giggles, barely suppressed, were heard. I have tried ever since not to make such dramatic entrances. I did continue to date periodically for the rest of my junior and senior years and managed a few movies with my arm (going gradually numb) around the girl's shoulders and some chaste but delicious good-night kisses.

I graduated valedictorian of my class (thus tying my valedictorian sister in the sibling rivalry department) from Austin Catholic Prep in 1961. The rector of the diocesan seminary presided over the event and I was pleased to receive my diploma from him, kneeling on the left knee to do so since true genuflection was reserved for reverencing the Eucharist in church. I gave my valedictory address with fear and trembling. It was built, appropriate to the times, on the image of astronauts launching themselves into space as we were launching ourselves into new lives. When I finished there was a moment of silence, which to me seemed to extend for an awkwardly long period, until my sister stood up and began applauding. She knew my address was over since she had patiently listened to me practice it for hours. Then the rest of my class cheered. When it was over many of them came to congratulate me. This surprised me, since I had not thought of myself as particularly popular, being a bit on the painfully shy side of the adolescent bell curve. It was a very happy, fulfilling moment in my life, and a most satisfying finale to my sibling rivalry with my sister. We tied.

The Seminary, Civil Rights, and the Second Vatican Council

I entered Sacred Heart Seminary College that fall, having attended Catholic schools for everything except kindergarten. In the seminary, I learned through courses in philosophy, theology and literature how to articulate the strong moral system which was my inheritance as a Catholic, as did the rest of my class. With them, I became intensely involved in the civil rights movement, at one point spending a week with a classmate, John Clark, living in the apartment-home of a black family in Chicago. Shortly thereafter, John and I organized SHREAC (the Student Human Relations Education in Action Committee) and put together a day-long race relations conference at the seminary

Wishing to share what had been for us a seminal experience in Chicago, John Clark and I organized a weekend experience for the whole seminary, putting two seminarians into black homes for the weekend. Each host family invited in friends and neighbors for a chat. There is nothing like personal experience to bring about a breaking down of one's stereotypes about other people. On March 9, 1965, SHREAC organized the entire student body and faculty to march in support of the Selma marchers. Proudly bearing both the American and papal flags, we walked down the very streets that were to explode into race riots two years later. I was at the rear of our long line of about a thousand white guys passing through the black ghetto. People came off their porches to join with us as we marched, and we linked up with a massive demonstration in downtown Detroit. Over 10,000 participants were addressed by the mayor of Detroit and other dignitaries

Wandering Between Two Worlds

While I was in college, the Second Vatican Council happened. It could not have come at a better time for me. The Council's documents, which we read and studied and debated as they came out in stately procession from Rome, blew away my childhood impression of what Catholicism was all about and replaced it with a more dynamic sense of a community chosen by God to change history itself and to improve the lot of all humankind. Salvation was not just a spiritual, personal thing. It was a challenge to humanity to overcome its own evil. College is a crucial time in one's life. During it, one chooses the basic values one will uphold for the rest of one's life. The Council thus permeated my being thoroughly and permanently. One could say that the way I experienced the Council and its remarkable teachings was not simply existential, but ontological as well. The Council's statements on ecumenism and interreligious understanding (*Nostra Aetate*) became, along with the rest, part of who I was.

After college, I attended St. John's Seminary for two years. There, I took some optional scripture and biblical Hebrew courses from Fr. John J. Castelot, SS, who had written a popular series of books on the bible. There were only two or three of us in these classes, which he held informally in his room in the evening. His evident love of the Scriptures and joy at probing their depths infused me. But what astonished me was the fact that the Hebrew bible, read in its original, had a whole lot more in it than any translation can really convey. Genesis, for example, even its elegant and poetic creation accounts, is filled with puns and delightful and provocative word play that satirizes elements of the common world-view of the ancient Near East and gives the reader a sense of the ironies of life. In Scripture, tragedy and comedy constantly intertwine. The Bible is a far more sophisticated (and funny) set of books than our rather straight-laced approach to it as Christians allows us to see. It's no wonder that Jews are over-represented in American comedy. They've got a 3000-year long tradition going for them!

In the summer between semesters at St. John's, I went to Ecuador as a chaperone for a group of local Catholic high school kids on an exchange program. This was a learning experience for me on a number of levels. I was struck by the starkness of the class stratification among "pure" Spanish descendants, *mestizos* (mixed ancestry), Indians, and blacks. It was nearly absolute. At a party given for us by the parents, it dawned on me that the family I was staying with (they were of relatively modest means, living above the father's shoe shop, he being Indian, she Spanish) was sitting isolated in a corner and that none of the other parents would go near them, since their mixed marriage had crossed the racial divide. So I went over to stand with them, and stayed there. Since the parents (who were wonderful people born into a society not of their making, of course) needed to meet the chaperone, they came over.

The level of poverty of the Indians and blacks in Ecuador was something I was unprepared for, even though I had lived with black families in the ghettoes of both Detroit and Chicago. These people had virtually nothing. Entire villages were without electricity or running water. In one, the people were tremendously excited because a Peace Corps volunteer had just donated a transistor radio to them. This would be their first contact with the outside world. Ever. I knew that things would have to change, once people began to learn that life could be different. That summer made achingly real for me essential realities of oppression and exploitation I had previously understood only intellectually.

It was that summer in Ecuador that I began to think, albeit very hesitatingly, about whether I was called to the priesthood. The natural sensuality of Hispanic culture, especially during the days we spent in the tropical port city of Guayaquil, raised some quickly suppressed doubts about celibacy in my mind. I had not really begun to deal with my own sexual needs when I entered the seminary after high school, and I must admit that I had not received much direction in dealing with them (other than suppression and sublimation) while there. Then, too, living with a family, I began to think of what it would be like to be a father.

As I write, the Catholic Church in America is embroiled in perhaps the greatest crisis in its history, the so-called priest pedophilia scandal. I really do not have any unique insights to contribute to the discussion of the implications of this scandal. I had no sense at all of any unusual "goings on" while I was in the seminary, nor, so far as I know, did my classmates. The only criticism I could have, as indicated above, is that the seminary training simply did not deal with sexuality head on, but in many ways avoided talking about it. I had, for example, absolutely no clue as to why we were being warned against "particular friendships." I believe the situation in seminaries is likely better today in this regard. In our time about half the guys had entered after grade school and the other half, like me, after high school. My sexual development simply went on hold during my six years there. Today, most vocations are older, more mature men who have had more of life's experiences to draw on. If there was one major problem in our time, it was an excess of innocence.

Returning to St. John's with some inner conflicts, but still feeling on course for the priesthood, I received another jolt. Seminarians at that time were required to have some experience with parish life, which was a good idea since the seminary rule was basically one designed for a 17th century monastic life. So, donning the collar once a week, I went from home to home in a nearby parish, taking census of the parishioners. Wearing a collar and having a sympathetic face, however, opened me up for the life-stories and tragic dilemmas of many of the people, mostly housewives, who opened their doors to me. It was an emotionally draining experience to be exposed to so much sadness and often to situations I could not help, but could not help relating to in my heart. I began to realize that I would have to adopt some internal measures to insulate myself from emotional overload, were I to go on. I was not sure I wanted to do that. To this day, I have a tremendous respect for my classmates who have been able to do this. A priest must perform a balancing act of opening his heart to the inner turmoil of others enough to be spiritually helpful, while at the same time preserving a sense of professional distancing in order to keep his own soul from burning out in the heat of their pain.

Even so, I was unprepared when, sometime around Easter of that year, my spiritual confessor, Fr. Castelot, gently but firmly informed me that the faculty committee had discussed me and concluded that I should not receive minor orders with my class but take a year's leave of absence to think my way through whether or not I really wanted to be a priest. As kindly and affirmatively as Fr. Castelot put this to me, I still felt a deep sense of rejection. But I was also galvanized to do precisely what the committee wanted me to do. And the more I thought about it, in sleepless, agonized nights, the more I felt that they were right to suggest that the life of a parish priest was not one I was called to by God, though I felt called to something. Part of what I wanted to be, I knew by then, was a scholar, though I was not sure in what field, save that it should be in some branch of theology, most probably Scripture.

When June came and we went home for the summer, I was able to say goodbye to a number of friends. This was a consolation. In that period, mostly, when guys were asked to leave, they just disappeared overnight. They were there for dinner, but not for breakfast. My leave-taking from the life I once thought to be my calling, was gentler than that of many, and without residual bitterness on my part, though the process was easily one of the most painful experiences of my life.

After the Seminary: A New Life in New York

Leaving St. John's but wishing to pursue theology, especially what I then called Old Testament studies, I took a master's degree in Catholic theology at the University of Detroit. One of my teachers was Professor Shlomo Marinof, who was, for all practical purposes, the university's entire department of ancient languages. I took every course I could with him and, as with Father Castelot, I was usually one of only a couple of students in them. He was the first Jew I ever really got to know, a brilliant and gentle man of letters whom I admired greatly.

Then I wanted to go on for a doctorate in theology. I had applied to, and been accepted by, both the Chicago and Princeton divinity schools, but would have had to take out major loans to pay for either. Dr. Marinof suggested I write to his good friend, David Rudavsky, director of New York University's Institute for Hebrew Studies. I found the idea of studying the Hebrew Bible with the people who wrote it quite appealing, so I dashed off a resume. Rudavsky responded with a generous scholarship covering not only tuition but modest living expenses as well. On a warm day in early September of 1968, I walked out of New York's Grand Central Station with the address of the school in my pocket and two large suitcases. I did not know where I would spend the night, but I did know that my relatively sheltered Midwestern life was about to change. I set the bags down for a moment to take it all in. A young man promptly picked one up and began to walk off with it, mumbling something about carrying my luggage for me. I chased after him, carrying the other bag and would have lost the race if a policeman had not intervened. Welcome to New York!

The changes and challenges in lifestyle, intellectual environment, and religious perspective that I experienced in New York were dramatic and formative. This was the period of massive anti-war demonstrations. I had been in the seminary just at the right time to go through the Second Vatican Council as it was happening and been fortunate enough to be actively involved in the Civil Rights movement in Detroit during the same period.

The winds of social change blew strongly in those years and carried me with them. They promised a new and more equal American society, as the open windows of theological *aggiornamento* promised a reformed and more open Roman Catholic Church. For us, the God-intoxicated, change represented hope, not something to be feared. One could acknowledge freely the shortcomings of the past, whether in society or the church, because both were actively engaged in rectifying what had gone wrong. Admitting American racism and Christian anti-Semitism, then, was not to risk becoming mired in the guilt of the past (as it has continued to be in some parts of Europe). It was simply to open oneself to hope for a better future.

Most, and sometimes all, of my classmates at NYU were Jewish. The tone, style, and content of the discussions were entirely Jewish. What people wrangled over were questions of what it means to be Jewish. The questions that framed the issues for debate were thus Jewish. I found this both refreshing and fascinating. If one is raised within a holistic world-view as is provided by ancient traditions such as Rabbinic Judaism or Roman Catholicism, entire sets of interrelated frameworks make sense of, and give coherency to, reality, even to the often fractious internal debates that can divide a community itself.

Fortunately, I was just at the right time of my life to be plunked down, intact and with a solid grounding in integral Catholicism, in the midst of an entirely different but no less interesting worldview. Virtually everything I had ever learned -- spiritually, culturally, philosophically, historically, or biblically -- was viewed from a very different perspective. Of all the religious traditions that had flourished in the ancient Roman Empire, Judaism alone had been allowed to survive Christianity's triumph in Europe. Jewish communities predated Christian communities just about everywhere the latter spread, indeed, most often providing its original members.

The Jewish memory of Christendom, therefore, is invaluable. It is the only non-Christian (but still "insider") perspective on Western civilization. These communities, I was to discover with a sense of infinite loss, were the communities, the memories, and the unique spiritual witness that Nazi genocide had sought to end.

Before immersing myself in the New York Jewish experience, I had known nothing about being Jewish, save what I had learned in biblical studies under Catholic auspices (which was, at best, about two millennia out of date, so far as Jewish history was concerned). While academically sound, this perspective was only marginally useful for understanding how Jews today read their Scriptures, understand their history, and live their traditions. It was all new to me.

I did not at first encounter the Holocaust (or Shoah) with great intensity at NYU. It was discussed as pertinent to a given topic of study. It did not dominate either the formal course work or informal discussions of my classmates. Rather, it seemed to brood behind and beneath them, dwelling in the silence of the unspoken yet not unthought. This was in 1968, well before the NBC miniseries *Holocaust* broke open the repressed memories and lingering fears of so many in the Jewish community in this country, especially the survivors. What I encountered, rather, was the vibrancy of American Jewry, especially the New York variety. (The two are not coterminous, it turns out, but I thought so then, as did most of my classmates.)

I encountered the richness of Jewish history and the depth of Jewish philosophy. It was profoundly different, yet not necessarily contradictory to my own faith. As I learned to respect Judaism and its traditions, various facts and events occasionally intruded from that long past. I had known about the destruction of the Temple in 70 A.D. It was, after all, of great significance to the authors of the New Testament, all Jews. I learned for the first time what happened to the Jews of the Rhineland during the first Crusade in 1096 and about the expulsion of Jews from virtually all of western Europe in the succeeding centuries (save for Italy, where the popes gave them refuge). In effect, the words of my predecessor in Catholic-Jewish relations for the U.S. bishops, Fr. Edward Flannery, turned out to be an apt commentary on my Catholic education: "The pages Jews have memorized have been torn from our histories of the Christian era."

I did not deeply reflect on this then. It was a relatively minor theme of my major endeavor, learning about Jews and Judaism, and how to reinterpret and re-integrate virtually every aspect of the theological and historical vision in which I had been trained and which gave meaning to my life. The result was an oddly familiar pattern. For with all the startling divergences in the definition of ultimate issues and the differing perspectives on shared issues, it was the same God, the same sacred history, after all, being studied, albeit in a way so different from what I was used to. The tragic, suffering elements of that ancient, sacred history were there, to be sure. But they did not predominate for us at NYU in the late 1960's, with the civil rights and peace movements capturing the lion's share of our nonacademic attention.

I became involved with draft counseling, for example, at a Catholic Worker storefront called the Thomas Merton House, but which soon became the Merton-Buber House. I met Dorothy Day again and attended a retreat with her. (She had come to St. John's and met with us in the parlor, the opulent furniture for which had been personally selected by Cardinal Mooney to impress visiting parents. She slowly looked over each piece, with a furrowing brow. Finally, she sat down and with a final sweeping glance said: "Yes. Well. Let's talk about Christian poverty.") I spent a weekend with the Berrigans, smoking pot (and inhaling!) with the Catonsville Nine, not long before their sentencing. I was there for that, too, spending the night in vigil before the courthouse. Phil Berrigan gave me advice. I had told him I just came out of the seminary and feared going into the structured life of prison, so was afraid to join them in peace demonstrations that broke the law and risked prison. "Don't," he said, "That is for those who can. You must follow your own conscience, and you can do great good outside as well as inside prison."

Two books given me by David Rudavsky, of blessed memory, riveted my attention on the Holocaust -- Elie Wiesel's *Night* and Andre Schwartz-Bart's *The Last of the Just*. These commanded a more personal response from me, as did a trip to Europe with my wife, Cathie, in the early 1970's. After some very pleasant days in Rome and Florence, we went to Munich. I became uneasy that night when I realized that the beer hall we were having so much fun in was *the* Munich beer hall. The next day we went to Dachau, a short train ride to a near-in suburb, as it was then. You cannot tell me that people in that town did not know that trains were pulling in full of tens of thousands of people and leaving empty. I had known it was real, intellectually; but confrontation with the reality was spiritually devastating. Although the Nazis never used the state-of-the-art gas chambers they built there (figuring it would save money on bullets), they regularly shot so many people they had to dig a system of trenches to drain off the blood from the killing field. A very high percentage of the people murdered at Auschwitz were Catholic priests, many from Poland. It is not accidental that Pope John Paul II had such a profound understanding of the Shoah or such a passion for dialogue with Jews.

I have since visited a number of other death camps and Holocaust sites, including Auschwitz. The sense of bereavement and bewilderment does not diminish. Nor can it be numbed. Each time, some new detail or perspective opens the wound again. All I can do, all *anyone* can do, is what the pope promised in 1987 to the remnant community of the Jews of Warsaw. He repeated that promise in my presence at Castel Gandolfo only weeks later. Later, I put that same promise into the speech I wrote for him to give to Jewish leaders in Miami -- to join our voices, as Church, to that of the Jewish people in permanent witness to what happened, so that it might happen never again. Never again!

Besides learning Judaism and Jewish history Jewishly, the NYU experience gave me some insight into what Jews know about Christianity. While there is nothing parallel to the ancient patristic teaching of contempt in Jewish understandings of Christianity, I learned that there is a surprising lack of accurate knowledge about Christianity in the Jewish community, even in the intellectual Jewish community I was experiencing. My first publication in the field of Christian-Jewish relations began as a paper for a class on the medieval Jewish thinker Bahya ibn Pakuda.

Pakuda wrote (in Hebrew) a small work entitled, *Hovoth haLevavoth* (*Duties of the Heart*). It was what we today would call spiritual reading, guiding Jews along the path to a deeper intimacy with God and each other. The class in which we studied this text was a rather interesting one. The teacher, Professor Gershon Appel, was Orthodox and the students (with the exception of myself) virtually all rabbis. The professor had been reluctant to accept me into the class because my Hebrew was nowhere near as fluent as that of the rest of the students. Professor Rudavsky had to intervene personally to get him to accept me. (He did so with an animated conversation back and forth in Hebrew, only snatches of which I could follow. I did catch the phrase, *talmid chacham*, which made my day and several thereafter, since it means "wise student.").

Dr. Appel kindly pointed me toward an edition of the book that had both the original Hebrew and an English translation. By working long into the night before each class, I was able to keep up and not hold back the whole group, as Dr. Appel had quite understandably feared. As it turned out, I ended up being helpful to the class. Pakuda, while writing in Hebrew, had written his book in the style and with the philosophical categories and understandings of medieval scholasticism, which was prevalent at the time, and which in fact created a chain of understanding between Christianity, Islam, and Judaism unparalleled up to the present day. There was a lot of "borrowing" of ideas back then. Aquinas often quotes "the Rabbi," Maimonides, for example. And the great 15th century Spanish Jewish thinker, Isaac Abravanel, was deeply influenced in his commentary on the Pentateuch by an earlier Catholic theologian, Alfonso Tostado.

I had just come from a Catholic seminary, receiving there a deep immersion in scholastic philosophy and theology. While my translation was slow and awkward, once I had down what Pakuda was saying, I knew with great precision what he meant and what his world-view was, since it was essentially an exercise in scholastic theology (and a brilliant one, at that). While Pakuda could presume that his readers understood the philosophical questions he posed and the scholastic categories in which he framed them, the modern rabbis in the class were in the main innocent of the thought world in which the book was written. Upon a number of occasions, therefore, Dr. Appel called on me to explain a profoundly Jewish text to a group of rabbis! That's dialogue, American style.

One thing did disturb me, however. While I was quite familiar with the spiritual path Pakuda worked out for his readers (since it was very similar to that in any number of Catholic spiritual texts I had pored over in my time in the seminary), the class (though not the professor) simply presumed it was quite different from anything Christian spirituality could possibly have come up with in any time frame. For them, to a real extent, for it to be "Jewish" meant that it had to be something other than Christian. To them, to a real extent, medieval Christianity was composed entirely of folks flagellating themselves, wearing hairshirts, and otherwise committing what Christianity actually teaches is the sin of self-mutilation. In other words, Christianity was described by its own extremes, as if the extremes were the whole. Christianity, defined by its worst, was set over against the best in Judaism to the detriment of the former.

There is, of course, a form of theological triumphalism inherent in such an approach. But now that I had thought of it, I realized it was pervasive among faculty and students alike, not only in this course but in others. So I wrote a paper for the class on that. I pointed out, among other things, that Jewish intellectual tradition tended (and, unfortunately still tends) to accept as true about Christianity as a whole just about everything that Catholic apologetics once accused Protestantism of believing (mostly erroneously) and, vice versa, just about everything that Protestant apologetics accused Catholicism of believing (again, mostly erroneously). The result is a caricature that neither Protestants nor Catholics would recognize as being "Christianity." It is a comforting vision for Jews, but it is wrong. Christians do not worship Mary nor do we believe that you can sin all you want and will be saved by "faith alone." This is often expressed in the false comparison that Christians believe that mere belief is enough while Judaism understands that one must live out one's faith ("creed vs. deed"). As a classic example of such thinking, I pointed to Martin Buber's Two Types of Faith (pistis vs. emunah). Well, nobody's perfect. In that book the master of dialogue, the mentor of all who are involved in dialogue today, allowed an unchallenged set of false premises to reduce a book to a polemic.

My paper was well received, indeed praised by Dr. Appel, who urged me to have it published. It came out under the title "Typical Jewish Misunderstandings of Christianity" in the Winter, 1973, issue of *Judaism*. Is it still applicable today? Yes. When I was asked by the Holy See to present a paper on the topic for the 1998 meeting of the International Catholic-Jewish Liaison Committee, I ran off my 1973 paper and presented it with only a bit of updating!

A Period Wedding. Then Back to Detroit

My wife and I were married on New Year's Eve, 1970, in the chapel of the Woodstock Jesuit Community. We had met when she took a summer course I taught on Martin Buber at the University of Detroit, where she also received a master's in theology. We corresponded about the shock of the assassinations of Martin Luther King and Bobby Kennedy and about the malaise in the movement following

Kent State. We found we had much in common, and shared that in the summer of 1970. Our route back to New York took us within a few miles of the other Woodstock, while it was going on, but we did not make that left turn into cultural history.

Cathie lived with her aunt and grandmother in a small apartment in Brooklyn. I proposed to her on a park bench in Washington Square one mild autumn evening. We went immediately to one of the small shops in Greenwich Village where the hippies hung out and bought two matching engagement rings with peace symbols on them.

We wrote our own wedding ceremony. The ceremony was later published in the 1974 Seabury Press volume *The Wedding Book: Alternative Ways to Celebrate Marriage.* So that was the first of our published collaborations. We later did a series of 12 articles on marriage for Catholic News Service. After the wedding, everybody took the elevator up to the common rooms of the Jesuits to imbibe the communal beer and the wine I had bought at the liquor store where I worked part time.

We had six priests at our wedding (an ecumenically mixed group of Franciscans and Jesuits) but were married by the local parish deacon. He tried to give us the marriage classes, but after the second night and after we had gently corrected his theology of marriage for the umpteenth time, he good-naturedly declared that we did not need more.

When I finished up my class work for the doctorate at NYU in the spring of 1971, I began to look for a job. I couldn't find anything appropriate in New York, so we returned home to Detroit. Cathie got a job as a religious education coordinator and I lucked into a position as Director of Catechist Formation for the Archdiocese of Detroit. I was hired by Fr. Bob Humitz, who wanted someone who would put together a teacher training program centered on Scripture, my long suit at the time. I was able to put into the training program a number of correctives on the traditionally negative portrait of Jews and Judaism, especially with regard to the New Testament, perhaps the first such diocesan-wide program to have tackled the subject seriously.

1971-1977 were good years to work at the diocesan level in Detroit. Cardinal Dearden had come back from the Council determined to make its vision a reality in the local church. We on staff participated in and took quite seriously the archdiocesan-wide consultation and, after it, the famous (or, to some, infamous) "Call to Action" program. Indeed, nearly everything we did was a first or near-first. Fr. Humitz was a key figure in the founding of a national association of religious education directors and its first president. Fr. Al Brunett (now Archbishop of Seattle), on whose ecumenical commission I served as a volunteer for Catholic-Jewish relations, was instrumental in founding the National Association of Diocesan Ecumenical Officers (NADEO), an organization I would work closely with in my future position. Detroit and Chicago were innovative centers looked to nationally by those wishing to implement the Council.

We were, of course, noticed by those who were dedicated to the cause of preserving the Tridentine Church and who abhorred the innovations -- ecumenical and social, catechetical and liturgical -- that we were happily making. Their newspapers, such as *The Wanderer*, delighted in catching us in the mistakes we inevitably made. This could have been healthy, actually, since innovators tend to make mistakes; but they went much further than fraternal correction. To them, Cardinal Dearden (hierarchical to the core, always in control, always "Iron John") was nothing less than a Communist. And we who worked for him were at best fellow-travelers, personifications of evil incarnate.

Bishop Tom Gumbleton was shoved to the ground while vested for liturgy at the Cathedral by the followers of Donald Lobsinger (a man seemingly dedicated to the cause of giving Catholics United for the Faith a bad name). Fr. Tom Hinsberg, who had taught philosophy to our SHS class and was then in charge of the Justice and Peace office, was a witness to this outrage. Fr. Hinsberg asked me to walk with him from the chancery to the courthouse for his testimony, since Bishop Gumbleton had quite rightly pressed charges against his attackers. Fr. Hinsberg feared that Lobsinger and his thugs would be somewhere along the route seeking to intimidate him, and *he* wanted a witness. He was correct. They were waiting near the entrance to the court. No police officers were in sight. I can recall reflecting on the irony of wanting to see a police officer, a thought which would not have occurred to me during the civil rights or peace marches I had been involved in. But here the law was on our side, if nowhere to be seen.

As we approached, they surrounded us. The language was foul. And I shall never forget the look in Lobsinger's eyes. Absolutely chilling. I resolutely walked on, carefully observing the "discipline of the eyes" taught to me at Sacred Heart, and not making eye contact. They danced around us, taunting us and spitting on us. We entered the courthouse. Tom gave his testimony while I gained appreciation for the American legal system and for the courage of these two dedicated men.

In Detroit I simultaneously worked full time for the Archdiocese, taught alternately at the University of Detroit and St. John's Seminary (one class hour short of full-time teaching in each case), and worked on my dissertation.

The dissertation consisted of a textbook analysis of Catholic educational material, on the primary and secondary level, for its treatment of Jews and Judaism. It showed that in the areas where the Council document *Nostra Aetate* was specific, progress in the textbooks was strong. But where the Council had not explicitly made a clarifying point to correct ancient misunderstandings, usually in the form of misinterpretations of the New Testament, invariably to the disadvantage of Jews and Judaism, ambiguities still remained in Catholic teaching materials. A follow-up study to mine, done by Dr. Philip Cunningham of Boston College, revealed further improvement. The presentation of Jews and Judaism in my daughter's textbook is vastly more accurate and positive than the anti-Judaic polemics that laced the religion materials I and my classmates received in the 1950's. This is comforting on several levels. Not only does it show that the work my generation has done in this field is having an effect in the parishes, where the reality of the Church resides, but it is also personally comforting. Since our parish church, like many suburban parishes in the late '70's, was under built and did not have enough rooms for our 1500 students, my daughter's sixth grade catechism class met in the synagogue next door. It would have been a tad embarrassing if the rabbi had picked up her textbook only to read one of the old-time anti-Jewish screeds that once, sadly, were abundant in them.

Unlikely as it sounds, my dissertation became a prototype for textbook changes in Europe as well as the United States. Tubingen University in Germany flew me over in the late 1970's to lecture on content analysis and how to improve Catholic textbook treatment of Jews and Judaism. At the end of the lecture, the Germans all banged their fists on the desks in the vast lecture hall. I was devastated. My host was wildly enthusiastic about the "huge, warm reception" I had received.

How I Got "The Job" and Found My Vocation

In 1977, doctorate finally in hand, I was again looking for a job, this time in academia. I interviewed at the American Academy of Religion meeting in Chicago in 1976. No go. Lots of interviews, lots of rejections. I sent in dozens of applications and received numerous nicely worded form responses, all of which promised to keep me on file. For all I know I still am. I got an acceptance from Villanova University of Philadelphia. Not much money, but with tenure possibilities. So I was planning to accept it, when fate intervened.

Due largely to Fr. Brunett's enthusiasm and prominence on the national ecumenical scene, Detroit had been selected to host the third annual National Workshop on Christian-Jewish Relations in 1977. As a member of the local planning committee, I was able to ensure a slot dealing with a topic I knew well -- the vast difference between the realities of the Pharisaic movement as a lay reformist movement of its time and the way "the Pharisees" are depicted in the New Testament, especially in Matthew's gospel. My topic drew about 100 of the 500 people who attended the workshop in March of 1977. I noticed in the back on the right three priests, whom I did not know, busily taking notes and conferring with one another. At the end of the talk one of them, Fr. John Sheerin (who had been editor of *U.S. Catholic*) came up and enquired as to whether I had a resume handy. The other two priests were Fr. Jack Hotchkin and Msgr.George Higgins. Fr. Edward Flannery had retired from his position as director of Catholic-Jewish relations for the USCCB and they were looking for a replacement. Though a layperson, they felt that I might have learned something about Jews and Judaism at NYU, which counted more for them than clerical status. Fr. Sheerin had been assigned by Paulist Press to work with me on translating my Ph.D. tome from "dissertationese" into English for my first book, *Faith Without Prejudice*, published in 1977, so he knew where I was coming from, and evidently approved.

I had a briefcase full of resumes. I told them about the offer from Villanova. Four days later I found myself in Washington being interviewed for a job beyond my wildest ambitions. Three days hence, Fr. Hotchkin, of blessed memory, then and for the next 25 years my boss at the Conference, called to tell me I had the position.

Sports people, in such a situation, announce that they are going to Disney World. Cathie and I went to Israel with a stop off in Rome on the way back. The vice-president of the Pontifical Council for Christian Unity, Msgr. Charles Mueller, met with us. He said that the U.S. Catholic community was vital to the Church's dialogue with Jews. "You in America must lead, Gene," Mueller repeated several times. "We in the Vatican will support you. But you must lead." Quite a burden to place on a 34 year-old fledgling ecclesiocrat who did not yet know how to work the elevators in his own office building!

In mid-July of 1977, I became the first layperson to become director of a USCCB secretariat, starting my job about one month before Dr. Dolores Leckey began as director of the Secretariat for the Laity. This did not go unnoticed by *The Wanderer* crowd either. I had listed among the goals of the secretariat a Lectionary Project. This would involve prominent Catholic biblical scholars in looking at the implications for understanding Jews and Judaism in the lectionary selections and translations. A separate goal was a dialogue with the

228

Synagogue Council of America, which represents Orthodox, Conservative, and Reform Judaism. Without calling our office to check, *The Wanderer* came to the conclusion that I was asking the rabbis to evaluate New Testament selections for the Catholic liturgy, which was not the case.

The Wanderer launched a four-part attack on me and also on Bishop Francis Mugavero of Brooklyn for letting me lead him around "by the nose" with my pathetically heretical "Fisherisms." I must admit that this made me a tad nervous, new to the job as I was, until I was reassured that Conference staff, especially our Justice & Peace types, were boringly regular targets of such screeds. Catholic News Service, *The National Catholic Register*, *The National Catholic Reporter*, and *Our Sunday Visitor*, on the other hand, all printed positive notices and seemed pleased with the idea that a Catholic with a doctorate in Hebrew Studies would be guiding the dialogue for the bishops.

The dialogue with the Synagogue Council went extremely well for several years, producing two volumes of essays on social policy in the Catholic and Jewish traditions and how we derive policy from biblical principle. Dialogue meetings were hosted by the University of Notre Dame. I held a very lengthy discussion with the manager of the Morris Inn on campus. He simply could not believe a representative of the bishops would be asking him to remove the crucifixes from the rooms where the rabbis would be staying. "It is a symbol of universal love and self-sacrifice," he quite understandably argued. "Not to Jews," I explained. "To them its meaning was defined by the Crusaders who turned it into a sword and slaughtered tens of thousands of Jews in its name." That re-definition of the cross was to rear up and ensnarl the international dialogue again in 1986 during the Auschwitz Convent controversy, a classic example of interreligious miscommunication. For the record, the Morris Inn did accommodate my unusual request, though the shadowy outlines of the crosses were visible.

In 1981, I received the Walter Romig Award for outstanding lay alumnus of Sacred Heart Seminary. I consider it my first major award. I've received others, including an honorary doctorate from St. Mary's Seminary and University in Baltimore, and several from major Jewish organizations. I was twice seriously nominated by a pair of professors from Hebrew University in Jerusalem for the Nobel Peace Prize (seriously enough for the Nobel Committee to have written back to them asking for further information on the civil rights work I had done at Sacred Heart). But the Sacred Heart award is perhaps my most cherished, since my father was present to see his son (and his name) honored. He died in 1983 from diabetes, a shattering experience for me since he was relatively young. Of all the people in my life, my father had the most influence in my development. One time, my father said to me, "You know, son, when you give your name to someone, you don't know what will happen to it. What happened to my name has been very good." That is the highest praise I expect to receive in my lifetime.

International Dialogue and Mundane Realities

I attended my first meeting of the International Catholic-Jewish Liaison Committee (ILC) as a guest of the Holy See in 1978 in Madrid. In 1980 I was made a member of the ILC, representing the Vatican, and also a Consultor to the Pontifical Commission. The latter appointment was reaffirmed every five years until I retired. So every five years I received a letter from the Cardinal Secretary of State announcing and stating, in quite elegant Latin, the presumption that I would "act accordingly." The first one arrived on April 1, 1980, encased in no less than three envelopes. I thought it was a joke until Fr. Hotchkin showed me his identically worded appointment as a Consultor to the Pontifical Council on Christian Unity. One year they forgot to send the letter, so I had to wait until August, when the *Annuario Pontificio* (the "red book" listing all of the curial appointments and offices) came out to see if I was still a member.

The 1978 Madrid meeting was the seventh, the first having been held in Paris in 1971. The seventeenth, which I organized on behalf of the Holy See, was held in New York in 2001. Subsequent ILC meetings I attended were in Buenos Aires and Cape Town, South Africa, the first such meetings on those continents so important to the future of the

Church. I cannot here narrate stories from them all, so a few vignettes from over the years will have to do.

My first reflection is that there is a distinct advantage in being a married layperson in the area of Catholic-Jewish relations. Most of the Jewish participants are rabbis and most of the Catholics are priests. At any given meeting a number of the rabbis would bring their spouses, as did I. Given the way people socialize on such occasions, this provided numerous situations where my wife and I would go out for a meal or shopping with another couple (invariably Jewish) or my wife would go out with Jewish spouses. This enabled us, as a couple, to establish an informal set of relations with Jewish leaders that was not possible in the more formal setting of the official sessions themselves. I can remember, for example, coming into the lobby of our hotel at one meeting to check in. Jewish delegates were in a group on one side, talking with each other while several priests were in a separate group by the desk. Our very presence broke the ice. Cathie and I were greeted by the Jewish group in typical Mediterranean fashion, with hugs all around and much back-thumping, while the Catholic officials looked on, a bit bemused by it all. We then brought the Jewish delegation over and the unofficial meeting (which is almost always more important than the official one) unofficially began. I don't know how long the two groups had been standing separated from each other by only a few feet of lobby floor.

I think it was at Regensberg in 1979 that the delegations were put up in a Catholic retreat house. Quite nice and clean, of course, as one would expect in Germany. On the other hand the single beds were not only on opposite sides of the narrow room but also fixed to the walls. American married people traveling in Europe quite often have the experience of having to move the two single beds in their room together, even in relatively expensive hotels. This has lead me to reflect upon how there could be so many Europeans. Here, however, Cathie and I were stymied. So we tried to sleep in one of the twins together, American style. The problem was that every time one of us turned over, we triggered a light switch. German technology had defeated our American romanticism! The next morning, we sat at the breakfast table with a very eminent American Reform rabbi and his lovely wife. "How did you sleep," he asked. "Not well," I cautiously replied. "You couldn't figure out the damn light switch either," he laughed, "We had the same problem. On and off all night!" This is not a conversation, I assure you, that the rabbi would have had with a celibate.

On a number of occasions, this personal link of shared matrimonial interest may have helped avoid or solve difficulties by enabling Cathie and/or I to float ideas or concerns from one side to the other to test their viability before putting them on the table for official discussion. I must note as well that among the veterans on both sides of the dialogue, whether clerical or lay, deep friendships were forged. The result was that, since the two groups knew each other better, they were less leery of giving offense and more skilled in raising sensitive issues than they were in the early years; so the "back channel" that Cathie and I represented is not needed as much anymore. This is as it should be.

The highpoint of my involvement with the International Catholic-Jewish Liaison Committee came in 2000. I was asked by the Holy See to coordinate the Catholic side of the dialogue for its 2001 meeting in New York, since the Pontifical Commission's secretary had had to take early retirement due to serious illness and had not yet been replaced. All of a sudden, it seemed, I was directing Catholic-Jewish relations not just for the U.S. Bishops but for the Church Universal! There were a number of heavy issues at hand, such as the implications of the document *Dominus Iesus* for the dialogue and the ongoing debate over scholarly access to the Vatican archives for materials related to the Holocaust.

The planning meetings, one in Washington, one in Rome, went well. Cardinal Walter Kasper, the newly appointed President of the Pontifical Council for Christian Unity, himself agreed to interpret *Dominus Iesus*. As Co-Coordinator of the ILC's International Catholic-Jewish Historical Team (see below), I arranged for its two most eminent scholars, Prof. Michael Marrus, dean of the Graduate School of the University of Toronto, and Fr. Gerald P. Fogarty, SJ, of the University of Virginia, to present the team's conclusions on the portions of the Vatican archives they had meticulously analyzed to date.

In any event, the meeting, though dealing with several of the most volatile and radioactive issues in the dialogue, exceeded expectations on all levels and produced two significant joint statements, one on international social policy and one on how to present "the other" in our respective seminaries and schools of education. So nervous was I about its outcome, I must admit, that when it was all over, I sat down and found myself quietly crying with relief.

Vatican Documents and Jewish Commentaries

Since the mid-1980's the public perception of Catholic-Jewish relations has been, at least as portrayed in the secular media, one of alternating controversies and grand papal gestures. In most of these, in one way or another, I have had a role to play, often minor, but with the stakes no less high for that. This perception of dramatic ups and downs, however, masks the ongoing, essentially more positive, reality.

In 1985, for example, the Holy See came out with its "Notes on the Correct Way to Present Jews and Judaism in Preaching and Catechesis in the Roman Catholic Church." This was only the second major statement of the Pontifical Commission for Religious Relations with the Jews after the Second Vatican Council. As is usual with Vatican statements, beginning with *Nostra Aetate* itself, the Jewish community subjected it to sharp scrutiny and, noting that it had some good points, pointed these out as well areas that needed improvement. The Holocaust, for example, while mentioned, was not fully grappled with as an event with consequences for our understanding *Christian* history. Again, such criticism is in the long run most helpful to the Church. But the media, being what it is, focused on critical aspects of Jewish responses and wrote up a "story" (When did they stop reporting on events and start doing "stories" instead?) of controversy, when in fact the "Notes" constituted yet another step forward, however imperfect.

The American dialogue played a role in the development of the document. Materials developed with the help of the Advisory Committee to my secretariat ultimately were made part of the text. In 1982, the Chair of the U.S. Bishops' ecumenical committee and I represented the U.S. at a meeting of representatives of bishops' conferences from around the world. We were called together by the Pontifical Commission to advise the Holy See on what should constitute the substance of a major teaching document on Catholic-Jewish relations. We primarily brought materials on religious education and preaching. But what they asked me to address specifically was the significance for Catholic teaching of the rebirth of a Jewish state in the Land of Israel in the 20th century (our conference had addressed this issue in 1975 on the anniversary of *Nostra Aetate*, as the French bishops had done in 1973).

I presented my understanding of the profound biblical and religious underpinnings of Zionism, which on the surface appears to be a secular movement for liberation not unlike those of other 20th century national movements rising for their freedom against the colonial empires of Europe. Indeed, the Zionists devoured and modeled much of their strategy on the literature produced by the Irish rebellion against British rule. Since the British held the Mandate for ruling Palestine, this makes perfect sense. I argued that while one should not overstate the theological implications of the ingathering of the Jews into their ancient homeland, in the sense of it being a harbinger of the End Time (as some fundamentalist Protestant Christians do), it could not be ignored among the "signs" of our times. Indeed, it implies a rather definitive rebuttal of what was left of the "divine punishment" aspect of the old deicide charge. Likewise, it was only the ancient Jewish longing for the Land given them by God which could explain how the remnant of European Jewry, two-thirds of which had been systematically murdered by the Nazis, could have found hope in humanity to dare to give birth to a new generation and a new country, given the odds against either ever happening. Even the most secular of American Jews, I have noticed, observes Passover in some fashion, passing on the deepest sense of Jewish identity to their children. And even the most secular of Israelis has an awareness of biblical history so profound that it would make the most pious

234

Bible Belt preacher jealous. It is, after all, their history, the history of the Jews.

A member of the Vatican Secretariat of State had been invited to the meeting. He asked a few pointed questions. After the session, Cathie and I went out to dinner with the chair of the U.S. Bishops' Ecumenical Committee, who had been watching the man closely and who predicted that there would be "not a word" on Israel in the document when it came out. But in its section 25, the Vatican *Notes* distilled all the themes I had taken some 30 pages to develop and wove them together into three tightly drawn paragraphs. And in a gesture unusual for the Holy See, the Pontifical Commission noted its reliance on a statement of a local bishops' conference for its key phrasing: the 1975 statement of the U.S. bishops which had been drafted by my predecessor, Fr. Edward Flannery, and which I had spun out in detail in my paper.

Even so, the document was destined to run into difficulties upon its promulgation in 1985. Parts of it, including section 25, were so carefully worded, so nuanced, and so tightly couched in "Vaticanese" that the Jewish community was bound to take a dim view of some of its statements. Father Jorge Mejia (later a cardinal), knowing I had contacts in the Jewish community I could rely on for complete discretion, shared an advance copy with me. I, in turn, shared their feedback with him. When the document was published in the Vatican newspaper, *L'Osservatore Romano*, Mejia published alongside it an article giving the proper interpretation of sections most likely to be misunderstood. This greatly facilitated my own efforts to explain its true meaning, at least to those who cared more about substance than controversy.

Reading the official documents of the Catholic Church accurately is an art that requires a level of theological background that very few reporters in either the American or European press have. One needs to understand the level and context of the document within the overall teaching of the Church, often going back centuries. In my case, the task is made a bit easier by the fact that the official magisterial context begins only with the Second Vatican Council, nothing said by any earlier Council, or even a Father of the Church, having any doctrinal relevance to its interpretation. *Nostra Aetate no. 4*, on Judaism, is virtually unique in this respect.

Compounding the difficulty of presenting to the public an accurate understanding of a Roman document is the media's appetite for instant analysis and commentary. Consider a more recent case, that of the document, *Dominus Iesus*, put out by the Congregation for Doctrine (formerly the Holy Office of the Inquisition). This document was put up on the Vatican's website concurrent with a press conference attended by a handful of people in Rome. It was written in High Vaticanese, since it was intended principally for the use of bishops and their theologians. It warned of certain excesses to be avoided ecumenically and interreligiously. The stories of most American newspapers, accordingly, were filed even before most American bishops and their theologians had ever seen it. The result was something of a nightmare, certainly for Catholic-Jewish relations.

While the document did contain theological caveats of significance for ecumenical (properly, the work toward *Christian* unity) and general interreligious teaching, it actually said nothing of relevance to the specific enterprise of Catholic-Jewish relations. It took me some months to convince Jewish leaders of this, since their first take on it was from the *New York Times*, which simply blew this aspect of the story. The document quite rightly, in my opinion, made a distinction between religions of "faith" and "belief." It defined the former as a response to divine revelation. The latter, while still having its own human validity and even beauty, were the result of human wisdom, albeit perhaps nudged by the inspiration of the Spirit, but not as a direct revelation as is Sacred Scripture (Hebrew Bible and New Testament). Thus, from a Catholic point of view, it is improper to place the Quran on the same level of revelation as either Testament of the Bible. So far, so good. But many reporters not trained in theology wrongly placed Judaism in the category of human belief rather than divine revelation. If so, of course, this would have meant that *Dominus Iesus* was guilty of the most ancient heresy in Church history, Marcionism, which taught just that. But the reality was that

Dominus Iesus did not take up in any way where to place Judaism. It presumed that its readers would be familiar with *Nostra Aetate* and the more recent *Catechism of the Catholic Church*, which states clearly: "The Jewish faith, unlike other non-Christian religions, is already a response to God's revelation in the Old Covenant." That is, one cannot presume that what the Church has to say about other religions in general is pertinent to what the Church has to say about Judaism. In other words, *Dominus Iesus* posed no difficulties whatsoever for Catholic-Jewish relations since it never addressed the issue.

It would have saved many, many hours of my time and that of the American bishops and their theologians, if there could have been some way to get the text to those of us responsible for explaining it before putting it up on the Vatican website for everybody to misinterpret. Indeed, that is how it used to be with a document such as this. Promulgated in Rome, it would have gone (as this one did, in fact) to the nuncios via diplomatic pouch and from there distributed to the bishops before the press around the world had it. In that way the local church can analyze the documents and, as it were, "translate" them into language understood by their communities. But the internet has changed the world faster than the Holy See's time-worn traditions have adapted to it. Now, the raw document, in all its undigested and uninterpreted glory, is cast to its fate in virtual reality, with anyone having internet access and a phone contact with the local paper able to present themselves as "experts" on its meaning.

The Pope is Coming! The Pope is Coming!

I met John Paul II seven or eight times over the years, usually in the company of Jewish representatives who were, of course, the point of the meetings. My most unusual meeting occurred not in the Vatican but in the papal summer residence of Castel Gandolfo on September 1, 1987. It had been a very difficult summer for Catholic-Jewish relations. The pope had scheduled a major visit to the U.S. for September, with a meeting in Miami with Jewish leaders as the opening event, the first ever of a pope with the leadership of the world's largest Jewish community. Planning such a meeting

237

presented enormous complexities and sensitivities, not simply between Catholics and Jews, but within the Jewish community as well. Who to invite? I suggested giving each of our major dialogue partners among the Jewish agencies and religious groups a certain number of seats and letting them choose whom they would. It was a religious meeting, so it should be in a synagogue. But whose? Conservative, Reform, or Orthodox? After consulting friends in the Jewish community, I suggested that it be held at the museum in Miami which was housing a major exhibit of items from the Vatican's Judaica collection – Jewishly neutral ground, but surrounded by sacred Jewish objects and books.

In the midst of these deliberations, the Vatican announced that a return visit from the President of Austria, whose predecessor had hosted the Holy Father the year before, was to take place. The new president of Austria, history records, was Kurt Waldheim, whose Nazi past was then leaking out to the world. In my humble judgment, this was not, shall we say, very good timing. The controversy that ensued was seismic and very much raised into question whether the meeting between the pope and American Jewish leaders would take place. Thousands of phone calls ensued, along with many behind the scenes discussions around the country and internationally.

Overseeing it all was the bishop of Harrisburg, Pennsylvania, now Cardinal William H. Keeler, who was the chair of the bishops Ecumenical Committee at the time. To go from a smallish diocese in rural Pennsylvania to the heart of an international, media-intensive controversy was certainly a baptism of fire, and one which he lived up to admirably.

One factor in the equation was to find a means whereby the Holy See, without appearing to back down from the diplomatic validity of the visit to Rome of the duly elected president of Catholic Austria, could reaffirm the importance of the pope's meeting with American Jews and the utter seriousness and respect with which he approached the Shoah and its victims. In a discussion in which I took no part, it was decided that the president of our Bishops' Conference would send the pope a copy of a book Rabbi Leon Klenicki of the Anti-Defamation

League and I had compiled of the pope's talks to date on Jews and Judaism. The pope's response could then say (as it did) what needed to be said. It would also serve to remind Catholics as well as Jews of the centrality of Catholic-Jewish relations in the current pontificate. And so it was that Archbishop John L. May, President of the National Conference of Catholic Bishops, received from the Holy Father a letter dated August 8, 1987. It began: "As my second Pastoral Visit to the United States approaches, I wish to express to you my profound gratitude for your kindness in sending me the volume containing the texts of my statements on the subject of Jews and Judaism. This significant undertaking is the result of cooperation between Catholics and Jews in America, which is a further source of satisfaction." The book was E. Fisher and L. Klenicki, ed's, *Spiritual Pilgrimage: John Paul II on Jews and Judaism*, which, in a second edition, went on in 1995 to win an award from the Jewish Book Society. Doubtless, this was the first time a volume of papal addresses had ever won a major Jewish award.

In any event, the letter from the pope, which reprised a number of his key themes on the subject over the years, was sent to Jewish leaders and served to break the ice. Further, it allowed them to accept an invitation to come to Rome for a meeting August 31 with Cardinal Jan Willebrands of the Pontifical Commission and the next day with the pope at Castel Gandolfo.

Laughing with the Pope

The meeting with the Pontifical Commission was tense but came to a satisfactory resolution the next morning. Cardinal Willebrands, who met with the pope that night, announced that the Holy See would undertake to produce a major statement on the Shoah and its implications for Christians. The statement was finally published in 1998, after much internal discussion and dialogue with the Jewish community, in much of which I was involved.

We met with the pope on a sunny, warm September morning. A cooling breeze was blowing off the lake through the window of the baroque receiving room. The room was set with great sensitivity. A circle of chairs, all exactly alike, surrounded a small table with a bible (Hebrew Scriptures only) open to a psalm. On one side the psalm was in the original Hebrew, on the other, in Latin. We prayed it, alternately, in both languages.

The pope came in and was introduced to us one by one. I was standing between Reform rabbi Alexander Schindler and Orthodox rabbi Henry Seigman. I was also the only Catholic not wearing clericals. When the pope got to me, I naturally bent over to kiss his ring. Looking startled at what he thought was a rabbi about to pay the obeisance only Catholics owe, the pope started to pull his hand away. Rabbi Mordecai Waxman, who was introducing the Pope to the Jewish delegation, immediately called out: "It's all right, Your Holiness. He's one of yours!" At which point everyone, the pope included, cracked up. And so it was that my wife woke up that morning, turned on the morning news, and saw her husband laughing with the pope.

After the historic and very pleasant meeting, the pope came around the circle of his guests again. Following him was a monsignor bearing a tray on which were arranged a pile of blessed rosaries in little plastic cases and leather boxes which it turned out contained memorial coins minted by the Vatican for the year. The Catholics received the rosaries. The Jewish guests received the more valuable coins. Again, the pope took me for a rabbi and handed me a box. Only when I had my hands on it did his eyes widen a bit in recognition. I held on. His eyes twinkled a bit as he let go of it. When I told Bishop Keeler of this during dinner on the Piazza Navona that night, his eyes twinkled too.

This story ends well in Miami. My wife and I ended up in a penthouse suite in the hotel in which 200 American Jewish leaders were staying. Security, needless to say, was tight. Secret service agents watched everyone getting into and out of the elevators. One had to be a guest to get in. If we had a visitor, he or she was escorted to our door. We had to verify the person's identity before he or she was let in. We needed the large suite in order to accommodate the people invited to a reception with Cardinal Willebrands the night before the meeting with the pope. The pope arrived on time in Miami on my birthday, September 10th. But Cardinal Willebrands, who flew in with him, was nowhere to be found. Bishop Francis Mugavero of Brooklyn, then the Episcopal Moderator for Catholic-Jewish Relations, took this in stride. He worked the room like a professional politician (which he could have been, Mario Cuomo and Geraldine Ferraro being among his proteges), while the Secret Service fussed and fumed and phoned all over the city. Finally, the Cardinal was found and whisked to the reception. He looked weary, but gave a spirited talk, which set a positive mood for the meeting with the pope the next morning.

I sat in the second row for the historic occasion, next to Rabbi James Rudin of the American Jewish Committee, with whom, like Leon Klenicki, I have also published a number of works and shared innumerable platforms around the country. We both paid very close attention to every word. It is traditional for the Holy See, when the pope comes to a country, to ask the local hierarchy beforehand for ideas as to what His Holiness should address, and sometimes (by no means always) for drafts which the pope can work over and make his own. I had written such a draft, and Jim had written the draft for Rabbi Waxman, who was to give the Jewish welcome to the pope. Afterwards, we compared notes. In both cases improvements had been made on our offerings, but the significant substance of what we had written was preserved. I like to quote *that* text of the pope's, for some reason.

I have had numerous occasions such as this, listening to bishops and archbishops incorporate as their own the ideas I and many others have worked out over years of careful study, building brick by brick what is today a rather impressive theological response to the doctrinal challenge of the Second Vatican Council. Often, I have been surprised, usually positively, sometimes humorously. When the late Cardinal John O'Connor came to New York, for example, he asked me for a draft for his first talk in a major synagogue there. I sweated over a text. He kindly invited me to be present. So I was there in the first row when he opened his talk with the words: "Dr. Eugene Fisher has prepared a wonderful text for me, from which I am sure you would benefit. But I want to talk to you heart to heart." At which point he dramatically tossed my text aside and began to tell stories from his life and his reading. He brought down the house, and a love affair (albeit sometimes a stormy one) between a Cardinal and the world's largest Jewish community began. The man was a natural.

Oh, yes. The text was not lost. A few years later, with a few updates, it was given as the keynote address by the President of the USCCB at a National Workshop on Christian-Jewish relations. He made it his own too. And it was very well received.

Pharisees and Apostles

In March of 1998, I went on a pilgrimage to Israel and Rome with a joint group of Catholic bishops, led by Cardinal Keeler, and rabbis, led by Conservative rabbi Joel Zaiman. The idea was for them to show us Israel from their point of view and for us to show them Israel as a Catholic experiences it. The trip was jointly planned by the American Jewish Committee and the Jewish Council for Public Affairs, on the one hand, and the Catholic Near East Welfare Association on the other, with me looking over their shoulders to facilitate what turned out to be a sprightly dialogue in its own right. ("Well, if we are going to Bethlehem University and visit with the Latin Patriarch in the morning, we must go to the Israel Museum and visit the President of Israel in the afternoon." Etc.)

We also visited, and prayed at, each other's holy sites. In Capernaum, we visited the site of the ancient 2nd century synagogue, laid out on the same foundations as the one Jesus preached in. As the group sat on the stone benches along the sides of the ruin, I could overhear a number of conversations, all of them religious in nature. It struck me that this was perhaps the first time that the successors of the apostles, our bishops, and the successors of the Pharisees, the rabbis, had held a meaningful conversation in that place since the close of biblical times.

And then we all went to Mass. The Catholics, of course, celebrated Mass every day, with the bishops rotating as celebrants. The homilies were dialogical in tone, geared to the fact that the congregation included a number of rabbis and one Catholic. As the days passed, the kiss of peace took on more and more meaning for all of us, as we wished each other "shalom" in the land of Abraham and Sarah, Jesus and Mary. It was Lent for the Catholics, and I must say that retracing the steps of Jesus in the Holy Land with this unique group of pilgrims made it the most prayerful and meaningful Lenten season of my life.

While we were in the air flying from Jerusalem to Rome for the second half of our pilgrimage, the Holy See released the long awaited, *We Remember: A Catholic Reflection on the Shoah*, the document which had been promised at Castel Gandalfo a decade and a half earlier. It had been prefaced by statements of a number of European bishops' conferences in 1995, coinciding with the anniversary of the liberation of Auschwitz forty years earlier, as well as an American statement by Archbishop Oscar Lipscomb, speaking as the chair of the Bishops' Committee for Ecumenical and Interreligious Relations (BCEIA).

The meeting at the Commission went quite well. Rabbis Mordecai Waxman and James Rudin pinpointed precisely and thoroughly the areas of weakness that would be reiterated time and again in subsequent months. Cardinal Edward Cassidy, President of the Pontifical Commission, listened very intently and stated his agreement with the key points. This face-to-face dialogue, its openness and honesty, enabled some good things to come out of the public controversy.

First, having had a chance to consider carefully Jewish objections before the media blitz inevitably escalated them into public polemics, Cardinal Cassidy was able to prepare a measured, constructive response. He gave it to the national meeting of the American Jewish Committee in May of 1998, filling in and clarifying a number of areas not sufficiently clear in the original text, and also providing it with a definitive interpretation responsive to Jewish concerns.

Second, this enabled our Conference to implement the text within the local church in the U.S. in a constructive way. In September of 1998, the Conference put out a small volume entitled *Catholics Remember the Holocaust*, which collected all of the European and American statements leading to the texts of the Vatican document and Cardinal Cassidy's own interpretation. The bishops also authorized the BCEIA to issue *Catholic Teaching on the Shoah: Implementing the Holy See's We Remember* (February, 2001). This statement mandated and provided guidelines for Holocaust education on all levels of Catholic education, from elementary through university. And again, with the wisdom of hindsight, it made sure to bring together the meaning of the original Vatican document with its authoritative interpretation by Cardinal Cassidy.

Our meetings in Rome with Vatican officials culminated in an audience with the Holy Father, who seemed to have been apprised of the concerns raised so ably by our rabbis, since some of what he said seemed to respond to them, though he did not, of course, directly acknowledge this. After the rest of the pilgrimage group left for home, Cardinal Keeler and I stayed on for a meeting the next week of the International Catholic-Jewish Liaison Committee. That conference, too, involved an audience with the pope. This is how I ended up meeting with the pope twice in the space of a week, hardly something I expected to happen in my life when I got off that airplane in New York in the late summer of 1967!

The International Catholic-Jewish Historical Team

I was asked in late 1999 by Cardinal Cassidy to "coordinate" the Catholic side of a team of six historians, three Jewish and three Catholic, appointed by the International Jewish Committee for Interreligious Consultations (IJCIC), on the one hand, and the Vatican, on the other. The team was to analyze the materials from the Vatican's archives pertinent to the Second World War and the Holocaust, those that had been released to the public over the years. This was only a portion of the collection, of course; and Jewish and other scholars had been requesting for years to be allowed access to the rest.

Normally the policy of the Holy See is to make available to scholars its archives by pontificate. They had made an exception, beginning in the mid-1960's, by making available a large portion of their materials for the World War II period, even though they were then working on preparing the archives of Pius XI. The reason for this was a play written by Rolf Hochhuth, a German Protestant, which virtually demonized Pius XII and tried to make him culpable for the Nazi Holocaust against the Jews. Reality, of course, is never found in such stark black and whites as Hochhuth presented it. Yet the secular media of the 1960's latched on to the simplistic belief that the pope could have stopped the German army and caused it to lay down its arms with a single command, if only he had dared. The response of Pope Paul VI was to release "everything pertinent" to the matter. The problem with Paul VI's approach, of course, was that since everything pertinent did not mean "everything," the suspicion arose that the Vatican was holding back materials that would not show it in a good light. To meet this ongoing objection, Cardinal Cassidy had suggested at the 1998 ILC meeting that a joint team of scholars be set up to look objectively at what had been released and to ask questions based upon their scholarly research.

This sounded good on paper and I agreed to co-coordinate the international team with the chairperson of IJCIC as my counterpart. The idea of having me as the co-coordinator rather than Cardinal Cassidy, I was given to understand, was that the Holy See could not in this way be accused of trying to exercise influence over the Catholic scholars. I was, in short, a "firewall" between the Holy See and the Catholic scholars.

So far, so good. The international team had several intense meetings in the first half of 2000 going over in detail the twelve volumes of published materials. But politics and media curiosity took their toll. When we went to Rome in November of that year to present our report to Cardinal Cassidy, we were betrayed by one European member, who leaked it to the French press before we could officially present it. We were in the midst of a rather delicate discussion, since the report had not come out in the form the Cardinal had expected. It was much more tentative and, even though it affirmed objectivity of the original collection, sought further archival material (as one might expect from a group of topnotch academics!). The Cardinal was called out of this meeting by a member of his staff. I shall never forget the look on his face when he came back in with a copy in his hand of the French newspaper containing a summary of our leaked report.

We all felt the betrayal, of course; but were helpless to undo it. We did meet with other members of the Curia, among them Cardinal Mejia, then in charge of the Vatican Library and its archives. A suggestion was made to him to alter the policy by which archives were released, a suggestion which was to bear fruit, but not until long after the demise of the historical team, which suspended its work in the summer of 2001 amidst a flurry of negative media accounts.

The remainder of the pertinent Vatican archives are indeed now being released in accelerated fashion, the Holy See having increased the number of archivists preparing the materials from two to ten, and the matter has significantly calmed down.

Cambridge Interlude

The US Catholic Conference did not provide for sabbaticals for its lay senior staff. Dolores Lecky, who headed the Secretariat for the Laity, was given three months to study at Tantur in Jerusalem, and I was allowed three months in the spring and early summer of 2003 to accept an appointment as a Fellow at Cambridge University in England, a program set up by its Centre for Christian-Jewish Studies. I was the first Christian in the program.

My wife, Cathie, and daughter, Sarah, accompanied me and together we experienced life in a culture at once like and most unlike our own and, together, punted on the Cam River. I lectured at the University's Theology Faculty and in London at an exclusive club. Both were places where my grandparents and those of most of my audience, who tended to be Catholic and Jewish, could only have gained entrance through the servants' door in the back. I also researched and wrote a paper comparing Catholic-Jewish relations in U.S. and British history, which turned out to be remarkably similar in ways I would not have anticipated. I also discovered that my one famous ancestor,

Daniel O'Connell, the great Emancipator of Ireland, is as well regarded in British Jewish history as he is in Irish history, since one of the first things he did on becoming the first Catholic to hold a seat in Parliament was to move for the emancipation of the Jews.

It was a wonderful, restful period, and almost (although not quite) prepared me for the maelstrom that was to come on my return. I had known what was awaiting me, since the drama had begun before I left; but the next nine months were something of a nightmare for me, professionally. I refer to the tremendous flap over the making of Mel Gibson's movie *The Passion of the Christ*.

The Passion of Catholic-Jewish Relations -- Mel's "Melstrom"

The story began some months before my Cambridge interlude, with an article in the Sunday *New York Times Magazine* interviewing Hutton Gibson, Mel Gibson's father. Hutton Gibson held extreme anti-Semitic views and also believed that the teaching authority of the papacy had ended with the death of Pope Pius XII, making Gibson a "sedevacantist." A sedevacantist believes that the See of Peter, the papacy, is vacant and the current holder illegitimate. Such a person, of course, is no longer Catholic; but the media never quite caught up with that fact.

It was well known at the time that Mel Gibson was in the process of making a major movie about the death of Jesus. Jews who knew their history (and a remarkably high percentage do) and Christians involved in the dialogue knew that such depictions, in the past called "passion plays," had over the centuries been occasions for vicious and deadly mob violence of Christians against Jews. Did Mel share his father's anti-Semitic views and would these influence his passion play writ large on the movie screen? Since no one had seen the script, fears and rumors escalated in the press and equally in emails to me. Mel was presumed to be a Catholic and therefore, somehow, my responsibility.

The idea came to me that the half-dozen Catholic and Jewish scholars with whom I was most deeply in correspondence and who had the necessary biblical and historical expertise might offer Mel some suggestions that could help him, without decreasing the dramatic impact of his film. The idea would be to make sure that it was reasonably historically accurate and, above all, could not be used to foster the dangerous notion that the Jews were collectively guilty for the death of Jesus.

I contacted an old friend, Msgr. Royale Vadakin of Los Angeles, who had been the ecumenical officer of that archdiocese back when I first started with the Conference. I knew he knew people in Hollywood. Roy did indeed know someone on Mel's production staff, a kindly and good hearted Jesuit, a scholar of the classics, who was translating the script for him into Aramaic (the language of the Jews of Jesus' time) and Latin (though he had told Mel that the language of Roman troops in the empire at the time would have been Greek, not Latin). I explained to him what I had in mind. A short time later my daughter came running into our kitchen, where I was having a snack, announcing that Mel Gibson was on the phone asking for me. I took the call.

The discussion with Mel, who also had three other folks on the line with him, went quite well, I thought. We spoke for almost an hour, the second half being in the car on the cell phone as I was driving my daughter to a school-related event she had to attend. He said he would welcome the advice of the scholars, though he could not promise to adapt everything in his movie since it was already being filmed. Mel asserted that he was not at all anti-Semitic. "How could I be," he asserted, "since I play golf with so many people with numbers on their arms?"

Shortly after Easter a copy of the script was delivered to one of the members of our little team, which was co-chaired by my counterpart in the Anti-Defamation League; and the scholars set to work making their comments and suggestions. I duly reported this to the Bishops' Committee for Ecumenical and Interreligious Affairs at their spring meeting and sent the scholars' report on to Mr. Gibson the day before leaving for Cambridge. The group, of course, was pledged to keep both the script and their report in strictest confidence, which they did.

Wandering Between Two Worlds

Shortly after arriving in Cambridge, I received a long distance phone call from my office saying, in effect, that all hell had broken loose. Gibson was threatening to sue the Conference and demanding the return of all copies of the script. These were, of course, immediately returned to him. I was enjoined to silence by the Conference, which was not difficult since I was in England.

The Gibson team itself, however, went public with the story, engendering a media frenzy in which several of the members of the scholars' team understandably stated their positions publicly. I returned to the office later that summer, still maintaining silence on the merits of the movie myself. Many in the Jewish community, however, wondered in public why the bishops had not come out against the movie (they did not do so even after it was released). The simple reason was there was no consensus on which to make a formal statement. Yes, it was a passion play writ large; but some bishops felt that bringing the story of Christ into the public sphere was a help to evangelization, even if it was not perfect.

What the Conference did allow me to do was to put together a book, rather substantial as it turned out, of official teachings of the Church from and since the Second Vatican Council, both those from Rome and those from the U.S. bishops themselves. These made very clear and in detail why one cannot conclude that the Jews, during Jesus' time or in subsequent generations, could in any way be held collectively responsible for the death of Jesus, which was at most the decision of the Roman governor, Pilate, in collusion with the Temple priesthood, who hardly represented the people of Jerusalem, much less all the Jews spread around the Empire. This is, in fact, the clear statement of the gospels themselves. So, as I joked, "Mel made a movie and I threw a book at it." I believe the latter, founded as it is upon the clear testimony of the New Testament and upon the solid teaching tradition of the Catholic Church, will prevail in the long run.

Indeed, the teaching of the Church prevailed even in the short run. Whereas passion plays over the centuries precipitated great waves of Christian violence against Jews, the movie did not. In an article I wrote for *America* magazine after the release of the movie on Ash

Wednesday, February 24, 2004, I noted this fact. Passion plays, I noted, had acted as triggers for violence. In a sense, *The Passion of the Christ*, a typical passion play, had once again pulled the trigger. But the Second Vatican Council's clear teaching that the Jews then, and now, cannot collectively be blamed for the death of Jesus, had so permeated the minds of Catholics (and, through parallel Protestant teachings, other Christians as well) that even though the trigger was pulled, the "gun" of anti-Semitic violence did not go off. Christians simply no longer have in their heads the notion of collective Jewish guilt. Jews in dialogue were just as mystified by Catholics who said that the movie did not trigger any animosity toward Jews as Christians in dialogue were mystified by the historically founded and very real fears of Jews that the movie would do just that. An incidental but very healthy by-product of the affair, I also noted, came with the intensification of Catholic-Jewish dialogues around the country discussing the movie and educating Catholics about the dark side of Christian treatment of Jews over the centuries. Subsequent statements by Mr. Gibson, of course, have raised further questions about his attitudes toward Jews, but that is a story I had nothing to do with and so is not pertinent here.

Life in Retirement

Not long before Christmas 2007, the Conference announced that, because of the necessity of budget cuts, largely due to the huge losses of money from the child sex abuse scandals, it would have to cut back staff rather severely and re-organize. Those of us of a certain vintage were offered quite reasonable retirement packages, knowing that the number of positions in our respective offices would, in any event, be reduced. The Secretariat for Ecumenical and Interreligious Affairs, for example, would go from five full time professionals on staff to just three. After some anguish and realizing I had little option, I accepted the package. Thirty of us, many lay professionals who had worked for the Conference since the time of, or in my case shortly after, the Second Vatican Council, retired by the end of June of that year.

I must say that my leave-taking did come with some positive notes.

My thirty years, it seemed, had not gone unnoticed. Not only did my office give me a very moving farewell dinner, but some very nice things were said, both then and in the Catholic press. One colleague, the head of the Conference's Department of Social Development and World Peace, said that when the history of the Conference came to be written, three names would be most prominent, Msgr. John Burke, the founding general secretary, Msgr. George Higgins, the great labor priest who was also a tireless advocate of Catholic-Jewish relations and, well, myself. I asked him the next day in the elevator how he could possibly have put me in such company. He responded simply, "You deserve it." In an article on my retirement in the *National Catholic Reporter*, John Allen said that it was a truism that no one is irreplaceable. But, he said, some are less replaceable than others. "Think of the Chicago Bulls without Michael Jordan."

I also received awards from the National Council of Synagogues, representing Reform, Reconstructionist and Conservative Judaism; Orthodox Judaism; the Anti-Defamation League; the American Jewish Committee; the National Catholic Holocaust Institute of Seton Hill University; the Center of Centers of Christian-Jewish Relations, representing almost thirty such institutes in the U.S. and Europe; and B'nai B'rith International. On my last day of work, June 30, I left my office for the last time and drove a half block up the street to Catholic University, where I received the 2007 Cardinal Bernardin Award "for promoting dialogue within the Church" from the Catholic Common Ground Initiative. Who am I to argue with all these perceptive people?

I have continued writing, lecturing, and participating in dialogues in retirement. In early September of 2008, I presented a paper at a major symposium in Rome on Pope Pius XII, arguing that the archives for the World War II period should be released to scholars as soon as possible. At the conclusion of the conference, the group met with Pope Benedict XVI at Castel Gandolfo; and, since I had given a paper, I was one of the twenty participants brought up to be introduced to him. Benedict is gentle and kindly in such meetings and is truly interested in what people have to say to him personally. Being told what I did, the pope took my hand to impress upon me the great importance to the Church of moving our dialogue forward with the Jewish people. It was, as it was when I was last at Castel Gandolfo to meet Pope John Paul II, a beautiful, sunny day, auguring well. I prayed for the dialogue that Benedict had just blessed.

Pain and Prayer

Most of the controversies between the Church and the Jewish people during my almost one-third of a century with the Bishops' Conference have come at us from Europe and involve, in one way or another, the Holocaust -- Bitberg and Waldheim, the Auschwitz Convent and the canonization of Edith Stein, Pius XII and the International Catholic-Jewish Historical Committee. It is no wonder. Two thirds of the Jews of Europe, one third of all Jews then living, were systematically hunted down using the most sophisticated technology then known (computers, for instance, were perfected for use in identifying Jews in occupied countries). All this was done in the heart of "Christendom." Virtually all of the perpetrators and bystanders were baptized Christians, at least in name.

Though I have dealt with the Shoah and its implications for the Church all of my adult life, I cannot get used to its horror. The details constantly shock, constantly surprise, constantly test my faith not only in God but even more so in humanity. I have seen the memos of major German corporations touting the cost-efficiency of their gas chambers versus the use of machine guns, and providing as appendices tests showing the superiority of Xyklon B gas over the products of their competitors. I have seen the trench dug in the killing field of Dachau to drain away the blood from the mass shootings. I have seen the crematoria of a number of death camps. Toward the end, to save gas and time, the Nazis began to throw babies live into the crematoria. Atrocity in the name of efficiency! How could anyone, however brutish, pick up a baby girl and throw her into the flames? Time after time? I have a daughter. One of those babies could have been my baby. One million children. Future Einsteins and Bubers and Mahlers. Murdered by genetic fiat.

The Holocaust was not perpetrated by illiterate louts and barbarians, as were the 10,000 Jewish victims of the first Crusade in 1096, but by the educated elite of Europe, the product of its best universities: engineers and lawyers, businessmen and doctors, elite and highly trained units such as the infamous Einsatzgruppen, by fathers (and occasionally mothers) who loved their own children, read Goethe and listened to Beethoven. How does one compute all this? How does one pray? Where is the God of love, or even justice, in the dreadful silence of Auschwitz today?

On one level, I believe, I can pray because I can pray with Jews in the face of all this. *Ani Ma'amin*, they pray. "I believe." And they prayed it standing in line to enter the gas chambers. We went to Auschwitz, Cathie and I, with a Catholic-Jewish group lead by Cardinal Keeler and Rabbi Jack Bemporad. At Auschwitz II (Birkenau, which was devoted exclusively to the killing of Jews, while Auschwitz proper more "ecumenically" killed Jews and Poles together), the group, which included members of the Polish hierarchy and local Jewish community, used a liturgy of remembrance of the victims that Rabbi Leon Klenicki and I had written several years before, and which has been reprinted in a number of languages. Leon was there, but he was unable to lead it with me. Another rabbi filled in for him as he stood quietly at the back of the group, his heart saying what his lips could not. We all said together the *Kaddish*, the Jewish prayer for the dead that praises God and nowhere mentions death. With us, too, was a man we had met earlier who turned out to be a Polish Catholic, now living in America, who had been interned in Auschwitz, and who had helped a member of our group, a Jewish survivor, in the camp when otherwise she would have been swept up and taken to her death. Prayer? Yes. I am a believer. *Ani Ma'amin!*

One of the most frequent questions asked of me at the socials after my talks is, "So, how did you get into all of this? I mean, you are a Catholic. How did you come to give your life to this cause?" My short answer is invariably: "The Word of God led me to it, by which I mean my love of the Hebrew Scriptures. Which I developed in the seminary." You now have my long answer. Part of it was sought. A bit of it was planned. Most of it was serendipitous. It is in the serendipity that I believe one can discern, however faintly, the finger of God writing one's life. Follow those faint stirrings in your heart and the ineffable hopes that murmur in your mind. Strangely wonderful things can happen.

A VIEW FROM THE PORCH
John P. Mulheisen

Where did all my curiosity and self-confidence come from? There were days when it wasn't so. I remember my first night as a Sacred Heart Seminary student, the beginning of a new adventure in my life. I was standing on the back porch of that beautiful Gothic building in the heart of Detroit…tears building up in my eyes. I don't know why. Was I afraid I couldn't make it there or was I afraid that I just plain didn't belong?

I didn't come to the seminary with the strongest academic credentials. I was a mediocre student at best, although graduating from Salesian High School did require some degree of competence. I came from a family where education was a product of the streets and parks more than the classroom. My father died when I was twelve. That left my mother and an older brother and sister. None of them demonstrated an interest in maintaining a strong family unit, and they soon got on with their own lives. I did too, but I missed not having anyone close.

My fortunes changed during my high school years. I was able to make up for a lack of family support by allowing a surrogate family to "adopt" me. I met Ed and Cath in my early high school years. Ed was our baseball coach, and the whole gang was invited over to his house after practices and games. As time went by, the others drifted away; but I stayed around because I had found a family. They let me in and loved me and gave me a place to be besides the streets.

Ed and Cath were the prototypical Catholic family of the fifties and sixties. They raised nine children on a Detroit Edison underground repairman's salary. They never had great wealth, but the love that came from that small home in Detroit permeated and spread throughout the entire neighborhood to everyone and everything they touched. Even before my seminary days I noticed that they were special. The young assistant priests from St. Brigid were attracted to their company, not unlike a good number of seminarians would be attracted to them in a few short years.

I first realized that the Church had the ability to create conflict as well as communion because of Ed and Cath. They were struggling with the major issue of the day -- birth control. As a young man, I could not begin to understand the struggle that these loving people were going through. As a surrogate son who loved them dearly, however, I recognized that the Church was not always a haven of peace in their lives. It was the first time I recognized that questions were allowed in the Church. On the other hand, the answers had better be right...or else.

I am sure that the confidence I needed to enter the seminary came from the association I had with Ed and Cath. It also helped that my best friend from kindergarten, Jim O'Brien, decided to join up as well. Jim lived across the street from St. Brigid Church. His family experienced a lot of tragedy during the years we were growing up. In the 1950's one of the biggest fears a family had was having a member come down with polio. Most families avoided this terrible disease, but the O'Brien family was struck twice. Both Jim and his sister Pat contracted polio when they were in elementary school. Jim's was a relatively mild case that resulted only in a deformed foot. His sister Pat, on the other hand, suffered a severe case that rendered her a quadriplegic for the remaining thirty-five years of her life. Jim also lost a sister to leukemia during those years. In addition his father was an invalid due to emphysema and died when we were in high school. This family bore unbelievable sorrows.

Jim and I took our experiences and insecurities and entered Sacred Heart in 1961. I had visions of belonging, of being respected like the young assistant priests at St. Brigid. These men were not only looked up to in the community; they were also free to continue to be accepted in Ed and Cath's life, even as adults.

I also had a deeper, subconscious motivation in my decision to enter the seminary. In retrospect, I now believe I was seeking the security of the institution. I had not been prepared to make serious decisions in my life, and the seminary seemed like the ideal place for me since all my decisions would be made for me. I was missing, however, a sense of spirituality and the basic skills required of a student to excel in the demanding environment of seminary life -- skills such as a basic curiosity and fundamental study habits. So that first night I cried. Was I afraid or did I just not belong?

My seminary experience was bittersweet. I loved the comradeship and the security of the structured life, even though I did start to grow out of the need for that structure. I look back on those days at Sacred Heart with great pride and warmth. Simple association with the loving, high achieving, full of life group of young men of that day rubbed off on me and made me a better person. The seminary also gave me the opportunity to get a higher education, something I never would have had otherwise. The entire four years had a profound effect on the rest of my life, more than for others, perhaps, because it caused a drastic change in my direction. I began to believe that I too could achieve something important. I had a long way to go, but the seed had been planted.

There was also a dark side to my experience at Sacred Heart. It started years earlier with my father's death and came to a head with three tragic deaths in my first two years of seminary life. Two fellow seminarians and my stepfather of one year all died within a very short period of time. These deaths, along with a strong case of insecurity, led me to an exaggerated fear of death and a severe case of anxiety. I was stricken with psychosomatic problems that served as a distraction to my studies and my efforts at developing a spiritual life. The seminary faculty was very supportive. They provided me psychological help and personal understanding that enabled me to get through that dark time. By my senior year I had overcome most of my fears and declared myself almost normal.

Like it did on most of my classmates, Vatican II had a profound
influence on me. I didn't think the old Church was irrelevant because
I didn't know any better; but when the sweep of changes came, I
embraced them all, simply because they made so much sense.
Nothing seemed more stupid to me than having to listen to lectures in
Latin. I was not a good student to begin with; to expect me to learn
that way was impossible. And the Mass made so much more sense
when you could actually hear the priest talking to you in English! To
me, the most important change in the Mass was the new emphasis on
the Word. For the first time in my life I saw the Mass as a learning
experience that would help me grow spiritually.

But grow I didn't, not yet anyway. I still had a sense that to be a good
priest you not only had to want to help people reach eternal life but
you also had to tow the line, follow the rules, remain celibate. By my
senior year I knew I couldn't do that; and so upon graduation I left for
another life. I didn't know what it was going to be; I just knew I
couldn't cut it as a celibate priest.

My first year as a secular college graduate was spent teaching seventh
graders at a Catholic school in northwest Detroit. I was also reintroduced to the social world of dating. It had been over five years
since I last dated, and I began to believe that I had made the right
decision in leaving the seminary. The fun and freedom of that first
year was short-lived, however, because in November of 1966, I was
drafted into the army. It was back to institutional life but with a twist.
It wasn't a life of idealism and laughter like the seminary experience
but rather a life of reality and anticipation. The anticipation was
Vietnam.

I carried what I had become in the seminary into the army. As a
naïve, socially immature soldier, I didn't make any waves and
coasted through boot camp and advanced infantry training. Then my
background kicked in with its first major influence on the course of
my life. Instead of Vietnam I was sent to Alaska for eighteen months.
I marveled at my good fortune of dodging Vietnam until I realized

that there were only two classes of solders in Alaska. The first class consisted of overage (23+) college graduates who would probably question every order on the battlefield. The second class consisted of solders whose questionable intelligence probably would have meant disaster under fire. It made for an interesting mix.

My military situation and the comparative isolation of Fairbanks, Alaska, gave me little chance for social growth; but it did afford me the time (and boy was there time, with twenty-three hours of darkness and minus 50-degree temperatures) to grow intellectually through reading and reflection. Because of my background and an unbelievable coincidence, I ended up being assigned as a Chaplain's Assistant.

It happened when I first arrived at Ft. Wainwright. I reported to post personnel for unit assignment and was directed to the next available assignment clerk. Not only was the clerk from Detroit, but it turned out we had a mutual former acquaintance. This clerk was a boyhood friend of Pat Vosberg, a Sacred Heart student in the class ahead of ours who had committed suicide four years earlier. Learning that I was a seminary graduate, he asked if I would have a problem working for a Baptist chaplain. In my best southern drawl I said that I would have no problem at all, and the rest of my army career was set. I worked for the Baptist chaplain for eight months and then was assigned to the Catholic chaplain for the remainder of my tour.

My association with the chaplains kept me in close touch with religion and the Church. My seminary training prepared me well for my duties, and I soon found all the chaplains and chaplain's aids turning to me for help. This empowerment was very fulfilling and renewed my interest in the priesthood. All of a sudden I discovered I was pretty good at ministering the Word. I began to feel that I might have sold myself short the last time around and should give the priesthood another chance. Consequently, I took an early release from the Army (two months) and entered St. John's in the fall of 1968, three years behind my original class.

At St. John's I began the intellectual growth of my life. For the first time I felt I was a student who was not only growing from within but also contributing to other people's growth. I dove headlong into theology and thoroughly enjoyed the freedom of thought that the faculty afforded us. But that freedom of thought that had its roots in the Vatican Council and was nurtured by three years of secular life experience was also the beginning of the end for me as a candidate for the priesthood.

I began to question. I questioned basic theological tenets. I questioned the Church's teaching on birth control and its inconsistency in other areas, including capital punishment and war. I could not reconcile the Church's claim to be pro-life on the one hand, yet approving of capital punishment and economic wars on the other. I came to believe that the Church was more a political institution than a beacon of faith.

Theologically, I began questioning the existence of God. To this day, I am not altogether sure why I came to such a drastic point. Perhaps part of it was that I started out with a poor foundation in faith. Add to that the credibility of the Church starting to crumble in my eyes, and a lot of questions came up. Was God real or was he created to give us a reason for our existence? At that time I would have become a full-blown atheist if it were not for Viktor Frankel. In reading Frankel's *Man's Search For Meaning* for the third time, one story struck me and gave me the wisdom to at least question my questioning.

Frankel spent three years in a German concentration camp during World War II. The premise of his theory, which concludes that there is meaning to life, is based on this experience. In one of his recollections he describes returning from a long day of hard labor and spotting a man lying by the roadside. This was nothing new for him. He would often see men lying by the side of the road ready to die; and they always did. But on that particular day he witnessed another emaciated inmate stop, take out his only piece of bread, his dinner for the day, and try to feed the dying man. The donor knew he would not save the dying man, but he was still compelled to try. This seemingly irrational act was a common experience in Frankel's world of that time. In the midst of all the agony and hopelessness, he witnessed hope and charity. Because men were willing to reach beyond what they could understand, especially during the most desperate of times, he *detected* that there was more to life than he could comprehend. Frankel's conclusion gave me a reprieve from the isolation of being a complete non-believer. There is a force beyond our empirical understanding. Why not define this force as God?

In effect, I had been given the green light to continue to search for God. But, because of my disillusionment with the politics of the Church, it would have to be in a different environment. The Church as a community of people is my heritage; and, like a magnet, I am always drawn to it. Yet I had lost patience with it as an institution and knew I was going to struggle to stay a part of it. The tiny crack opened by Vatican II was just enough to let me out screaming, to let me think for myself for the first time in my life.

After a year and a half of growth away from the Church, at the expense of the Church, I left the seminary for the final time. I was a different person from the one who had left in 1965. This time I left much more mature intellectually but still treading water socially. I took a job with an automotive aftermarket company and decided to get on with my life -- in a hurry. I was in a hurry because here I was, 27 years old and not married. (Remember my social immaturity?)

I met a girl at work and we had a whirlwind courtship. We were married within a year. I suspect it did not take long before we both felt we had made a mistake, but by then we had two beautiful children. The Catholic influence on my life (I still couldn't shake it) determined that I would make the best of it and raise a fine family. I think the fact that my dad died so early in my life gave me a strong desire to be a good father. But, after fifteen years, when my son was twelve and my daughter was eight, my wife told me she didn't want to be married any more. The subsequent separation and divorce made it impossible for me to be a full-time father. I moved close to their house and tried to be there as much as possible, but I could never be the full-time influence I wanted to be. It was, and still is, the biggest disappointment of my life.

During the time of my first marriage, I worked for six years as a

Religious Education Director. Even though I was struggling with the Church's authority and had questions regarding some of the Church's teachings, the intellectual climate of the times allowed me to be a part of it. I never compromised any of the articles of faith, because I felt they were valid for those who believed. I had neither the inclination nor the authority to contradict the Church. Indeed, I wished I had the faith.

I believed strongly in the community, and I worked very hard to help the people understand that their faith had to be something they lived every day and every minute. I spent three years with SHS 1965 classmate Roman (Skip) Duranczyk at Guardian Angels in Clawson, where he was associate pastor. Then, when another 1965 classmate, Phil Calcaterra, died, I replaced him for three years at St. Mary Magdalene in Hazel Park. During this time I had the opportunity to teach adult education courses, and we brought in heavyweight local thinkers as guest speakers on many occasions. Such experiences afforded me the opportunity to grow to the point where I finally achieved the self-confidence that made me an effective teacher. The freedom of Vatican II finally paid dividends in helping me to become a man.

By the time of my divorce I had also grown socially. I wasn't in a hurry to make a new commitment. I knew I had time to find the right person who could love me and share my life. I have always had a longing to be loved. I know that sounds simplistic (because who hasn't?); but I have been told that, because I did not experience strong love bonds as a child, it became more of an obsession with me. Maybe that is why I was in such a hurry to get married the first time. I wasn't in a hurry anymore; but, wouldn't you know it, I met that right person immediately. Mutual friends introduced us.

Jeannette was also a divorcee with two children. She has twins six months older than my oldest. Her daughter is a special child who is mentally impaired. When we met, Jeannette was taking care of her daughter and working full time. It was an unbelievable burden that she handled like a pro. We had many things in common, including a Catholic background and a shared feeling that the Church looked down on those who divorce, no matter what the circumstances.

Jeannette and I married in 1986. She has been, and always will be, the love of my life. The experience of unqualified love is the most redeeming experience there is. Without it I cannot imagine anyone truly understanding the love of Jesus. That is just another reason why celibacy is such a misguided policy. How much more effective could a priest or a bishop be if he truly experienced the love of a woman?

Through the years Jeannette and I have done our best to be parents and stepparents. It is a difficult project because you cannot be one hundred percent to anyone. We believe that being good role models is our best chance to positively influence our children. The Church has not played a role in this effort. Jeannette raised her son in the Catholic faith. I did not raise my children that way. I regret it now only because they never were given the opportunity to experience the dynamics of a religious community. None of our children is a practicing Catholic. Yet they are beautiful people. My daughter is a good mother, my son is a good husband, and my stepson is a good man.

I still struggle with the God question. To me God is in the details. Of all the passages in the Bible, I am most influenced by Matthew 25, the Sermon on the Mount. You don't have to participate in the idiosyncrasies of an institution to live as Jesus lived. As a matter of fact, it can be a distraction. The primary function of an institution, out of necessity, is self-preservation. And self-preservation breeds politics and bad decisions and loss of purpose. To me the answer is to feed the hungry, help the poor, take care of the sick; and then, if there is eternal life, you will see it.

I do not have the gift of faith. I wish I did. It would be so easy to have definitive answers to fall back on. I am, however, still strongly influenced by my heritage. When I go to church, it is a Catholic church, because that is what I understand. Sometimes Jeannette and I even discuss going back on a more regular basis, not because it is required for salvation but because the community can help you grow.

For most of my formative years the Church ruled me with an iron fist. Truth was absolute. Everything was black or white. I allowed the Church to be my guide, my leader, my mentor. Vatican II freed me from that rigid bond that stifled creativity. It opened the door to freedom of thought, a chance to make mistakes and learn from them rather than be ashamed of them. It gave me the choice to believe that every encounter in life is an encounter with God. As Karl Rahner said, "Unless nothing is profane, can anything be sacred?"

As I look back on my first day on the back porch of the beautiful Gothic building that was my home for four years, I think of that young guy who was so anxious about the future; and I smile. I smile because the future is good. I realize that I did indeed belong. I realize that I was fortunate to be a part of it all. I wasn't ready for all of it, but most of us weren't. Besides, who could have possibly been prepared for what was to come?

My seminary experience was a primary influence in any success I have had over the past forty years. It gave me an association with many intelligent, high-principled individuals whose influences are still with me today. It was the steppingstone to the world of ideas that makes my life more interesting and exciting. And it gave me a gift that I will always cherish. It taught me to love myself; and therefore it made it possible for me to easily love others. That is the greatest gift of all.

MY DAD IS PINK
Michael J. Callahan

"Day Dog" were the words of greeting which reached me on my first day of high school at Sacred Heart Seminary. The class was unevenly divided between those of us who used public transportation to reach the school and boarders, who came from the neighboring Detroit suburbs and from other Michigan dioceses. I went to school there because my family could not afford another private high school for me and because I believed I had a vocation to become a priest.

Detroit had reached the zenith of its population in the 1950 census with just over two million inhabitants. Many Detroiters worked in automobile manufacturing and belonged to various unions, especially the Teamsters and United Auto Workers. Many were devoutly Catholic, including those in my family. I had two sisters. All three of us attended the parish school and heard our pastor often preach that it was at least venially sinful for parents not to send their children to Catholic grade schools and high schools.

So each morning I rode two buses from northwest Detroit to the seminary high school, a trip repeated even on Saturday for morning classes. The education was mediocre at best. The majority of faculty members were parish priests with master's degrees in some field, usually obtained after the archbishop assigned them to teach at our school. Latin was our only class taught by a true professional, Fr. Walter Markowitz, who had a Ph.D. in Classics from the University of Michigan. His funeral in the seminary chapel was my last visit to the Gothic structure.

Following high school graduation, many in our class, boarders and "dogs," left the seminary. Those who stayed lived together. In those days seminarians numbered in the hundreds. The Catholic Church had a seemingly unending stream of young men to fill the ranks of its priests.

The four year college scholastic program was thoroughly a matter of liberal arts. Priests taught us philosophy classes in Latin and a class in logic, along with chant and speech classes designed to help us with preaching and liturgy.

Everything about college life agreed with me, because life and study was a competition to be the best student with the highest grade point average. We all knew that the students who finished at the top of the class would be rewarded by the archbishop with a full scholarship to Rome or to Louvain in Belgium.

I spent an enormous amount of time learning Spanish. My goal was to become bilingual. Señor Gordon Farrell taught our Spanish classes. He was Argentinean and a full-time faculty member at the University of Detroit. On my final exam, he wrote that I could only learn more Spanish by living in a Spanish language country.

Fr. Paul C. Berg, known affectionately as " Paul C minus," taught most of the philosophy classes I took. He lectured in Latin on all the theorems of cosmology, epistemology, and ontology. Our class labored through the material, despite its apparent irrelevance. For me, those classes were hurdles to be jumped on the way to a scholarship.

Louvain and Vatican II

At the end of my senior year in college, Fr. Gerald Martin, aptly known to the students as "Meany Martin" because he was at one time the Dean of Discipline, told me I finished second in our class. Likely, I would be assigned to studies in Rome. Years later, I found out the registrar had miscalculated my grade point average. Still, I was rewarded with the coveted scholarship and four years of study at the American College of the University of Louvain in Belgium. The American College housed one hundred fifty students from dioceses all over the United States. Seminarians attended theology classes at the larger university of more than 30,000 students.

Language was the first barrier to be overcome by new men who arrived in 1965. Classes were taught in French, and oral exams were taken in French, although students could elect to answer the questions in Latin. Thanks to Fr. Markowitz's years of drilling, I chose this alternative.

By now the Catholic Church had begun to change. The Second Vatican Council, convoked by Pope John XXIII, continued under Pope Paul VI. John Dearden, the Detroit archbishop, was a leading light at the Council; and the final session took place during my first year at Louvain.

Louvain's professors played important roles in the "aggiornamento" of Vatican II, where many of them served as *periti* or experts to European bishops. So pervasive was their influence that *Time* magazine called Vatican II "Louvain I."

Professor Louis Jannsens taught the notion of "responsible parenthood." Parents could use artificial contraception to limit the number of children. Curia officials tried to censure Jannsens because Rome believed use of the pill to be "unnatural" compared with the rhythm method. Jannsens disagreed, reasoning there was no difference between spatial barriers to fertility and temporal ones. Archbishop Dearden agreed with Jannsens, but his interventions at the Council for responsible parenthood were met with intrigue and ultimate failure.

Rome's morality came from the natural law which was developed in the high Middle Ages when the Church was the dominant institution in society. This natural law morality made the Pope and his curia the ultimate law givers. Both were invested with infallibility for their pronouncements. We should recall that the Pope and curia were charter members of the Flat Earth Society. Some might observe that they still are.

Louvain's influence at Vatican II helped weave into the fabric of Council constitutions and pronouncements the radical moral notion that the individual's conscience, not the papacy, was the ultimate basis for deciding what's right and what's wrong. That teaching rocked the foundations of the institutional church. For four years at Louvain, my classmates and I were schooled in this radical theology.

After suffering through the incomprehensible lectures of the first year, Sacred Heart Seminary classmate Brian Haggerty and I set out for a summer in France. In 1966 and throughout our years in Europe the American dollar was very strong against the European currencies. As a result, students could afford extensive travel.

Our first destination was Lyon, built first as an ancient Roman fortification. There we worked at a camp for blind children who showed us their games and activities, but mostly they spoke to us and spoke and spoke. The children made no allowance for the fact that neither of us could speak to them except in halting and infantile French.

Next, we journeyed to the Norman coast and lived at an orphanage in Dieppe. The town was the scene of a famous "raid" by Canadian forces in 1942. They tried to seize a port in the Nazi-held Atlantic wall. The Canadians failed to make it off the rocky beach. Once again, both of us immersed ourselves in the activities of French children, who did us the great favor of talking endlessly.

At the close of the summer of '66, Haggerty and I travelled to Rome to spend ten days with neighbors of mine from Detroit. My friend Peter was stationed there with the Veteran's Administration. He gave us numerous guided tours and introductions in the Eternal City.

I began my second year of classes with great trepidation. What if I still could not understand the lectures in French? The first morning back at Louvain I heard and understood the lecture, and I was forever grateful to the blind children of Lyon and the orphans of Dieppe.

Spain became my destination for the summer of '67 and '68. I stayed with an Australian family named Ryan in the hills above Malaga, on the Costa del Sol. The family sponsored self-help projects among the poor and destitute. At that time, Spain was ruled by Generalissimo Franco. It was unmistakably a police state.

I was assigned to a geriatric hospital in a dangerous slum of Malaga, which the *guardia* would not enter after dark. I never stayed after sunset. Each day I would take a number of paraplegic children to the beach, carrying one on each hip. One child was a gypsy. I was warned to watch her closely because gypsies would try to steal her. They did eye her closely but never attempted any abduction.

By the end of my second summer in Spain, my Spanish was good enough to allow me to travel freely. So I hitchhiked from Gibraltar back to Louvain with a lengthy detour through Munich. There I met a number of classmates at the Oktoberfest, the largest carnival for beer drinkers you could ever imagine. On my sojourn to Munich, I would often stop at a local tavern for lunch. My accented Spanish would cause the bartender to call out to other customers. They would laugh at this obvious American using local slang.

My decision to hitchhike was motivated by personal economics. Either I could ride a train back to Belgium and arrive two weeks before school started, or I could save the money for German lager. As I started out, the weather was quite mild, so I slept outside in a sleeping bag. One morning I awoke to the sound of a ringing bell coming closer and closer. I sat up and saw I was in the path of a horse-drawn plow.

I arrived at Barcelona where I found myself stranded at the side of an eight lane highway, a rarity in Spain. No one stopped. I hopped a train for France and stopped at Avignon, famous for the French captivity of the medieval papacy. France was in the midst of a record rainfall. The youth hostel sat beside the Rhone River, which flooded that night. I joined dozens of other students evacuating to higher ground and to avoid France's worst flood in fifty years.

Switzerland was my next destination where I had to hitchhike around Lake Constance. I took my first and last ride in a motorcycle sidecar, which places the passenger only a few inches above a bumpy roadbed.

A young reporter for a Munich daily newspaper gave me a long ride toward my destination. En route we spoke about religion and the Church. He asked my views on *Humanae Vitae*, Pope Paul VI's encyclical on birth control. The reporter said that Catholics of Bavaria were the most loyal and conservative in the world but they would never follow the Pope's teaching on birth control. He echoed the sentiment of Prof. Jannsens who, when asked if Catholics would follow the Pope and practice rhythm, answered "Le train est déjà parti". "(That train has left the station)."

Our final year at the American College forced the class to confront celibacy. The rector called us together before ordination to subdiaconate and explained that we must each sign a rescript pledging to remain celibate for the remainder of our lives. The rescript was in Latin. An Oklahoman observed he could neither read nor understand nor sign the oath. The rector told me to translate the document so each one could sign with due deliberation and understanding.

Then, as now, celibacy was a less than welcome condition for ordination to the priesthood. Through the decades since 1968, the requirement of celibacy has been relaxed for some. Bishops may dispense from celibacy, though they don't like to consider the possibility. Apparently bishops feel that, since they had been good celibates, the priests they ordain should be too.

1969 was the year I was ordained a priest. The institution of the Church was very different from the Church 40 years later. In '69, priests were so plentiful that even a small parish had one or more assistant priests. On ordination day, June 26, 1969, with my hands gripped firmly by Bishop Weldon of Springfield, Massachusetts, I promised faithful obedience to Archbishop Dearden and his successors in Detroit. Some promises, I learned, were more difficult to keep than others.

Back to Michigan

Re-entry to Detroit meant that five newly ordained priests from Rome and Louvain were introduced to the chancery departments and the workings of the institutional church. Bishop Tom Gumbleton was iconoclastic in his assessment of the chancery's impact when he asked how many parishes would even notice if the chancery shut down.

St. David was my first parish assignment. The urban church had 2,500 families and 12 grades of school. I quickly became involved with anti-war protests because three or four recent grads from our high school returned from southeast Asia in body bags.

I attended anti-war demonstrations with St. David students. I marched on The Mall in Washington, with a crowd of 400,000, to protest the bombing of Cambodia.

My involvement in anti-war protests was not exactly the stuff of the Berrigan brothers, yet it did divide the parish. I joined a group of Michigan clergy who met with Congressman Gerald Ford. He told us Nixon's strategy was correct and America's youth were not being slaughtered needlessly.

The parish high school closed because of a lack of funding. The number of nuns declined precipitously, and the parish could not hire replacements for the women religious who had taught for free. I left the parish to begin a Hispanic ministry in the northern counties of the diocese.

Hispanics came to Michigan as agricultural workers and stayed to work in the auto plants. Pastors of parishes where I worked with Mexicans continued to ignore these minorities, yet the ministry I undertook was left unfunded by the diocese. I taught college courses at Marygrove and Mercy to keep my car on the road and the prospect of my Hispanic ministry alive.

Feeling an acute need for professional credentials, I took the Law School Acceptance Test and began law school at Wayne State University in September, 1972. I paid the tuition there on my own, since the archdiocese would not fund a "secular" degree. Whoever enjoys law school and its intimidating pedagogy should seek mental health treatment. This law school class, however, turned faculty intimidation upside down. Several Vietnam vets began the first year of law school with me. They retaliated against an abusive property law professor by hiring an old "hippy" to sell popcorn in the lecture hall during one of his classes. The popcorn vendor was dressed only in the box that held bags of the hot, buttered corn and nothing else. The professors quickly realized the time-tested methods of intimidation no longer worked.

During the second two years of law school, I worked as an intern for Peter Deegan, St. Clair County Prosecuting Attorney. When he first asked me to take the internship, I explained my Hispanic parishioners might be the defendants. He asked, "What better way do you have to help them solve their legal troubles?"

Tribunal Detour and Saginaw Assignments

The Church had been displeased with my legal studies. Then, as I neared the finish line, the archbishop told me I would go to Catholic University in Washington to study *canon law*. Cardinal Dearden intended that I work full time in the Tribunal dealing with marriage annulments.

There are many similarities between Roman Law and the Common Law of U.S. Courts. In both systems, a contract is a contract. A tort is a tort. A crime is a crime. Judicial opinions are critical in both systems. Both court systems are adversarial. Both systems employ professional lawyers. Each system relies on legal precedents for advancing and expanding the law. The highest Church court is called the Sacred Roman Rota which, in the 1970's, issued some startling opinions on the indissolubility of marriage.

One opinion of the Rota held that a marriage could be annulled if the parties were psychologically incompatible. A second opinion held that the marriage bond could be ruled a nullity if either party lacked due discretion. These precedents were very different from the age old tradition which said that the marriage of two Catholics before a proper priest and two witnesses, which was followed by sexual intercourse, created a sacramental bond which no authority under heaven could set aside.

Aided by these precedents, annulments increased from 700 for the entire nation in 1971 to more than 17,000 in 1976 and over 20,000 just one year later. The Church's teachings on the permanence of marriage completely disintegrated. The marriage within the Holy Family between a pregnant sixteen year old and a man of thirty, who was not the father of the unborn child, would have been annulled as a routine matter in 1980.

After graduating from canon law studies, I returned to Detroit's Tribunal as Defender of the Bond, the canon lawyer that argues against an annulment. Cases found rapid resolution in six months or less if the $300 fee had been paid. If the fee went unpaid, the case languished for a year or more. Such hypocrisy became intolerable, so I resigned my Tribunal position after 17 months.

As punishment, I was stationed in Westland in a second assistant pastor position. But in the spring of '79, Mr. Deegan called and offered me a full time assistant's position as a prosecutor in Port Huron. For the first time in my life, I had a real job which paid a decent wage and permitted me to live in a place where I did not work. I no longer felt I was a fungible person. I was a skilled individual. Within six months, Mr. Deegan promoted me to senior trial attorney handling major felony prosecutions.

On weekends I celebrated liturgies in a parish sixty miles north, in the Saginaw Diocese. The parishioners of Our Lady of Lake Huron in

Harbor Beach were very conservative, but they accepted my dual ministry.

In the fall of 1981, I returned to full-time ministry as vicar for Hispanics under the late Ken Untener, Bishop of Saginaw. I became involved in migrant health concerns and summer schools for migrant children. I even received an appointment to the National Migrant Health Committee from the Reagan administration. All these activities involved endless rounds of meetings and community organizing which can best be summed up with the motto: "When all is said and done, a lot more is said than done."

For five years, I served the people of Sacred Heart, a racially diverse inner city parish. The parishioners were African-American, Anglo, and Hispanic; and they labored diligently to improve conditions for the poor of Saginaw. The rectory even housed a Saginaw police mini-station and a project called Emmaus to assist women released from jail and prison to return to drug-free lives through education, health care, and hope.

Sacred Heart parish had a substantial endowment, consisting of several thousand shares of AT & T stock. Dividends funded the parish's diverse ministries. The diocese eventually closed Sacred Heart and confiscated more than a half million dollars. The bishop used the money to refurbish a suburban church which had fallen on hard times. Once again, the Anglo institutional church abandoned the inner city and its poor.

During the efforts aimed at parish consolidation, I met my wife, Susan. She worked on the committee to consolidate. She was a single mother, raising three children (Jarrod, Maribeth, and Kim) on her meager salary earned as the cathedral's bookkeeper and financial manager. At the same time that I left Saginaw for a position at the Wayne County Prosecutor's Office, she also left to begin studies at the Business School of the University of Michigan, where she earned her undergrad and MBA in a four year program.

Before leaving Saginaw, I served as chairman of a prison site

274

selection committee. The group eventually chose a site near two mothballed General Motors foundries. A new prison there would provide more than three hundred recession proof jobs to unemployed auto workers. Though the local paper praised our choice, local citizen groups charged that the choice was racially motivated. The site was then moved to a prosperous rural township which has continued to reap economic benefit from the prison.

On March 23, 1987, I began work as an assistant prosecutor in Wayne County. John O'Hair, the prosecutor, had called me at Sacred Heart rectory to offer me the job. The bishop told me I would have to leave the parish immediately and I could no longer be covered under the diocese's health insurance plan. I guess this exchange was the diocese's version of an exit interview.

Judgeship, Marriage, and a Large Family

I lived at St. Cecilia's, a parish landmark in Detroit, with Msgr. Finnegan, an ebullient Irishman who seemed to know everyone. As an assistant prosecutor, I handled some high profile murder cases involving children. One case was chronicled in a *Detroit Free Press* special entitled, "Why did Tanea Have to Die?" Msgr. Finnegan read the article and then began to encourage me to run for judge.

People magazine published an article entitled, "Father Mike Callahan is a Man of The Cloth and the Law." In 1990, I agreed to run for an open seat on the Wayne County Circuit Court. I obtained more than 5,000 nominating signatures at St. Cecilia's and by walking door to door in my Redford neighborhood.

The diocesan newspaper learned of my candidacy for judge and labeled it a "bad idea." My only opponent was the son of the archdiocesan attorney, himself a former circuit judge. He complained bitterly to the archbishop, Cardinal Edmund Szoka, who did little to hamper my campaign. I spent less than $300 dollars on the campaign and won the election by 58,000 votes. I now am in my fourth six-year term on the bench.

In the spring of 1991, Susan and I purchased a home in Belleville where she moved with her three children and with Chiara, our first adopted African-American child. Susan's three children readily accepted me as their "dad." We married on June 22, in Gatlinburg, Tennessee, in an effort to avoid local publicity. In October, however, a local reporter confronted me about our marriage, which defied the church's rule on celibacy. *Larry King Live* featured Susan and me in an interview opposite an archconservative priest claiming to be an authoritative voice for true Catholicism. Reba McIntyre also had a segment on *King* that night and praised Susan's calm responses to the rants of the "real" priest.

Our efforts at adoption continued. Susan, the older children, Chiara, and I went to an adoption fair where we met our sons, Emmanuel and Jonathan. Emmanuel came up to our family group with his arm around Jon and announced, "My name is Emmanuel and I'm four. This is my brother Jon and he's three. And we can be adopted." I turned to Susan and said, "Where do we sign up?" The boys had never lived together until they came to live at the Callahans. Susan and I began as their foster parents as we pushed mightily to become what the children call their "forever family."

Chiara, Jon, and Emmanuel attended Bethany Bible pre-school. When they reached first, second and third grade respectively, we allowed them to ride the school bus together with the instruction to get on the same bus. They complied. And on the first day after school they all climbed on the same *wrong* bus. Susan and I waited at home with a video camera and a digital camera to record their first ride home. We waited and waited for the bus to arrive. When it finally came, I heard a young voice on the bus ask our children why they lived with those white people. Emmanuel answered matter-of-factly that they were adopted, then added some precision by observing, "Besides, my dad is pink."

A number of years later Susan was surfing Michigan's adoption website and saw the pictures of twins we had met three years before at a retirement party for Chiara's foster dad. Susan asked me if I had ever thought of adopting twins. I answered honestly that I had never entertained such a thought. We met Treana and Trevon and brought them into our forever family six months later.

In February, 2001, our adoption worker contacted us about Ramaul, age 10. He was in foster care with an elderly woman who could care for him no longer. Ramaul was very quiet and guarded. Throughout the adoption process he called us "Susan" and "Mike." He came to live with us full time and, in no time, we became "Mom" and "Dad."

Jon and Ramaul and Trevon have overcome the problems of Attention Deficit Disorder. All the children have bonded well. For Susan and me, these children are the joy of our lives; and their progress is the source of great personal satisfaction.

Reflections on Today's Catholic Church

I believe historians of the church will point to the last two decades of the 20th century to chronicle the demise of the professional clergy. Since 1973, there are ten thousand fewer priests in the U.S. In Detroit, St. John's, the major seminary, closed, and Sacred Heart became both the major and minor seminary. Today Sacred Heart Major Seminary has about 90 seminarians for its entire program. Our class alone had more than 40 on graduation day in 1965.

Celibacy is the number one reason why men decline to become priests. Pedophilia, its constant companion, further tarnished the Catholic priesthood in local and national exposes. Widespread child abuse by so-called "celibates" has unearthed a scandal which the profession of clergy cannot survive.

In the 80's, I represented Saginaw at the national meeting of diocesan attorneys. Strategy sessions outlined defenses for bishops in lawsuits filed by abuse victims. Defense lawyers for insurers urged bishops to hang tough and deny any involvement by priests. Delay was also a good defense as the statute of limitation might run out. Yet, dioceses have paid out billions to settle the claims.

Catholics have contributed handsomely to these settlements. In 2005, church officials admitted to spending three billion on plaintiff's claims. I believe the true figure is three times that amount.

Gerald Shirilla's case illustrates the extent of the problem and the church's effort to cover it up. Before his admission to SHS, Gerry taught at St. Ladislaus High School. He abused a student named Tom Paciorek, performing oral sex on him at Belle Isle Park. He repeated this sexual activity on Tom's younger brother, Jim. Tom and Jim became major league baseball players, high profile victims of child abuse by a priest.

Shirilla entered SHS and eventually was ordained a priest in the class just ahead of ours. He joined the seminary faculty in the early 70's but had to be removed in the face of accusations by students that he had molested them. He entered therapy and was pronounced "cured." Gerry subsequently went to Rome, received a doctorate in liturgy, and rose to become Director of Worship for the Archdiocese. As pastor of a small suburban parish, Shirilla again found himself accused of sexual indiscretions with male teenagers who answered phones at the rectory after business hours.

This time, Gerry's "cure" took him to a residential facility in Maryland. Despite a subpoena for a deposition in a case against him brought by one of the "houseboys," the embattled priest refused to cooperate and claimed his fifth amendment right against self-incrimination. The strategy of denial and silence was still the favorite path of our bishop on the advice of diocesan attorneys.

In one final irony, convicted pedophiles and defrocked priests receive monthly checks for early "retirement," while retirement benefits are denied to priests who still serve parishes well beyond their seventieth birthdays. There are no priests to replace them and only a depleted pension fund left to pay them.

Final Remarks

Sacred Heart Seminary certainly has had an enduring influence on me. I have tried to weave recollections of my formative years there with observations about church and society, based upon my personal history and the story of my family. The story of my family, of course, is not over.

In 2008, I was elected to my fourth and final term as circuit judge. Susan is a CPA and director of accounting at Ford Motor Company. Jarrod, an industrial salesman, lives in South Caroline. Kim and Maribeth are teachers in North Carolina. Emmanuel is a junior at the University of Michigan. Jonathan is in engineering at Michigan State University. Chiara attends Washtenaw and wants a career in law enforcement. Trevon, Treana and Ramaul are finishing high school in Belleville. So far, we have five grandchildren. I expect we will have many more in the future.

Wandering Between Two Worlds

THE CIRCLE OF LIFE
Thomas W. Krell

Maybe it's the realization after 9/11/2001 that life is fragile and we can never know what might happen next. Maybe it's part of the residue from turning 65 this year. Maybe it's the fact that the deaths we've been experiencing lately come not from our parents' generation, but from our own. Whatever. Somehow it seems ever more important today to reflect on who we are, where we've been, what we've come to, and in what direction we might be going. For me it seems that the process is circular.

> *"And the seasons, they go 'round and 'round*
> *And the painted ponies go up and down,*
> *We're captive on the carousel of time.*
> *We can't return, we can only look behind*
>   *from where we've came,*
> *And go 'round and 'round and 'round in the circle game."*
>   Joni Mitchell

A bit of family background first. My folks lived in a two-family flat in Royal Oak when I was born. They moved a few short blocks in 1945, when I was two years old, to a two-story frame cottage-style home. And, contrary to the old saw, you <u>can</u> go home again. My wife, Sandy, and I bought this house from the family estate after my mother died in 1989. *"Everything old is new again…"*

As many of my other classmate-brothers have mentioned in these shared reflections, every family has its own degree of dysfunction, mine included. My dad fought, till the day he died, a battle with bipolar disorder, manic-depressive cycles that left all of us wondering at times which way he would swing next. Dad taught us all -- my two sisters and me -- strong liberal political values; and Mom provided a deeply religious tie to the Catholic faith and its traditions. Sometimes they clashed. My father always joked that when my mother voted for "Ike" in 1952, he forced her to move to the garage for six months. At least I think it was just a joke! But he sure did have strong political opinions. If Mom ever crossed the Democratic-Republican line again, she didn't tell any of us.

After I had received eight years of parochial education in our local parish grade school, my folks sacrificed to send me to the University of Detroit High School. Its strong Jesuit academic background and its deeply Christian social philosophy stated clearly and strongly that all of us were to become "men for others." My values were shaped irrevocably during those four years.

I decided that I would like to become a physician, even though my years of Catholic education and service as an altar boy kept drumming the idea of the priesthood into my brain. I began pre-med studies at Xavier University in Cincinnati in 1961. Of course, it would have to be a Jesuit college! Coming from a strongly protective family-centered youth, then attending university nearly 300 miles away, I suddenly found that I had to make my own decisions. Even though I hungered for an intimate sexual relationship and desired deeply to discover the special someone with whom to share my life and to start my own family, my gut kept telling me that if God was calling me to the priesthood, I had better not say "No." It would be at my own peril. The words of the Adrian Dominican Sisters from my grade school years and the Jesuits at U. of D. High and Xavier echoed in my brain. I decided that at least I had to give the seminary a try. After one year of pre-med at Xavier, I was on my way to Sacred Heart Seminary.

In September 1962, I became a college sophomore, in my classmates' mocking phrase, a "new cucumber," joining a tight-knit group of young men who had been together at least a year, and many of them five years, since they began in the seminary high school. I had a difficult time fitting in, but I knew that I belonged there; and so I grew to love the place, and the training, and the "brothers." I tolerated philosophy classes and stuck with the program.

A couple of college memories stand out, in those pivotal years when the Church and the world were beginning to come undone. This was the time of the Second Vatican Council, the Civil Rights revolution, and the beginning of the Vietnam War. The seminary was celebrating one of its periodic family days, on Sunday, November 24, 1963. My parents joined many others, along with brothers and sisters of the seminarians, for Mass and socializing. All of us were still numb with grief over the assassination of the first Catholic president just two days earlier. As family groups were standing on the back porch of the seminary building, the shocking news blared out that the accused assassin, Lee Harvey Oswald, had been shot by Jack Ruby. We all went to a parlor where a TV was replaying the event over and over again. We knew instinctively that our nation and our lives would be changed deeply by the seminal events of those November days.

In 1965, the seminary faculty sent two of its finest, Fr. Paul Berg and Fr. Bill Cunningham, to Selma, Alabama, to join in the march to the state capitol in Montgomery. Perhaps there were others, but these professors stand out in my memory. These two forward-looking men (prophets?) came back to share with all of us the power of the events, and we all sensed that our lives would never again be the same.

The four years of theological training at St. John's Provincial Seminary went by in a blur, highlighted by beautifully simple minor ordination rites, as many of us advanced through the gradual process of becoming priests. It's amazing to me that the strongest memories I have of those years center on events of shocking magnitude. Our class was in the midst of our first parochial internships as second year seminarians in July, 1967, when the Detroit riots shattered our Caucasian complacency, exposing us to the deep racial chasm in our midst. In February, 1968, the nation reeled with the death of Dr. Martin Luther King, Jr., the one leader who seemed able to help bring about the changes needed in our divided society. And then, in June of 1968, shortly after ordination to the diaconate, we had a few days off before going to our first parish assignments My mother woke me up on the morning of June 6 with a cry: "Bobby Kennedy has been killed!" I can still taste the salty tears that choked me on that day. *"When will they ever learn?"*

Priestly ordination for me and my Detroit classmates took place on June 7, 1969. I felt at the time that it was the happiest day of my life. Cardinal Dearden, already a towering figure in the American Church, laid his hands on my head; and I knew that this was where God wanted me to be. I was clearly aware that God had called me to be a priest, and now I had become a part of that very special Catholic Christian vocation.

I had served as a deacon at Visitation parish in the heart of the city of Detroit. The 1967 riot in Detroit began within our parish boundaries with a raid on an after-hours "blind pig." I felt fortunate to be called back there as a priest. These were exciting times to minister in a city parish; my life was deeply enriched by our African-American parishioners, their traditions, and their rich culture. Motown music. "Soul" food. The wondrous ease with which my new black friends approached all the vicissitudes of life, even in a divided and declining city. And their deep and amazingly strong Christian faith. My years under their tutelage, even though I was called to be *their* teacher, helped me to become a better, more open person.

Luckily, I also was privileged to serve my first years in ordained ministry with Fr. Gerry Britz as my pastor. When he left the parish in 1971, our friendship was cemented; and we became traveling buddies, confessors, and spiritual directors for each another. I also grew in my understanding of the intensity of the black struggle in our society from Joe Dulin, who was principal of St. Martin De Porres High School, a consolidated parochial high school which was located in our Visitation church building. Joe was and is a dynamic, tell-it-like-it-is African-American leader.

One day in spring 1970, this "still wet behind the ears" assistant pastor went over to church to celebrate the early Sunday morning Mass. I found that the church doors were locked from the inside. It seems that Mr. Dulin, many of his faculty members, and a number of the parents of the De Porres students were worried that the Archdiocese might close this pre-eminent urban Catholic high school because of funding issues. In order to protest that possible closure, these black leaders decided to "close" the church instead. I went back across the street to the rectory, awakened Gerry Britz to tell him we were locked out and I couldn't celebrate Sunday Mass. He called out from his room, "Well, that's OK; we just get to sleep in a little longer!" TV news cameras soon arrived; the story got fairly big publicity, and we celebrated Mass in the convent chapel for the next week or so, until the protest was over and we could return to the church building.

The Archdiocese, by the way, did not close De Porres High School at that point. Ironically enough, it was moved a few years later to the closed Sacred Heart Seminary High School building – the Cardinal Mooney Latin School -- and later further north and west in the city. It was finally shuttered by the Archdiocese in 2002 because of the lack of funds and the declining student population.

A rich sidelight of those days at Visitation was made possible by Fr. Denny Moloney --Sacred Heart Seminary college class of '63 -- who lived in our rectory while ministering as a chaplain for three hospitals in the neighborhood. Denny was a peace activist in the growing opposition to the Vietnam War and a member of the "D.C. Nine," who poured blood on the records of the Dow Chemical Company because of that corporation's manufacture of napalm. Through Denny, I was introduced to the Berrigan brothers and many other committed "peaceniks." I vividly recall one evening when Phil Berrigan was staying at our rectory. We drank scotch into the wee hours of the morning, discussing the war and the nuclear arms race and the challenge this presented to the Church and her leaders. During another evening gathering at Denny's family home in the neighborhood, I sat across from "Hanoi" Jane Fonda, struck by her beauty and moved by her passionate commitment to the cause. *"Those were the days, my friend, we thought they'd never end..."*

I ministered at Visitation first as Deacon, then as Associate Pastor, and finally as Co-Pastor with Fr. Ted LaMarre. Ted, a powerful leader in Church and state, served as one of Michigan's Civil Rights Commissioners. He came to the Archdiocese on loan from the Diocese of Saginaw.

I left the inner city to become co-pastor of St. Ambrose Parish. That parish's boundaries straddle the border of a predominantly black, poor, and decaying Detroit lower East Side neighborhood, and white, affluent, and elegant Grosse Pointe Park. My partner in the pastorate was seminary classmate and good friend, Fr. Bob Ruedisueli. We concelebrated our first Sunday Masses at St. Ambrose on the weekend of the U.S. Bicentennial, July 4, 1976; what an invigorating beginning to a parochial assignment. Our shared ministry was an exciting chapter in my priesthood. We grew together with our people and with one another in wisdom, age, and grace.

The four years at St. Ambrose Parish changed my life in ways that were deep and profound. Friendships were created and nurtured that last until this day, out of the matrix of the Christian Family Movement chapter in St. Ambrose. I treasure the impact these very special men and women and their children have had on my life.

We also were involved in a pioneering ecumenical covenant with the neighboring Episcopal Parish of St. Columba and its pastor, Fr. Bob Bickley. Joint worship services cemented the covenant; our common sacramental understanding led ultimately to concelebrated ecumenical Eucharists. Both parish families appeared to love the growing bonds of unity until the Archdiocesan Ecumenical Commission and Cardinal Dearden told us we had gone "too far" and we were mandated to stop the joint Eucharistic celebrations.

An avocation that still brings joy to my life began with a presentation of the musical *Godspell* that I helped direct in St. Ambrose Church. This theatrical production led to the organization of a community theatre group called the St. Ambrose Community Players. Connected with both of these groups, the St. Ambrose Players and our strong parish Christian Family Movement, was the woman who would become my friend, my soul mate, and, ultimately, my lover and my wife, Sandy Stevenson.

I knew that God was calling me to be a priest, but I always found it difficult to live alone. I ached for intimacy and connections. Family was important in my roots; I wanted it to be mirrored in my extensions. And so the agony began. Priesthood or marriage; solitude or intimacy; celibacy or conjugal relationship. I truly loved this woman, Sandy. Being with her made me feel happy and complete. Apart from her, I felt half-full. I wrestled for years with the dilemma. If God wanted me to be a priest (and I truly did believe that God had called me to the sacramental priesthood), then why wouldn't God help me to live celibacy? If God wanted me to be married, then why did God nag me with the desire to remain in the celibate Catholic priesthood?

Sandy's two children, Jim and Beth, also became very special to me. They were bright and enthusiastic, loved music, theatre, and life, much like their mom and me. When the four of us were together, it truly seemed like family to me and the fulfillment of a lifetime of dreams.

Jim and Beth's father is James Stevenson, a jazz musician from Detroit, whom Sandy married in New York City. She and James split up when the kids were five and four, and she returned to Detroit. She raised the kids alone, without any financial support from their father. She went back to school part-time and was able to get her Master's Degree in Social Work from Wayne State.

I hoped to be able to live the so-called "Third Way," about which I had heard so much: men who felt called to the priesthood as well as to an intimate relationship with another person and who lived out that duality in their day-to-day lives. I tried. We tried. But it just didn't feel right. Guilt, "the Catholic gift that keeps on giving," nagged at me when I'd celebrate morning Mass after spending the night in the arms of my beloved. I counseled with my friend Fr. Gerry Britz. I went on numerous directed retreats. Sandy and I started seeing a Catholic psychiatrist whom Gerry had recommended to me. I prayed and I wrestled with my God.

I left St. Ambrose Community when the Archdiocese informed Bob Ruedisueli and me that, because of the growing shortage of ordained ministers, ours would become a one-priest parish. Both of us decided to leave the parish that we deeply loved to allow a new pastor to find his own direction for the community. I hoped and prayed that distance would help break the bond that was deepening between Sandy and myself. I was assigned as pastor to St. Gabriel Parish in the heart of Detroit's southwest side, a multi-ethnic enclave where Spanish and Arabic were as likely to be heard on the streets as English. I even went to Mexico to learn *Español* in order to serve my Latino parishioners more effectively. And just as in Visitation parish, I received more than I gave from my multi-ethnic parish family. My parishioners reminded me of the wondrous diversity of God's family and the Kingdom promised in the Gospel.

But the hunger for intimacy remained; the desire deepened. Sandy and I attempted numerous times to separate from one another, but I always felt compelled to return to her loving embrace.

Finally my confessor-friend Gerry Britz told me that it was time, if you'll excuse the expression, "to shit or get off the pot." He recommended a 30-day Jesuit retreat using the Ignatian *Spiritual Exercises*, insisting God would speak to me there. I was unable to take 30 consecutive days off from my parish without telling the bishop the reason for the retreat. (I wasn't ready for that one!) I went out to Colombiere Center, the former local Jesuit novitiate, in the hills of northern Oakland County, for one to two days each week. There I struggled with silence, continued the wrestling match with my God, assisted by my Jesuit spiritual director in choosing scriptures on which to meditate. After fifteen weeks of this regimen, I truly do believe that God spoke to me, in a more personal and intense way than I had ever previously experienced. As I reflected on Matthew 14:21-33, the passage where Jesus walks on the water and invites Peter to join him atop the waves, I heard Jesus telling me, "Don't be afraid, Tom; if you want to walk toward me, you can." I walked to him, and was relishing, indeed delighting in, the experience as long as I looked directly at him. When I looked down at my own feet, I started to sink. As the water came rushing up to my head, real terror set in. Jesus, however, picked me up and carried me tenderly in his arms back to the boat. He spoke to me and said, "You don't have to be afraid. I will never abandon you as you attempt to make a decision in this struggle. If you choose to stay in the ministry, I will carry you; but if you leave the active ministry and get married to Sandy, I will carry you as well and will show you how to live your priesthood in a new way. It's your choice. But, whatever you do, don't be afraid!" If someone had told me that I'd hear the Lord talk to me in this way, I'd have thought he or she was some kind of fundamentalist "kook." But I truly do believe that Jesus *did* speak to me on that special day. And He helped me make my decision.

And so I called Cardinal Edmond Szoka, John Dearden's successor as Ordinary of Detroit, and asked him for a leave of absence. Archbishop Szoka requested that I take my time making a final decision, that sixteen years as a priest deserved at least six months to a year more of reflection. He offered a temporary leave as an option. I was pretty sure where the Lord was leading me, especially after my hill-top conversation with Him at Colombiere; but again I went along Cardinal Szoka's recommendation, and began my temporary leave. Sandy and I decided that it wouldn't be a real decision-making time if we were to move in together, so I got a one-bedroom apartment and went about the business of finding a job. What do you do when you grow up and have to figure out a new form of employment at age 42?

To the rescue -- as the "*seasons*" and the "*circles*" continued to go "*round and round*"-- came mentor and friend from my seminary days, Fr. Bill Cunningham. Following the 1967 Detroit riots, Bill had helped found a civil and human rights organization called FOCUS:HOPE. Responding to the critical issues of the day, the group offered education and support to city and suburb alike in dealing with the racial divide. The agency began to deal with hunger and joblessness as two of the major issues which segregation had helped to create and nourish. Bill had offered agency positions to many men who had left the seminary or the priesthood, figuring he could count on their idealism and, to be honest, that he wouldn't have to offer a high salary to them. I networked with Bill at FOCUS:HOPE; and he offered me a position as a job developer for the fairly new Machinist Training Institute, which was offering training in machining and tool and die making to people formerly shut out of the system, especially African-Americans and women. I didn't know a thing about machining, couldn't tell a lathe from a mill or a grinder; but I thought I could sell prospective employers on our special breed of graduates. I accepted the position.

After a year of living independently and working in the "real world" for a living, and after lots more struggling with the Lord, including another directed retreat experience at the Jesuit formation house in Guelph, Ontario, I knew God was calling me to move on and realize my priesthood "in a new way." I went back to the Cardinal and asked for a permanent leave.

Sandy and I joyfully planned our wedding for September 19, 1987; but we changed the date because Pope John Paul II came to Detroit on that day and we didn't want our proposed downtown reception marred by crowds. (Sandy thought that the Pope was out to get us; I only somewhat jokingly proposed that we invite the Pontiff to be the official witness of our vows since he was going to be in town anyway!) Instead we were joined in the Sacrament of Matrimony the next Saturday, September 26, 1987, in a beautiful celebration witnessed by two dear Episcopal priest-friends, a married priestly couple, Meredith Hunt and David Lilvis, at St. Columba's Episcopal Church. That lovely Gothic church, whose parishioners had shared the ecumenical covenant with St. Ambrose, seemed perfectly fitting as the site in which to proclaim our marriage covenant. Our guests were the very special people who had stood by both of us during my agonizing, decision-making struggle; these friends joined our families in a wondrous celebration of God's love. Sandy's 88-year old mother walked her down the aisle. Our daughter Beth led the singing and soloed in a beautiful rendition of the "Alleluia" from Mozart's *Exultate Jubilate*. The day and the liturgical celebration were, along with my priestly ordination, the happiest moments of my life, and the times that I felt closest to the Lord with whom I had engaged in such a long wrestling match.

Shortly after our "Episcopal" wedding, I got a letter from Pope John

Paul II, extending to me a dispensation from my priestly responsibility. For the sake of my Mom -- Dad had died a few years earlier while the decision-making struggle was going on -- we renewed our vows in a simple "Catholic" ceremony in our home in Grosse Pointe Park, with dear friend Gerry Britz officiating. Some of our friends said to us: "Just how many weddings are you going to invite us to?"

The delirious days of newly married joy came crashing down a month after our wedding when daughter Beth was diagnosed with Hodgkin's disease. Was God punishing us for the indiscretions of our days of pre-marital intimacy? Or was He planning to strengthen us for a new commitment? Fortunately, Beth had discovered the small lump in one of her lymph nodes very early. She was found to be in the beginnings of Stage Two Hodgkin's lymphoma. After abdominal surgery, including a spleenectomy, and six weeks of radiation therapy, Beth was officially declared to be in remission. Happily, Hodgkin's disease is said to be "cured" after five years of remission. We had a "Cure Party" for Beth in early 1993. The support group who stood by us in our courtship and on our wedding day now joined in celebrating our daughter's health.

Beth's brother, my stepson Jim, had been recruited by and joined the Unification Church of Rev. Sun Myung Moon -- the "Moonies" -- while his mother and I were deepening our relationship. Keeping in contact with Jim was difficult, often impossible. The Moonies purposely separate children from their parents, and Jim was traveling the country selling flowers by the side of the road. Jim was "fixed up" by Rev. Moon for an arranged marriage with Japanese-born Chitomi Yokoi. Their legal wedding in New York City preceded ours by just a few months. They had a religious marriage ritual later in Korea, joining hundreds of other couples in one of Rev. Moon's mass weddings. Jim and Chitomi left the Moonies shortly after their first son Jatomis, a.k.a. J.T., was born. They have since had two other boys, Joseph and Sammy. I don't think it's just typical grandparent's prejudice to say these three boys are wonderful, smart, and very beautiful Eurasian children! Our sadness is that the youngsters and their parents, Jim and Chitomi, live in California; and we only get to see them once a year or so.

In the weeks and months leading up to our wedding, Sandy and I searched the metropolitan Detroit area for a parish community that would provide a "fit" for us. It was important that the parish be multi-racial and multi-ethnic, that it provide a deep sense of community, and that the pastoral leadership proclaim Gospel justice values. We settled on St. Patrick's Parish Community in the heart of Detroit's Cass Corridor. Group home folks worshipped next to doctors from Grosse Pointe. Elderly residents and visitors from far and near were served by a wonderful senior center and its charismatic founder, Sr. Mary Watson. Our pastor, Fr. Tom Duffey, was truly a minister, a servant-priest, in the model of Jesus. His humble leadership and his prophetic ability to cut through the "crap" and get to the heart of the matter touched both of us -- and all of his people -- very deeply.

"Duff," as he was affectionately known by friends, family, and parishioners alike, was diagnosed with throat cancer in the early 80's. He needed assistance in proclaiming the Word in order to save his voice, and he began calling his people to share the preaching ministry. Preaching had always seemed to be such a central part of my call to priesthood, and I really missed it. I eagerly accepted Duff's invitation to be part of a rotation of preaching parishioners, proclaiming the Word about once a month at Sunday celebrations. I was living my priesthood again, in a "new way."

Fr. Duffey suffered from diabetes in addition to his other health issues and often was forced to go to the hospital or to stay home and miss Mass on Sundays. He also tried to take a month of rest each summer. On one of these times when he would be away from St. Pat's, Duff challenged his people to accept the fact that bringing a "stranger" priest into the community didn't make sense when there were priests in the congregation. He invited, indeed he challenged, me to celebrate Mass on one of those August Sundays. To lead the congregation in liturgical prayer, to celebrate the Eucharist once again, was a profound joy for me. And I invited my wife to join me in the recessional, with tears streaming down both of our faces. Duff also invited some lay women from the parish to celebrate the sacraments, but most of the time the responsibility was given to me or one of the other ordained married priests in the congregation.

One Christmas Eve, Duff had an attack of diabetes-induced cellulitis on one of his legs. Sandy and I came to church for the evening celebration. It was, I recall, at 7:30 PM, not midnight, since the Cass Corridor neighborhood did not attract lots of suburban folks later in the evening. Fr. Duffey's Pastoral Associate, Floria, asked if I could celebrate the Christmas Mass since he was in the hospital. It was, and is, one of my most profound Christmas memories. I was graced by the Lord, who had invited me to share his priesthood, to celebrate His Supper in honor of His birth; and our little "rag-tag" congregation was more beautiful than any grand cathedral Christmas community could ever be.

After working at FOCUS:HOPE for four years, I decided it was time to find the lifetime career or profession in which I could live out my priesthood "in a new way," as I was doing in my parish family. I left FOCUS:HOPE and worked for a couple of years as a Vocational Rehab Counselor for a private agency, but this just didn't seem to be where God was leading me. I heard about an opening at Sacred Heart Rehabilitation Center for a Spiritual Counselor. (SACRED HEART?! Sounded good to me!) Sacred Heart Center was founded by Basilian Father Vaughan Quinn. The agency had an excellent reputation as a treatment center where "Skid Row" type drunks found sobriety next to "respectable" alcoholic doctors and lawyers, and inner-city crack addicts shared their stories and their healing with suburban housewives. Espousing a treatment philosophy based on the Twelve Steps of Alcoholics Anonymous, spirituality was and is an important component of Sacred Heart's program. I was hired as the Spiritual Counselor in the downtown Detroit center of the program, where the clients "detoxed" and began their recovery program before they progressed to finish their treatment at the agency's long-term center in Memphis, Michigan. God graced me with a job that was truly a ministry. Leading ecumenical worship services, proclaiming the healing words of recovery, providing "Fifth Step" opportunities that echoed the Sacrament of Reconciliation in its very best sense, I truly believed that God had helped me find my niche.

Budget cutbacks in the program eliminated the position of Spiritual Counselor at the Detroit branch, but I was invited to become a regular treatment counselor at the Memphis Center. Leading groups of men and women who were attempting to find healing in their lives, I experienced God's healing grace in my own life. But again the budget ax struck as the State of Michigan cut back radically on social services to save taxpayer dollars. No longer able to serve as many indigent clients, Sacred Heart was forced to lay off more than half its staff members, myself included. For the first time in my life, I was unemployed; and I discovered what it was like to join the lines at the Michigan Employment Security Commission in order to get my unemployment check.

At the same time as this layoff, our cost-cutting governor was also in the process of closing Lafayette Clinic, the premier research mental health facility in downtown Detroit, where my wife Sandy worked as a clinical social worker. She received word about the Clinic's shutdown the very same week that I got my layoff notice from Sacred Heart Rehab. Needless to say, we were not too happy with our elected officials in Lansing.

I accepted a couple of part-time positions, thanks to the kindness of friends, and explored the idea of going back to school in order to get some new letters after my name. Somehow a B.A. in Philosophy and an M.A. in Religious Studies just didn't make it in the "real world." (I had applied for various positions in the "official" Church, but could never seem to land an interview, much less a job offer.)

Wayne State University, Detroit's urban campus, had begun a program that offered a Bachelor's Degree in nursing, after an amazingly brief 16 months, to women and men who already had another bachelor's degree. Both of my sisters are nurses, and I had always felt something of a call to work in the health care arena. I took the prerequisite science courses, was accepted into the program, and at age 51 became an undergraduate once again. Most of my classmates were less than half my age. When one of the few other men in the program dropped out early on during our clinical rotations,

Wandering Between Two Worlds

I became the class elder, the "grandfather" of the nursing program. I recall, with mixed emotions, a lovely summer day when one of our nursing class discussion groups was meeting outside, sitting on the campus green. My stepdaughter Beth was at the University taking a graduate class in education. She walked by, saw me, and giddily shouted out a greeting, "Hi, Dad!" I looked around at my fellow nursing students and realized that all of them were younger than Beth. I never felt quite so old!

Our class graduated in December, 1995. I took my Nursing Boards, became an R.N., and accepted a position as a Staff Nurse on the Geriatrics Unit of Henry Ford Hospital, which had helped pay for my nursing education. I felt drawn throughout my nursing education either to Obstetrics/Labor and Delivery or to Hospice Nursing. Both seemed to be life-affirming, generative ministries. The former was probably an unrealistic dream, since our hospital, like many others, hired few, if any, men to work as nurses in its O.B. department. But the hospice model of comfort care was calling me ever more insistently.

We had signed a commitment to work 20 months at the hospital's main campus in downtown Detroit. I "paid my dues"; and, as soon as possible, after almost two years on the hectic hospital unit, I started looking around for a nursing job in a hospice program. Happily, I was offered a position in the Henry Ford Health Care system with a hospice team dedicated to the care of terminal patients who reside in nursing homes.

Within days of my hire, I felt deeply that this was where God had been leading me all along. Standing at the side of dying patients, ministering to them and their families as they completed their journey here and faced a new life beyond, I experienced the hand of the Lord in a profound and intimate way in my life and in my new career. I recall being with my first dying patient, a fairly young man succumbing to the ravages of liver failure after a life of alcoholism. He took my hand, looked upward, and said something like "Thanks for being here. Don't be afraid. 'Cause I'm not." Within hours, he expired. And I'm not afraid. Death and dying do not frighten me in any way. I'm honored to minister in this very special way.

I had always accepted as part of my religious faith a belief in an afterlife, a shadowy acceptance of a heaven or hell beyond our earthly sphere. Privileged to be present at the deaths of dozens of men and women, I can now confidently say I have "seen" the *Beyond*. I know it is true. Dying is only a "passing over," not a "passing on." And the dead but risen Lord is present in the moment as He is in no other of our human passages.

Hospice has given me the opportunity of being priest once again. Offering the Sacrament of the Anointing of the Sick on various occasions, being invited to lead services or to preach at funerals, but most of all in a celebration of presence, a healing not of physical symptoms, but of spiritual realities, my hospice nursing career is truly a ministry in the best and deepest sense of the word. A *priestly* ministry.

Every hospice worker can share myriads of "miracle stories" about death and dying. One of my favorites is the time I was asked to offer the Sacrament of Anointing to "Margaret," one of our patients who had begun to crash quite quickly. Her sister was present, along with the convalescent home nurse and nursing assistant and two of my fellow hospice team members. We didn't have time to bring an "outsider" priest to the bedside, so we counted on the "nurse-priest" present. We gathered around Margaret's bed, prayed the ritual together. The community joined me in the laying on of hands and the anointing of her head and hands. As we finished the ceremony, we linked our hands with one another and with Margaret, and prayed the Lord's Prayer. I leaned over and whispered in Margaret's ear, "It's OK, Margaret. Jesus is ready for you now. Don't be afraid to go to him." She looked up at me, took a deep breath, ... and died. "Awesome" is a word that is overused nowadays. This was an *awesome* experience.

Sandy and I also have treasured our call to assist in marriage preparation and the sacrament of matrimony. Through the auspices of the Federation of Christian Ministers, a faith-filled community made up mostly of former Catholic priests but also of laywomen and men who feel called to liturgical ministry, I am able to officiate legally at weddings. We have mutually prepared couples for marriage, calling on both of our professional backgrounds, Sandy as a social worker and myself as a priest and counselor. We have celebrated the nuptials jointly, just as Meredith and David witnessed and celebrated our wedding, husband and wife ministers. We have not done this ministry as a job; we never hung out a shingle or had a web site or an 800 number. But many friends and family have asked us to offer this ministry for themselves or for their children. It has been a joyous extension of our marital commitment as well as a response to the call of a sacramental priesthood.

Again the stories are many, but a very special one was the joint marriage service of our Catholic friend Laura and her Jewish partner Matt, co-witnessed officially by myself, my wife, and a female rabbi, Tamara Kolton. An ecumenical celebration of love and commitment in the best and deepest sense of the word. A deeply "Kingdom" experience.

Another Christian community that has accepted me as a married priest is the ecumenical version of the Cursillo movement, "*De Colores en Cristo.*" Having been the spiritual director of many Cursillo weekend retreats during my years in the active Catholic priesthood, I thought that those special experiences in the Christ-message and Christian community were over for me, since I could no longer serve officially in this capacity in the Roman Catholic Cursillo. But many of my "Cursillista" friends felt drawn toward a more open ecumenical expression of the movement, which is contained in the "*De Colores en Cristo Ministries*" experience. I have regularly been asked to serve on teams with Protestant ministers or Episcopalian priests as co-spiritual directors. I treasure the growth in my vision that has come from sharing ministry with female priests like Meredith Hunt and Rebecca Lepley as well as from numerous brother ministers from a garden variety of Christian churches. These retreats continue to provide wondrous and powerful experiences of the Lord's love and his call to discipleship and community.

I also have treasured the pastoral ("priestly") call to a Clown or Mime ministry. While still at St. Ambrose Community, Sandy and I and her two children joined with other parishioners in learning how to use mime in liturgical ministry. We formed a Clown Ministry troupe and together celebrated the sacraments: Eucharist, Reconciliation, and Healing. My clown *persona*, whose name is "Twinkle Toes," continues to minister liturgically at *De Colores* retreats as well as in nursing homes as part of my hospice career. This "ministry beyond words" reminds me of how very wordy we preacher types often become; many folks continue to tell me years later how the clown celebration of Communion or Confession was the most powerful liturgical rite that they have ever experienced.

After our friend Fr. Tom Duffey retired from the active ministry, the Archdiocese of Detroit sent a new pastor to St. Patrick's, a young man who held a more conservative understanding of liturgy, of priesthood, and of parish community. We attempted to remain as members of the parish, but our new pastor's vision just could not jibe with our own; we didn't feel at home at St. Pat's anymore. And so we sought out a new parish family, becoming "Roamin'" Catholics for six months, sampling the treasures of a dozen or more urban Catholic parishes that shared our vision and understanding of Gospel and community. We settled on another embracing, inclusive Christian family, joining the parish of Our Lady of Fatima, located fairly close to our home. Another pastor in the model of Jesus, Fr. Paul Chateau, truly listens to his people and openly shares his priesthood with them. We're happy we have found a home church ... or a church home.

And so, the circles have indeed gone *"round and round."* What often seemed like a roller coaster in the end was really a carousel. And what a ride it has been! I have learned that it's more important for me to be *catholic* than Roman Catholic. I have grown in my understanding of a Creator whose embrace is always inclusive, never exclusive. And I (or we) envision a church that celebrates a truly pluralistic society. How boring the journey would have been if everyone looked or acted the same. How can one possibly imagine a world without gay fellow travelers? Or a journey where all the riders had the same skin color or spoke the same language? Or a religion whose Savior-Brother would exclude his Moslem or Hindu or Jewish or agnostic sisters and brothers from the ride?

I have treasured many friends and associates over the years who have helped broaden my vision of society, of church, and of priesthood. Ordained priest brothers like Gerry Britz, Bill Cunningham, Tom Duffey and Phil Berrigan –all of whom have gone to glory. And Bob Ruedisueli, Denny Moloney, Bishop Tom Gumbleton, and Cardinal John Dearden. And, yes, I cannot leave out my sister priests from the Episcopalian tradition, like Meredith Hunt and Rebecca Lepley. *"When will we ever learn"* in our official church family that the priesthood cannot be limited by gender, any more than by marital status or sexual preference?

I'd like to offer a word here for some very special women in religious life. I truly believe that the vision of Vatican II has been lived more powerfully and vividly by religious women than by either my brothers in the ordained ministry or by the emerging lay leaders. These women have shown me the way to community and to Gospel discipleship by their word as well as by their example. I thank God for my aunt Sr. Clare Nicolai, who recently "passed," for Sr. Mary Watson from St. Patrick's Senior Center, and for Sr. Susan Van Baalen, a charismatic chaplain in the prison system, and long-time Director of the U.S. Federal Prison ministries, with whom I shared many Cursillo experiences. And on and on. Each one of these women has been a "priest" to me and to the various communities in which they served, even if the official church doesn't recognize their priestly ministry.

My lay friends, including my family, are legion; and their baptismal priesthood shines forth in so many ways that it would take another chapter or chapters to tell their various stories. I am deeply grateful for all the wonderful, caring friends God has placed in my life.

And, of course, my most intimate priestly companion, Sandy, my fellow minister and wife, has helped make the journey always interesting, occasionally frustrating, but consistently exciting. I thank God for her... and for all the rest.

And for the carousel ride itself. What an incredible journey it has been. To our Creator, the Father and Mother of us all, to our Redeemer, and to our Sanctifier, I say *"gracias"* … *"arigato"* … *"danke schon"*… "thanks." I look forward to the next circle.

SEMPER FI
Jerome N. Nadolski

I left St John's Provincial Seminary in June, 1966, after First Year Theology. My decision to leave the seminary was pretty much made about half way through college; but I kept thinking that a decision of that magnitude should not be flippant, so I decided to make a final decision after college graduation. College life at Sacred Heart was about 98% academic (which I liked) and about 2% priesthood; so at the conclusion of college, I decided to spend one more year in seminary, since I felt St. John's would be about 2% academic and 98% about priesthood -- and it was. As a result I felt very confident about half way through that first year at St. John's that my decision to pursue another career was a good one. At that time I began applying to graduate schools of social work and gained acceptance to the University of Michigan as well as Wayne State University. I ultimately chose Wayne State over Michigan because Wayne State would allow me to defer my admission until after I completed military service.

In retrospect, my decision to go to the seminary was greatly influenced by three things I experienced while growing up living with my parents and siblings in my grandparents' home (duplex) in the part of Detroit which is referred to as "Pole Town." My grandparents lived downstairs and we lived in an upper flat.

First, I always seemed to be interested in helping people. I felt a great deal of compassion for people who were in pain, either physically or emotionally. My mother was a very caring person who seldom, if ever, had a negative thing to say about anyone. My paternal grandmother was the same way.

Second, I think family pressure played a great part -- not wanting to disappoint my parents or grandparents. I came from a strong ethnic family which felt obligated to send at least one of its children into the religious life. For some reason, I felt singled out for this -- perhaps because I was a good student who liked hanging around the parish, helping my grandfather with a lot of his volunteer work. We were parishioners at Sweetest Heart of Mary Church in Pole Town; and my family had helped found that incredibly ethnic, staunchly faithful parish. The parish had actually broken away from the Archdiocese of Detroit when a non-Pole was appointed pastor. The parishioners, including my family, mortgaged their homes to purchase the church from the Archdiocese; but eventually things came back to reality and the break was healed. My grandfather was in charge of everything from the credit union to the ushers to the Knights of St. John, etc. He was held in high esteem by priests, nuns, and parishioners alike. We basically ran the place. I can still remember seeing my grandfather on his deathbed in our home being visited by an official of the Archdiocese so that he could sign the papers (as Secretary of the parish council) releasing the parish back to the control of the Archdiocese.

Third, an older cousin whom I was quite fond of was the first in the family to go to seminary. He eventually left but returned some years later, was ordained, and is currently a pastor in the northern part of the state. His leaving seminary sent shock waves through the family. My relatives felt a certain amount of disgrace in the community and a loss of status in the parish. I may have gotten caught up somehow in this whole thing and "was sent in off the bench" as a replacement. My family wanted to send me to Orchard Lake St. Mary Prep School, which was a boarding school for young Polish men who were considering priesthood; but I did not want to live away from home. As a compromise Sacred Heart came into the picture. I should also mention that my late father, who retired from the Detroit Police Department as a Detective Sergeant, had tried seminary after high school; but he dropped out after one semester. So the tradition of service to the Church was deep-seated in my family.

I left the seminary with a clear goal -- a career in professional social work. Again, I had always been interested in helping people, so the goal of social work came quite naturally. It started to more clearly evolve about half way through college, when I realized that I really did not want to dedicate my whole life to the Church but simply wanted to help people. Priesthood requires a lot more than just helping people. I began to understand the awesome spiritual responsibilities that are the essence of priesthood and which I realistically did not feel called to nor did I want to develop.

Another factor that helped me to decide that priesthood was not for me was celibacy. As time progressed I felt a strong desire to marry and have a family. That's not to say that if a married priesthood were permissible that I would have stayed in seminary. I would have left anyway, since I simply did not feel that I wanted the priesthood. I have never second-guessed my decision, and this confirms in my mind that I did the right thing. I must say that after 40 years of marriage and 39 years as a professional social worker, I feel very fulfilled and would have chosen no other life.

To properly pursue a social work career required a master's degree in social work, which at that time meant two years of full time study as well as two internships. Before starting into my formal social work studies, I wanted to complete my other goal of a commission in the Marine Corps. I was accepted into Officer Candidate School for the Marine Corps for a class commencing in January, 1967. Between leaving St. John's and starting OCS, I took a management position with the Ford Motor Company.

I enjoyed the opportunity to work in industry. After a rather brief but intensive Ford Motor Company orientation/management training program, I was assigned to a position at the Woodhaven Metal Stamping Plant in Woodhaven, Michigan. In that job I worked primarily in safety engineering and production. In the production area I supervised fifty hourly employees. Our job was to produce parts which ultimately were shipped to the Rouge Assembly Plant and made into automobiles. This was a time of extremely high production; and, as a result, ten-to-twelve hour days, six-to-seven day weeks comprised the normal work schedule. This routine was certainly quite a contrast to the rather relaxed atmosphere of seminary life. The pressure to reach high production quotas was intense; but this job convinced me that I had the ability to manage people in a very demanding environment and gave me the confidence to tackle a leadership position in the Marine Corps. I actually enjoyed the challenge of leadership and problem-solving which filled my workday. I gained great satisfaction from both.

After the military I was offered continued employment with Ford Motor Company but declined in favor of pursuing my graduate education at Wayne State University School of Social Work. Other than missing at times the more lucrative salary that a career in the auto industry would have provided, I have never regretted that decision.

My decision to enter the Marine Corps prior to going to graduate school was not impulsive. As far back as I can remember, I was attracted to the notion of not only becoming a Marine but also becoming an officer in charge of other Marines, not necessarily as a career but at least through one tour of duty. Perhaps it was the exposure to World War II stories of glory and heroism that I heard from returning veterans that sowed that seed; but I'm not really sure. Two favorite uncles who served in the Navy during World War II spoke of their high respect for the Marines that they served with; and I listened with great interest in their stories. After high school I had considered seeking appointment to Annapolis (the U.S. Naval Academy) to pursue that goal; but I decided to enter Sacred Heart Seminary College instead. I felt pulled in both directions and ultimately decided to continue in seminary and if it did not work out, later pursue a commission in the Marine Corps.

I was commissioned a Second Lieutenant in the Marine Corps in 1967 and, after further training at Infantry and Transport schools, was sent to Vietnam in 1968. During my 13 month tour in Vietnam I served as a Platoon Commander with 30 enlisted Marines under my command and later as a Company Commander with more than 100 Marines under my leadership. We operated in such strange sounding places as Danang, Phu Bi, An Hoa, Gia Le, Hue, Quang Tri and

Khe Sahn..

While with the Fifth Marine Regiment during the Battle for Hue during the Tet Offensive, I had the honor of serving with Sacred Heart Seminary classmate Ken Eason who, like myself, was a Second Lieutenant Platoon Commander. Ken was sent to reinforce my unit, and we were together less than 24 hours. My last image of Ken was of him heading into another battle area right after our units were ambushed. Ken had this strange look in his eyes, kind of empty -- like he and his men would not get out alive from this terrible month long battle that had already cost the lives of hundreds of Marines. Some call this the infantryman's "thousand yard stare – 'cause you've seen beyond." In other words you are sure that your days and moments are numbered. When I recently heard of Ken's personal struggles after his return to the States, I strongly suspected that he had left some of his soul back in Vietnam.

My time in the Marine Corps brings me no regrets, only the pride that comes with the feeling of a job well done. I attained the rank of Captain at final discharge from service which was difficult to do for a Marine officer who did not graduate college from the Naval Academy. During my college and theology days, there were no actual organized protests against the war. I left seminary in 1966 and the war had not really escalated to the point of generating much protest – at the seminary or any other place. This came much later -- probably after my return from Vietnam. For me it was a non-issue. When the significant protests against the Vietnam War began, my reaction was (and is) that everyone was entitled to his opinion about the war. Conscientious objectors, war protesters, draft card burners, escapees to Canada had every right to their beliefs and the expression of those beliefs. In retrospect I must admit I have concerns about not only why the war was fought but how it was fought. As a former commander in the field, I must admit our objectives were not always clear or well thought out and I feel this led to a lot of needless casualties.

As a commissioned officer you view your role as that of a professional manager of men and material—much like my job in industry but, of course, with a much greater potential for danger and

305

disaster. Your sense of responsibility to your command, not only to the assigned mission but to the men and material entrusted to you, is profound and takes precedence over all else, especially in combat situations. You simply do not have a lot of time for philosophical debate. My moral imperative was pretty simple -- to see to the needs of the men under my command. When you consider that at one point I had command of over 100 enlisted Marines and three junior officers, my focus had to be 100% on the task at hand.

For this book, I was asked if I would be willing to expand on some of my experiences in Vietnam. The telling of "war stories" is never easy for veterans unless we are together with other veterans at the VFW Post, American Legion, or the Marine Corps League, all of which I have membership in. Or when I meet another veteran and we simply share experiences. Combat veterans share a "brotherhood" and no one else can really understand what we are talking about. I think we are afraid that we will be viewed as exaggerating, looking for praise, sympathy, or whatever. Some veterans are afraid of the "mind flooding" which sometimes occurs when recalling these events, where one's mind is overwhelmed with memories well beyond the ones being discussed. This can be very uncomfortable and lead to needless upset.

There are many experiences that I could share in addition to the one already mentioned with Ken Eason. Here are a few.

One of the finest officers that I served with in Vietnam was our chaplain, Fr. Lyons, a Jesuit. He was critically wounded during an ill-fated, ill-advised frontal assault by our lead platoon against dug in machine guns. The platoon was decimated; and during the assault, with heavy fire from the guns raking the area, Father Lyons was wounded numerous times while ministering to the Marines. The last time I saw him he was being loaded on to the back of a battle tank with a number of other critically wounded. Due to heavy enemy ground fire and limited visibility from monsoon rains, helicopters could not evacuate the wounded. As a result, the seriously wounded were given the choice of remaining with our unit or being carried by tanks which would have to fight their way out of the battle area in which we were surrounded by a much larger force of North Vietnamese regulars. The majority chose to fight their way out. As the tank pulled out, he gave us a "thumbs up." This was very typical of him. We could always rely on his encouragement and positive attitude despite terrible circumstances. Fortunately, he did make it out; but he never returned to our unit due to the severity of his wounds. Father's attitude was pure and simple—to meet the spiritual needs of the men in our unit despite the complications of the situation.

Two other tales give good examples of how ironic and confusing things can be in war. These experiences lead to a lot of "head scratching" in terms of how or why things happen.

On one occasion our unit (2nd Battalion of the 5th Marine Regiment) was surrounded by a much larger force. I was told to take one reinforced platoon (approximately 50 men) and attempt to break out and do a reconnaissance of the area to our south in an effort to determine if we could move the larger unit and equipment through or at least re-supply our battalion. I had only been "in country" for two months and was therefore inexperienced; but I quickly decided that we probably would not make it back alive. I mustered the courage to ask the senior officer who was issuing the operational order to myself and another second lieutenant who was to reinforce my platoon with his thirty Marines what to do if the bridges that we had to cross were blown up by the enemy. I got the rather nonchalant response, "I guess you will figure that out when you get there, lieutenant." The other lieutenant refused the mission saying, "This mission is suicidal." He was immediately relieved of his command (which is a great disgrace and probably a court martial offense with prison time). I often wonder what became of him and wonder if maybe he was the real hero and was just trying to save his already battle weary Marines from certain death. Not only did we complete the mission but we returned with minimal casualties.

On a separate occasion I was having a smoke with another officer in an area quite a few miles from any hostilities when a Marine, angry at the other officer for some discipline that he had just received from him, threw a live hand grenade at us. Fortunately we saw it coming and dove into a bunker, escaping unharmed with the exception of being knocked silly from the percussion.

The irony exhibited in these two incidents is obvious. Death was certain in one situation but never came. But in another seemingly safe situation, death came very close, at the hand of another Marine.

Despite this kind of craziness, I view my time in the service as a positive one. It certainly leaves you with a profound appreciation for life and a realization that it can be snuffed out in an instant -- so, put it to good use. I seem to have an almost super sensitivity to people who waste their lives on self-destructive things like drugs and alcohol. I become upset when I see a talented person waste his or her talents due to laziness or other bad habits. When you consider all the young, talented people who were killed in service of their country before those talents could fully flower, it makes it all the more upsetting.

I often think back to my 500 classmates from Marine Corps Officer Candidate School and the Naval Academy at Annapolis--especially the 50 who were killed in Vietnam and the many others who were seriously wounded. These were exceptional men from some of the finest universities in the country, where many had distinguished themselves as scholars and athletes. A book, *The Boys of '67*, was written about our class due to its high achievement during some of the most intensive fighting of the war. Five of my classmates became generals, one of whom, James Jones, a highly decorated Vietnam veteran, was appointed by President Barack Obama to serve as his National Security Advisor. Jones previously served as Commandant of the Marine Corps and in other high level assignments. I have often wondered with amazement and some confusion how I happened to get involved in that life situation (a Marine officer in Vietnam) and with that group of incredibly gifted and dedicated young men. Life can be interesting!!

During my last year in the Marine Corps, I married; and my wife Loretta and I lived in Jacksonville, North Carolina (Camp Lejeune), until my discharge in December, 1969. I began dating Loretta after I left St. John's. Because she was the sister of a friend and classmate of mine, Ed Nowakowski, we had known each other for quite some time. While in North Carolina we lived off base and Loretta taught school in a small farming community. This was a great time for us. We traveled a lot throughout the East Coast, taking full advantage of the leisure time before we had to return north to the busy lives that awaited us.

My return to life at home after the military was not that difficult. Newly married and fully absorbed in graduate school and work made the transition fairly easy. My military experience allowed me to help other veterans who found the transition more difficult.

In January, 1970, I started graduate school at Wayne State University and completed my master's degree in social work in June, 1971. During graduate school I worked part time as a social worker for Wayne County Juvenile Court and continued working there after receiving my masters degree. In November, 1979, I moved to a position with Detroit Edison (now DTE Energy) as an Industrial Social Worker in the Employee Assistance Program. I finally retired in June of 2008 after almost 40 years of professional social work. For approximately 28 years after completing my master's degree, I also worked evenings providing individual, group, and family counseling as part of a private practice.

The ten years that I worked for Juvenile Court as a clinical social worker included working with Juvenile Court wards and their families in a wide variety of situations including delinquency, abuse, and neglect. My work with DTE Energy included working with employees and their families who had a variety of issues, including emotional, substance abuse, and family life problems. I served as group leader to a team of five other employees. I had the opportunity for three years in the 1990s to work in a developmental assignment in the customer offices. I managed seven different customer offices and supervised about 50 employees. This experience helped me gain a better understanding of the day-to-day frustrations of both employees and customers.

Wandering Between Two Worlds

My wife and I have two children, Andrew, 36, and Marian, 32. We
are proud of the fact that both are professionals, living productive,
independent lives. Both have Bachelor of Science degrees. My son
works as an RN and my daughter works as a Physical Therapist,
having completed her Master of Physical Therapy degree after
graduating from college. Both are married and we are expecting our
fifth grand child.

My wife also retired in June of 2008, after 40 years as a teacher. She
worked as a school teacher for the Chippewa Valley School District
for over 22 years. Prior to that she worked for the Hamtramck School
District and also for the Richlands School District in North Carolina
when I was stationed at Camp Lejeune. She has two master's degrees;
and, besides teaching, she has mentored new teachers. She also
served as a union representative. We were pleased that she was able
to take a leave of absence from teaching during our children's early
elementary years and feel that this has helped them to be the well-
adjusted, high achievers that they are today. We are a very close
family; all live within ten minutes of each other. Sunday dinner at our
house is a weekly event and gives us a chance to share our lives.

My wife and I are not only spouses but also best friends. We are
amazingly similar in personality, likes and dislikes. We are looking
forward to our retirement and spending the rest of our days together.
We plan to travel a lot and spend time at our vacation home in
northern Michigan but not spend too much time away from our
children or close friends and extended family.

Ed, my wife's only sibling, has retired and lives with his spouse in the
Grand Rapids area. We share time together whenever possible.
Unfortunately my four siblings are some distance away. Two brothers
live on the East Coast, a sister lives in South Carolina and another
brother in the Traverse City area. My wife's parents are deceased, as
are mine. We miss them as they were wonderful people. My siblings
are with their original spouses and leading good, productive lives.
One is a FBI agent, another is a retired journalist, another a realtor.
All of our siblings' children, with the exception of one who has not
entered college yet, are in college or already graduated from college

and leading good, productive lives. I can truly say that, as a family, we have been very fortunate. I believe that it has to do with the tradition of our two families -- that is, heavy emphasis on faith as well as education. Our parents had a very strong faith to complement their solid work ethic; and it was the expectation that we would follow suit.

Looking back at my seminary days, I have no regrets. In fact, I feel the better person for it. The liberal arts education was outstanding and prepared me well for life. The people I associated with were, for the most part, fine individuals, with a depth of character that one seldom finds in such numbers. I had no trouble adjusting to life after the seminary and attribute this not only to personal strength but also to the faculty and to my fellow students. Sacred Heart was a very progressive institution for its time and encouraged freedom of discussion and exposure to the outside world. The administration saw the wisdom of not sheltering the students from the world that they would have to function in, whether they decided to pursue priesthood or not. For this I am very grateful.

As to the scandals that have rocked the Church recently, I don't really have any special insights. I would say this, however: men who become ordained bring with them the same problems of personality and mental health that affect many other people -- be it substance abuse, sexual abuse, depression, anxiety, or whatever. After all they are human. Ordination does not change the human to the divine.

As far as my own belief system, my wife and I are very strong Catholics and attend church weekly where we serve as Eucharistic Ministers. We do our best to live our faith in every part of our lives. A criticism that I share with my wife is that our religious -- priests, nuns, and brothers -- have taken such great pains to assimilate into the mainstream that they, in far too many cases, have forgotten what their real role is. We as Catholics don't need for them to be social workers. There are enough of us already. We need them to devote their lives to becoming our mentors as far as developing our spiritual lives. There seems to be such concern about the dwindling numbers of priests and religious. Perhaps the emphasis should be on quality rather than on quantity. There should be a greater expansion of lay persons' roles in an effort to free priests from administrative details. This then would allow them time to devote themselves to the spiritual needs of the parish and allow them to become the spiritual leaders that we lay people so desperately need. As Christ's strong spiritual leadership allowed the early Church to grow and develop, such guidance is needed in today's society to bring us back to strong biblical principles and ethical behavior to guide us on our road to salvation.

Again I recall the example of my old Marine chaplain, Fr. Lyons. At crucial moments, such as when he was being evacuated from the battlefield, he gave men hope as they prepared for the next life. It seems to me that this should be the essence of the formally religious life -- that is, meeting the spiritual needs of the people without being sidetracked by worldly and mundane issues.

PASSAGES AND MIRACLES
William E. Richardson

On New Years Day, 1969, I drove into the small university town of Auburn, Alabama, where, for that entire year, I would pursue a master's degree in electrical engineering. If you had told me at the time of the 1965 Selma support march in Detroit that a mere four years later I would be in college in Alabama, I would have told you that you had been smoking something very strange indeed.

<u>My Early Years and My Time in the Seminary</u>

I was born in Saginaw and raised in Flint, the firstborn of John and Betty Richardson. My father was a lawyer, my mother a grade school teacher, although she never taught full-time after I and my two younger sisters, Ann and Marybeth, were born.

I made the decision to become a priest at a very early age, probably in the second grade, much too early to be settling on such a long-term choice. Nonetheless, I stuck with that decision throughout grade school at St. John Vianney in Flint. All my teachers, mostly nuns, as well as most of my grade school classmates, understood what I had planned to do once I finished eighth grade. I was going into the seminary and not just any seminary. I was going to Sacred Heart Seminary in Detroit.

I had first become exposed to SHS through my seminarian counselors at Camp Sancta Maria in northern Michigan. I spent a mere two weeks for three consecutive summers at the camp, but I met many

313

future clergymen from Detroit there, including at least three future bishops -- Thomas Gumbleton, Bernard Harrington, and the late Kenneth Untener. So when the time came for me to take the seminary admissions test, I prayed first that I would pass it and second that I would not be sent to the Grand Rapids seminary.

The next eight years were the most formative of my life. I discovered I was a good student and that I truly loved learning. I began to mature as a person. I say "began," because there were clearly parts of the maturing process that could not happen in a Catholic seminary, most notably how to deal properly with members of the opposite sex. I made many friends, friends for life, other men who became the brothers I had always wanted as a youth. Finally, over that eight-year period, I became aware that the priesthood wasn't for me.

Leaving the Seminary

When I left the seminary after college, in 1965, I had to decide what I was going to do next. I had a degree; but, outside of social work, there was probably little I could do with a B.A. in Scholastic Philosophy. It is important to understand one of the main reasons why I left the seminary. It was my impression that many of my classmates looked upon the priesthood as ordained social work. I did not see the priesthood as simply this. Yes, I understood that much of the priesthood involved serving the faithful, a function that had heavy social work elements to it. Beyond that, however, I saw priests as persons called to holiness. In the mid-1960s, because of all the social activism of that time, the social work part of the priesthood was clearly dominant. The holiness part had taken a back seat, or so it seemed to me.

I certainly am not implying that I was a holy person. Far from it. Anyone who would sleep in while Mass was going on, deliberately skip the communal rosary, and spend little non-mandatory time in chapel could not be considered holy or devout. When I had my conference with the dean, Fr. William Sherzer, to discuss whether or not I would continue to St. John's, he told me that the faculty had some misgivings about me. They felt that I had a good intellectual

314

grasp of philosophy, theology (as much as we had been given to that point), the teachings of the Church, indeed the priesthood itself; but there seemed to be something missing on the spiritual side. Nonetheless, they were going to recommend that I continue. I told him that I had already made up my mind to leave. He readily accepted that decision. Fr. Sherzer and the faculty had me pegged right.

I must make a few remarks about the "ordained social worker" vision that I thought most in the class had in mind. I knew that this was not my calling. That is not to imply in any way that I did not share the views of my classmates regarding civil rights, worker rights, the Vietnam situation, capital punishment, social justice in general. I absolutely did.

I grew up in a family of staunch Roman Catholics of what we would now call the "old school." Both of my parents, cradle Catholics themselves, were devout in their faith. I never received mixed messages about the seriousness of religion in one's life. There was never any doubt about Roman Catholicism being the one, true religion, although neither of my parents disparaged the beliefs of those of other faiths. Personal holiness was an objective. Saving one's *own* soul was the ultimate objective; and that was accomplished by praying a lot, not breaking the commandments, generally avoiding sin of all sorts, and hoping that Jesus granted one a "holy death." As far as service to others goes -- good works, if you will -- that element was present, but more as a subset of "not breaking the commandments," following the Golden Rule, the "faith *and* good works" requirement. It wasn't particularly emphasized as a key element of how one "saved one's own soul." The good nuns at St. John Vianney grade school reinforced this same viewpoint in me.

When I left my home at the age of 14 to enter Sacred Heart, then, I carried with me the vision of a priest who facilitates the above for others. A priest was a person who was always personally holy; and, through that personal holiness, he led others to personal holiness. The ideal priest said Mass, preached meaningful sermons, heard the confessions of the faithful, converted outsiders to the one, true faith, in short he was a "St. John Vianney" type.

I learned Catholic social doctrine at the feet of my seminary professors. By the time I had finished high school, I had absorbed a new set of life guidelines based upon *Rerum Novarum* and *Quadragessimo Anno.* One of my most vivid memories from high school is of Fr. Kenneth MacKinnon, a history teacher, loudly proclaiming to our class that only the Democratic Party espoused Catholic social teaching in its political agenda. The message I got was clear – I needed to be a Democrat in order to be a good Catholic! I secretly became a Democrat when, as seniors in high school, we had a mock presidential election and I voted for Kennedy. Later, with my politics much more open, my father, the Republican lawyer, was not amused. He even claimed (to me only) that he thought I might "have been brainwashed by those liberal seminary priests."

Thus I became the raving liberal Democrat in my family of Republicans, all because my eight years in the seminary had given me a strong dose of liberal thinking, along with a true sense of outrage regarding the social inequities rampant in American society. No, my not wanting to be an ordained social worker had more to do with my extended vision of the priest as a father-counselor, a spiritual leader, an intellectual man of God, an apologist for Catholicism, a teacher. Intellectually I knew I could probably do those things. I also knew that the spiritual fervor was indeed missing.

Then there was the celibacy issue. I had known for some time that I had a strong attraction to females. A little voice in the back of my head kept telling me that some day I would personally enjoy a sexual relationship with a woman. I could not move forward toward a life of celibacy feeling that I would be unfaithful to it someday.

So, there I was. I had a degree that I could not directly use. I knew I was inclined toward the academic. I also knew that I was inclined toward the technical.

I always had an interest in science and technology. That interest led me to become involved in handling the seminary audio/visual equipment. At that time SHS had a fully equipped sound room, complete with a studio for recording, located beneath the stage in the auditorium. By my senior year in college, I had become the school's chief sound engineer. My classmate George Wesolek and I, ably assisted by many others, began a taped radio program called *Current*. The program, which featured discussions of many issues of the day, accompanied by a liberal dose of folk and rock music, was broadcast weekly on WXYZ radio in Detroit. *Current* survived as a seminary "apostolate" for many years after we moved on with our lives.

Yet, the seminary had taught me a true love of literature, especially fiction. If the English major option had been open to me (it was introduced for the class behind ours), I would have taken it in a heartbeat. While it is true that one can study life through philosophy and history, to me it is much more fun studying it through poetry and fiction. Most true literature becomes very hard to understand unless one has the great liberal arts background that I obtained at the seminary. I still recall (and believe) what Horace said about art: it must both delight and instruct. I love learning and I love being delighted. What could be better?

Thus two roads beckoned. One would have taken me toward a Ph.D. in English with a subsequent life as an academic teaching in a university. The other would have returned me to school to study engineering, eventually carrying me into the world of industry and business. I had less than a summer to make a choice.

I wrote a letter to Michigan State University, inquiring about their graduate studies in English. Before I could get a response, my father, who knew what I was considering, announced that he could get me into General Motors Institute (GMI) through a friend of his who was on the faculty. My dad also had connections at AC Spark Plug, where he had worked during World War II. I would need such a GM unit to sponsor me in order to get into GMI.

There was some sense of urgency for me to find a college home somewhere, since, by leaving the seminary, I had lost my draft deferment. Vietnam was really heating up and I had no interest in going there. In short, I jumped at the GMI opportunity. Nonetheless, I promised myself that I would one day pursue an advanced degree in English somehow, somewhere.

Studying Engineering

The decision to study engineering presented me with a more pressing and immediate problem. My science and math experience, with the exception of the college chemistry course I took at SHS, was five or more years old, dating back to high school. I had some catching up to do. GMI, as it turned out, could not admit me until the winter semester; so I signed up for some courses at Flint Junior College in an attempt to get a jump on what I would need at GMI.

In February, 1966, I entered General Motors Institute in Flint to study electrical engineering. These were the three most stressful years of my life, up to that point. My situation was made worse by my previously-earned liberal arts degree. I was given credit for all of GMI's liberal arts requirements. The good news was that I started as a sophomore. The bad news was that all I took for three years were science, math, and engineering courses. I ate, slept, and breathed equations, formulas, and engineering principles for my entire time at GMI. Some semesters I was carrying 27-28 credit hours (six classes).

During my three years at GMI, I probably went out on dates only three or four times. This is an important fact, since it meant that I delayed any true dating until I was in graduate school, deacon year for those still in the seminary.

One of the deans at GMI was a man named Harold Baker. He had a very bad reputation with members of the student body, since it was he who called in poorly-performing students to dismiss them from the school. One day I received word that Dean Baker wanted to see me in his office. I was not worried since, despite the pressure-cooker environment, my grades were more than good (excellent study habits practiced in my early seminary days helped me greatly). I was, however, curious. Dutifully, I showed up at the dean's office at the scheduled time. I was ushered into the inner sanctum where we engaged in the obligatory small talk. Eventually, he started in with

318

that famous cliché, "I suppose you are wondering why I sent for you." As it turned out, the administration leaders were aware of my background as a Catholic seminarian and they were curious as to why I had left pursuit of the priesthood for engineering. I did my best to explain my reasons to the gentleman. At the end of the explanation, he revealed the reason for his question: the single most common profession that students left GMI to pursue was the ministry! I had gone in the opposite direction and they wanted to know why. As I was leaving, he, only partly in jest, answered his own question of why students left for the ministry: "After several years at GMI, you *need* God!" I could concur with that.

In those days, GMI (since transmogrified into Kettering University, a private college) meant doing a five-year stint, not just the normal four. For most students, the fifth year was spent in the sponsoring unit working on a significant project. The ensuing write-up amounted to a bachelor's thesis. If, however, a student was able to keep his or her grades up to a certain high level, he or she spent the fifth year attending a graduate school to get a master's degree. The award of the master's degree, strangely enough, then became a prerequisite for the award of the bachelor's degree!

Throughout my three years at GMI, my stress levels were so high that they forced me to study constantly. This intensity resulted in good grades. To me it was an either/or dichotomy. I *either* studied all the time (result: excellent grades) *or* I flunked out. There was no middle ground. Thus, my stressing out got me sent off to Auburn University in Alabama to get an M.S. in electrical engineering. A nice reward for three years of pure agony. My choice of Auburn as a graduate school was, as these seemingly simple decisions always are, a fateful one that would affect much of the rest of my life.

Alabama was not what I expected. The people with whom I came into contact were very cordial indeed, didn't seem to be racists, nor did they resent the Yankee from Michigan invading their university. They were, in fact, quite used to it. Many northerners from GMI did their bachelor-master program at Auburn. I had picked Auburn, not for its academic excellence (even though the engineering school is well respected) but for more practical reasons: (a) it was in warm weather territory and (b) the football team was pretty good. As a precaution against real rednecks coming after someone with Michigan license plates, however, I emblazoned the rear window of my 1968 fire-engine red Pontiac Firebird with a very large "Auburn University" decal.

1969 was a very good year for me. I met my future wife at Auburn, obtained my master's degree, and Auburn beat Alabama in football for the first time in many years (The final score was 49 – 26; a true Auburn fan never forgets!). It was Pat Sullivan's first year as Auburn quarterback (two years later, he would win the Heisman Trophy) and it was also the year the football team was integrated. In those days, the Auburn-Alabama game was played in Birmingham, normally strong Alabama territory. When we came out of Legion Field after Auburn's triumph, we were greeted by groups of black kids cheering our team and our school. The reason was simple. Auburn's team had just been integrated while Bear Bryant had yet to integrate Alabama's.

With eight years in the seminary not that far behind me and coming off three years of pure studying with no dating to speak of, my comfort level at interacting with members of the opposite sex was low. So it was not unusual that I sought out social connections through the local parish. As it were, this parish ran a number of programs for the Auburn students. I was directed to one involving graduate students. Thus, I met my first wife within a week or so of landing on the Auburn campus.

Sarah Benz, studying for her master's in psychology, was from Mobile. Her mother's maiden name is Marston, an old Mobile family. One of her Marston forebears founded the *Mobile Register*, a daily newspaper, back in the 1800s. Sarah's family lived in the long-time family home, an antebellum mansion on Mobile's fabled Dauphin Street. Unfortunately, the family's wealth had long ago dissipated (gone with the wind?), so the house was not in the best of shape. In the guidebooks it is listed as the Green-Marston House or Termite Hall. The second name was the one we all knew it by.

320

Termite Hall is an interesting place, not so much for the architecture or the history, but more for the inhabitants, both permanent and temporary. At the time of my marriage to Sarah, in February, 1970, the permanent occupants included Sarah's mother and father, her aunt and uncle, several children of each family, and Sarah's grandmother, the venerable Mrs. Marston, affectionately known as Grandy. Grandy was a wonderful woman, very friendly, very southern. Years after her death, her life (and Termite Hall) would be fictionalized in the historical novel *In the Hope of Rising Again*, written by her great-granddaughter Helen Scully. Occasionally Grandy and I would talk about books. One time she began to recall a book from her youth that she still remembered, a now-dated novel entitled *Houseboat on the Styx*. When I told her that I had read it, she was amazed. Yes, I told her, the seminary library had a copy of it and I had read it there. I told her I had enjoyed it. That cemented a firm friendship that outlasted my marriage to Sarah.

The Marston family was well educated and very cultured, despite the lack of money. All the children of Sarah's generation had gone to college, many of whom had advanced degrees. Mrs. Eleanor Marston Benz, Sarah's mother, was not a college graduate, but she was the long-time librarian at Mobile's large Catholic high school, McGill-Toolen. She had read more than most college graduates. Termite Hall, then, became an informal gathering spot for many old Southern intellectuals. You never knew exactly whom you were going to run into there. The home was large enough (and the family in need enough) so that extra rooms were often rented out to family friends. Eugene Walter, poet, novelist, actor in Fellini movies, was a temporary resident for a number of months after he returned from his extended European stay.

I mention Eugene deliberately. He was a good example of the open-mindedness of the entire Marston/Benz family. Being openly gay in the conservative south was not always a safe thing. Eugene, however, was a family friend, therefore welcome at Termite Hall at any time. Mobile, as it is, is culturally closer to New Orleans and the rest of the formerly French Gulf Coast, than it is to the rest of Alabama. On more than one occasion I have had to politely point out to friends from the north that not everyone in the south resembles the characters portrayed in the movie *Deliverance*.

The World of Business and Marriage

Sarah and I dated throughout my year at Auburn. We were married in Mobile's Spring Hill College chapel. Spring Hill, where Sarah went to undergraduate school, is the oldest Jesuit college in the south. The ceremony was performed by my classmate, Rev. George Wesolek, who was then assigned to my old home parish in Flint, St. John Vianney. Sarah and I subsequently returned to Flint, where I continued to work for AC Spark Plug, this time as a full-time employee.

In 1971 I left AC to work for a company named Teleflex. I followed a former AC supervisor to eastern Pennsylvania, where Teleflex has its headquarters. The facility to which I was assigned was in Limerick, not far from Philadelphia. Although I stayed with this company for only two years, they were two of the best of my life. My son, John, my only offspring, was born in Lansdale, Pennsylvania, in March of 1972. This was clearly the highlight of those years.

I also learned a lot about myself during that time period, although some of the lessons did not fully reveal themselves for several more years. My new (and former) boss made me a group manager in charge of a small number of technical and manufacturing resources. This gave me a really big head. I decided that I was pretty important in the world of business, that I could hold my own with anyone, and that all I had to do to rule the industrial world was to make the right moves. This is precisely what I *didn't* do.

I next took a job as a marketing manager with ITT Semiconductors in West Palm Beach, Florida. My cockiness was still with me. I never had any formal training in marketing; but, because I had hung around with salesmen at Teleflex, making numerous customer calls with them, I fancied myself as an expert in the art of marketing. Actually, I barely knew marketing from sales. It's a wonder I was hired by ITT at all. The only thing I can put it down to is that I interview very well.

I took something else besides cockiness away from my Teleflex experience: a significant drinking habit. As I usually tell it, I fell in with evil companions, namely those same salesmen who gave me my marketing lessons. Under their tutelage, I grew to enjoy scotch and water at lunch. Soon I was buying scotch for my home and began to drink one, then two, each night after work. As the years went by, those drinks became more scotch than water. When I finally quit, cold turkey, one day in 1988, 17 years had gone by. I had worked my way up to three or four drinks every night, whether I was alone or with someone else, often followed by one or two beers. I had begun to wonder if I was an alcoholic. Until I quit, suddenly, unexpectedly even to me, that night in 1988, I did not know for sure. I can now state safely that I am not now, nor have I ever been, an alcoholic, for the simple reason that I could quit and never return. I know alcoholics. They *cannot* quit, at least not that easily. I was a heavy drinker, but not a drunk. Liquor never made me mean; it made me sleepy. In my later single days, many, many nights were given over to having my fill of scotch, eating dinner alone, and going to bed, sometimes as early as 6:30 PM. I wasted a lot of time drinking…too much time.

My Florida sojourn, in the employ of ITT, the multinational corporation accused at the time of engineering the overthrow of several South American governments, was mercifully short, only about 14 months. I was no longer in the same business sector as before. I was in the semiconductor industry, and I found that things worked somewhat differently there. Further, that industry was just seeing the leading edge of the largest business change it would ever see. Yet no one was quite sure what was happening.

In 1973, the year I joined ITT, the hottest product on the market was the hand-held calculator. These devices were then selling for $100 or more. In West Palm Beach, ITT made the chips that drove the power-hungry red LED displays. ITT did not make the calculator chip itself. Too bad. The calculator chip begat the microprocessor; the microprocessor begat the personal computer; the personal computer begat the World Wide Web as we know it today. Change was in the air. ITT was not on the plane. Soon,

I left to "pursue other options," as they say. Six months later, ITT closed the West Palm facility.

I returned to Michigan, to a tiny town in the Lower Peninsula, Reed City, joining a small company there, Nartron. Nartron was in the business of selling electrical and electronic products to the auto industry. This job experience was the worst of my entire career. Up until the point that it ended, it was the most miserable ten months of my life. Once again, it taught me significant life lessons. "Cocky" left my vocabulary. "Humility" took its place. When you work in a small remote town for a small company that is owned by a single individual, you truly work at that individual's pleasure and according to his rules. If he does not choose to treat his employees with respect and dignity, then you have the choice of going elsewhere. I chose elsewhere.

By this time, my wife was getting weary of me dragging her and our three-year old son around the country, seeking out continuing employment in the automotive component industry. She insisted that I look for employment in her hometown of Mobile. International Paper had its technical headquarters there. I started on July 1, 1975, and stayed with them until I retired in 2001. After Nartron, I was extremely grateful for the chance to return to the position of working engineer.

My work with International Paper provided me with the most satisfying job experience I ever had. As a computer control engineer, I was a key player in the design and construction of the company's Mansfield mill in Louisiana. Mansfield was the first mill ever built that was totally dependent upon computer systems to make paper. I wrote critical software that endowed those systems with the reliability to perform that feat.

I was promoted to supervision in 1983 and remained in management from that time forward. With the exception of 1994, when I was in an environmental assignment, I spent my entire career at IP as either a member or the leader of the corporate Process Control group, the same group I had first joined in 1975. As leader of that group, I became the top technical professional in IP's process control world. When I started with the company, I never aspired to go any higher; so I met my own expectations. When I left that post to retire in July of 2001, I could look back at a rather simple legacy. I performed software feats some thought impossible. I lead a group of dedicated professionals, sometimes well, sometimes not. I tried to be compassionate in my management of people, another trait I carried from the seminary. I often had to preach, be a father-confessor, even fire employees. To those entrusted to my managerial care, how I did my job was most important. Shortly after I retired, some of my former employees told me they wished I were back, that they appreciated the way I went to bat for them and cared about their welfare. My former secretary of many, many years paid me the ultimate compliment on one of my last days of employment. She told me that I was the boss against whom she measured all her subsequent bosses. And she had worked for vice-presidents since she last worked for me. It's the human things, like these, that are important to me, not the technical achievements.

Mobile, Moviemaking, Divorce, and Beyond

At the time I arrived in Mobile to assume my job in 1975, I had been married just over five years. I had a young son, John, who was just over three years old. Sarah and I bought a house in one of the less expensive new subdivisions in western Mobile. One day there was a knock on the door. A man identifying himself as a representative of Columbia Pictures informed us his studio had purchased a house across the street from us and would be filming there during the summer of 1976. The movie, called *Close Encounters of the Third Kind*, was to be directed by Steven Spielberg, who had become famous because of *Jaws*.

When filming began, all three of us were able to be extras in the movie, although our "roles" were left on the cutting room floor. John, however, gained a profession at the age of four. He currently lives in Los Angeles and works in the film and video industry.

As it turned out, I must have gotten my ideas of love and marriage from the movies. Sarah was quite an attractive lady, and I pursued her relentlessly the year we were at Auburn. I believed that all I had to do was to get her to marry me and the rest would take care of itself. Boy meets girl; boy pursues girl; girl stops fighting it; girl marries boy; they live happily ever after. It ain't necessarily so, as the old song goes. It wasn't in our case.

The year after the movie shoot, she left me. Thus, the next phase of my life began. For awhile I saw my life in four to eight year segments. Seminary: eight years. Engineering school: four years. First marriage: nearly eight years.

The following eight years would comprise, as Don Henley says, "the wild, wild nights of running." I was searching for my next mate. I looked high and low, often too low in the moral sense. At the time of my divorce, Sarah had agreed to apply for an annulment (she brought the divorce action against me, so I thought that was only right). We were turned down. This was truly a soul-searching time for me, because my conscience told me that I had to have an annulment to remarry. If I didn't get it then I had no business out chasing women (only way to really put it). During this time, my rationalization machine was working overtime.

I had a tearful discussion with my pastor during which we prayed together for a resolution. He advised me to file an appeal, which I did. In those days, the court of second instance for Mobile was New Orleans. A successful appeal would mean reversal of the local decision. A turn-down meant that a further appeal went to Chicago, maybe even Rome. (I know that the rules have since been changed.) After probably another year, an order to reverse came from New Orleans. My advocate told me that it was the first case that he had personally been involved in where that had happened.

I now had my annulment, so I continued the hunt for a new mate. My tactics didn't change much, but I felt free to marry now. Finally, in 1983, I met the lady who would become my second wife. It took months of dating her, during which time I was still seeing other women, to realize I had found someone special; but I finally saw I had the real thing in Katherine Elliott.

Bermuda

Katherine, like me, was a divorcee. She was not Catholic but I had no problem with this. During those years, I had dated plenty of girls who were not Catholic, probably the majority. I didn't keep track. Mobile, while a heavily Catholic city for one in the south, had a lot more Baptists. There were plenty of folks from other Protestant denominations as well.

Katherine came from a Presbyterian family that could not have stood in sharper contrast to Sarah's. Although she had lived in Mobile for many years, Katherine was originally from Gardendale, a suburb of Birmingham, in the northern part of the state. If Mobile represented the old French-influenced sophisticated south, Birmingham represented more of the south that northerners had learned about during the civil rights struggles of the sixties. Katherine's family still lived in Gardendale. Her parents lived in a simple home that her father had built with his own hands.

Like her parents, Katherine was an independent woman. Unlike her parents, both of whom had worked hard all their lives, she had the benefit of a good education. She lived alone in the home she had owned with her husband prior to their divorce. She had no children of her own, but she was fully dedicated to the children of the area. She worked for the Mobile County Board of Education. She drove weekends to Tuscaloosa (about four hours, one way) to take courses at the University of Alabama leading to her education doctorate.

As a white child growing up in the south of the 1960s, she had experienced the civil rights revolution from an entirely different perspective than that of her black neighbors. For that matter, her experience had been considerably different from my own. I not only grew up in the north, I grew up in the seminary. Most of us can recall where we were when we heard that President Kennedy had been shot. Katherine was no exception. She was in class in Gardendale High School. The announcement of Kennedy's violent death was made on the public address system. The students in her class cheered, all except Katherine. She burst into tears and hurried home brokenhearted. She was upset over the loss of the promising young president, whom she supported, but maybe more so over her classmates' reactions. I doubt she ever marched in a civil rights demonstration, but that incident told me a lot about her character and where her heart was.

When Katherine and I began to talk marriage, I explained to her about the Catholic annulment process. She was not overly enthusiastic about going through it; but, after some thought, she willingly did so. After her annulment was granted, she remarked to me that the process was actually a cleansing one for her. She was required to face a number of unpleasant facts about her previous marriage. The process helped put all that behind her.

The wedding date was set for October 5, 1985.

We had agreed that the wedding would take place at my home parish, Holy Family in Mobile, but would be officiated by both a Catholic priest and Katherine's pastor, Rev. Joe Donaho of the First Presbyterian Church. There was to be no Mass. Classmate Fr. Steve Makranyi agreed to come to Mobile to perform the ceremony; and it was well done by both clergymen. A reception in the church hall followed. The next day we left for a honeymoon trip to Bermuda.

Bermuda was Katherine's only choice. I had suggested alternative locations, such as San Francisco or Vancouver, BC. I was not that enthusiastic about Bermuda, not because I foresaw disaster, but because Bermuda is a standard tourist location. Katherine stated that we would have many opportunities to go to the other cities, but this might be the best time to go to Bermuda. I acquiesced.

We arrived without incident and checked into our accommodations after a resort-provided bus ride from the airport. Visitors to Bermuda are not allowed to rent cars. Further, the streets and roads are all very narrow and winding, with traffic proceeding on the left side of the road, in the manner of Britain and many of its territories and former colonies. Visitors may rent small motorbikes, however. Most resorts, including ours, had rental outlets associated with them.

The first day we bused into Hamilton, the largest city on the island. After doing some shopping, we returned to our resort. We had talked about renting motorbikes the next day and traveling to the northernmost of the islands, to the smaller town of St. George. Again, I was not enthusiastic. I had never been on a motorbike (only once on a motorcycle) and was concerned about the length of the trip. Several hours, round trip, of riding on an uncomfortable bicycle seat did not excite me. I did not argue vociferously, however. I was solicitous of my new mate's desires and so went along with the plan.

The next day was Thursday, October 10, 1985. That morning we rented the bikes. Besides the obvious, to drive on the left side of the road, we were given only three instructions that I can recall. First, we had to wear the provided helmets. Second, we were not to exceed twenty miles per hour, which was ludicrous, given that the bikes had no speedometers. Finally, we were not to turn around to look behind us while the bikes were moving. It was tough not to do this, since the bikes also lacked rearview mirrors.

In retrospect, we should have stopped right there and abandoned our plans. We had, however, already made a series of decisions that, in the sum, would prove fatal. We had come to Bermuda, where people drive on the left. We had decided to rent motorbikes. We had decided to rent two bikes instead of one with two seats. We had agreed to accept bikes that were ill equipped for the journey. Since we had two bikes, we also decided that I would lead and Katherine would follow.

We struck out on the road and for awhile our plan seemed to work well. I would start out and after 15 minutes or so, I would pull over and let Katherine catch up. She was never very far behind me. The last stop we made together was at a stop sign. The arrow pointed to the right for St. George. After a few moments of conversation, with traffic at the intersection cleared, I pulled out into the left lane and accelerated up the road.

Wandering Between Two Worlds

Within a few minutes, I sensed that something might be wrong with my front tire. While still moving forward, I stood up in the seat several times to peer down at it. It appeared to me to be going soft. Since I couldn't tell for sure, I decided to stop at the first convenient place to check it. Within a minute, a service station appeared on the right; so I pulled into it to await Katherine's arrival.

I am not sure how long I waited at the service station before I decided something must be wrong. To the best of my recollection, it was only a minute or two. Worried, I restarted the bike and headed back the other way. I suddenly came upon a scene too impossible to imagine. A broken motorbike lay in the road alongside a body, a form that I could not clearly see. There was a crowd of 10 or 12 people hovered around the accident. I didn't have to be told who it was. I came off my bike in an instant and began running toward the crowd. Immediately two young men grabbed me and held me back. I remember telling them in agonized tones that I only wanted to be with her. They continued to force me back, telling me that an ambulance was on the way. I was led to the porch of a nearby residence, where a kindly lady brought me a glass of water. There I sat, stunned, teary-eyed, frightened. For the next several days, I would stay in that other-worldly dreamlike state, where one can almost stand outside his body, observing his own actions under great stress and emotion. The thoughts that one has at such times are almost always strange, unreal, often banal, even inappropriate.

And so, at that terrible moment in my life, as I sat on a stranger's porch step on a beautiful sunny Bermuda day, waiting for an ambulance to come for my wife of five days, a wife who was lying unmoving in the road, knowing absolutely no one on that island, a black man wearing a clerical collar came up to me and put out his hand to do what he could to help. This man was my Good Samaritan. His name was Rev. Stuart Lambert. He was a native Bermudian and an Anglican minister (he is now a priest of the Ethiopian Orthodox Church). For the next three days, he seldom left my side.

Once the ambulance came (it took forever, it seemed), Fr. Lambert drove me to the hospital. On the drive I told him a little about me and

Katherine. He learned I was Catholic. We prayed together as we drove. As we drove into the hospital yard, I saw ambulance attendants outside hosing blood off of a gurney. We had only been in a special waiting room a few minutes when a doctor entered and gave me the news I had expected but had been praying I would not have to hear. Katherine's injuries, especially those to her head, had been too much; she could not be revived. I cried for a few minutes, holding the doctor's hand tightly in one of mine and Fr. Lambert's in the other. I remember making the rather stupid statement that death was part of life, the last part. I think that was me standing outside myself, trying somehow to remain philosophical in the face of enormous tragedy. I also remember muttering, over and over through my tears, "What am I supposed to do now? I don't know what to do!" Eventually, I went down the hall to see Katherine's body, a terrible experience that is difficult to describe; so I won't try.

At some point the engineer in me, the part that is ever-organized and ready to attack every problem one step at a time, seized control, if only temporarily. I knew that the first thing I had to do was call her parents. I got through to her father, who, thank God, was shocked and upset, but not hysterical. I remember his last words to me were, "Bill, bring her home." I promised that I would.

By this time, a Catholic priest had arrived, called to the hospital by Fr. Lambert. Incredibly, his name was Fr. Tom Kirwan. He was kind and compassionate, asking about Katherine's religion. I remember telling both clergymen that I had a priest classmate in Detroit named Tom Kirwan. Both Fr. Kirwan and Fr. Lambert offered to let me stay at their homes. I elected to stay with Fr. Lambert. I felt a comfort with Fr. Lambert and a need to stay close to him. He had come to me in my darkest hour. I wanted to stay with him, not anyone else.

This wonderful Anglican priest, this new-found friend, then took me first to the resort so that I could gather all of our possessions and transfer them to his home, where I would stay that night. He handled dozens of the details for me. He went to the resort manager and explained what had happened. He talked to the motorbike concession owner. He arranged for Katherine's body to be transferred to a mortuary (although that did not occur until the next day, since an autopsy had to be performed). Everywhere he made it as easy as he could for me. As it turned out, before he became a priest, he had been a policeman on the island. He had good contacts in Bermuda's government and with a lot of other locals whose help would be needed. Since Katherine was a foreign national in Bermuda, getting her body back to Birmingham would not be straightforward.

I had to make other phone calls, to key friends and relatives who could relay the word to others. I made some of these later that day at Fr. Lambert's home, near his church. There I met the priest's wonderful family. Margaret, his wife, turned out to be white. They had two beautiful children, David and Rachel, both in their teenage years. They welcomed me into their home as if they had known me forever.

During a number of these calls and on a visit to the U.S. Consulate, several people, all well-meaning, suggested that I return immediately to the United States, without Katherine's body. I steadfastly refused. I had told Hugh Lawrence that I would bring his daughter home. I was going to do just that. Further, I was concerned about the priority all the red tape would be given if I were not there to keep after people.

One of the calls I received was from my other Good Samaritan, my brother-in-law, Dick Hanson. Dick, at that time married to my sister Ann, called me from Detroit Metropolitan Airport. He was on his way to Bermuda to assist me in everything. Despite all my mental bravado and telling people that I could get through everything alone (with Fr. Lambert's help), when Dick said he was on his way, I was so relieved and thankful. He arrived the next day and took over *everything*, just as he said. With the assistance of Fr. Lambert, he connected with the proper people in both governments, with the local funeral home, and with Delta Airlines. He had to slip the funeral home manager $100 to move some detail or another forward, he told me. I didn't care. I was just so grateful that he was there, handling any and all issues, big or small.

On Saturday, October 12, 1985, we were on our way back to the

United States, back to Gardendale, Alabama, where we would lay my new wife to rest the following Monday. A priest friend, Fr. Peador Dalton, drove my son up from Mobile for the funeral. Many others from Mobile made the nearly five-hour drive to Gardendale as well. Dick Hanson arranged for my parents to fly down from Michigan.

The funeral was a simple one, officiated by the Lawrences' minister. Before we reached the gravesite, which was only a few hundred yards from the funeral home where the service had been held, Fr. Dalton asked me if there was a particular bible passage I would like him to read. I mentioned a passage from Job. A few minutes later, when we had reached the gravesite, I found him madly paging through his bible, trying to find the passage I had asked for. I called over one of my employees from International Paper, Mike Cottrell, one of those who had driven up from Mobile. Besides working for me as an engineer, Mike was an ordained Assembly of God minister. Because we had had many discussions about religion in the office, I knew Mike probably had both Testaments memorized. I asked him to help Fr. Dalton find the proper passage. Sure enough, within a minute or two, Dalton calmed down. When he was asked to say a final few words, he had exactly the right passage: "The Lord gives, the Lord takes away. Blessed be the name of the Lord."

The next few months consisted in a jumble of details for me. Just a few recollections:

I found myself having to deal with the remnants of Katherine's earthly life, her possessions. She died intestate, without a will. As her husband, I was named administrator of her estate by the court. Although I barely knew those in her family, I helped them recover money from insurance policies that Katherine had. I helped divide her earthly possessions among these fine people. I arranged for the sale of her car and her home. I arranged for payment of her outstanding bills through the system the court had set up. I had the strange experience, more than once, of coming across something or other in her house, not understanding what it was or what should be done with it; and, without thinking, telling myself that I would have to ask her about it when she got back.

I awaited the report from the Bermuda courts on the accident. Called an Inquiry, I hoped it would answer questions that I had about what happened. The wait went on and on. Through friends, I found myself in contact with Sen. Jeremiah Denton's office. I talked to my congressman, Rep. Sonny Callahan. I even spoke to the U.S. Attorney, Jeff Sessions, now one of Alabama's senators, about somehow putting pressure on the Bermuda government to deliver the Inquiry results.

Finally the results arrived. I found that Katherine simply lost control of her bike (Had I distracted her when I was standing up in my seat, looking at the tire? I will never know.) Her bike moved erratically on the road, crossed over into on-coming traffic where it was hit head-on by a car. Her helmet flew off before she hit the ground, so when she came down, her head hit the pavement with no protection. This probably caused her death.

It took me a good deal of time before I recovered from this terrible experience, if one actually ever does. I think about Katherine often and sometimes wonder what life with her would have been like. Yet, I have never been one who looks back or does a lot of "what if-ing." The recovery time from this experience was longer than for some of my more minor crises; but eventually I got there, with a lot of help, both divine and human.

Married Again

In December, 1987, I took my third dip into matrimony. Marilyn Clark was a girl I had known for a long time and dated some during the eight years between Sarah and Katherine. She was, in fact, at one time my ex-wife's best friend. At the same time that I was dealing with the immediacy of Katherine's death, Marilyn was ending a troubled relationship with a local judge. We got together again, maybe at first just to comfort each other. Marilyn, like Sarah, was Catholic and a Spring Hill College graduate. She also had a previous marriage to deal with; so there was another annulment to go through.

Marilyn, despite being a cradle Catholic, had been away from the regular practice of her religion for some time. As we began to get serious about each other, she returned fully to the faith. In the process she reintroduced me to a number of the practices of Catholicism from days gone by. She remembered the emphasis on rosaries, holy hours, and novenas; so she sought out opportunities to participate in these and similar things. Suddenly I found myself doing them right along with her, things I hadn't done for years. Some of it felt very strange, especially at first. Although we didn't turn the clock all the way back to the Fifties (we never wanted to go to Latin masses, for instance), some of it felt as if Vatican II had never happened. Although Marilyn still enjoys these "older" practices, she is up-to-date with the newer ones as well. She acts as a Eucharistic minister at our parish while I do my thing as a lector.

Marilyn was employed by the State of Alabama as a social worker. She worked in a department called Quality Control. This was a euphemism for a group of people who ran around the state, chasing down all the food stamp fraud. She came from a family of Irish Catholics (out of Rochester, New York) who had migrated to Mobile in the 1940s. Joseph Byrnes, her father, was a self-made businessman who was involved in many different enterprises over his lifetime. In Mobile, there is a street in one of the more posh districts called Byrnes Boulevard.

In 1970, I had been married to Sarah in the main chapel on Spring Hill's campus. This time I was married to Marilyn in the very old, very small Sodality Chapel on the same campus. This chapel was the first built by the Jesuits in the mid-1800s. It only seats about 25 people. This was fine with me. When you get married the third time, I think a small, close friend and family service is best. I didn't even ask a priest-classmate to do this one. My pastor came over from Holy Family to say the Mass and administer the wedding vows.

Marilyn retired from her state job several years after we married. She gets a nice little pension check each month, which is indeed welcome. Since 1997, when International Paper moved about 200 of us out of Mobile, we have been living in the Cincinnati area. Marilyn continues her social work by providing a cooked meal monthly for a homeless shelter in downtown Cincinnati.

We have been married now for more than 21 years. Our love is stronger than ever.

My Faith Life and How The Seminary Experience Continues

For as long as I can remember, I have always "wanted" others to be Catholics. From my earliest years, I can remember that I associated being Catholic with being good and being moral. I didn't associate being non-Catholic with the opposite state; I just wasn't sure about the others. Kids that went to Catholic schools were assumed to be good and moral and could be counted on to treat me right. Kids that went to public school were at least suspect. Naïve and simplistic? You bet. My seminary days and subsequent experiences helped me turn this youthful outlook on Catholicism to a more formal way of life.

Even when I wasn't completely true to its vision, I always kept the Christian ethic in sight, with the Catholic version always in mind. If you ask me what I believe in, that's really easy. All you have to do is go to the Nicene Creed and read it. That's what I believe. None of this has changed from my days in the seminary. While it is true that I have found myself disappointed on occasion with rulings out of Rome or with the actions of certain clergymen, I remain very, *very* Catholic.

I wish that Paul VI had chosen to write a different directive on artificial birth control than that contained in *Humanae Vitae*. I feel that there were adequate philosophical and theological grounds for a different result. The fact is that he *did not* write another directive; he wrote the one contained in *Humanae Vitae*. I accept that.

I wish that the Church would relax the requirement for a celibate clergy in the Roman rite. I have problems with allowing married Episcopalian ministers to enter the Church and be ordained as married priests, when we have a vast number of men who have left the priesthood because of the celibacy requirement and who would return to the ministry in a heartbeat if they were allowed to stay married. I object to this apparent injustice, but I accept it and pray that it will be different in the not-too-distant future.

I wish we didn't have to bear the seemingly constant barrage of sex scandals among the clergy. They are not only embarrassing and scandalous; they have harmed many individuals, primarily the victims of the abuse, and harmed the Church as a whole.

I must admit that my former unquestioning respect for members of the Church hierarchy has been greatly damaged by the revelations of cover-up by some of the bishops. Sadly, I now look with suspicion upon these men, men that should be above reproach in every way but who clearly have often failed those whom they are supposed to be serving.

But the Church is made up of fallible human beings, sinners all. I expect that such sinful actions on the part of clergymen have been going on since Christ's time. They are just far more visible now. They are sad. They are shameful. But they have not driven me away from my home, the Roman Catholic Church. I trust in the Holy Spirit to guide us out of this terrible mess.

As you might expect, the biggest challenge to my faith, to my entire belief system, came with my having to deal with the death of my second wife.

Was it anger with God? No, not really. As Job states, the Lord gives and the Lord takes away. He is God, master of life, master of death. It is his right. Further, I should not necessarily expect to understand why.

No. What scared me more than anything was the thought, the possibility, that Katherine was really *completely* gone, body and soul, that death was truly the end. I was struck with the silence of death, with the inability of my loved one to communicate with me. Why would God allow that to be so? Why must there be such silence? Could it possibly be because there is *nothing* after death, no afterlife, just final and eternal extinction? These thoughts gnawed at my mind, haunted me, frightened me. I was more disturbed with the possibility of nothingness than with the possibility of eternal damnation.

Of course if there was truly nothing after death, then all that I had been taught and believed was a mere sham. I needed reassurance. I needed it badly.

As it so happened, Fr.Tom Kirwan (the classmate, not the priest on Bermuda) was associate pastor at my sister Marybeth's parish in Sterling Heights, Michigan. On a visit to her, I walked around the corner to Tom's rectory and asked to speak with him. He knew, of course, of Katherine's death. I told him of the difficulties I was having and asked him to recommend some reading material. He suggested a book entitled *Afterlife*, by an Episcopalian priest named Morton Kelsey, who taught at Notre Dame for awhile. I immediately purchased the book and read it cover-to-cover. While it didn't allay all my fears immediately, it calmed me down. It told me that there are other intelligent people out there that have considered these questions and have concluded that death is not extinction. Intellectually, of course, this was not news. Emotionally, I found it comforting and reassuring.

In addition to my formal Catholic beliefs, I have adopted one or two of what I call "operating principles" for my spiritual life. These are beliefs that stay with me daily, that directly affect the way I live my life. The first of these is an easy one. I believe in the power of prayer. I believe that it works...always...even when I don't get the result that I want. I have discovered that sometimes what I pray for is not at all what I really need. [As Aimee Mann sings, in the soundtrack of the movie *Magnolia*, "Yu got what you want. Now you can hardly stand it."] So, in many cases now, I simply pray for God to handle my problems. It has only been in recent years that I have been able to pray this way.

The second principle is a little harder to explain, but it helps me deal with that age-old issue, "The Problem of Evil." Why did God allow six million Jews to perish in the Shoah? Why does God allow vast populations of people to perish in Africa by famine? Why did I have to have that traffic accident this morning? Or, why did God allow my wife to be killed in an accident when we had only been married five days?

I usually refer to my principle as "process theology." I am aware there is a formal system that has that name in theological circles. I first heard the term, in fact, from a good female friend in Mobile sometime after Katherine's fatal accident. An educated Methodist, she talked to me about it for only a few minutes. What I developed in my own mind from the conversation was the following:

1) Life is a process. Free will life decisions are part of that process. We don't always choose wisely. When we make mistakes, errors, bad decisions, these normally take us down a new fork in our life's road. Even good decisions take us down new forks. Eventually we are faced with a new decision that we would never have been required to make had we not made the earlier one. Again, we must choose. Again we take a new path. These ever-branching decisions may make us better people or they may make us worse. Some are simply neutral. But every day, every month, every year, for good or ill, we make them. The marvel is that no matter how far out on that tree (out on a limb?) we get, one step will always bring us back home, back to God. At every branch in our path, there is this possibility. Why? Because God has built it into the *process*.

2) During this on-going life process, we occasionally have bad things happen to us (see my short list, above). Why? What's going on here? Is God testing us? Is he challenging us? Yes, I believe he is. These problems, these difficulties, are not necessarily aimed at us one-on-one personally. I doubt anyone would claim that the Shoah happened to challenge him or her personally. Yet, we feel these things personally. How many times have we heard someone express a thought such as this: "I cannot believe in God. Any God who would allow six million innocents to die cannot be a just God. Therefore, He cannot exist." The person who makes such a statement is *absolutely* taking the Shoah

personally! That person is saying that *my personal belief* cannot exist because of something as terrible as the Shoah.

There is a common saying in the business world that <u>every problem is really an opportunity</u>. That's what I believe. I believe it is part of life's process that we be faced with problems and that what God is waiting to see is what we do with them, what decisions we make because of them, how we react to them. These are the challenges of life, the pitfalls that can lead us to growth or to despair.

Looking at things this way has worked for me and is part of my everyday practice of religion. True, there is nothing in this "system" that addresses those directly affected by an evil (such as those slaughtered in the Shoah). This operating principle works only for survivors, ones who must look back on the evil and try to determine what its meaning is.

Liberals and Conservatives, Democrats and Republicans: Personal Reflections

As I described earlier, I became a social and political liberal simultaneously, through the strong teaching of Sacred Heart Seminary's faculty. At about the same time, I thought of myself as a Church liberal as well. Today, I sometimes describe myself as conservative; but, in truth, I believe I am really just an orthodox Roman Catholic. I realize now that I never truly left the orthodoxy of my earlier days. An explanation is called for.

"Liberal" and "conservative" are labels that seem to defy definition, since people argue about them all the time. Perhaps it's more reasonable to state that, if one is going to use such definitions in a discussion, written or spoken, one had better be certain that everyone that is a party to that discussion understands the terms in the same way. This forces me to define, or at least attempt to describe, what I mean when I use those terms. To complicate matters further, it is my observation that the meanings have tended to shift in significant ways over time.

Prior to Vatican II, a liberal was a person who argued for certain changes within the Church brought about through accepted Church procedures. A conservative would argue that changes were not needed and shouldn't occur; but, if they were to occur, they must do so under accepted Church procedures. Liberals and conservatives, therefore, were in agreement that *accepted Church procedures* were the key. Examples of such procedures were (a) papal decrees, (b) validation through the operation of the universal magesterium, or (c) the actions of an ecumenical council. Of those three procedures, only the first was a true possibility for Catholics of the 1950s. The second was barely understood by most Catholics and the third was a possibility so remote, it was discounted altogether.

Examples of issues upon which Catholics tended to choose sides were celebration of the Mass in the vernacular, the requirement for abstaining from meat on Friday, and the requirement for priestly celibacy. The liberal and conservative positions on these issues are obvious.

Enter Pope John XXIII. Things changed, to say the least.

The fact that the Council occurred at all made the second two *accepted Church procedures* a reality for 20th century Catholics. The problem was that there was significant disagreement about how they worked, especially in relationship to the pope's authority. Once the council began to issue its documents, some began to act as if the pope were no longer relevant. This situation was later exacerbated by Paul VI, when he issued *Humanae Vitae*. To many, that encyclical confirmed that the papacy was simply out of touch with modern reality. It also confirmed to many that collegiality, one of the products of the council, was a sham. Another group concluded that, since the pope had ignored the advice of many theologians and bishops, there was no problem ignoring what the pope had said, at least regarding birth control.

But once the genie of ignoring the pope was out of the bottle, the door to wider dissent opened on many other topics. This phenomenon was not limited to either the left or the right. Thus the shift in meanings for the terms "liberal" and "conservative." On the far right were the Lefebrists, who claimed that both the pope and the council were illegitimate. On what authority they based this claim is beyond me. On the far left were numerous dissenting theologians, certainly not an organized "movement" like that led by the French archbishop, all of whom claimed that neither the pope nor the council went far enough. Unlike the Lefebrists, who clearly put themselves outside the Church via the standard schismatic route, the leftist dissenters continually insisted they were still inside the Catholic Church; but they then became quite irate when Vatican authorities called them to account. Again, on whose authority these dissenters based their actions is beyond me.

The result of all this was to widen the meaning of the terms "liberal" and "conservative" to include a number of Christians who, by their own actions, had removed themselves from the Roman Catholic community. I have always believed that any organization has the right to set the terms of its own membership and to clearly state who meets and who does not meet those requirements.

The logic of ignoring or marginalizing the pope based upon the work of Vatican II escaped me. The pope was required in order to call Vatican II; but once the Council spoke, the pope was no longer required? Had those that felt this way forgotten that the pope also had to *approve* the council's actions? So how was it possible to ignore the pope? To me, doing so made no logical sense. And logic is very important to me for I am still an Aristotelian at heart.

I once heard a priest say that the Jews of Jesus's day expected someone to "show us a sign." Thus the gospels, especially Mark's, are full of miracles. The Greeks, on the other hand, expected someone to "explain the logic of it to us." The letters of Paul, therefore, are full of explanations. In my personal spiritual life, I have never expected to "see signs," although I admit that would be nice. Therefore, like the Greeks, I crave explanations. And the explanations need to be logical, need to be consistent, need to hang together, as it were. Otherwise they are not explanations at all.

Wandering Between Two Worlds

Ralph Waldo Emerson once proclaimed: "A foolish consistency is the hobgoblin of little minds." The first two words are often left out by those who would argue that consistency is not important. Worse yet, the same people forget the last words of the passage from which this famous quote comes: "Speak what you think today in hard words and tomorrow speak what tomorrow thinks in hard words again, though it contradict everything you said today." To me, whatever truth is contained in the "hobgoblin" part of Emerson's statement is totally undercut by his final words.

So, I look for explanations, for logic, for reasons, even though I, like Kierkegaard, know that logic will carry me only so far. This fits right in with what Fr. Sherzer told me so long ago in my final conference with him. It also fits well with what I chose as my new vocation -- engineering, a profession dependent upon logic, reason, and consistency. The engineering profession, not surprisingly, is also notably heavy with "conservatives," at least the political kind.

For years, wherever I worked, I was one of very few Democrats in the salaried workforce. In most cases, I kept my party affiliation to myself. I saw no sense in getting in arguments with other employees, especially my supervisors, about my politics. Yet, early in my industrial career, I served for a time as a member of the Genesee County (Michigan) Democratic Party Committee and went to several Michigan State Democratic Party Conventions as a delegate.

I still vote. I expect I always will. I seldom vote for Democrats now. This is a fairly recent development. Ever since the Democratic Party made being pro-abortion part of their litmus test for higher office, I have been unable to support their national candidates. In my view, only so-called Catholics remain at the national level: Kennedy, Kerry, Pelosi, all of whom presume to know better than the Church and thus have put themselves outside of it, whether or not they are willing to admit it. They say that they have never left the Catholic Church. Well, like Ronald Reagan, I have never left the Democratic Party. It left me.

Frankly, I have problems with the other guys too. If the Democrats don't speak for me on abortion and related life issues, the Republicans don't speak for me on the death penalty or gun control; and until recently they missed the boat on critical environmental issues.

The Little Miracle

I think it would be appropriate to conclude my story by telling you of an occurrence in my life that I consider a miracle. No, I have not been having revelations or visitations by saints and angels. Further, it does not involve "an interruption of the scientific laws of nature," which is one way of defining a miracle. It does, however, involve a *highly unlikely* event that is *extremely difficult* to explain under normal circumstances and whose result brings good out of bad. For this reason I call it the "little" miracle. See what you think.

Immediately after Katherine's death, I subconsciously began to look for, and find, the good that came out of that bad event. The main thing I found was the outpouring of love that people exhibited for me. Beginning with Fr. Lambert and Dick Hanson, to Katherine's immediate family (who *never* blamed me in any way for what happened), to people who worked with me, worked with Katherine, were simply friends or sometimes people I hardly knew, this outpouring of love was palpable. It was genuine. It was real.

I got to know the entire Lawrence family. We grieved together. We shared our feelings openly. In one picture taken at our wedding, Katherine is standing in Holy Family Church. Behind her can be seen a banner picturing a butterfly and proclaiming "I am the Resurrection and the Life." Her mother later called it to my attention. I talked to my pastor about getting it. A kindly lady at the parish volunteered to make a duplicate. It was sent to the Lawrence's church in Gardendale, a gift of Catholics in Mobile to Presbyterians in Gardendale. The more I looked for good things such as this, the more I found them. But there was a bigger one to come.

We were only married five days and, for most of that time, we were in a foreign country. Now when people get married, they normally wait until after the honeymoon to take care of changing beneficiary names on insurance policies. Consequently, when I began to go through Katherine's papers and other personal effects, I found all of the beneficiaries were her family members. No surprise there. If the situation had been reversed, she would have found the same with my policies.

I began to think about the policies that International Paper provides for their employees and their families. I talked myself into thinking that, just because I had not had time to put Katherine's name on my work policies, the company should still have covered her automatically, whether or not I had a chance to pay my small portion of the first premiums. There were two policies covering spouses: one small term life policy and a much larger Accidental Death and Dismemberment (AD&D) policy.

I approached the Human Resources benefits clerk with my request that these policies be honored. She listened to me carefully and told me she would forward the issue up the line.

Weeks went by. I heard nothing. Then one day I got a call from the clerk to come and see her. When I arrived in her office, she carefully explained that, in order for the policies to pay off, the premiums had to be pre-paid, including the portion payable by the employee. Eight years before, when Sarah and I divorced, I had cancelled premium payments on the term life policy. For some unknown reason, however, I was still making the premium payments on the AD&D policy. I apparently had been doing so for eight years!

I am not sure whether Sarah's name was still on the policy or whether there was *no name* on the policy. It didn't matter. The insurance company had ruled that, since I had been paying the premiums all along, the policy would pay off for Katherine's death.

Now I know myself. I am meticulous, sometimes to a fault, about spending money for no reason. When I cancelled the small policy in 1977, it was my full intention that the larger AD&D policy be cancelled as well. So why wasn't it cancelled? I don't know. But it wasn't. Why didn't I notice for eight years that I was paying for something that had no value? I don't know. Would the money have been paid to me if I had not made an issue of it? Of course not. No one would have even noticed. Could there have been a human clerical error? Yes, of course. That is the most reasonable explanation. But even if that's exactly what happened, the fact that it happened to me, the only person who could benefit from it, is beyond human belief. That's why I call it the little miracle.

Then again why do I call coming into a substantial sum of money under such tragic circumstances a miracle at all? Because of the good that came out of it and for no other reason. I sent a portion of the money to the bishop of the Episcopal Diocese of Bermuda in Fr. Lambert's name, in gratitude for the love and friendship he showed to me, a perfect stranger. I donated another portion to the University of South Alabama to establish a scholarship in Katherine's name. This scholarship has since paid out thousands of dollars to deserving education and English majors. I still participate in the annual recipient selection process. Finally, a very large portion of the money was used to send my son to a proper college where he could pursue his dream of becoming a moviemaker.

Before we married, Katherine and I talked about John's college education. I explained to her that I could not afford to send him away to school. In fact, I had been encouraging the boy since he was small to study hard, since he would have to earn a scholarship in order to go anywhere other than a local, state-supported college. When Katherine heard this, she told me very clearly that somehow or another she would do whatever she needed to do to see that John went to the college of his choice. *How could she ever have known what this would mean?*

A miracle? In my mind, yes. Small, maybe, but nonetheless as real as it could be. I believe there are many more where that came from.

Back to the Future

In the end, I am a believer and continue as a practicing Catholic. I am not claiming great enlightenment. I simply have come to terms at this time in my life with certain aspects of existence that are beyond human understanding. Note that I say "come to terms." Note further that I say "at this time in my life."

My religious views are without a doubt less sophisticated than those of my classmates who studied, and still study, theology. I am hardly the picture of a model Catholic. My mind still wanders at Mass altogether too often and I am not as active in parish life as I probably should be, despite serving on several parish councils and one archdiocesan pastoral council. But I wouldn't even be this far along in a maturing process if it hadn't been for the marvelous training I received at Sacred Heart in the fifties and sixties. I will prize those days forever.

You may recall that long ago, just prior to my entering GMI, I promised myself to someday pursue an advanced degree in English. I was finally able to do that in Mobile, where the University of South Alabama is located. I completed my master's degree in 1982. Upon the faculty's invitation, I later taught evening courses in Technical Writing at South.

Learning is a life-long enterprise, in my view. I was first taught that in my seminary days. The lessons were different then. At that time, I had no practical experience with the world outside. Now I do. So if life is a continuing learning experience, then I truly am a perpetual student. Bless all my seminary professors who put up with me but taught me so well.

Very early in my seminary days, I read an article about a young man who had entered the seminary, then left after several meaningful years. He said he felt he had a vocation to the seminary but not a vocation to the priesthood. That summarizes my feelings about my time at Sacred Heart very well. I was meant to be there but for reasons other than becoming a priest.

As for the future of the Roman Catholic Church, despite the liberal-conservative swings of the past 45 years, I have no worries or concerns. Long ago one of our seminary professors told us that after every general council of the Church, there is a period of great agony and upheaval that sometimes lasts for decades. We are in that period now. Our Church is made up of humans. But I am at peace, knowing it is also a divine institution. I fully trust the Holy Spirit to guide us safely through this troubling time. *"And behold, I am with you always, until the end of the age."*

WHO WOULD HAVE THOUGHT?
Robert A. Ruedisueli

It has always seemed to me that the hardest part of a writing project is the first word. Once I had typed "**that word,**" I knew I could do the rest. "**That word,**" in this case, had to be deleted from the page since it was an expletive; and that's what I learned to do with expletives! I don't often start with such language, but I usually get one in before I am through.

Two dates have special meaning -- graduating as a member of the class of 1965 from Sacred Heart Seminary, Detroit, Michigan, and being ordained to priesthood in June of 1969 by the new Cardinal, John F. Dearden.

Since that day in June, I have struggled to live out the vision and words of the Second Vatican Council, not as though they were written in stone forty years ago (because they weren't), but as they have grown and developed since then. In spite of ceaseless attacks from a variety of sources and for a variety of reasons, I believe that the vision of that council was not only valid for its time but, in a newer and fresher form, will more fully manifest itself in the future of Catholicism. We can never "go back" to live our future.

I write from the tranquil environment of my home in Port Sanilac, where I will retire, at least for a while. I look out in the woods and watch the deer, wild turkey, squirrels, rabbits, all the flora and fauna, with my friend Carole, for whom I am guardian, and our dogs, and think that life gets little better than this. Christmas carols are playing on my CD and it is the middle of January. I usually don't get time at

Christmas to listen, so my season starts late. I think priests generally celebrate after normal people are through. I also write from the perspective of being a priest in good standing in my diocese for almost forty years. Little do they know!

I grew up the middle child in a middle class family. My dad worked for his uncle in a "mom and pop" hardware store. My mother was a stay-at-home mom for the most part. Two older brothers and two younger sisters complete the picture. We moved from the city to the brand new suburbs in 1949, and we and our friends played in the mud for several years -- a lot of mud as the building boom continued!

My father was a conservative, my mother more progressive. The following example always jumps to mind when I think about the roles my parents played in my formation, my "growing up." On my First Communion Day in 1950, there were so many students in the class at St. Joan of Arc Parish that we were spread over three Masses. Only our parents could be our guests. I got up, got dressed, and went to brush my teeth. Boy, did that glass of cold water taste good going down! Oh no! I broke my fast on my First Communion Day!

FATHER: "You will just have to wait until next week. Your mother will talk to Sister and explain and make other arrangements."

MOTHER: "No, no, that's not fair. It was only water, after all. You make your First Communion today, and I will take responsibility with God!" (I think my mother created the concept of the Pastoral Solution!)

I knelt to receive my First Communion with my parents on either side. As the priest, an extremely stern and authoritarian pastor, leaned over to place the host on my tongue, he leaned over too far and tipped the vessel. I was showered with hosts from the seemingly bottomless ciborium! I had hosts inside my new suit coat pocket, between my coat and shirt, lying on my shoulders, in my hair (stuck to the Wildroot Cream Oil, Charlie – or were those my Brylcreem days?). Anyway hosts were everywhere. (I think my mother then and there hatched the plot to get me to the seminary. It was a sign -- a

Eucharistic shower – like being baptized with milk and thus destined to be a bishop!)

The pastor nearly collapsed as I helped him locate the hosts and politely handed them back to him, his face becoming redder and redder with each host I handed him. My father looked straight ahead as if nothing had happened or that he had never seen me before in his life; but (horror of horrors!) my mother helped me with the hosts. (I believe that that day my mother gave birth to the notion of Extraordinary Ministers of the Eucharist!) Within a few years that church building was soon replaced by another. I am fairly certain, however, that there was no connection between those two events.

Another sacramental formative point came at my Confirmation. In those days many priests were gathered together to assist the bishop, their numbers based on the size of the class to be confirmed. Priests were the only ones who could perform a variety of sanctified ministries involving the conferral of the sacrament. Usually the priests had dinner together, often with several cocktails…or more. Two of the functions they performed made them known as "pushers" and "wipers." The wipers would wipe the Chrism off the foreheads the bishop had just anointed. The pushers would urge, with a shove, the newly confirmed away from the communion rail to make room for the next. I was the victim of an overzealous "pusher" who pushed me before the "wiper" could make his move. I returned to my seat with Holy Chrism still on my unworthy forehead. After the ceremony my father was beside himself with confusion about what to do. My mother kissed my forehead and simply said, "Don't wash your forehead until morning." Wouldn't she have made a great pope?

In the midst of this family setting, I was taught to be both a worrier and a chronicler. The challenge to see (really, to worry about) the consequences of actions, behavior, attitudes, and ideas was a major part of my growing up. I was also taught to watch closely and observe and, like Boswell, to analyze and be objective, free to comment on the wisdom or folly of the moment. What these skills equipped me to do, I am not sure. They are just part of me. I worry and I watch – and I do both very well, thank you. Here is just an example, if you will bear with me.

Not long ago, I ordered a new stackable washer and dryer, to be delivered on the weekend. Since I had writing this autobiography hanging over my head and not really knowing what that first word would be, I thought, "Why not get the spot ready for the new installation?" And so I began. Never in eleven years had I turned the valves or adjusted the water connections to the old washer/dryer. Yet I courageously faced the challenge.

As I worked, I became more and more anxious because the connections were not coming off very easily. I became even more determined: I MUST get it done; there is no turning back; I must be successful at this. My eyeglasses came apart and a lens fell into the sink. My back had been bothering me all week and I found myself almost paralyzed with disc pain. Finally one line loosened and came off successfully. I was encouraged. But I was immediately challenged by the second one – the more reluctant of the two. I had two wrenches at play, and sweat began to form where it should. With all my might I bore down on the second connection; and, of course, the line popped apart! (I hate PVC "pipe.") Water began to shoot everywhere. Kind of pretty in a way, I observed, although it was creating quite a mess. Then I began to worry. Something more serious was about to happen! Immediately the pump went on, signaling that it would not go off again until I did something. Actions have consequences; inactivity does too.

I threw the electric switch off and turned on a faucet to drain the lines. I retrieve my lens, the water pressure was relieved, *my* pressure was way up, and my back provided killing pain. Rags soaked up the water. Then the thought hit me: you are getting a new washing machine. It uses water. This is a problem that must be fixed. You are here for another week. When the pump is off, there is no water. Remember…you can flush but once. Suddenly my need to release water grew and I headed for the cedar grove nearby the side of my house, near the forsythia bushes right over by the fuel tank. Once back inside, I opened the yellow pages and saw ***"Same Day Plumbing – 'Ask for Mark.'"*** I called. Suddenly, surprisingly, I had a new best friend. He was on his way. God bless Mark. (Will he do it right – I worried!?!) I thought about throwing away every wrench I had! I became convinced they do more harm than good. Those things can kill you!

My obtuse point is that the skills I learned growing up in my family taught me to live at two levels: get into life, deeply and fully, but don't get sucker punched in the process. Also, when water is shooting everywhere, turn off the damn pump!

In early adolescence I was moved by, of all things, two papal encyclicals. They were *Mystici Corporis* (*On the Mystical Body of Christ*) and *Mediator Dei* (*On the Sacred Liturgy*), both written by Pope Pius XII. I was moved by the vision he created as he described the Church as a fundamentally spiritual reality, a mystical body. I saw in these pastoral letters a body of dynamic holiness that exists in universal and cosmic dimensions. I saw a bond that exists among the people of faith. The Church (not denomination) that is marked by unity and holiness is real and lives and is effective. What I do, here and now, makes a difference to you and to all, there and then. And his Holiness called for new directions in the Liturgy and new participation in this Prayer. Many friends with whom I have shared a commonness of vision in these forty years were affected by that same vision. Each of us had been given a sense of Church that was cosmic yet personal. I guess that is why Teilhard de Chardin appealed to me. I believe in the movement of holiness and mystery that unfolds in time and beyond and, in that unfolding, draws all things together. This movement calls each of us to enter into it and experience it fully and deeply just as soon as each of us is ready. I believe that we all will grow in that readiness and share this vision in and out of time. This sense of Church beyond time has only grown stronger through the years, especially when it was tested and risked.

My biggest memory of graduation from college is surprise. I was a poor student. If you are busy worrying and observing, there is not much room for study. Study actually gets in the way. I was surprised that I was graduating, that I had become the first in my family (both sides) to achieve a degree, and surprised that I was recommended to go on to St. John's Provincial Seminary in the fall of 1965 to begin theological studies. Surprised, pure and simple. Who would have thought?

The eight years of seminary life leading up to college graduation – yes, I am a "lifer" – made every good sense to me in the historic context. Head Prefect, Recreation Prefect, Beadles, demerits, etc. (all Harry Potter-esque), never taken too seriously. (Actually, I received only five demerits and it was in the final week of high school.) Getting the cassock in the third year of college was a point of arrival, a kind of indicator of things to come. By the way, I ripped my cassock during the first week running late-for-something from my room and catching the pocket on the doorknob. Maybe that was an indication of things to come as well! My biretta was stolen off my door in the third year of theology. I used it for a door marker so I wouldn't get lost searching for my room. The seminary community no longer used birettas anyway.

Studies at St. John's Seminary were easier since theology fascinated me. I loved studying it and I loved the reflection, the contemplation into which it led me and drew me. The movement of the community to Holy Orders and all that very serious business was captivating. Finally, I thought, we were getting down to brass tacks.

In those years, we were drawn into a series of life-changing events and experiences that affected the whole world. Even those of us in our closed, academic, kind of monastic life could not escape the impact of such amazing events.

The Second Vatican Council had been called and began serious deliberations in Rome. Its progress in discussions and the preparation of documents for universal teaching held promise of enough fresh air for all.

The Civil Rights movement had begun in earnest. People were living and dying for the rights of all men and women, races, creeds, and lifestyles. The energy engendered in this struggle offered the promise of success. Could the Age of Aquarius be far behind? I think it was at the Vest Pocket Theater where I saw *Hair.* I joined the cast on stage for that final scene of dancing and singing. I was convinced that all the ideals, all the possibilities were just that -- possible, and that I had found a part in it worth singing and dancing about.

My classmate Jim Lavigne and I took a long permission in our college days and ended up downtown at a music store on Woodward Avenue, in a picket line demonstrating for equal rights and against tokenism. We had the opportunity to meet James Farmer, Director of the Congress on Racial Equality, at a rally at Fort Street Presbyterian Church that same afternoon. It was exhilarating. In one sense, it was naughty. We were breaking out of the pack. Some other seminarians walked by and saw us in the picket line and later asked us what we thought we were accomplishing. Further, we had entered a Protestant church! WOW! There was a cross in that church and pews too! Oh, my!

In another sense, it was life changing. It affirmed, at least, the fundamental attitudes of equality that had been introduced to me in my family as I was growing up. I was excited. I had expressed the part in all this that I had claimed for myself. As a child, I remember asking my mother what she would do if my older brother started dating or even married a woman of a different race. Without blinking, she said: "I would try to love her just like any girl he might marry." Fundamental attitude. Foundational as well. We have now seen the Inauguration of Barack Hussein Obama as the 44th President of the United States. In every sense this was for me a celebration of victory in a war which I helped to fight. There is satisfaction in this action. Another change has been effected, another corner has been turned; and it feels so good. There were no attack dogs, no fire hoses for crowd control, another victory that moves everyone forward.

We were ordained on June 7, 1969, and began our first parish assignments as priests on June 26.

- On June 27 I buried a 45-year-old woman who had died of cancer.
- On June 28 I buried an 11-year-old boy who had drowned at

his family cottage.
- On June 29 I had two weddings (I didn't know any of them from Adam and Eve.) and
- On the weekend I had a Saturday Mass and a Sunday morning Mass. The Sunday Mass was held in the gym – the "Folk Mass" – as distinct from the one not for "folk," which was celebrated in the church.

In the midst of this schedule, I celebrated the Sacrament of Penance (heard confessions) for the first time. During an intense conversation with a penitent, there was a startling knock on my confessional door. It was the high school girl from the rectory come to tell me that there was an "emergency," a woman is dying who needed to be anointed. The pastor said that I am to go.

Well, I had never even looked at the ritual for Anointing of the Sick. I would fly by the seat of my pants on this one! I didn't know the territory or where Joann Street was. I didn't have oils. I didn't have a ritual! What color stole do I wear and where is it? I AM A BAD PRIEST – as Lou Costello might say! I discovered an oil stock (container – probably Chrism!), a ritual, and a purple stole on a table on the landing of the stairs to my room. As I drove in search of the street and the house, I thumbed through the ritual to see what happens during an anointing. When I arrived, I thought for sure she was dead. No one spoke English; but I learned the word for 'aunt' in Italian: "Zia, Zia," over and over again. I began to pray the ritual. When the part came for the oil, I unscrewed the cap and discovered that the oil stock was empty, the cotton dry. I was worried, big time. Then I heard a voice, God whispering in my ear: "I will provide what you lack." I thanked him, touched my thumb to the cotton, and it actually made a squeaking sound! The good news: "Zia" lived six months longer – through the anointing of the dry cotton – so I got to anoint her again. That second time I used oil and she died properly that day. Maybe I missed the point and should have stuck with dry cotton!

In the sixties, as a nation and a world, we were in the throes of the Vietnam War. More and more it became an indefensible action. My opposition to the war, my commitment to demonstrating against the war, calling the government to end it, grew. The momentum increased. I worked with a group that targeted suburban housewives and began to convince them to actively work in their neighborhoods and among their social circles to end the war. Body bags came home by the score, funerals were celebrated, families grieved, communities were wounded, questionable secret military operations became public information, and the outcry grew louder and would not go unheard. When the war ended, the troops were brought home, many in the middle of the night while the nation slept. They had no homecoming for heroes, then or ever. There is a remaining great sadness here. My evil Boswellian/worrier side was filled with glee, and I rejoiced when that president had to resign, as the result of a multiplicity of hateful, disdainful, arrogant behavior toward fellow humans and fellow countrymen. I shared that moment with the townsfolk of Port Sanilac, and with classmates Charlie Fontana, Al Kuras, and Jim Cronk, at a local bar and grill, since I had no television. It was a glorious moment for a worrier, a warrior, a wannabe righter of wrongs. Actions have consequences.

Right after the election of Ronald Reagan, the hostages in Iran were released, to much relief and great rejoicing across the nation. At the following Sunday liturgies, I called on the people to rejoice fully in the event of the hostages' release. I also asked them for one additional thing – not only to welcome home the hostages but also to look around their families, relationships, and neighborhoods to see if they might know someone who was a Vietnam veteran. I urged them to write, call, or visit those people that day and welcome them home as well and thank them for what they had risked for the nation. The people responded with enthusiasm, and I received thank you notes and calls from vets for the next several weeks. One Vietnam veteran also told me that it was too little, too late; this is still part of that lingering sadness.

Through the Sacrament of Reconciliation, I learned a lot about what really happened to the men and women in the Vietnam War, what choices they thought they had, what choices they were forced to make, and how their lives would never be the same. I buried several who returned but could not continue to live. There was a vast emptiness in the heart of a man who told me that he had ordered the massacre of a village. He was still using heroin. He was dead within a year of his returning home under cover of darkness.

All these great movements affected what was going on in the priesthood and earlier in seminary life. In those days in the later sixties, seminary life "relaxed," as new rules were developed, We could actually go out to approved lectures and entertainment on certain evenings (or sneak out to a baseball game after signing out for a lecture on Immanuel Kant). Parish priests grew wary of seminary life and seminarians. They worried about the future of the Church and the priesthood. These were the early signs of the distrust that grew after we were ordained and began parish ministry. This attitude would bleed over to the people and remains to this day. Several years ago Fr. Gerry Martin, one of our best seminary professors, told me that he would never be able to accept this automatic mistrust and that it would remain a source of real pain for him. In past times trust was given automatically, simply because the guy was a priest. Now distrust is given just as automatically. Neither is healthy in and for the Church.

The enormous national and international issues caused rifts in the fabric of the class and the seminary community. Seminarians took sides and politics began. There are divisions in the class that have never been mended to this day. For a worrier/chronicler, this is not a good thing.

In the early seventies mothers began going to work outside the home in ever-larger numbers. Families were looking for ways to limit their size and still receive Holy Communion. *Humanae Vitae* was published by Pope Paul VI and went against the popular trend in the Church and even among those expert faithful from across the world that he had asked to advise him. The decree stated that the teaching of the Church would remain the same. Artificial means of birth control would not be allowed. It remained *in se* evil ("evil in itself"). I spent many hours with couples discerning their options. My spiritual directors gave a direction of conscience to counsel these good people. Some simply, without discussion, let their birth control and their sacramental life live side by side without resolution. Others simply left the Church, seeing it as yet another irrelevant institution. I can't say that I can recall a single family that gave up artificial birth control because of *Humanae Vitae*. I know of many for whom it was a source of great anxiety and thus an opportunity to grow into a more adult faith life. This does not mean they accepted the teaching.

I found that my real education began following ordination. Vowed religious women shared their joys and struggles with me. I learned about the connection with the people that priests had talked about and found it challenging and wonderful. I shared a rectory with four other priests and learned how to live with four other sets of expectations and visions of priesthood and life. This was tough. We lived in the splendor of the "old Church," with cooks, laundresses, and housekeepers. It was a strange world for a worrier/chronicler. In spite of the difficulties, it was in this first assignment that I learned to love the Church and the priesthood. In those days the archdiocese worked hard to implement a vision of the Council. By 1969 the liturgy was completely in English. I have never celebrated the Liturgy in Latin.

The good news of the Council, along with proposed and forecasted changes, was not such good news to *all* people. Some people questioned everything. Others dismissed any priest under 35 years of age. It was a difficult time. Without the support of still other people, those would have been impossible days. I was busy all the time. I pulled "door duty" every Sunday and Thursday. Every call and drop-in was mine for the taking on those days. They were very long days. Wedding rehearsals were scheduled for each Thursday evening. I took them all because all the other priests were off for the day. Sometimes my Thursday evening schedule went like this: 7:00 PM Mass; two, three, or four rosaries in funeral homes; and up to three or four wedding rehearsals, each followed by confessions for the wedding families.

Don't ask how I did this. It remains a blur. But I do remember two distinct events on the same Thursday evening. One had to do with a confrontation with the pastor. When I said that there was no way I could do all these services in such a short span of time, he simply told me to do my best. The second, again that same Thursday, was my conducting three wedding rehearsals simultaneously using the three aisles in the church, keeping the folks laughing throughout. We played aisle leapfrog and each wedding party got their turn in the main aisle. We were laughing very hard when the pastor came in to offer to help hear confessions. Afterwards he insisted on knowing what was so funny. Further, how dare we be so loud in church! (There were three rosaries that evening as well: two right across the street, the other around the corner.)

What kept them laughing, I found out, was that they didn't like the pastor either and were willing to do anything to help me out of the jammed schedule, to get through the rehearsals, so they could have good weddings that weekend. They really were there to help me through it. I appreciated it. I slept well that night: no worries.

Sixties liberals had a field day. Often, too often, they were led to believe that Church teachings were up for grabs and that it was safe to say that the Council said we could do this or that, when it wasn't true. Many of the faithful suffered greatly in those days simply trying to get their parishes and their parish priests to look at what were the implications of the Council, to tell them what the Council was about. But the polarization among clergy was so great that many priests simply refused to look at the Council, much less learn about it or teach about it. Involvement of the faithful and ways to become involved in parish life grew rapidly -- too rapidly, I think, to prepare people well. Often, ignorance was king and confusion reigned. The impact of this confusion on religious education programs is unquestioned. Without too much exaggeration, the largest budget item in such programs seemed to be money for crayons and pictures to color, as well as balloons and felt banners. The music reflected an oversimplification too. "Joy is Like the Rain," for example, springs to mind. And how many different lyrics were set to the sing-song of children's music? Most of the music at my first Mass was secular in tone or in nature. My closing hymn was "Turn Around, Look at Me," for God's sake!

Religious education was almost wiped clean from the face of the

Church. The "second class citizens" who attended public schools were a casualty of the "Council Wars." All more the pity, since now that group is the majority of Church membership. Not only can they not count the sacraments but they can't articulate or appreciate the lushness of the centrality of Baptism in faith and in all ministerial life. But, regarding the latter, neither can most clergy nor pastoral ministers.

I have had one specialized assignment. I was a hospital chaplain for three years. There I learned some really powerful things about myself, about life, and about heroes and heroism. Rusty was eight years old and his parents were violently separated. I never met them until I prayed Rusty's funeral. When I met Rusty, he was well into the processes leukemia brings to a little guy. The picture I have of him is one of his school pictures. He had already lost his hair to chemotherapy. Over the course of a year and a half, we became friends. I baptized him, with one of his friends who was a nurse as a witness. That's the way he wanted it. When he was a patient in pediatrics, I would visit him and we would play. He made me laugh and feel free. I would put him in a wheelchair and cover him head to toe with a blanket so he could not see out and therefore not be seen. Then I would head to the doors of the unit to help him "escape," waving to the nurses at the station as we passed so they would know he was with me and that we were off on an adventure. I would take Rusty around the hospital, to the administrative offices, to the volunteers' offices, etc., and all would simply be charmed by this little kid who was dying. It was on one of these occasions that he called me "Daddy."

As the disease progressed he lost the use of his facial muscles and could no longer smile; laugh, yes, but not smile. With great courage, he would prepare for seemingly endless and always painful spinal taps. When the staff approached him, he would climb onto the table, assume the position, and not even whimper. Soon enough he ran the risk of catching whatever germ us healthy folks were carrying. "Enteric Precautions" means that a visitor has to gown up, face mask, gloves, etc., to protect the patient. Use of these became the rule. When I tried to get away with that, Rusty would insist that I remove the mask so he could see my face and beard and remove the gloves so he could hold my hand flesh on flesh. Late one afternoon he asked me to hold him on my lap; and moments later there he died. The nurses had been watching extra carefully that day; they had expected his death and were so gentle with him and with me.

Rusty is such a hero to me. He taught me so much about the nature of suffering. While it can't be avoided by anybody, it can be dealt with, it can be endured, and, in the end, it can be conquered. One day shortly before his death, Rusty asked me, "When I die, will my sickness go away?" I said it would. His answer: "That's good to hear. I'm tired of it." He was absolutely confident in the truth of my response.

My next assignment was shared with my classmate Tom Krell, in an experimental arrangement called co-pastors. The experiment, attempted by several priests in the diocese in those days, is now officially deemed a failure. For me it was a highlight of my priesthood. Tom and I grew in friendship and lived those four years making the Council come alive in the parish. I learned about effecting the future by the decisions I made in the present. We prepared and implemented a five-year plan, the results of which were achieved after we had moved on. It worked! The parish built a community center and freed itself of many of the obstacles we carried in our days there. All of this was once thought impossible. This assignment also gave me the courage to believe that the vision of Vatican Council II just might have a chance to be achieved in the parish setting.

I reached a point in my priesthood when I needed to get out of living in a rectory and to learn to live like a normal person. I had arranged with the pastor to create an apartment in the school and take over the position of Adult Religious Education Coordinator. The Parish Council agreed. The auxiliary bishop caught wind of it and didn't agree at all. Cardinal Dearden was preparing to retire and was busy getting his ducks in order. I think the auxiliary sensed that the hammer was coming down on the diocese. He simply said: "NO! It is not possible." So I then asked him for a leave of absence and he said: "OK!" He had to check with "the boss," but he didn't think there would be a problem. Within days I received a letter informing me that my request for a leave had been granted and that another, soon-to-be auxiliary bishop would handle the details and make the final arrangements. In March the phone call came and I was told that my last check would be April first and that by the first of May I would be dropped from health and auto insurance and would be on my own. No conversation, no meeting, no face to face. I simply wept. Well, I simply wept and worried and watched!

I ran into a former college teacher, Thomas Hinsberg (horrible philosophy professor – I told him so too – *after* my surprising graduation), who had left the active ministry and married Connie, a wonderful former vowed religious woman. He asked what I was going to do, and I said that my first hope would be to survive. At that point, however, I was not sure. I was down to less than 125 pounds. A few days later I received a call from Connie, who said she thought I might be able to get a job working for someone in her family who owned a restaurant, The Club 500. I grabbed at it because they were willing to give me medical insurance right away.

I hurt in every joint, muscle, ligament, bone; even my hair hurt by the end of the first week. I stood on ceramic tile flooring doing the work of prep chef all day. I sliced and diced, kneaded and broiled my little fingers to the bone. My supervisor was 21 years old and a jerk. But I had health insurance. A priest of the archdiocese, Fr. Larry Pettke, invited me to move into his parents' home, which he had inherited upon their deaths. It was a very generous gift and conveniently located within walking distance of the restaurant, so I saved on gas too. A classmate, Fr. Tom Kirwan, offered me one month's salary if I needed it – anytime, no questions asked. It was very kind and generous of him.

Within a few months, I heard of an opening at the Samaritan Health Center, a landmark Detroit hospital that had just opened a residential detox/rehabilitation program for polyaddicted people, mostly from the streets, and a psychiatric unit. Don Novak, a former seminarian, was the director. He interviewed me and I was hired as counselor and lay chaplain to both units. My pains began to go away immediately.

Wandering Between Two Worlds

That year we were making $8900 as priests in parish ministry – whether we wanted to or not. In my new position I began at $20,100 – but I did have to pay my own auto insurance!

I was newly born into a different world. Psychiatrists sent their sickest chronic patients to the new unit, and the staff turned over about once a month. It was grueling work for the professionals. I would waltz in and spend my time speaking with those able to communicate and see what I could offer. I had a supervisor, a psychologist, who helped immensely to give me a sense of purpose in the psych unit. I came to know the faces of mental illness and the goodness in the hearts of those so stricken. I appreciated at a new level the nature of that beast that lives in the minds of so many. One guy spoke in symbols only. He was a big and very black and beautiful person. One day, for fun, I began to try to follow him in his symbols. Suddenly I caught it and off we went for about 10 seconds. When he realized that I was getting it, he became more obscure and he was once again safe in his symbolic world. As he went off into that world, he winked at me and laughed, as if to say: "Nice try, kid."

I worked very hard, but it seemed less like work than anything else I have ever done. I feared my first evaluation, thinking I would be fired. I wasn't and shouldn't have worried. The alcohol treatment unit was a challenge as well. We were so inundated with clients that the counselors fell behind in taking client histories. Without those histories we could not apply for Medicare payments, and we would run into real trouble financially. I volunteered to take the histories since I had time on my hands. What stories I heard! What sad and tragic lives these men and women had lived. Again I saw the face of the beast. I learned a lot about the illness and the cure, about those who turned around and those who died. A young black man of 26 years entered our program three times in the year I was there. As he left the third time, I prayed with him and he wept with me. Three days later he was brought to the medical floor after drinking one shot of whiskey. He died that day. I wept again.

The Sisters of Mercy built another hospital in the city to replace Samaritan's outdated building. They also carried the hospital for many years, although the deficit was in the millions at each year's end. It was a real gift to the city and the eastside Detroit community. I was proud to have been a part of their effort.

Another stop along the way was my taking advantage of some wanderlust that I shared with a friend named Terry. We decided to go to Florida and began by looking for work. A position opened for a probation / parole officer, or PPO, in Fort Myers District, Collier County Office, in Naples, Florida. I flew down and interviewed and got the job. Terry went through training as a correction officer and began to work in a local state prison.

As a PPO I carried a permanent caseload of 70 to 80 felons and worked on Pre-Sentence Investigations, work release programs, release on recognizance, three contacts with each client each month, etc. Any aspect of community life that convicted felons related to, so did we. I had a combination of murderers, rapists, drug dealers, and bad check writers. I liked Florida, except in the summer. I enjoyed the job but it was high on the paper work and low on the interpersonal. I was warned that my job was not a counseling position. It was supervision, pure and simple.

One day I was answering a letter from a friend from Michigan. Kathy had written and brought me up to date on what was going on up there, and in the course of the letter asked if I had made a decision about priesthood. In answering her letter, I shared some of my thinking about experiences in priesthood in the past and what I was experiencing in probation work. I reflected that I was missing that dimension of helping the people I was working with. I missed the sense of ministry. Before I knew it, I was writing that I had made up my mind and that I had decided to contact the archdiocese and would probably be back in Michigan the following spring as a priest. I did and I did. My working in Naples had taught me a valuable lesson -- I could make it. I could survive outside priesthood. I had choices. I would never feel trapped in the priesthood. I would never say what I had heard from others: "I can't do anything else."

After my leave of absence, I was given a brief "reorientation" assignment that lasted for one year. The assignment that followed was the most difficult of my priesthood. It lasted five years. It began with Parish Council members angrily criticizing which office I chose to use and concluded with a mere 25 people at my farewell reception. One year following my transfer, that parish was closed.

It was during this assignment that I realized a woman who was a member of a former parish where I had ministered some years before was stalking me. The fact that it took years for me to realize this is a further example that I am not the brightest button on any vest! The stalking progressed so far that, each night before I went to bed, I could see her in the parking lot by my car; and each morning she was there as well. Our confrontations were ugly and merely served to feed her psychosis. Some of her friends supported her fantasies and allowed her to speak about our "relationship" at meetings, etc. At one point, she even claimed that her youngest child was "ours."

Eventually the police had such a rap sheet on her that they were able to arrest her based on their own knowledge and experience. Following her arrest, she caused such chaos that the Watch Commander ordered her taken to Receiving Hospital to begin her processing as a psychiatric patient. She was remanded by Probate Court to a hospital for treatment.

The rest of the story gets muddled and confused. The very day she was released, she came to the parish and disrupted the Sunday Liturgy. The police had to be called and she was returned to the hospital. Somehow her husband was able to keep a distance from all this. What had lasted for several years at this point began its final 12 months. This final year frightened me greatly. By its end, I experienced such deep feelings that I had trouble sleeping, lost my appetite, and was filled with a rage that only one affected by being a victim could recognize. I felt held hostage, helpless, afraid of what the next day might bring.

Once, during Confession time, the door opened and in she walked. She promptly sat across from me and hiked her skirt over her knees and leaned forward with this strange flushed look on her face (I think this might be called a fetching glance?!). It made my blood run cold. As she began to speak, I realized that this situation was more than unreasonable. I was afraid at what she might do. I stood up, opened the door (luckily there were others in the church!), and ordered her out, never to return. She slowly rose and with great nonchalance walked out and went over to the others there for a quiet conversation. God only knows what she told them! I have rarely felt such rage. A stroke would have been a welcome relief! For a man (and probably for a woman, too) unfamiliar with such suggested intimacy without any foundation or participation, I was blown away and remain to this day confused by it all. It was in the midst of this that I realized that I was no alcoholic. I didn't *need* to drink. I *wanted* to drink. I really did want to drink, especially when these confrontations occurred. Instead I continued to drink in my normal pattern. Finally the saga ended.

After a long absence, she reappeared at a morning Mass after I had moved to another parish. She walked up the main aisle to the very front pew with her son (the "our" son one) and took her seat in the pew. She stared and I became frightened again. She won that day. After Mass a very wise woman of the parish, a good friend of mine today, came up to me and asked: "What was going on between you and the woman in the front pew?" I told her the story, in brief; and she said that the air was thick between us and she just knew something was wrong. Then she assured me that "my stalker" was powerless to do anything to me. She could not hurt me. She could do nothing except frighten me, if I let her. Those words that day made sense, and sunk in to a deep level within me. I knew I had won the war. Several days later the stalker came to Mass once again, sat in the same seat, with the same son, and stared. I felt very calm, peaceful, and prayed the Liturgy. Boy, did I! At one point, I am not sure when, she rose and stepped into the center aisle and stared, then slowly turned and walked out. I have not seen her since. I have seen newspaper accounts of instances of her stalking other priests. Rarely a week goes by when I don't pray for her health and thank God that my mental health is manageable – to this day anyway.

My next assignment was as an associate. The pastor was going on sabbatical; and the diocese felt that a priest/associate with experience was necessary to handle the responsibility, since it was a large parish. I arrived rather broken and beaten up from my previous assignment. The people at this temporary assignment were wonderful. They offered healing and nourishment. In fact they breathed new life into the possibilities of ministry for me again.

I mentioned that my mental health was manageable; but it was not so for Fr. Robert (not his real name), another priest with whom I ministered in this parish for a very short time. He was a religious order priest looking to find a home in the Archdiocese of Detroit. Robert was so very ill-equipped emotionally to be a parish priest. Although a professional, he had few people skills and even less skill at handling his own life. His problems manifested themselves in chronic heart problems, for which several doctors had prescribed a variety of pain killers. Washed down with vodka and juice, the pain was manageable for him! I found him at the end of a Tuesday off, after staff members told me that they had not seen or heard from him all day. He was sitting on his couch and very cold. Pills were still visible in his mouth.

Robert was raised by distant relatives whom he thought were his parents until he was ordained. He had joined a religious order that was mostly composed of Irishmen, even though he was Persian! Robert never really found acceptance in his community. Thus rejected, orphaned, and screwed up, he was ordained. He promptly changed his name, at 27 years of age, to his real father's name. He floundered for years and was afflicted by all the elements of denial. In the priesthood, it is very safe to be addicted to pills and alcohol.

Struggling in the work of the Order, in parish work, in one diocese after another, Robert finally came to me to die. I had known him a month and a half. His Order wanted to bury him quickly. I refused. They wanted short services. Again I refused. I demanded that the superior general fly in for the Vigil Service. Somehow, I got my way! We welcomed Fr. Robert (his body) to the parish church on Sunday at Evening Prayer, as a "Father" to us all. We celebrated his fragile priestly ministry and his brokenness. Just before the funeral Mass the following Monday, the county coroner announced that Fr. Robert had indeed committed suicide. I informed the Cardinal, who was presiding at the funeral, and he said, "How the hell do they know what went on in that room?"

One of Robert's favorite postures was to sit with his head in his hands and moan, sometimes for fun, sometimes not. One month to the day after his death, I was asleep when I suddenly heard movement in the hallway outside my room. I turned my head; and in walked Robert, in full habit, which I had only seen once. He sat at the foot of my bed and put his head in his hands. I heard myself say, "For God's sake, Robert, get your damned head out of your hands and go home! It's over and you are safe! God loves you like no one else ever has!" He did just that and left. Three months to the day after his death, long after his family had removed all his belongings, the housekeeper (my last experience of a housekeeper!) brought clean laundry to my room and set it down on my bed. As I put the items away I noticed an article of clothing that was not familiar. When I looked closer (with my glasses on!), I found Fr. Robert's laundry nametag sewn along the edge. Like I said, I didn't need to drink, I just wanted to.

During the next two years, I began to seriously study the documents that seemed to pour out of the Vatican and the national offices of the Catholic Church in the U.S. on a daily basis. These documents addressed opportunities for ministry for the faithful – lay ministries. Much work had to be done to study, prepare lesson plans, formations sessions, etc.

I brought this interest and enthusiasm with me to my longest assignment: St. Mark Parish, Warren, Michigan. I began 20 years of very intense formation, discernment, and development of ministry teams. Cardinal Roger Mahoney's pastoral letter on lay ministry gave new strength to my work, new enthusiasm to the ministry groups in formation. The focus on baptism as the principle sacrament of ordination in the Church brought so much of what the people of St. Mark Parish had been working toward. It crystallized and affirmed our hard work. We have developed ministry teams that have substantial responsibility for a variety of church and social needs. Along with this ongoing formation program, we sold our old school building and poured the money into a major renovation of our remaining building. It is a church in the round, with a right-sized Worship Space. Consequently we now have room for a good-sized Outreach Center, an excellent Gathering / Welcoming Space, offices, and multipurpose rooms, all in a circle and under one roof. It is working amazingly well.

More so the process of the renovation – the very last thing I ever really wanted to do – brought the parish members to a new level of relationship. Smaller spaces in our temporary "churches" as the building was being renovated forced us to be physically closer together for Liturgy; and we began to find that we liked it. We began to build on our experiences of wandering in the desert of Exodus and to the homecoming that the Kingdom will be. In short, we declared that we have become a new creation, a community where all are welcome.

Our move back into our main building was such a homecoming. This new spirit led us to survey the people to see what needs were being met and what still needed to be developed. This survey resulted in the formation of a Parish Family Commission, which is composed of fifteen groups that parish members requested -- from exercise, to sewing, to Protecting God's Children, to the hospitality / social concerns of parish life – and much, much more.

All the groups work in tandem with the pre-existing ministry groups. The focus of the work we have begun at St. Mark's is in recognition of the nature of the Church that flows from the teachings of Vatican II. Principal among these ministry groups:

- One group addresses food and clothing needs of the community and explores social issues; currently the members are exploring opening a warming center.
- A Marriage Ministry Team works with all those who share or seek to share the Sacrament of Marriage.
- The Christian Formation Program fulfills the needs of families, adult and elementary religious education, youth ministry, sacramental preparation as a separate track,

R.C.I.A., and infant baptism catechesis of parents and godparents.

- The Bereavement Team works with families who have lost a loved one, assists them in planning and leading vigil services and at the funeral Liturgy. Follow-up communication with immediate family members continues for a year.
- A Pastoral Care of the Sick Team visits the parish sick and hospitalized and coordinates the Sacrament of Anointing.
- All of the liturgical ministries are fully expressed.

In the beginning of this assignment, I started at square one for about the seventh time in my priestly ministry. I choose not to do this again. The people involved in these ministries fear that their work will be in vain and a new pastor will overturn our hard work. I guess I will stay on as long as I can so I can support their growth and the expression of their ministry. It's a beautiful thing. The Faithful continue to develop their faith lives, they continue to become more informed than ever, more articulate, more challenging to nonsense. This is a great sign of hope and the promise of ongoing vitality for the Church.

St. Mark Parish and the response of the people – and the struggle with clarity of vision – have re-energized me. I believe that the Council worked and worked well. I don't kid myself that I am on the same page as many in the college of bishops. Yet, I believe I am on the page of *some*. I am glad for that and for them.

So what if the Council didn't get it all done and that the follow-up has been choppy and inconsistent and filled with contradictions? Maybe that is the point. No one thing, one moment, one council, could do all that – all those lives, all those mistakes, all those attitudes and ideas that took 1900 years to develop. But I have a fundamental belief that we are on the road. Those who seek to undermine the vision, the mystery of the Spirit moving in our Church and in the world, are as powerless to accomplish that goal as I am to stop them.

I believe that they have taken on the Spirit and She is always victorious . . .

I don't know what the Church will look like in fifty years, or in a hundred; but I believe that it will be what the Spirit wants it to be, and the current struggle will be a part of that creation.

We continue to stand in the midst of the sexual abuse and leadership crisis in the Church. Confusion, clashing ideologies, much re-arranging of deck chairs everywhere. New (old) practices are being resuscitated in the name of "correcting" abuses. The people are very confused. All in all, we are clergy that are weary to the bone. Weary of the denial, of being adrift as a people, weary of overwhelming responsibility with little or no voice. I think it was to this level of weariness that Matthew spoke when he penned: "Come to me all you who are weary and heavy-laden and you will find rest." I never thought I could become so tired in my soul.

I read a comment recently about the mental or intellectual schisms that exist in the Church today. This thought hit me like a ton of bricks. I find it easy to acknowledge that I am in a kind of "schism" with my Church. I love the CHURCH. I love that compassionate, warm, loving, reconciling, welcoming, ever-wider embracing, healing, expanding, wonderful movement of the Divine called the Body of Christ. Simply put, I wish everyone could see what I see in the dynamic reality of the CHURCH. It is wondrous and healthy; it is servant; it is fragile but unafraid; it is confident but not arrogant. I paraphrase St. Paul: "The CHURCH (my CHURCH!) bears all things, believes all things, hopes all things, and endures all things. It never fails."

I relish the opportunity for this review of these forty years. It has been a good life to date; and I fully expect to outlive my parents' years, both making it to 94 years old. I plan to enjoy retirement as well.

For the last several years I have been appointed by Probate Court as a guardian for Carole. She is 65 years old and was born with cerebral palsy. We put an addition onto my retirement home, and Carole and I spend as much time there as possible. We enjoy vacationing together. Our major trip was a 16-day tour across Italy with a group from the parish. We often had to use a wheelchair, but seeing the sights through her eyes was like seeing all the sites from a new perspective. Typically, I was responsible for her falling out of the chair and landing on the cobblestones at St Peter Basilica. We were on our way to an Ordination Liturgy for new priests who would minister in Rome. With my luck I found that the grates for draining rainwater have openings that perfectly match the distance between the wheels of a wheelchair. We were moving at a good clip so we wouldn't be late, and then suddenly we stopped dead as the wheels caught in the grate openings. Carole was tipped right out of the chair and onto the cobblestones. There were no injuries except to her pride and a wound to my concern for her safety. Several people offered assistance, and we proceeded to the Liturgy and had a great view of Pope John Paul II as he presided.

Many other things could be told in these pages, things too numerous to tell without driving you nuts. But all true, all a part of the mystery that surrounds each of us and ushers us forward. Some days, in some ways, I can feel the embrace and the refreshing aroma of the lived Church. It is comforting, like Limoncello fresh from the freezer – wonderful, refreshing!

"For the vision still has its time, presses on to fulfillment, and will not disappoint; if it delays, wait for it, it will come, it will not be late." (Hab.: 2:3)

Who would have thought?

Wandering Between Two Worlds

THE HISTORICAL CONTEXT:
A CONCLUDING AFTERWORD
Gerald P. Fogarty, S.J.

In the essays above, members of the class of 1965 from Sacred Heart Seminary in Detroit recount their stories from the time they entered that college seminary to the present. These men provide snapshots of the history of the American Church over the last forty years. Some went on to the priesthood and are still active. Others left the active ministry and are still angry at their experiences. Still others cherish the education they received and their association with this group of talented young men, as they pursued careers outside ecclesiastical life. Others, still, found, as Vatican II would affirm, that service to the Church did not necessarily mean ordained priesthood. As one reads these disparate stories, one wonders if members of that class of 1965 any longer have anything in common after so many years of change. Yet, despite their varied attitudes toward the institutional Church, they still do hold something in common—when each of them entered Sacred Heart Seminary College forty years ago with the intention of studying for the priesthood, during four years, they forged bonds of friendship that remain to this day.

As the Preface to this volume indicates, one could easily produce similar stories from alumni of other diocesan seminaries or religious orders, where the narrators look back on four decades of tremendous change. Some changes in the American Church, indeed, had parallels elsewhere, but others were unique to the American Catholic experience. Americans in general and Catholics in particular suffer from a lack of historical sense and are prone to make the immediate past the norm for all the past. The American Church of 1960 was a subculture of fairly recent vintage. It had a vast educational system that taught its youth from kindergarten through university; it operated as if it really did not need anything outside itself to achieve its purpose. Yet, intellectually, it was deficient. What seemed to be the expression of perennial Catholic teaching was in fact something of recent origin.

375

In the early twentieth century, American Catholic intellectual life was only in its infancy when it was cut off. First, in 1899, came the condemnation of Americanism, which seemed, in the minds of certain theologians, to hold the American Catholic support of religious liberty suspect, although recently available documents in the Holy Office in Rome make evident that Leo XIII forbade the actual discussion of the American separation of Church and State. Then, in 1907, came the condemnation of Modernism, which ended intellectual endeavors at the Catholic University of America and Dunwoodie seminary in New York. The American Catholic Church lapsed into an intellectual somnolence that presented as timeless verities of philosophical and theological theses which were, in fact, of recent origin. The American Catholic subculture and intellectual life provide one frame of reference for placing these essays in a broader historical context. Two of the contributors were sent to Louvain for theology. Both note the refreshing courses in Church history they took based upon the historical-critical method used there.

But there is another frame of reference, a structural one. The bishops of a century before these young men entered the seminary asserted a strong sense of collegiality, a term they used in the nine national councils they held from 1829 to 1866—by the tenth, in 1884, such language had disappeared. By 1962, when Vatican II opened, few, if any, American bishops had any knowledge of the concept. For them, the council was a learning experience. John Dearden, who became the Archbishop of Detroit in 1958, was a prime example of one bishop who took to heart the orientation of the council. Yet, some of these stories also show the "dark side" of this paragon of Vatican II.

But the American Church in 1961 was not a homogeneous subculture. It was multi-ethnic. Within the main subculture, therefore, they were yet other subcultures: Italian, German, Irish, or Polish, to name the principal ones. As Catholics moved upward socio-economically, they also moved outward from the urban—and many times national— parish of their parents to the suburbs. In the cities, Catholicism was reinforced by ethnicity and vice versa. With suburban affluence, religion and ethnicity took on new meaning or lost all meaning. Two Polish-American writers, for instance, describe how they chose to go to Sacred Heart Seminary rather than to Orchard Lake, the seminary for Polish-American students; they saw themselves more as Americans than as Polish-Americans. Whether consciously or not, the American Church was in many ways an important agent of Americanization.

But the American Church had another characteristic. It drew its clergy from every economic class. Several of the writers note that they were the first ones in their families to go to college. Others noted that they came from some affluence. In the seminary and in religious orders at the time, all were equal. While several of the contributors rightly decry a clergy class of privilege, it is also important to recall that this class was not drawn from wealth and privilege. Cardinal Richard Cushing of Boston once remarked that he knew no bishop whose parents had gone to college. On the eve of Vatican II, a more scientific survey was made and, in general, bore out the cardinal's observations. The negative side of this was that many candidates for the priesthood may well have been attracted to the seminary because of the desire for upward mobility and education. In 1961, the year our authors began college, the priesthood was a respected profession, and a priest was an automatic leader in the Catholic subculture. That would all change.

When the class of 1965 entered its freshman year, the American Church was in a state of euphoria. A Catholic had finally been elected to the White House, but few American Catholics carefully analyzed John Kennedy's famous speech to the Houston Ministerial Association and recognized that he embraced an un-Catholic notion that "church" and religion were fundamentally private, the very issue that the Jesuit theologian, John Courtney Murray, was then trying to combat and that catapulted him into international fame as a framer of Vatican II's declaration of religious liberty. Those were heady days, with John XXIII, a grandfatherly peasant on the throne of Peter. Not only had he been photographed as nuncio to Paris with a cigarette and a cocktail glass, he had also called a council, only the third one since Columbus had stumbled upon two continents and thought he had reached India. But few examined the pope's Synod of Rome that called for clerics to wear the tonsure, or his compliance with the prohibition of two professors at the Biblical Institute, Stanislaus Lyonnet and Maximilian Zerwick, from teaching, or his largely ignored edict that Latin should be the language of seminary instruction. The myopia of so many Catholics, American and others, prevented them from seeing that good Pope John was not quite the revolutionary they envisioned. But the American Catholic euphoria, nourished by Kennedy's election after so many years of second-class citizenship, rapidly came to an end.

Many American Catholics recall the enthusiasm of the opening of Vatican II and the way in which the bishops wrested control of it from the curia, but many also forget that the council almost came to a halt in its first week as the United States and the Soviet Union came to the brink of nuclear war in the Cuban Missile Crisis. Throughout the council and the later years of these seminarians, the Cold War hovered in the background.

In the meantime, as the Church universal was engaged in the council, the United States was engaged in a two-fold campaign. On the one hand, it went through the civil rights movement and witnessed for the first time priests and religious marching in demonstrations about issues that did not, moreover, directly pertain to the welfare of Catholics. On the other, the nation found itself enmeshed in an increasingly unpopular war in Vietnam. Soon, the anti-war movement adopted some of the tactics developed in the civil rights movement. For the first time in history, American Catholics engaged in an extensive anti-war movement. Whereas patriotism and loyal service in the nation's wars had long been an instrument for acceptance and assimilation of Catholics into American culture, now priests and nuns were being arrested in protests. But there was a difference between the civil rights and anti-war movements. In the former, protesters sought to test the constitutionality of state and local laws against federal law; in the latter, the federal government itself was sometimes challenged. American Catholics were moving beyond their narrow parochial interests and taking their places as major players in reshaping American society. But not all American Catholics were in agreement. The division over the war was evident in the Sacred Heart class of 1965 as two left the seminary to serve in

Vietnam, while most remained to protest it. Whatever the judgment on Catholic participation in the civil rights and anti-war movements, the enthusiasm surrounding the council and the election of Kennedy came to a halt.

The assassination of Kennedy in November, 1963, brought "Camelot" to an end. The short Kennedy years engendered enthusiasm and a sense of service, but they were also as mythical as the imagined pontificate of John XXIII. Historians are leery of dealing with hypothetical cases, "what if"—what if Kennedy had lived; what if John XXIII presided over the council until its completion? What historians can do is point to the decade of the 1960s as a period of loss of trust in government over Vietnam and in the Church over perceived failings of the council or Paul VI's reinforcement of the traditional teaching against artificial contraception. Seldom has there been so dramatic a change in so short a period. A decade that had begun with such optimism ended with skepticism toward all authority, whether in Church or State.

In 1960, the American Church seemed a bastion of stability. Its members were obedient—orthodoxy was a word seldom heard, since only John Courtney Murray had voluntarily undertaken silence in face of opposition to his views and some biblical scholars were deemed dangerous by certain theologians. In Europe, however, the "new theologians," Jean Danielou, S.J., Yves Congar, O.P., and Henri de Lubac, S.J., had been silenced; the Pontifical Biblical Institute in Rome was under fire in Rome; and theological turmoil was seething just beneath the surface of apparent calm. But the American Church was unaware of any of this. The American people were also generous—the American contribution to the Peter's Pence collection was one way of influencing Roman decisions, even if there was little theological influence. But the challenge to authority in the 1960s came close to making the Church one more human institution, like the state, which should be reformed only according to society's norms. As American Catholics became assimilated into American society, they sometimes adopted a Protestant ecclesiology that the real Church is invisible, that the visible Church is merely human, and that, therefore, existing ecclesial divisions make no difference. As some of the essays reveal, the once revered—and obeyed -- institutional church now became secondary to individual freedom, as celibacy emerged as an issue. Even before the sex abuse crisis of 2002, therefore, trust in the Church and its leadership was being eroded. And, it might be added, the bishops' handling of that crisis only exacerbated the erosion of that trust.

For whatever reason, most of the members of the Sacred Heart class of 1965 who were ordained and remain in active ministry chose not to make any contribution. The two who did contribute both indicate their lack of trust in Church officials. One remarks about the lack of respect and trust in the priesthood. He also brings up another important issue. The priesthood ceased to have the respect of the people and be a source of identity. For that reason, he took a leave of absence to see if he could "cut it" in the secular world. He could and he returned to ministry. One wonders how many other priests may have doubted whether they could "cut it" in the outside world of their parishioners.

The question of identity pertains to more than profession and respect. It also raises the issue of sexual identity. Almost all the contributors mention the lack of any real discussion, much less education, on sexual issues in the seminary. Diocesan seminaries and religious houses of studies guarded against "particular friendships," the code word for homosexual relations, by prohibiting less than three seminarians from recreating together—"numquam duo" was the refrain in Jesuit novitiates, where the novices were probably more familiar with the meaning of the Latin than the danger that lay behind the adage. Relationships with women presented no problem because they did not exist, except with mothers or sisters or a glimpse of a classmate's sister. Seminarians and priests, for that matter, were sexually isolated. That situation would end.

Again, the 1960s were a turning point for the role of women in American society. In 1959, for example, aside from nursing programs, only two of the twenty-eight Jesuit colleges admitted women. By 1970, every Jesuit institution—as well as former male bastions like Notre Dame and the Ivy League schools—admitted women. On a practical level, priests and priests-to-be had to accept women as equal co-workers. Seminary life did little to prepare young priests for this new relationship.

At the same time, the sexual revolution challenged celibacy and each priest's sexual identity. Gays came out of the closet; straights severed the connection between sex and marriage, so that "Sex and the City" could become a staple of the under-thirty television viewing audience of the twenty-first century; and young Catholic couples saw nothing wrong with living together before marriage. How could this new attitude toward sex not affect seminarians and priests?

Most of the contributors call for an end to obligatory celibacy. While celibacy is a requirement only for clergy of the Latin rite and is a discipline that exists only by Church law and there are already married priests in the Latin rite, the issue is more complicated. Why does the Catholic culture no longer support celibacy? Have the past forty years brought insights to which previous generations were completely blind? There is a tendency to want the Church to conform to American mores. I say this because two years ago I had preached on the sex abuse crisis for over five months. One parishioner argued with me that the issue was celibacy, because it was unnatural. I pointed out that monogamy was unnatural in our present society. To say that the Church should accept only what is "natural" is dangerous, for it would do away with sacraments, grace, and, ultimately, the Incarnation. The changing attitude toward celibacy, I believe, has to be placed within the broader context of the changing role of religion in western society. Forty years ago, Protestant divinity schools recruited from the best and brightest of college graduates, but by the 1990s were having severe problems in recruiting qualified candidates. In other word, recruitment for the ministry has to be placed in a context beyond the Catholic focus on celibacy.

Something else has been lost over the past forty years. The late William X. Kienzle, a former priest who at one time edited the *Michigan Catholic*, the Detroit diocesan newspaper, gained fame as a mystery story writer about a priest who helps the police solve murders. Kienzle's protagonist was an able pastor, who easily related to his parishioners and was steadfast in maintaining social contacts with his fellow priests. Are his fictional accounts of priestly gatherings for dinner and golf reflections of a by-gone era or nostalgic recreations of a situation that never existed? Much was wrong with a clerical caste, enamored with authority and nurtured by an uneducated and largely immigrant laity. Yet, it also provided a fraternal support system that countered the individualism of American society.

These stories, with their pathos and hope and sometimes strident criticism, present a slice of American Catholic history. They tell of the transition from a Church certain of itself to a people in pilgrimage with its certainty now being tested against the world of which it is, and always was, a part.

ACKNOWLEDGEMENTS

I would like to gratefully acknowledge my classmates from SHS65 in allowing me to lead this writing effort. Because of the contributions and kindnesses of my sixteen co-authors, this project became a labor of love for me. All the writers were infinitely patient with me, as I urged (and sometimes badgered) them into completing their parts of this book. None ever told me "No."

Special thanks are due to the only two previously published authors in the group, Dr. John A. (Jack) Dick and Dr. Eugene J. Fisher. It was Gene who first surfaced the idea of writing this book. As the process of actually doing so went forward, Gene also obtained the services of Gregory Baum and Gerald Fogarty in writing the insightful pieces that begin and end the book. Jack, who was regularly available to me as a consultant, via email or transatlantic call, put me in touch with Robert Blair Kaiser, a published author in the area of religion. Kaiser, as his friends call him, gave me numerous leads as well as considerable encouragement in submitting the book to as many publishing houses as possible. He taught me to never become discouraged by a rejection notice, something that I received multiple times.

We couldn't have properly completed this project without the special skills of classmate-author Bob Thomas. At the very last minute, Bob took over the not insignificant task of producing the photos that appear on the title pages of every story. He cropped all the "before" photos from our graduation picture of 1965. That was the easy part. He then produced the "after" photos from many diverse sources – snapshots, formal sittings, group pictures of all sorts – ovalized them, and forwarded them to me so that they could be placed within the text. I am an old "computer guy," and I know what a big job this was. Yet Bob remained dedicated to rapidly getting it done, at the price of hours, nay *days*, of his time. His efforts were essential to getting this project properly completed.

Finally, my thanks go to George Van Antwerp. George may consider himself a small time publisher; but, to the SHS Class of 1965, he will never be "small" in any way.

William E. Richardson
February, 2009